EMPIRE
MAKER

ALEKSANDR ANDREEVICH BARANOV. A shipboard artist drew this portrait of Baranov in 1819, shortly before his death. It was originally published in St. Petersburg as a lithograph in P. A. Tikhmenev's *A History of the Russian-American Company* in 1861. The only image we have of the chief manager, it shows him wearing the ribbon and medal for the Order of St. Anna, 2nd class, his most treasured reward for his services to the Russian Crown.

EMPIRE MAKER

ALEKSANDR BARANOV AND
RUSSIAN COLONIAL EXPANSION INTO
ALASKA AND NORTHERN CALIFORNIA

KENNETH N. OWENS

With Alexander Yu. Petrov

A Samuel and Althea Stroum Book

UNIVERSITY *of* WASHINGTON PRESS

Seattle and London

This book is published with the assistance of a grant from
the Samuel and Althea Stroum Endowed Book Fund.

UNIVERSITY OF WASHINGTON PRESS
www.washington.edu/uwpress

LIBRARY OF CONGRESS CATALOGING-IN-PUBLICATION DATA
Owens, Kenneth N.
Empire maker : Aleksandr Baranov and Russian colonial expansion into Alaska and
Northern California / Kenneth N. Owens, with Alexander Yu. Petrov.
    pages cm. — (Samuel and Althea Stroum books)
Includes bibliographical references and index.
ISBN 978-0-295-99459-8 (hard cover : alk. paper) 1. Baranov, Aleksandr Andreevich,
1745–1819. 2. Russians—Alaska—History. 3. Russians—California, Northern—History. 4.
Rossiisko-amerikanskaia kompaniia—History. 5. Alaska—History—To 1867. 6. California,
Northern—History. I. Petrov, A. IU. II. Title.
F907.B23O94 2015
979.8'02092—dc23
[B]
  2014041601

Paperback ISBN 978-0-295-74172-7
Ebook ISBN 978-0-295-80583-2

CONTENTS

PREFACE AND ACKNOWLEDGMENTS

IN AUGUST 1790 ALEKSANDR ANDREEVICH BARANOV, SON OF A merchant trader from a remote small city in northern Russia, clambered aboard a waiting ship in Okhotsk, Russia's main Pacific port, and set sail for North America. A balding, rather stout person, short in stature and already well into his middle years, Baranov did not then appear to his contemporaries as a man with any extraordinary talents. Yet for the next quarter century and more, he was the leading figure in guiding the growth of Russia's overseas colonies in Alaska and northern California while shaping in them a distinctive, multiethnic society that in various ways endures into the present.

Bearing the title chief manager first for an Irkutsk-based merchant fur trading company, then for the imperially chartered Russian-American Company (RAC), Baranov proved to be something of a commercial genius. He combined shrewd business sense with a kind of buccaneering bravado. Under his management, a small Russian and Native Alaskan workforce engaged in predatory hunting and trading for sea otter peltry, seals skins, and the furs of foxes and other land mammals, making immense fortunes for company directors and stockholders in Siberia and European Russia. These activities extended Russian authority from the Aleutian Islands and maritime Alaska as far south as California's Bodega Bay. Despite hardships and setbacks of every sort, amplified by a pitiful lack of support from his homeland, Aleksandr Baranov imprinted his personality on an epic age in North American frontier history.

Baranov's career has not sufficiently engaged the attention of the history profession either in the United States or in Russia. His first biographer, Kiril Khlebnikov, met him in Sitka (New Archangel) near the close of his career, when Baranov was at last being allowed to retire. An office manager for the RAC, Khlebnikov developed intense admiration for the veteran chief manager. The book he later wrote was a slender laudatory account, lacking any critical perspective to modify the author's glowing praise for his subject.

Based almost exclusively on Baranov's oral recollections, Khlebnikov's publication is remarkable as much as for what it omitted as for what it included. This work, in other words, is an exercise in biased historical storytelling, selectively describing a limited number of events in ways most favorable to Baranov and to Khlebnikov's employer, the RAC.

By default, Khlebnikov's *Life of Aleksandr Andreevich Baranov* has remained the main source of information about this man and his career for more than a century and a half. When, as a western frontier historian, I first became interested in the history of Russian America forty some years ago, I was disappointed to find only two other biographical accounts, both relying almost exclusively on the Khlebnikov work.[1] And like Khlebnikov's *Life*, these other few volumes also proved to be silent about cultural interchanges between the Russian and Russo-Siberian newcomers and the Native peoples of Alaska and northern California. Plainly, a great deal more needed to be known about Baranov and his times.

Subsequently, a sustained burst of scholarly translations has greatly eased the problem of finding English-language source materials on Russian America. Led by the late Richard A. Pierce, an indefatigable researcher, translator, and publisher, and by the Oregon Historical Society team of Basil Dmytryshyn, E. A. P. Crownhart-Vaughan, and Thomas Vaughn, a host of scholars and skilled linguists have endowed Russian American studies with a wealth of documentary works in English. And yet in the absence of any collection of Baranov papers or any RAC archive covering his administration, an obvious gap of knowledge remained.

Shortly after retiring from academia, I began to contemplate the possibility of writing a life-and-times biography of Baranov, despite my unfamiliarity with the Russian language. This possibility became a realistic undertaking once I met Alexander Yu. Petrov, a senior research fellow in the Center for North American Studies, Institute of World History, at the Russian Academy of Sciences and a member of the history faculty in Moscow's State University of the Humanities. The author of a seminal study on the founding of the Russian-American Company, Alex was then a visiting professor at Oregon State University and nearing completion of a volume about Natalia Shelikhova, a primary figure in the history of the Siberian–North Pacific fur business. Because of our mutual interest in Baranov and his times, Alex immediately agreed to join with me in a full-scale research and writing project.

Together we drafted a collaborative research plan that was subsequently funded by the National Endowment for the Humanities (NEH). As we had proposed to the NEH, Alex traveled about western Russia and Siberia in pursuit of Baranov materials for fourteen months; then the two of us spent an additional two months together in the United States, touring the Pacific Coast states to investigate other possibilities. In the end we found little of documentary value in U.S. collections, but Alex's careful work in Russia made possible for the first time a full appraisal of Baranov's background and experiences before he arrived in Russian Alaska. Joined with the abundance of documentary publications now available in translation, these materials enabled me to move past Khlebnikov's adulatory work and write this far fuller, more inclusive factual study, intended to convey a balanced interpretive view of the Baranov era in Russian America within the context of North American frontier history.

In particular, I have aimed to provide an improved understanding of two often controversial matters: the history of the first Russian Orthodox spiritual mission in Alaska and the fur company's evolving relations with two key groups of Native Alaskans, the Alutiiq peoples of Kodiak Island and Chugach Bay and the Tlingit peoples of southeastern Alaska. Among other topics, this volume also presents a detailed account of Baranov's interactions with the British and Anglo-American merchant shipmasters who were his rivals and sometimes partners in the fur business of the Northwest Coast and northern California. Additionally, the book describes the chief manager's paramount role in founding the Russian establishment at Bodega Bay and Fort Ross and his responsibility for the RAC's short-lived Hawaiian misadventure. Most fundamentally of all, I have hoped to make a scholarly contribution to our knowledge about the cultural dynamics that resulted from the meeting of diverse peoples within North America's northernmost frontier borderlands.

Readers will find that I have a particular concern for matters of material culture and the methodologies of work among Russian America's ordinary people. The hows and whys of daily activities among hardworking people, such as the Russian contract workers and their Native compatriots, seem to me as important for historians to understand as the grand talk about great deeds by those who gave the orders. Baranov, to be sure, was an exceptional man, a great man, but he certainly did not stand alone on history's stage.

During the years I have been engaged with this project, Alex Petrov has remained a valued friend and consultant. And of course I've accumulated obligations to many other people. First among them are the four scholars, now departed, to whom this book is dedicated. Alton S. Donnelly, a onetime colleague and longtime comrade, years ago encouraged and aided my interest in Russian America as an integral part of the North American frontier. Nikolai N. Bolkhovitinov, Alex's mentor, supported our cooperative work from afar. Lydia T. Black, never reluctant to share her views, welcomed Alex and me into her home in Kodiak for a memorable evening of lively discussion. Richard A. Pierce, a career-long advocate for Russian American history, gladly lent his expertise and assistance to our project.

While Alex and I traveled together, we were able to take advantage of the expert advice and warm hospitality of many other scholars. Devoted Fort Ross supporters John Middleton and Lyn Kalani were our hosts during a coastal California research visit. In the Portland area we were aided and entertained by Basil Dmytryshyn and Thomas and Sherry Vaughan. At the University of Alaska Fairbanks, the hospitable Katherine Arndt guided us to sources at the Rasmuson Library and Molly Lee toured us through the Museum of the North. In Anchorage we were cordially entertained by historian Katerina G. Solovjova. At the Alaska State Office of History and Archaeology, State Archaeologist Dave McMahan went far out of his way to accommodate our Baranov-related inquiries, as did Alaska State Museum curator Steve Henrickson and Bruce Merrell, Alaska bibliographer at Anchorage's Loussac Public Library. During our stay in Kodiak, Ellen Lester, curator of collections at the Baranov Museum, was a pleasant and very helpful guide. A weeklong visit to Karluk—eventful in salmon and a certain large Kodiak bear—was made possible by Larry Sugak's genial hospitality. In Sitka during the Tlingit two hundredth anniversary commemoration of the peace with Baranov, we were pleased to meet Nora Marks and Richard Dauenhauer, leading authorities on Tlingit myth and history, as well as David Nordlander, the historian in charge of the ambitious bilingual Meeting of Frontiers website for the Library of Congress. We were also made welcome by Greg Dudgeon, superintendent of Sitka National Historic Park, and impressed by his adept costumed dancing during the public potlatch proceedings.

As this book took shape, close friends were generous in boosting the project along. At an early point Jean Hurtado, then an editor for a leading western university press, was firm in her opinion that Baranov deserved not a mini-biography but a full-scale study. Al Hurtado, who has traveled with me along many scholarly trails, did not turn back when my footsteps led into the far north. Steve Crump gave me the benefit of his decades of experience as an editor, clarifying my prose in ways that readers should cheer. For tech support I have relied on the charming Victoria Owens, a redheaded St. George who slays digital dragons with a right click.

At an advanced writing stage, I was fortunate to have the manuscript reviewed by three outstanding authorities on Russian America: Steven Haycox of the University of Alaska Anchorage history department; Richard Dauenhauer, emeritus professor of native languages at the University of Alaska Southeast; and the Reverend Dr. Michael Oleksa, editor of *Alaskan Missionary Spirituality* and a foremost teacher and writer about Native Alaskan peoples and cultures. Their perceptive comments, corrections, and suggestions have rescued me from many blunders. At various points they have each nudged me in different ways to rethink my interpretations and modify my conclusions about the Baranov era. They will not find me always in perfect agreement with their perspectives on Baranov, but I have given them each quite serious consideration.

The staff at the University of Washington has worked diligently to ease the publishing process. Senior acquisitions editor Ranjit Arab and his predecessors, Julidta Tarver and Marianne Keddington-Lang, were models of patience while waiting for a finished work. Mary Ribesky, assistant managing editor, has ably kept the book on schedule, while marketing director Rachael Levay brings a true promoter's spirit to her role. The skillful copy editing of Jane Lichty has earned my admiration and deep thanks. I am grateful also to cartographer Barry Levely for his excellent map work.

As every writer knows, a project like this entails countless hours of self-imposed solitary confinement. I have been transfixed in front of a computer keyboard for days on end, virtually oblivious to the world around me. The challenges to normal life caused by this conduct have been wonderfully met by Sally Owens. She not only has managed our marriage for these many years, but with her expertise as a microbiologist, Sally has made significant and welcome contributions to my understanding of the medical aspects of Russian American history. And with good grace, she has tolerated the presence of Aleksandr Baranov as an unbidden guest at our dinner table. Yet I believe she will now not be sorry to see him gone.

KEN OWENS
Sacramento, California

EMPIRE MAKER

I

A MAN OF THE NORTH

Aleksandr Andreevich Baranov was born during the winter of 1746 in Kargopol', then a prosperous trading town located on the Onega River in northern Russia. His upbringing as the oldest son in a prosperous merchant family provided him with the early experience and emotional underpinning for a successful business career. Following a suitable marriage, when he was more than thirty years old ambition and a taste for adventure led Baranov, his wife, and his younger brother to move to Irkutsk, the capital of eastern Siberia, where great fortunes were being made by the talented and shrewd.

IN WINTER, IF NO STORMS ARE BLOWING, RUSSIA'S NORTHLANDS are profoundly silent. Throughout the countryside a blanket of snow covers tundra, marshlands, meadows, rolling hills, and gently sloping low mountains, muffling every sound. Rocky shores along the northern coast front onto a motionless frozen ocean. Stepping softly, reindeer graze the lichens that spread across thin-soiled taiga lands as clouds move south and bring fresh snowfall to drift over open marshes and fields. Layers of white fall quietly onto the stands of pine, fir, and birch that grow here and there throughout the region. Small streams are frozen through, their banks hidden behind thickets of willow. Dense ice tops shallow lakes and the few broad rivers whose sluggish currents continue to flow, hidden and unheard, northward toward the sea. In the woods a fox may be stalking a terrified vole, each animal focused with quiet intensity on its own survival. During short winter days no bird sings. Hibernating bears sleep soundlessly in their hidden dens. In the coldest weather occasionally a loud crack may echo through the woods, the sharp, gun-like report of a bursting limb. If people are about, their voices will carry a great distance in the cold air. So too will the repeated thud of an axe in strong hands cutting through a tree. Otherwise, the land is hushed, a vast and still territory that at first appearance may seem almost deserted of life.

Settlements were far apart in the eighteenth century as they still are today, usually near the seashore, alongside a river or lake, or bordering one of the crude wagon roads that crossed over the highlands. Peasant villages and trading towns wakened noisily to the daily rituals of work and worship, islands of sound in a quiet landscape. Church bells rang out in the darkness of winter mornings, a signal for the devout to trudge through the cold to an early service. While some recited their prayers, other villagers looked to the household chores, tended animals, hauled water, chopped wood, helped children get dressed. At some point family members would sit together, ask a blessing, pour cups of black tea from a steaming samovar, and perhaps share a loaf of dark, dense rye bread. Soon enough each person would rise and go about the day's activities, guided by the bells marking the proper time for every spiritual duty.

Weather, physical environment, and cultural history had shaped in the north a distinctive region of the Russian nation. The White Sea and the Barents Sea form a northern margin. Seashore, tundra, and taiga covered with mosses and a low growth of shrubs curve around bays and inlets, with river estuaries offering slight harbors for small boats. Although ice-locked during winter months, as early as the tenth century these waters brought Norsemen and other adventurous traders to the White Sea coast in search of salt and furs. To the east are the Ural Mountains and beyond them the vast spaces of Siberia, a rough country of legendary cold and isolation, inhabited by tribal peoples whose ways seemed strange and primitive to early European observers. On the west is a border area long disputed with the Finnish people, a district of lakes, rivers, and forested low hills known as Karelia. On the south, the land rises gradually to a divide separating northward-flowing rivers—principally the Neva, Onega, North Dvina, and Mezen—from the immense river systems that drain central Russia on their way southward toward the Black and Caspian Seas. Along these waterways heavily laden riverboats on long summer days traveled routes that connected northern Europe with ancient trade centers in Persia and India.

This northern country is the homeland for a diverse mix of peoples. Along the shores of the White Sea and extending inland are the Pomory, an indigenous population who have maintained their identity despite strong pressures for assimilation in modern times. Skilled fishers, ocean hunters, and watermen, expert in building and sailing small boats, the Pomory also worked seacoast salt-extraction sites well before the era of recorded history. They carved walrus ivory and became woodsmen, farmers, and herdsmen of the genetically unique Kholmogor cattle.[1] Farther south the region was colonized from the tenth century by Slavs and Finnic tribes, including the Beloglazaia Chud', Karelians, Sami, and others: self-reliant herders, farmers, and craftspeople who held strongly to their separate traditions.

While ethnic Russians predominated, early census tabulations for the northern region identified people of nine distinct cultural nationalities who customarily spoke their native languages within their own communities. Many peoples of the region were adept in trading, sailing, boatbuilding, and hunting. Generally, they had no fear of traveling long distances either over-land or by sea. They blended the legendary hardiness of Russia's common people with an adventurous spirit especially prominent among the durable folk who live alongside the rivers and oceans of northern lands.[2]

The rural population in the eighteenth century was composed almost entirely of free people, so-called state peasants who avoided the long-term process of enserfment that had eroded peasant freedom in Russia's richer agricultural areas to the south and west. Although their independence of movement was legally restricted (a law many northerners found ways to evade), state peasants controlled their own property and their own lives. Usually they paid no taxes but owed annual levies in kind and service duties to the state. Until 1764, when Empress Catherine II (Catherine the Great) issued a secularization decree, some portions of the northern countryside and their peasant villagers belonged to Orthodox Christian monasteries and churches. Following secularization, the common folk of the former church lands also became state peasants, sharing the status and obligations of other free rural residents.[3] The powerful Stroganov clan with its headquarters at Solvychegodsk near the White Sea, the center of the northern salt industry, retained valuable lands and control over a peasant workforce. But nowhere else in the north was there a dynasty of great hereditary landowners com-manding armies of serfs; nowhere else did people find themselves compelled to bow low before the tyranny of demanding lords.

Throughout the north, the Russian Orthodox Church was well estab-lished in its spiritual supremacy. No town was too small, no village too poor to maintain its own place of Orthodox worship, its wooden spire or onion-shaped dome rising above the surrounding square-built wooden homes. In larger towns, each neighborhood, almost a village in itself, had its own church. Richer churches in the wealthier sections supported a more ambitious architecture, with multiple domes and elaborate furnishings, standing alongside the imposing stone residences of the merchant elite.

The people of the Russian north were loyal in their devotion to the true faith, religiously observant and conservative to the core. Here and there, remnants of pagan practices persisted in isolated rural communities, carefully hidden from the priest's sight. But in public view peasants and townsfolk alike made their church the focus of faith and the infallible guardian of social order. The priest heard every confession, baptized every child, consecrated every marriage, and officiated at every funeral. He kept even the darkest secrets of the congregation. Seldom a man of learning, usually married to a local woman, he was no richer than the people he counseled from day to day. He labored to inspire the respect and affection of his congregation, and if he was blessed with a strong, melodious voice for leading the choir's liturgical chants, his popularity was likely assured.

* * *

The Kargopol' district, where the Baranov merchant family had situated itself by the middle years of the eighteenth century, was famed as a farming region. Moderate winters and good soil—clay and sand with abundant limestone—made this the prime agricultural area in northern Russia. The traditional three-field system remained in common use, with one field left fallow each season on a rotating basis; but ambitious farmers were attempting to improve their holdings. Peasant families worked together, men and women shoulder to shoulder, to extend their fields by draining marshlands and clearing away forest fringe areas. The more progressive increased their yield by intensive application of animal wastes as fertilizer. These efforts paid dividends. The Kargopol' district became the region's granary, raising barley, rye, oats, flax, and peas for local markets. Although peasant landholders in the north did not approach the immense production of grains for export that characterized the serf-farmed estates in Russia's black-earth territories and the southern steppes, by the end of the eighteenth century Kargopol' crops were feeding other northern provinces as well.[4]

Cattle and sheep raising and dairy farming were also expanding in this region during the eighteenth century. Herders had access to broad, well-watered meadows for grazing and for hay crops that fed cattle during the northern winters. At the end of the eighteenth century, the first general land survey in the Kargopol' district calculated that meadowlands amounted to more than six hundred thousand acres, over twenty percent of the total.[5] Farm-raised beef and veal as well as increasing amounts of butter and cheese

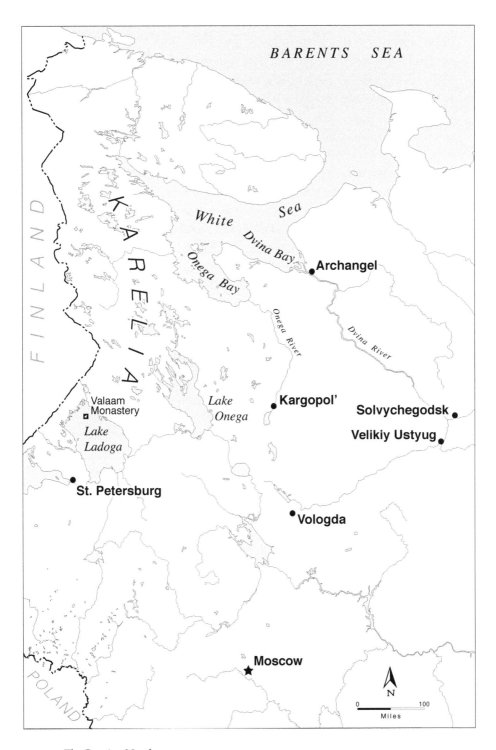

MAP 1. The Russian North

found buyers in the region's urban centers. Yet even within larger towns many families kept a cow or two for milk. Flocks of sheep supplied both meat and wool for village use. In most localities the villagers observed Ram Sunday: a day when the men slaughtered and roasted a ram with appropriate ritual and everyone feasted. The villagers' cows or sheep could serve another purpose as well. With no locks for their doors, cautious wives would make sure each evening to have a family animal staked nearby as a sentinel, able to warn against prowlers who might come skulking in the dark of night.

The northern forests provided all Russians a natural wealth of timber, supporting an eighteenth-century technology built on solid wooden foundations. Timber served a thousand purposes. Logs from the forest provided household fuel and the raw material for charcoal, burned whenever intense flames were required. Wood was the basic material for all types of construction; iron and steel remained dear in price, while building stone and bricks were scarce, too expensive for common use. Skilled workers in wood made tools and farm equipment, ox wagons, carts, sledges, and the durable flat-bottom boats that carried heavy cargoes along the rivers during the summer.

Their log houses were usually huge, elaborate structures, two or more stories tall, where dozens of people lived together in a multigenerational patriarchal family under one sharply pitched roof. Between these homes a network of wooden walkways offered secure paths over snow and mud during the wet seasons. Close by, elaborately crafted wooden churches—the older churches typically built with high, tentlike central towers and domes decorated with fish-scale shingles made from ash—were a striking and justly famed feature of the region's country villages.[6] Many villages also had a wooden windmill of distinctive design, with all the machinery and sometimes even the millstone itself fashioned of wood.

Peasants frequently carved their own eating utensils from wood and fashioned their furniture—benches, tables, chairs, bedsteads—from timber. Their hands could craft clever wooden toys prized by children and wooden crests or other decorations for the wooden walls of their wooden homes. Kargopol' carpenters, northern artisans in wood, traveled widely, their reputation creating a demand for their labor in St. Petersburg, Moscow, and other distant places. Even today, though many old skills have been lost, the region around Kargopol' is renowned for some of Russia's finest examples of log architecture and wood-crafted folk art.[7]

Throughout the north, the natural world carried a living inventory of fish, birds, and mammals made useful in one fashion or another by the peoples of the countryside. In Pomory territory on the White Sea, herring, cod, seals, whales, and immense annual spawning runs of Atlantic salmon were part of the northern country's exploitable wealth. On their island and cliff-side rookeries, seabirds laid a bounty of protein-rich eggs that might be gathered by agile searchers. Migrating geese, ducks, and swans provided a similar bounty as they arrived in great flocks during the spring to nest on the tundra. Semi-domesticated reindeer were year-round sources of meat, milk, and clothing for those who lived on the tundra, and they could be used for pack animals and powering sleds and sledges. Meadowlands and forest were home to a great variety of fur-bearing animals—bears, wolves, otters, beavers, squirrels, foxes, and lynx—whose pelts were valued for household use and for exchange in the marketplace. More for home consumption than market, grouse and migrating geese were fair game for hunters, their kills ignored by government authorities. As a by-product of hunting and herding, leather making was a small-scale, low-skilled peasant industry that added to the household output of marketable items.

On weekly market days in the villages, the principal goods for trade were foodstuffs, local crafts, and a few essential clothing items made of homespun linen and wool woven by nimble-fingered wives and their daughters. During winter months weaving was a favored occupation for housebound women, particularly if there were girls in the family who each would want to accumulate a substantial dowry of clothes and household linens.

Also during the winter, when animal pelts were in prime condition, traders arrived from a distance to purchase local products. They offered cheap vodka and a small selection of manufactured wares in exchange for dressed furs and home-tanned leather. Often in winter and summer, a peddler or two appeared in the village marketplace, bringing ribbons and rings and bright scarves, steel needles and thimbles, mirrors, perhaps snuff and pipes and smoking tobacco, perhaps also knives, pots and pans, and samovars for brewing tea, along with other trinkets and low-cost merchandise to attract village women and their menfolk. They traded in an economy with little or no cash. Barter was the rule, and accumulated wealth, if it existed, was seen most often on feast days in the form of gold earrings, finger rings, and bracelets adorning the wives and daughters of the more prosperous peasant households.

Arriving like honored visitors, peddlers and traveling merchants from the region's larger towns linked the villages of northern Russia to a wider world of commerce, national events, and slowly changing cultural fashions. Literacy was rare among all except a small, socially select educated class. Even in St. Petersburg's royal palaces there were officials and courtiers unable to read. Without any public media, reliable information was elusive. Rumor was rife, gossip a powerful force, hearsay and speculation almost as important as authenticated fact in determining popular opinion.

Townsmen received news and exchanged information mostly by personal contact in their regular gathering places—merchant guild halls, taverns and inns, the city hall, the public market—and in the front rooms of their homes where their shops were located. Rural people relied mainly on the reports brought to them by travelers and traders. Villagers would trust their priest— likely no better educated than his parishioners—to explain and interpret the stories that reached them from the outside, however garbled these accounts might be. But the commercial men who carried the news to the rural folk were not disinterested. They came with something to sell; in exchange they looked for something to buy at a good price. To this extent, villagers were all too vulnerable to false reports, deliberate misinformation, and the sharp practices that shrewd, grasping men might try on them. They were right to be suspicious.

In the larger towns, merchants and traders had a wary understanding of one another. They shared with other townsmen a distinct classification within Russia's eighteenth-century social hierarchy. They were part of the *meshchanstvo*, a category of urban residents that also included artisans and craftsmen. The *meshchane* were property owners; they paid taxes, made church contributions, provided properly for their families, and managed the day-to-day economic life of urban Russia. Merchants were organized as well in their separate associations, the merchant guilds. Each town had three, with financial requirements that reflected the comparative economic status of their members. These guilds promoted the interests of the resident merchants as a whole and mediated the inevitable disputes between partners or competitors.

Empress Catherine II instituted in her Guberniia Reform decree of 1775 a code of municipal reorganization that brought order and hierarchy into Russia's urban structure. The new rules gave special privileges to an elite class of great merchants, the *kupechestvo*, who were exempted from payment of certain taxes. The less privileged had to register in their separate guilds and pay a tax of one percent annually on their declared wealth.[8] No matter how far they might travel or where they might relocate, all merchants remained enrolled as citizens, taxpayers, and guild members within their original home jurisdictions, with annual obligations that were at once patriotic, legally necessary, and commercially astute.

With its diverse peoples and broad-based economy, its independent peasantry, orderly townsfolk, and ambitious traders, the Russian north was a land apart, distinctive in its society and cultural styles during the eighteenth century. It was relatively independent from control by noble autocrats in Moscow and St. Petersburg. Not a rich land, it was no prize for armies to fight over. Never had a huge, harsh military campaign devastated this countryside. And for anyone who came to know it in detail, it might appear a land of many virtues. Here was a living ideal: a blueprint of sorts for the society that Aleksandr Baranov, a man of the north, would attempt to bring into existence when he came to manage Russia's North American colonies.

* * *

Kargopol', the place of Aleksandr Baranov's birth, is one of the oldest towns in northern Russia. Its origins are obscure; even the meaning of the town's name remains a matter of dispute. The generally accepted statement is that the town was founded in 1146, a year before the establishment of Moscow. An unchartered settlement of traders from medieval Novgorod may have existed at the site decades earlier.[9] Kargopol' townsmen long sided with Novgorod in its rivalry with the emerging Muscovite state. In the fourteenth century Prince Gleb of Kargopol' joined with other princes to defend their homeland against Tatar invasion, only to die a glorious battlefield death in 1380. Supported by a surge of settlers from the south, Moscow's rulers triumphed over Novgorod during the fifteenth-century reign of Ivan III (Ivan the Great). In the mid-sixteenth century his grandson Ivan IV (Ivan the Terrible) assimilated the Kargopol' district into his personal domains and ordered a census that documented the town's prosperity. By the seventeenth century a Crown-appointed military governor controlled the region.

Further changes came early in the eighteenth century with the ambitious reforms of Peter the Great, who instituted regional governments called *guberniia*s that placed authority in the hands of local administrators. Only partially successful, this structure was refined by Empress Catherine's 1775 decree.[10] Her reorganization made Kargopol' the district center of Olonetskaia province within Novgorod guberniia.

Kargopol' stands on the west bank of the upper Onega River, where Novgorod merchants coming from the west crossed the river on their way to Velikiy Ustyug and the Ural Mountains. The northward-flowing Onega is a critical river link in the centuries-old trade route that connected Moscow and Vologda to the south with Karelia and the Pomor'ie region. It offered convenient access by water to Archangel and the nearby Solvychegodsk salt-producing district. At this commercial intersection, traders profited by dealing in salt, furs, locally produced foodstuffs, and vodka. A major hub and a lively river port, Kargopol' was never very large despite the wealth of its merchant elite. No more than six thousand people may have lived there at the time of Baranov's birth.[11]

Fire, the scourge of northern Russia's wooden towns and cities, periodically swept through Kargopol', devastating homes, businesses, and government offices and destroying the records that they sheltered. According to the sketchy surviving evidence, at midcentury the Baranov family residence was a substantial stone mansion set near the riverbank close to many similar structures, each surrounded by abundant land and the outbuildings necessary for a wealthy residential estate. Downstream, wharves, docks, and warehouses filled the commercial waterfront.

Close by, bordering a square known as the Old Market, stood the Church of the Holy Spirit, the Baranov family's place of worship. A stunning high-walled white structure built of locally quarried limestone, it was completed in 1692. Its architecture is distinguished by large windows with carved surrounds rich in elaborate, fanciful detail, and an ornate blind apse, all topped by five domes with their crosses pointing upward toward heaven. Though now abandoned, this structure and Kargopol''s other extraordinary examples of limestone-walled churches give glorious testimony to the wealth of the town's merchant elite, their spiritual dedication, and their cultural aspirations.[12]

* * *

Aleksandr Andreevich's father was Andrei Il'ich Baranov, a native of Solvy-chegodsk.[13] We know little about him except that he was a merchant and married to Anna Grigor'evna, a woman of his same age who probably came to Kargopol' with him early in their marriage. His business must have prospered; he provided well for his family and saw two of his children make favorable marriages among the small circle of merchant families that dominated business and public affairs in this provincial capital. Anna Grigor'evna appears to have been a virtual partner in his enterprises, participating with her advice and counsel. After her husband's death, her oldest son called on her to manage the family's remaining business interests at Kargopol' after he left home and moved first to Siberia, then to North America.

A lack of church and family records leaves unknown the exact dates of Aleksandr Baranov's birth and his christening. Indirect evidence indicates that he was born in late 1747.[14] Following Russian custom, during his adult years he and his colleagues celebrated as a personal holiday his name day, December 3, the day dedicated to St. Aleksandr Nevskii, rather than his actual birthday.

Three other children were born to Andrei Il'ich and Anna Grigor'evna Baranov. The oldest was Evdokiia, a sister nearly two years old at the time of Aleksandr's birth. His brother, Petr, born in 1756, was nine years younger than Aleksandr. The youngest was another sister, Vassa, born in 1760 when Aleksandr was thirteen and Petr was four.[15] With remarkable consistency, the personality traits and family dynamics among the four Baranov children reflect recent findings concerning the influence of birth order. Throughout their adult lives Petr—Petya would have been his childhood nickname— gladly followed the lead of Sasha—the customary affectionate name for young Aleksandr—taking the expected role of the admiring younger brother. From a psychological perspective, Aleksandr's lifelong self-confidence, his adventurous spirit, ease with others, and his obvious sense of his own competence in any situation were all traits that imply he enjoyed as a youngster the nurturing attention of his older sister, who would continue to be the family's dedicated caregiver throughout her life. From early in his career Aleksandr demonstrated a practiced habit of command that likewise may have been rooted in childhood, with a much younger brother and sister, neighboring children, and the Baranov family servants willing to do his bidding.[16]

The children, especially the two boys, must have been raised as favored members of this substantial household, with servants and doting parents to look after their needs and heed their whims. Russian families cherished their children. Birth was risky, and infancy and childhood were full of dangers from disease and mishap. Especially in winter, colds, coughs, and fevers were endemic, with pneumonia an ever-present menace. Other seasons brought their own hazards, including the constant danger of serious intestinal afflictions due to tainted water and faulty sewage disposal.

Eighteenth century medical practice had little to offer except a body of traditional household remedies, supplemented by questionable medicines often worse for the patient than no treatment at all. In the north, long exposure in a *banya*, a steam sauna, followed immediately by a plunge into icy water or a romp in the snow, was considered a sovereign remedy. Learned physicians advocated copious bleeding and purges, supplemented mayhap with a regime of narcotic-laced potions, chemical poisons in pill form, and heavily alcoholic tonics. Among the common people, vodka was a cure-all.

Childhood diseases such as measles and mumps and severe epidemics of diphtheria and influenza took a heavy toll. For good reason, Russians especially feared smallpox, a disfiguring and frequently fatal disease that spread along trade routes from city to city and from region to region with terrifying swiftness, its cause and mode of transmission then unknown.[17] In addition, a century and a half before the development of germ theory and antisepsis, any wound or accidental injury, natural risks for active children, could prove fatal. With so many perils threatening their youngsters, parents and all members of the extended household customarily treated them with a doting concern that placed them in a treasured status. Sasha and Petya Baranov—lively, intelligent, and apparently in robust health—would have been such treasures for their parents.

As an adult, Aleksandr Baranov was a man of great emotion, openly expressed. On various special occasions he wept with gratitude for favors he had received. More often he flew into an angry, yelling, cursing rage, shaking his fists and threatening violent harm to those who defied him. These highly dramatic displays of temperament, not uncommon in Russian male society, must have been conditioned by the undocumented emotional history of his childhood. Although his anger was easily roused, it was also easily set aside. After one of these emotional storms, if he had been able to outface his opponent, within a few days Aleksandr Andreevich was quite likely to forgive those who had provoked him. This well-established pattern of towering anger, followed soon by a resumption of cordiality, suggests that as a boy this oldest son had learned to get his own way by an adroit use of temper tantrums. In later years he was not self-deceived; he would readily admit his character weaknesses and wrongdoings, including outbursts of anger, in letters to trusted friends. His parents' pride in their oldest boy may well have been accompanied by a sense that young Sasha Baranov was indeed a handful.

Among other distinctions, Kargopol' is famed for its brightly painted toy whistles, *Kargopolskie igrushki*, small simple figures made from the local clay in shapes and colors appealing to children. Fish, horses, and other creatures are popular, along with a traditional centaur figure that represents a man and horse together, the man's head adorned with a wide-brimmed clay hat. We can easily imagine such fanciful creations, horses and centaurs in particular, in the hands of the Baranov boys, first Aleksandr and later Petr. Hobbyhorses would have been a natural next toy for each of the boys in turn, allowing them to gallop about their home in high glee, banging into furniture and dismaying the household. They each may soon have had their own well-mannered pony to ride along Kargopol''s streets and out into the countryside, perhaps with a servant to look after them and keep their adventurous urges in check. On occasion, during drunken sprees at Sitka, a much older Aleksandr Baranov took hilarious pleasure in playing at horse races around his dining table with visiting American sea captains, equally drunk. This behavior could well have been cued by fondly recalled childhood experiences.

With the riverbank close by their dooryard, Sasha and Petya Baranov would have been dull youngsters indeed not to take an interest in the busy world of men who sailed from Kargopol' and the other men who built the boats, kept them in workable order, and handled the cargoes arriving from distant places. Boys would know that the Onega warms enough for swimming during the long, hot days of the northern summer and that toy boats will float easily on its current.

The river and nearby lakes abound in fish that can be caught with simple gear suitable for youngsters: a long pole, a sturdy plaited horsehair line, a bobber, and a baited hook. *Palia* (the region's trout-like species), pike, *okun'* (perch), roach, and various whitefish would be fine trophies to take home to the kitchen. A more imposing catch during fall spawning runs might be a silvery, shiny-scaled nelma, a white-fleshed salmon of Arctic waters that can weigh forty pounds or more.[18] As they expanded the range of their youthful rambles, the docks, the wharves, and the workshops and warehouses along the river must have been irresistible magnets. And what father, himself immersed in the town's trading and shipping business, would not have been proud to introduce his sons to the scenes of his prosperous activities?

A rowboat or small sailing skiff should have been perfect for two young men becoming accustomed to life on the water. It is easy to imagine Sasha initiating his younger brother into the delights of sailing and taking responsibility for looking after Petya as they went farther and farther from the docks and wharves of Kargopol'.

From the time he first left Siberia to sail to Alaska, only to be shipwrecked on the way, Baranov demonstrated that he was secure and handy at the helm of boats and small ships. When necessary he proved able to repair or even rebuild them. For years he sailed his own boat, unaided and often alone, on long voyages in all seasons through the waters around Kodiak Island and

Sitka Sound with never a serious mishap. He understood boat construction, and he was able to improvise in Alaska a kind of tarry pitch for shipbuilding purposes, no doubt reflecting his experience with another of Kargopol''s well-known industries, the manufacture of Kargopol' tar for ship's stores and for use in processing high-grade leather and furs. These were skills and knowledge that an alert, clever fellow could have gained while visiting the boatyards of Kargopol' and that would be developed as he sailed the Onega northward to the coast and along the shores of the White Sea.

We know none of this with the certitude that documents might grant, but Baranov's obvious skills as a small boat sailor and the ease of his adaptation to maritime Alaska, after having spent more than a decade in Siberia, give compelling evidence for crediting Kargopol', the Onega River, and the White Sea as his school of practical preparation for a career on the watery margins of Russian America.

The formal education of the Baranov sons is another topic lost to history. If we can judge the experience of the youthful Aleksandr Andreevich by the attainments of his adult life, plainly he received the substantial training necessary for success as a merchant. He wrote well and enjoyed corresponding with friends in long, chatty letters. He sent detailed orders to literate subordinates and careful reports to superiors, all in his own hand. At the end of his career an audit of his accounts at New Archangel showed that his bookkeeping, though far from meticulous, was accurate and honest. Except for rudimentary German, he spoke no foreign languages, and he did not indulge in philosophical discussions.

In short, the mature Aleksandr Baranov was a practical man. His knowledge and understanding were the results of a practical commercial education in a provincial town of northern Russia. Whether he and his brother studied with a tutor at home or were pupils at a local school remains unknown. Working as an apprentice with his father or other Kargopol' merchants must have been a big part of his advanced education. In August 1805, writing a letter of deep gratitude to Emperor Aleksandr I for honors he had received, Baranov summarized his training and career expectations in succinct, elegant language: "Being born in the merchant class and educated almost by nature alone, being devoid of the necessary learning and knowledge of the sciences," he declared, "I could never hope to acquire the distinction that your Imperial Majesty . . . has bestowed upon me."[19]

Although there is no reason to suppose that he knew the essays of Voltaire or the political treatises of John Locke, we might guess that in the homes of his parents and their friends the young Baranov was exposed to a provincial Russian version of western Europe's enlightenment culture. Visitors to his last Alaskan headquarters—a substantial wooden structure set on a hill overlooking the harbor at New Archangel on Sitka Sound—found that he appreciated art, was fond of music, and enjoyed the companionship of intelligent, affable men able to discuss world affairs. With educated guests his manners were, in his generation's phraseology, cultivated and unfailingly courteous—even though they might all be emptying far too many bottles of wine or hard liquor. He was a provincial, but certainly neither an ignoramus nor a boor.

* * *

Just before Baranov's eighteenth birthday in 1765, Kargopol' was leveled by fire. Only a few limestone churches and other stone buildings remained standing, and even these structures suffered heavy damage: foundations cracked, the wooden domes badly burned, icons scorched, and priceless frescoes on sanctuary walls ruined beyond repair. We do not know Aleksandr Andreevich's whereabouts during this great conflagration, but the consequences were significant for all Kargopol' citizens. The town needed to be rebuilt from the ground up. Already the growth of Archangel and St. Petersburg had begun to diminish Kargopol''s importance. As in other such urban disasters, some burned-out residents must have abandoned the town permanently, to start over again at a more promising location. The Baranov family remained, taking part in a reconstruction effort that lasted well over a decade. Town design, building construction, and precautions against fire and other urban dangers would be no mysteries to the mature Aleksandr Baranov.

Midway in her reign Empress Catherine II decreed that Russia's towns be reconstructed and new towns laid out according to a rectangular plan, following enlightened principles. Kargopol' leaders implemented the empress's wishes by rebuilding their town on a simple grid pattern, with large square blocks and wide streets aligned to the course of the Onega River. A special rule banned log houses close to the town's churches, both for safety's sake and to maximize the architectural viewscape that had become Kargopol''s pride.

Town planners designated a freshly cleared area as the New Marketplace, a name still in use after more than two centuries. Between 1772 and 1778, Kargopol' craftsmen erected in the center of this space a three-story stone bell tower, which the townspeople dedicated as a monument to the empress. With its blending of baroque and neoclassical elements, the bell tower stood as a striking visual affirmation of Kargopol''s recovery.[20] But Empress Catherine never came on tour to see it, nor did Aleksandr Baranov ever return in later years to marvel at this newest architectural masterpiece in his place of birth.

* * *

At age nineteen, when the paper trail for his career begins, young Aleksandr Andreevich was already well established in business. The evidence is a document dated October 1, 1767, drawn up in Kargopol' and preserved in the Russian State Historical Archive in St. Petersburg. This document is a contract between Baranov and another Kargopol' merchant. In vague terms it provided for a trading partnership between the two men, with the other man promising to fulfill his obligations to Aleksandr Andreevich, indicating that Baranov had supplied the capital for this partnership.[21] The circumstances for this agreement are obscure. Perhaps his father had died by this time, with Aleksandr Andreevich administering the estate and carrying forward the family's business interests. Or perhaps the young man was acting on his own, having already accumulated enough capital to deal independently in loans and trading speculations.

A similar partnership contract dated ten years later demonstrates the wide geographic sweep of Baranov's business ventures. The document records an agreement between Aleksandr Andreevich and Ivan Grigor'ev Pozdeev, another Kargopol' businessman. Baranov was advancing Pozdeev a substantial sum. With this money, Pozdeev agreed to purchase goods at a regional trading fair in the Nizhegorod district, in the Volga River basin of western Russia. According to the contract terms, these goods should be "appropriate to sell in St. Petersburg and in Ladozhskai-Uspenskaia fair, but just such things [that could be sold] without any delay and for cash." The contract further stated that Pozdeev would do his best for the partnership, "so that [they would] have cash by autumn." Upon Pozdeev's return to Kargopol', the partners agreed "to split the profit, hoping it won't be a loss, into two equal parts, or according to the amount of capital involved."[22] Further provisions make it clear that Baranov and Pozdeev were trading in vodka and other alcoholic spirits—all termed "wine" in Russian official usage—with the necessary license to be obtained from the Kargopol' magistrate for five thousand rubles. This high price reflected the government's expectation of large profits from the liquor business. Although the records are sparse, these documents support the statement by Kiril Khlebnikov, Baranov's first biographer, that until 1780 he engaged in trade in Moscow and St. Petersburg.[23]

Baranov's early business ventures were aided no doubt by personal and family ties to the Kargopol' merchant community. Sometime during the 1770s he made a socially appropriate marriage to Matreona Markova. Her father, merchant Aleksandr Markov, was at one point the town's mayor. He had prospered as a traveling trader in salt and spirits, operating with the expensive government license required for this business.[24] Aleksandr Andreevich's new mother-in-law was Irina Prigodina, who likewise came from a well-to-do Kargopol' merchant family. With their home situated close to the Baranov residence in the Dukhovskoi district, the Markovs most likely became a second source of business advice and potential financial backing for the ambitious young entrepreneur and his wife.

While the date of the couple's marriage is not shown in any documents, town records show that Matreona was seven years younger than Aleksandr Andreevich.[25] This age difference indicates that the match was likely not based on the sentimental emotions of romantic love that only became widely popular a century later. Instead, it must have been a marriage grounded in social propinquity reinforced by family approval.

Circumstances indicate that the couple were married while Matreona Aleksandrovna was still in her adolescence, perhaps no more than fourteen or fifteen, not an uncommon age for Russian girls in the merchant class to marry at the time. Hence the dominant leadership role that Aleksandr Andreevich had learned to take with his younger siblings might naturally be extended to his young bride, shaping a dynamic that assigned Matreona a position of dependency. But as events would prove, she would not always remain content to find satisfaction as a dutiful and obedient wife to the ambitious, perhaps emotionally inattentive, older man whom she had wed. It may be telling that the couple remained childless, although in time Aleksandr Andreevich would have children with another, possibly more devoted, female companion.

Aleksandr Andreevich's younger sister Vassa likewise made a socially appropriate marriage, becoming the wife of Kargopol' merchant Aleksandr Kuglinov, ten years her senior. The Kuglinovs, like the Baranovs and the Markovs, lived in the prosperous Dukhovskoi district, in a house inherited from the bridegroom's father. Over the years the Kuglinovs maintained close personal ties and possibly financial connections with Aleksandr Baranov. In due time their son Athanansius (Afanasii) Aleksandrovich would join his uncle in North America, where he served as a leader of trading parties in

Alaska, the Hawaiian Islands, and as far away as northern California. In 1819 he accompanied his uncle from Sitka aboard the navy ship *Kutuzov*, sailing for St. Petersburg on what became Aleksandr Andreevich's fatal last voyage.[26]

Neither of the two other Baranov siblings married in Kargopol'. Evdokiia, the older sister, remained at home after their father's death, a companion for their mother. Sometime after the great Kargopol' fire, Aleksandr Andreevich built a home of his own in the Dukhovskoi district. This became the residence for his immediate family. By 1784, when Aleksandr Andreevich was thirty-seven years old, Kargopol' city records indicate that both Petr and Evdokiia were living in this home, although their mother maintained a separate residence. At that time, according to the same records, Aleksandr Andreevich was elsewhere, "absent and living according to [municipal] passports [in Irkutsk, Siberia]."[27] Although Matreona joined Aleksandr and Petr Baranov in a quest for Siberian fortune during the 1780s, she later returned to Kargopol'. It is not clear where she then took up residence, but Evdokiia lived in the house built for Aleksandr, as a local chronicler states, for a very long time.[28] Petr meanwhile married and lived with his wife in an isolated outpost in the northern area of eastern Siberia, carrying on business as a trader in partnership with Aleksandr Andreevich.

During his early business career, from 1767 to 1777, Baranov was under obligation to pay ten thousand rubles to the Kargopol' magistrate. This hefty sum may have represented a tax on his father's estate, or perhaps it was in part the cost of Aleksandr Andreevich's membership in Kargopol''s second merchant guild. Unable to manage the whole amount, he did make a half payment of five thousand rubles on June 1777, after he had been working at least ten years to sustain the family fortune and improve his own finances.[29]

While remaining in his native town, Aleksandr Baranov learned a great deal about the opportunities for wealth that could be found in northern Russia. His trade activities extended at least as far as St. Petersburg and Nizhniy Novgorod, and very likely to Moscow as well. He maintained the family's good relationship with the Kargopol' local authorities. No doubt with coaching and active assistance from both his father and later his father-in-law, he became familiar with Russia's so-called *otkupnaia* system of licensed trade monopolies in salt, spirits, and a few other high-value commodities.

Rigorously enforced by imperial officials, this system was a type of indirect excise taxation intended to benefit the imperial treasury. It resembled on a limited scale the exclusive trade rights in foreign lands granted by the English Crown to the Hudson's Bay Company and East India Company. Even

though Empress Catherine was adamantly opposed in principle to commercial monopolies, her endless need for royal revenues convinced her and her
advisors not to interfere with this somewhat antiquated, extortionate, but
highly lucrative source of income. While still in Kargopol', Baranov secured
such a license for the sale of both salt and spirits in distant places. Not yet
thirty years old, he had opened what might become his gateway to riches.

In Kargopol', however, there remained his large debts. The five thousand
rubles Baranov owed to the local authorities must have been a great burden,
crippling his ambition for riches. Other businessmen had claims against him
as well. Years later another Kargopol' townsman petitioned the empress with
a complaint against Aleksandr Andreevich and his mother, saying they had
not paid him money due for his services and for their mutual interest in
the salt trade.[30] Despite the best efforts of Aleksandr Andreevich, after his
father's death the Baranov family fortune may have begun to dwindle.

The most attractive solution was a move to Siberia. While the Kargopol'
region was declining, Siberia was gaining a reputation as a place where great
fortunes could be made in a short time. It was the "golden bottom" in the
Russian phrase: a huge, harsh territory that attracted the courageous and
enabled them, God willing, to return home with purses and pockets well
filled. Because of his experience as a licensed trader selling vodka and other
spirits, and perhaps because of influential friendships that would help him
secure the same type of privileges east of the Urals, Aleksandr Baranov could
well expect to make greater profits there than in northern Russia. Moreover,
since he and Matreona had remained childless in Kargopol', it might not be
too inconvenient for her to make the move with him. Petr Andreevich, still
single, likewise would be an able assistant and constant support in meeting
the challenges of Siberia.

In 1781, most likely in winter, these three family members set out together
for Moscow and then across the Urals toward Irkutsk, the distant commercial
and governmental capital of eastern Siberia. According to custom, in Kargopol' there would be dozens of social calls before their leave-taking. Their
last day at home must have been filled with emotional moments, tearful
farewells and earnest pledges to sustain friendships and family ties despite
the great distance that would separate them. Finally, following a last round
of embraces, they would have departed as evening approached and traveled
through the night, when the roads were frozen hard, riding in an enclosed
horse-drawn sleigh. They were leaving behind the familiar surroundings of
the Russian north for the altogether strange setting of Russia's farthest east.

II

SIBERIAN MERCHANT CAPITALIST

—————————— ❋ ——————————

During the 1780s Aleksandr Baranov acquired and then lost a considerable fortune in Siberia, primarily as a merchant trader and government agent for collecting liquor taxes in Yakutsk guberniia. He pursued many different ventures, including the establishment of a glass factory and opening a trading business with the Chukchi people in the farthest northeastern region of Siberia. With a substantial estate in Irkutsk, the capital of eastern Siberia, he became a member of the local mercantile elite and a particularly good friend of Grigorii Shelikhov, the ambitious, farsighted managing director of the most successful fur business in the maritime North Pacific.

—————————— ❋ ——————————

FOR SIBERIAN BUSINESSMEN, TRADE MEANT TRAVEL, AND travel in Siberia was never easy. In Aleksandr Baranov's time, winter was the least difficult travel season. During spring months the roads became all but impassible due to the treacherously deep, glue-like mud of the Siberian countryside. Rivers choked with ice floes and swollen by snow runoff added peril to any journey. In summer the mud turned into knee-deep gritty powder that slowed struggling horses to a torturous pace. Choking dust and swarms of insects—mosquitoes, black flies, and tiny, stinging gnats—tormented summertime travelers and their animals. Fall rains again brought mud and swollen rivers, stranding those who were waiting for ferries or hoping to float partway by riverboat rather than trudge the roadways' bottomless sticky mire by horse and cart.

In wintertime the mud, dust, and bugs were gone; roadways and rivers were frozen, and sturdy Siberian horses could pull loaded sleighs with some speed across ice and hard-packed snow. But the intense cold of the brief winter days and long winter nights was a cause for concern. Fahrenheit temperatures of forty and even fifty degrees below zero were common enough to occasion no special remark by those experienced with Siberia's weather. With the cold, sleigh accidents, equipment mishaps, and injuries to animals, drivers, and passengers were constant worries. At the extreme, the trip could be fatal. Such was the fate, for example, of the royal chamberlain Nikolai Petrovich Rezanov, who died apparently from pneumonia at Krasnoyarsk in March 1807 after falling from his horse into a partially frozen river as he was traveling from North America toward St. Petersburg.

In any season, the trip from northern Russia into Siberia was long, tedious, and exhausting. Going first from Kargopol' to Moscow and then eastward across the Ural Mountains to Irkutsk, the route apparently taken by the Baranovs, the distance was nearly four thousand miles—a thousand miles farther than between New York and San Francisco. The terrain included great mountain ranges, broad lowland bogs, rapidly flowing rivers, and mile after empty mile of tundra, forested taiga, and grassland steppes interrupted by sharp highland ridges.

The only through route was the Trakt, the Great Siberian Post Road running between St. Petersburg and Irkutsk. Although the road itself was scarcely more than a rutted wagon track in most areas, by imperial order posting stations were located every ten to twenty miles apart. Maintained by residents of the countryside, these crude way stations allowed an exchange of worn horses for fresh and offered rough facilities for eating and lodging. Savvy travelers depended on their own provisions and arranged to sleep in their own sleighs or tents, thus avoiding some common hazards. A few towns along the way—Perm', Yekaterinburg, Omsk, Tomsk, and Krasnoyarsk—afforded weary visitors a chance to pause, perhaps enjoy a good meal or two, and sleep securely within four walls. Town merchants typically charged high prices to replenish the stores of these wayfarers.

Theft and assault were added dangers for the unwary. Many post station tenders and sleigh drivers had arrived in Siberia as exiled criminals, sentenced as murderers or habitual thieves; they may not have been fully rehabilitated by their banishment from European Russia. Some sections of the route were notorious for assaults by roving bands of escaped convicts or tramps who might waylay and rob their victims, then kill them to avoid detection. For those easily frightened, stories of attacks by bears and wolves were yet one more argument against venturing across the Siberian wilds.

It was hard to predict how long the journey would take. An exceedingly positive report issued by the government near the end of Empress Catherine II's reign said that an express message carried horseback between the imperial palaces at St. Petersburg and the regional capital of Irkutsk could reach its destination in less than two months. But this did not reflect the realities of movement across Siberia by most people.[1] At the time the Baranovs made the trip it took ordinary travelers at least three months to reach Irkutsk from Moscow with short pauses along the way.[2]

Beyond Irkutsk, travel in central and eastern Siberia was still more unpredictable because of climate and primitive frontier conditions. The main route led northward, beginning as a wagon and cart road that ran approximately 150 miles across a wide steppe to Kachuga Landing, the head of navigation on the Lena River. At this point all freight and travelers went aboard river barges. Once the ice broke in May, these vessels floated 1,500 miles downstream to Yakutsk, eastern Siberia's second-largest town and the world's coldest area of civilized habitation. It was located at the junction of the main routes that connected Irkutsk with far northern and far eastern Siberia. Following the Lena River downstream, travelers could reach the scattered Russian riverside outposts in the tundra country bordering the Arctic Ocean—a journey that Aleksandr and Petr Baranov must have made often.

Most traffic from Yakutsk went eastward toward the port of Okhotsk and the Kamchatka Peninsula. This was a hard journey, more than seven hundred miles by rough trails or no trails, along routes that varied according to weather, travel conditions, and the good judgment or unchecked whim of guides and drivers. Only packhorses and mules were able to cross the rugged mountains, wade through icy swamps, and ford the many swift streams that separated Yakutsk from Russia's Pacific seaboard.

In the mid-1730s it had taken Vitus Bering nearly two years to move the men and supplies for his second North American exploration voyage from Irkutsk to Okhotsk.[3] During Baranov's era all the men, equipment, and supplies necessary for outfitting North Pacific voyages and all returning freight still had to be packed over this haphazard, unimproved passage, perhaps the riskiest line of trade and communication regularly traveled anywhere in Europe or Asia.[4] If unburdened by heavy freight, Baranov and his contemporaries might be able reach Okhotsk from Irkutsk in three months or less, compared with the minimum of two months it took royal messengers to complete this trip.[5]

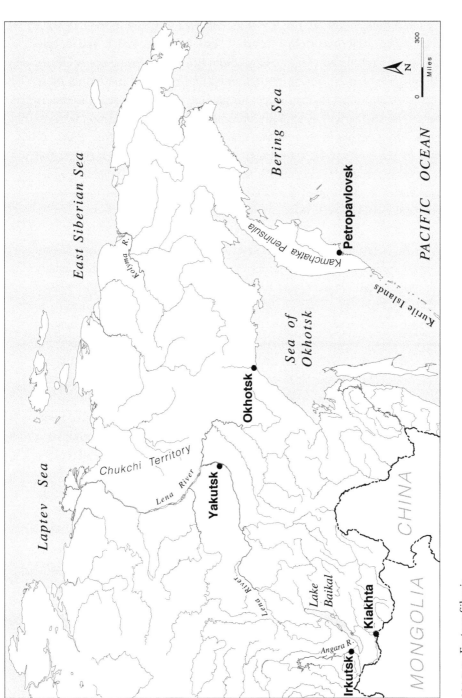

MAP 2. Eastern Siberia

Until the construction of the Trans-Siberian Railroad in the late nineteenth and early twentieth centuries, distance, discomfort, and danger walled off central and eastern Siberia from the luxury-loving upper classes of European Russia. But for the Baranovs and others of their kind, these obstacles improved their prospect for gaining some of Siberia's legendary wealth for themselves. East of the Urals, there was no competition with the great lords who dominated western Russia's economic affairs from their palaces in Moscow and St. Petersburg. So long as the royal treasury received a steady income from tax collections, Siberia in the late eighteenth century was a commercial frontier favorable for bold merchant enterprise, with only minimal attention from Russia's ruling class.

* * *

From the beginning, furs were the primary motive for Russian expansion into Siberia. Since early medieval times the Russian north had supplied quality furs to domestic markets and for export to western Europe. But heedless hunting practices, driven by high prices and insistent tax demands from Crown officials, undercut the fur economy. By the mid-sixteenth century the region's major fur-bearing animals were almost extinct. Exports slumped and tax revenues declined. To the east, Siberia's tundra and forest lands offered a new source for prime furs—black fox, white fox, red fox, ermine, beaver, squirrel, wolf, wolverine, and, above all, the dense and lustrous sable pelts. A ruthless rush began to turn Siberia's animals into Russian wealth. For hunters, traders, and government agents alike, Siberian furs were soft gold.

The conquest and colonization of Siberia began in the last decades of the sixteenth century as a speculative enterprise financed by the wealthy Stroganov clan. Small independent bands of mounted fighting men—Cossacks in the Russian terminology—and other free-spirited adventurers advanced eastward with astounding speed. Moving along river basins from west to east, they led a rampage after furs with strong support from an imperial authority whose officials took a full share of the plunder. By the early decades of the eighteenth century, aggressive fur hunters—Russia's *promyshlenniks* (proh-mísh-luh-nix)—had brought under the imperial government's nominal control all of northern Asia eastward to the Sea of Okhotsk and Kamchatka. Although the broad, fertile drainage of the Amur River on the southeast remained a land disputed between Russian royal officials and China's Manchu rulers, Siberia's central and northern expanses were loosely integrated into the Russian empire.

With the Crown's authority so rapidly and recklessly extended, Russian control over Siberia's Native societies was maintained by force of arms, the seductions of trade, and what could appear to Native peoples as the Russians' technical wizardry. It was a cruel conquest, as forceful and heedless of the consequences for Siberia's diverse cultures as any episode in the annals of early European imperialism. Nor was it always effective in quelling resistance. In the most remote areas, small numbers of Russians lived precariously amid large Native communities.

Typically, the Russian empire was represented in a frontier garrison by a mere handful of underpaid, demoralized, and dissolute soldiers and perhaps two or three equally debauched government agents and traders. Uniformly, the Russian invaders demanded that Native women serve them as domestic drudges and sexual partners, while their men were forced to make dangerous winter expeditions to bring more furs into these isolated outposts. "God is far above and the tsar is far away" the invaders said, coining a classic adage to excuse their most heinous acts. In such circumstances, minor disturbances could flare into violent protest against decades of mistreatment and injustice.

The only surprise is that Native uprisings were relatively rare. For the most part the Siberians, lacking firearms and divided among themselves, with their communities afflicted by newly introduced diseases and soon ravaged by alcohol, submitted more or less meekly to the Russian yoke. Equally important, as inevitably happens in every meeting of cultures, harmonious marriage unions between the invaders, all male, and Siberian Native women moderated every sort of social difference and created a community of interest especially in the children resulting from these unions.[6] Although some Siberian Native men might be resentful, these cross-cultural unions generally eased frontier social frictions, while many of the Russo-Siberian progeny of these unions—recognized as loyal subjects of the Russian Crown—would continue generation after generation to follow their fathers' line of work as promyshlenniks in the fur business.

In economic terms, Russian exploitation of Siberia's fur wealth was starkly predatory. Royal officials, backed by Cossacks or other military forces, demanded an annual levy from Native communities. Called *iasak* (yeáah-sahk), this tax was paid in furs, with the amount fixed by an arbitrary sliding scale meant to extract the maximum possible returns for the imperial treasury. Along with iasak, the Russians also demanded *pominki* (poh-mínk-kee), an additional fur donation supposedly made as a voluntary gift to honor the emperor but which in fact became a compulsory surtax expected from every Native community.[7] These levies forced Siberian peoples to supply the Russians all the furs they could gather, meanwhile neglecting their own needs.

To enforce their demands, imperial agents exacted an oath of allegiance from every Native community that came under their control, registered all men between the ages of eighteen and fifty, and recorded the fur receipts from each registered person. By swearing the oath of allegiance as they were arbitrarily required to do, the Native tribesmen legally became imperial subjects, but it was a status with no apparent benefits. Russian officials frequently took village elders hostage to ensure cooperation, imprisoning them in jail-like quarters. If the able-bodied hunters in a Native village were slow to deliver their assigned fur quota, their wives and children might also be taken captive until iasak demands were met. Other punitive measures sometimes included the confiscation of the Natives' domestic livestock or reindeer and in extreme cases even the burning of their villages.

Imperial officials also collected a ten percent excise tax on all the furs taken by private hunters and traders, to be paid in kind—one fur in ten on all grades of peltry—before any trading could be conducted legally. To manage these collections and the plunder from iasak and pominki, the imperial government created a special agency, the Fur Treasury of the Siberian Department. Its operatives manned customs posts in all main towns. From these bases, customs agents created an inspection system to detect smuggling of untaxed furs. Working for a share of any illegal fur they seized, they patrolled the main travel routes and conducted heavy-handed searches of everyone leaving the fur-producing districts, including even royal officials. Among other intrusions, their instructions required them to search for furs sewn into the voluminous petticoats worn by women travelers.[8] Such rules led to a regime of habitual bribery and official complicity in tax evasion at every level. And yet, despite its flaws, the fur tax system was vital to the empire; it brought in an estimated one-tenth to one-third of all royal revenues throughout the seventeenth and eighteenth centuries.

By 1781, when the Baranovs reached Siberia, the fur business was changing. The principal market now was China, whose Manchu overlords had agreed to open trade with Russia in the 1689 Treaty of Nerchinsk. Within months after seizing the throne in 1762, Catherine the Great abolished the state monopoly on the China trade. Private merchants took over this commerce, paying high duties not only on the furs they sold but also on imported Chinese goods. Along with Siberian peltry, Russian merchants exchanged

Siberian-grown ginseng and Russian-made linen fabrics for China's teas, silks, dried rhubarb root, and fine cottons. These items were in great demand among the upper classes of the two countries, while cheap Chinese black tea became the staple drink in peasant households throughout Russia.[9]

But just as had happened in northern Russia a century earlier, by the 1780s overhunting, combined with a sharp decline in Siberia's Native populations, were cutting back the supply of sable and other land mammal furs. Meanwhile, rising prices continued to encourage further depredations on fast-dwindling animal stocks. Excessive taxes and the empire's free market system were fatal to animals and indigenous people alike.

The Baranovs witnessed a radical shift in market conditions. As Siberia's prime peltry became scarce, Chinese merchants turned their attention to sea otter pelts and the skins of fur seals. Russian and Native hunters killed these animals in the coastal waters along the northern rim of the Pacific. The most valuable by far were the sea otters, found throughout an original range that extended from the Kurile Islands and Kamchatka eastward to the Aleutian Islands, all along the maritime mainland of Alaska, and southward as far as Vancouver Island in modern British Columbia.

This business began as an outgrowth of Russia's North Pacific explorations led during the 1740s by Vitus Bering and Aleksei Chirikov. By the 1780s the sea otter fur business was solely a Siberian-based enterprise, largely beyond the control of the imperial government. It was managed by small merchant companies with their headquarters in Irkutsk.[10] When the Baranovs arrived there, the successful merchant entrepreneurs in these perilous North Pacific ventures were emerging as a distinct commercial elite, the latest parvenu Russian entrepreneurs to build their fortunes in Siberia's "golden bottom."

Under treaty terms, Russia's Chinese trade could be conducted only at a single site on the Siberian border with China, four hundred miles south of Irkutsk and Lake Baikal. It was the most isolated and inhospitable location imaginable: a barren, wretched piece of ground with two rudimentary towns situated 250 yards apart. The Chinese town was Mai-mai-cheng (translated as "buy-and-sell"), a carefully planned outpost with large houses and wide streets. Because Manchu potentates meant to discourage their subjects from settling in a place where they might be exposed to corrupt foreign influences, by imperial order the town was totally devoid of women.

Kiakhta, Russia's "town built in the midst of nowhere," had been put up by soldiers from Siberia's Tobolsk Regiment a year after the signing of the 1689 trade treaty. Surrounded by wooden palisades and a moat, it gave the appearance of a beleaguered frontier fort. In addition to its small military garrison, the town contained a wooden church, a large enclosed marketplace, a storehouse for dried rhubarb, a vodka distillery, and a few grand houses that were residences and places of business for the merchants.[11] Although political differences between China and Russia sometimes brought a temporary trade closure, in Baranov's time this desolate place was the most important focus for moneymaking in Siberia and perhaps in the entire Russian empire.

* * *

It is likely that the three Baranov family members made the journey from Kargopol' across Siberia at a moderate pace. Even if they were traveling light, with little personal baggage and no cargo of trade goods for their business ventures, they would have been tempted to linger at Nizhniy Novgorod, Perm', and the series of trading towns along the post road east of the Urals. At each of these places they could have seen regional fairs that offered an introduction to Siberia's profit-making opportunities. More than tourists, the Baranovs were immigrants who expected to settle and participate in the business world of Russia's eastern territories.

As they neared the end of their journey the Baranovs would have traveled upstream along the Angara River to reach Irkutsk, the commercial depot that controlled Russia's access to the Kiakhta trade. Located on the river's right bank at the junction of the Angara and Irkut Rivers, Irkutsk is forty-five miles downstream from Lake Baikal, the world's largest and deepest freshwater sea.[12] This inland ocean is so huge that it significantly moderates summer and winter temperature extremes throughout the region.

Russian settlement at Irkutsk had begun in 1651–52, when government officials arrived to build a garrison fort and collect the fur levy from the region's Buryat people. By 1724 the town numbered about three thousand souls, with four out of five residents being merchants. Three decades later nearly seventy percent of all Siberian merchants lived in Irkutsk.[13] The town remained little more than a military and trading garrison at that time, built around a palisaded square. Its principal urban amenities were a wooden cathedral erected in 1693, a trade bazaar, a meat market, several all-night saloons, and a bathhouse for traveling merchants.

Shortly before the Baranov's arrival Irkutsk experienced its own trial by fire. A hayloft blaze in 1779 grew into a massive conflagration that leveled two-thirds of the town. As in Kargopol', rebuilding was carried out according to Empress Catherine's urban planning decree, producing an orderly configuration of wide streets bordered by new brick and stone structures. Yet the streets went unpaved and the sidewalks remained only plank causeways built over open sewer ditches. The result, as one author declares, was a strange mixture of squalor and grandeur, with construction continuing throughout the decade the Baranovs lived there.[14]

During this era of rebuilding, a booming fur trade economy reshaped Irkutsk and greatly improved the quality of life for its inhabitants. Rich merchants and their families dominated civic affairs. The city's population had reached an estimated ten thousand to twelve thousand by the time of the Baranovs' arrival. Its attractions included more than a dozen churches and several imposing stone mansions, many of them owned by men who were active in both Siberian trading enterprises and the North Pacific sea otter business.

Like the newly rich the world over, these merchant moguls ostentatiously displayed their wealth with imposing new homes filled with luxury goods from China and European Russia. Close to the Angara River an imposing two-story stone structure housed the Irkutsk provincial chancellery. Nearby the Spasskaia Church stood next to the city's administrative headquarters. In 1781 Irkutsk also became the capital for a governor-general who represented the Crown throughout eastern Siberia.[15] A year later the Imperial Academy of Sciences donated thirteen hundred books to the city as the foundation for Siberia's first public library. Although health facilities were minimal, Empress Catherine established a center for smallpox vaccination in Irkutsk, one of the first in any nation.

A city of opulent display and even some small claim to cultural distinction, Irkutsk gained repute as "the Paris of Siberia." This cosmopolitan northern metropolis caused a later American visitor to exclaim over its beauty. "Irkutsk," this adventurous tourist wrote, "looked so pleasant and comfortable, with its fine wide streets, its substantial and spacious buildings, and numerous churches, that it appeared to us more like a pleasant dream than an actual, enjoyable reality."[16]

Although built on a larger scale, Irkutsk in many ways resembled the reconstructed Kargopol'. The Siberian capital displayed a style of wooden architecture that would be familiar to any emigrant from northern Russia. Here also local limestone provided the material of choice for the richest churches and the stately mansions of its wealthiest residents as well as government buildings. Its riverside location must have pleased the Baranovs, and its society and cultural ambience may also have suggested home to them since some thirty percent of Irkutsk residents during the 1790s were natives of the region between Vologda and the White Sea, including Kargopol'. Among the wealthiest Irkutsk merchants were immigrants from Vologda and from Tot'ma, Archangel, Velikiy Ustyug, and Solvychegodsk, the principal trading towns in the Russian north. Speaking in a familiar accent, these men and their families would have been able to welcome the Baranovs and guide them in their adjustment to their new place of residence.

* * *

Despite the debts he had left behind in Kargopol', Baranov arrived in Irkutsk with ample capital to start business as a Siberian merchant trader. As his basic enterprise, he made an arrangement with Archangel merchant Fedor Lobanov to take over Lobanov's profitable franchise as a Crown agent for the sale of vodka and other spirits throughout northeastern Siberia. His trading territory extended as far north as the Arctic Ocean and eastward to the shores of the Bering Sea. Although the financial details are not on record, Baranov must have paid Lobanov a considerable sum for the royal license and his established commercial network. Subsequently, Lobanov retired, sold his Irkutsk estate, and returned to Archangel, while Aleksandr and Petr Baranov took over his operations. It was the same type of business that they had operated from their original base in Kargopol', but now their activities expanded over a far wider and wilder territory.

The concept for their business was simple. The Baranovs bought alcohol from three state distilleries all founded near the Angara River in the Irkutsk region during the mid- and late eighteenth century. They sold wholesale to licensed drinking houses mainly in Yakutsk. From this central point, the Baranov enterprise extended to include the port of Okhotsk on the east and distant small settlements such as Zashiversk and Zhigansk in the northernmost districts of Yakutia. Remote and hard to reach even by Siberian standards, with severe weather conditions and virtually no amenities, these locations demanded from traveling traders the utmost physical stamina to carry on their business. And these were also the places where fur merchants might still secure the highest-quality and most abundant Siberian furs from Native peoples and Russian hunters.

In addition to their inventory of vodka and other spirits, the Baranov brothers handled a range of basic items. According to a 1786 inventory, the goods in their post at Angarsk included a large amount of rye bread, a supply of flatiron suitable for fashioning into tools and household implements, and plenty of tea—the low-quality Chinese black tea loosely packed or pressed into bricks that served as an everyday drink for Russian settlers and Siberian

Natives alike.[17] They were, in effect, running a small general store—an eighteenth-century mini-mart—for this little Russian settlement on the Angara
River and for trade with the region's Buryat people. Their other trading outposts most likely were stocked in similar fashion, catering to the needs of
small Russian and Native communities.

As mentioned by his first biographer, Baranov ventured into many related
lines of activity, developing a horizontal integration of his Siberian business
enterprises. One of these operations was the management of government
distilleries at the three small settlements in the Angara district that supplied
spirits for all licensed traders in eastern and central Siberia. Records for this
branch of Baranov's profit-making activities have not survived, but most of
the principal Irkutsk merchants involved in the North Pacific trade in sea
otter pelts also took part in the alcohol franchise business. It may well be that
Aleksandr Andreevich formed his earliest business ties with the members of
Siberia's emerging North American fur aristocracy through his management
of these state distilleries.

Another Baranov venture in Siberia also related to the trade in spirits. He
became a government tax farmer, so-called, appointed by imperial authorities to collect excise duties on alcohol sales in the Yakutsk district. For lack
of documentary evidence, this facet of his activities has likewise remained
obscure. In essence, the job required the appointee to act as a government
agent in making tax collections. Instead of working for a salary or specified
contract payment, the tax farmer took part of the money he collected as his
return for the investment of time and labor and for the financial and personal
risks involved in the position. A successful tax farmer had to have the confidence of government officials. (On this point, Baranov's later wry comment
concerning the St. Petersburg bureaucracy may be relevant. "Petersburg," he
observed, "appreciates money most of all.")[18] He also needed the ability and
boldness to deal firmly with difficult cases. It is reasonable to assume that
Aleksandr Andreevich possessed these qualities in abundance and that he
made a good profit from managing the government's tax collections. But the
truth of the matter was probably well hidden, since Aleksandr Andreevich
would have been his own prime client, responsible for collecting taxes on his
own trade in spirits throughout Yakutia. Certainly, the job carried with it a
self-evident opportunity for artful evasion of the tax laws.

One additional Baranov project is well documented: building and running a glassware factory for the Siberian market, mainly making the bottles
needed by the Angara distilleries under his management. In this business

Baranov joined with Kirill (Erik) Laksman, a Finnish savant and professor of science who was an honorary member of the Russian Academy of Science. Nine years older than Baranov, Laksman supplied the technical expertise, while Aleksandr Andreevich apparently provided funding and handled the buying and selling.[19]

The project began soon after Baranov's arrival in Siberia, when the two men asked the then governor-general of Irkutsk guberniia, Ivan V. Iakobi, for a permit to build the factory at a site named Taltsinsk. A piece of meadowland alongside the Taltsy River and near the Angara River, Taltsinsk was twenty-eight miles upstream from Irkutsk. On Governor Iakobi's orders, Baranov and Laksman got their lease. A surveyor marked out a twenty-four-acre tract for the glassmaking plant, with an extra eight hundred acres (three hundred *desiatinas*) set aside to house twenty exile workers who would be the factory's labor force. Each worker and his family had room for a house and a farm lot of slightly more than forty acres (fifteen desiatinas).[20] The two partners paid Irkutsk guberniia the nominal sum of sixty-three kopeks a year for rent, a more than nominal fee of twenty-five rubles a year for each worker, and a small excise tax for each bottle they made.

Construction began in autumn of 1784. Apparently working under Baranov's direction, the workers finished a small laboratory building, a 1,400-square-foot factory with a large glass furnace at its center, a pottery building, barns, a bakery, and a bathhouse, as well as their own small homes. They also built a wooden dam and waterwheel on the Taltsy to provide power to the factory. Laksman soon created glass in the laboratory from local sands with a process involving Glauber salts—a crystalline salt used to generate high temperatures.

To succeed under factory conditions, the partners needed someone familiar with industrial glassmaking. In August 1785 they hired a master glassmaker from Russia's Barnaul glassworks. This expert signed a one-year contract that fixed his salary at 120 rubles a year, double the standard wage rate.

The glassworks began limited production in October 1785. The following April, Laksman boasted to the Irkutsk city council that "Taltsinsk has become the place where the first glass from Siberian bitter salt is being produced. . . . It is significantly better than other types of glass that are produced by using alkaline salt of the vegetable kingdom." His claims even showed an embryonic ecological consciousness, rare in that age. "I consider all factory owners who produce glass from potash in Russia," Laksman declared, "to be enemies of Nature, since they destroy our woods."[21]

In January 1786 Baranov and Laksman hired a young apprentice from Irkutsk to join the factory workforce. His employment contract said that he would learn glassmaking, and in return he would receive food, shoes, and clothes from the factory owners.[22] Apparently, this youngster worked only one year. But when the master glassmaker completed his original contract year, Laksman and Baranov kept him on the payroll. The wording of his new contract indicated that Laksman's claims for the factory's success had been somewhat exaggerated. "The glass factory was not put in order during the year that I worked there," the glassmaker wrote, "and so I did not manage to show my skills at work." He again pledged to work if necessary even on Sundays and holidays, "thus trying to prevent any losses because of somebody's absence or carelessness." Among other promises, he pledged to "prevent time wasting and avoid situations when students or other workers can be lazy and idle at work. And as an honest man, I will monitor all work with diligence." Should production come to a stop "under any unfortunate circumstances" during his absence, the glassmaker also said, he would do everything in his power to find and prepare the needed materials and equipment to resume work. "Everything is to be done in a timely fashion," he agreed, "and the shutdown time is not to be wasted, since the manufacturing process requires a great investment of capital and support. And because our sluggishness can cause considerable losses, I promise to prevent this with all my effort and diligence."[23]

This expert soon had the factory working at top speed. The Taltsinsk plant turned out a basic line of bottles for vodka and other spirits. It also manufactured sheet glass, icon lamps, glass beads in different shapes, cups, and a variety of glass dishes. Irkutsk was the primary market, but the factory's products reached buyers throughout Irkutsk guberniia and beyond Lake Baikal in northern and eastern Siberia. In time, some of these items may even have reached Russian North America.

* * *

The small company settlement housing the workmen and their families much resembled a traditional country village. The homes were log structures built in the northern style, each with a large clay stove in one corner. In animal barns and adjacent barnyards the residents kept a noisy, smelly collection of horses, cows, and pigs. Ducks, geese, and chickens added to the clamor and mess as they scrabbled for food. In small garden plots each family raised vegetables for the table, mainly root crops suitable for the northern climate.

The workers shared access to hay fields and woods, but they lacked tillable lands for raising grains or the leisure time that full-scale farming would require. For this reason, factory families bought their bread from a community bakery. During the long summer and early fall days, outdoorsmen among the workers could enrich their family's table by hunting and fishing. Family outings on holidays and feast days might include picnics or in summer months even an excursion to Lake Baikal, where mild temperatures and genial breezes offered a pleasant respite from factory labor.

According to a local tradition, Aleksandr Baranov kept a small house on the Taltsinsk factory grounds, set on a bluff overlooking the river. He could live here while supervising plant operations. It would be surprising if he did not socialize with the workers and their families. Though it was not his major investment in Siberia, certainly the project interested him greatly.[24]

Yet it failed to become a source of profit. Baranov and his partner even attempted to sell the factory in 1789.[25] After the sale fell through, Aleksandr Andreevich assumed major responsibility for keeping the factory going after his departure for North America. In a 1798 letter to a friend he declared, "My glass factory in Irkutsk is in poor condition." Laksman and his new partners had run the business, he said, "so long as materials left by me lasted," but when these materials were used up, they abandoned it entirely.[26]

As late as 1799 Baranov invested an additional five hundred rubles in the factory.[27] Despite its poor financial record during these early years, the glass factory's eventual success provided the Irkutsk region with an extremely useful industry, and for Aleksandr Andreevich it represented an innovative venture both in business terms and in creating a workers' community. His experience with the Taltsinsk project was a direct forerunner to his later community building on the wider stage of Russian North America.

* * *

As was often the case among merchants everywhere during the eighteenth and nineteenth centuries, Baranov added to his business activities by making occasional loans. The smallest shown in surviving records was a short-term loan of 250 rubles made to an Irkutsk widow. After she defaulted, her son paid off the debt in part by assigning to Baranov his share in a trading voyage headed by the Irkutsk merchant Pavel Lebedev-Lastochkin, a leader in the North Pacific fur business.[28] Other transactions on record include a 1784 loan for 1,900 rubles made to a local official and a 1787 loan for 2,441 rubles to a Mr. Kravtsov, taking furs as a security.[29]

In dealing with most Irkutsk merchants, Aleksandr Andreevich accepted promissory notes, indicating his knowledge of their business and his confidence in their ability to repay on schedule.[30] Presumably, Siberia's high interest rates made the loan business a profitable sideline when Baranov had capital available to put at risk. Sometimes, though, his judgment failed. He received pledges for payments that went long overdue and remained unsettled until friends or close relatives of the borrower made good on the debt.

Even as he was making loans to others, Baranov contracted one considerable debt of his own. In March 1787 he borrowed twenty-nine hundred rubles from Irkutsk businessman Mikhail Krasnogorov for one year. The following January, when he had paid off only seven hundred rubles, he entered into a new arrangement, promising Krasnogorov seven hundred rubles a month drawn from his profits in the wine and vodka business. To cover this obligation, Aleksandr Andreevich told his Yakutsk agent to make sure to pay this sum when it came due every month. "In case you don't have enough cash (which I can't know for sure)," he directed, "sell some of the remaining spirits at any price to get the necessary funds, or give the bill from Mr. Krasnogorov to Gomukov. He [Gomukov] will know that no matter how low a selling price he may be forced to set, he should never default on this promissory note, and that will be very certain."[31]

Despite their best efforts, Baranov and his agent could not meet this payment schedule. When he was arranging to leave Siberia in 1790, Aleksandr Andreevich deeded his Irkutsk residential property to Krasnogorov. A document of 1801 contains a further note on this transaction: "The house, and tallow-melting and candle factories belonging to the Kargopol' merchant Aleksandr Baranov in the first city area in the *Arkhangel'sk* parish #29 were abandoned after the departure from Irkutsk of bourgeois Mikhail Krasnogorov. The owner [Baranov] is away in America."[32]

Although the details are obscure, apparently by the winter of 1787–88 Baranov was struggling with a cash flow problem. He had much of his capital invested in the Taltsinsk glass factory. Other substantial funds were out on loan or tied up in his inventory of trade goods, mainly wine and vodka. With his resources stretched thin, in February 1788, a month after renegotiating his loan from Krasnogorov, he borrowed an extra three thousand rubles for a short term from Lebedev-Lastochkin. This sum he repaid within three weeks.[33]

* * *

As these transactions show, by the late 1780s Aleksandr Andreevich was becoming closely involved with prominent Irkutsk figures in the maritime fur seal and sea otter business. Baranov's operations inevitably drew him into the circle of Siberian traders who were building their fortunes by exploiting the fur resources of the North Pacific.

The most important of these men, both for the future of Russia's commercial and imperial expansion and for Aleksandr Baranov personally, was Grigorii Shelikhov. Approximately the same age as Baranov, Shelikhov was a native of Ryl'sk, a small trading center in the Kursk region near the western border of European Russia. He had moved to Irkutsk in 1772 or 1773, when he was about twenty-five. First he worked as an agent for Ivan Golikov, an older merchant who was also a Kursk native. Golikov's Siberian fortune came from his success as a liquor tax farmer for Irkutsk guberniia.[34]

Backed by Golikov's capital, Shelikhov entered the North Pacific fur business in 1774. He joined with Lebedev-Lastochkin to acquire a seagoing vessel from another defunct trading partnership, and the two men sent a fur hunting and trading expedition to the northern Kurile Islands. They made a handsome profit. Shelikhov then formed a series of partnerships with other merchants experienced in this type of enterprise, joining with them to sponsor hunting and trading voyages both to the Kuriles and to the Aleutian Islands.[35]

From his home in Irkutsk, Shelikhov often traveled to Okhotsk to manage the construction and outfitting of his ships. He then dispatched them on their voyages and took charge of the cargoes and all the partnership business when they returned. Presumably at Okhotsk he met the young woman who in 1775 became his wife. Natalia Alekseevna Kozhevina was the daughter of Aleksei Kozhevin, a prominent navigator and mapmaker in Okhotsk, and his wife, Fiokla. Thirteen years old at the time she wed Shelikhov, Natalia Shelikhova was half the age of her new husband, and she was ardently devoted to him.

After the wedding, the bride's mother moved to Irkutsk to live with the Shelikhovs.[36] The young Natalia would have been fortunate to have the benefit of her mother's coaching in the many aspects of domestic life that became her responsibility as the wife of a prosperous merchant. Support must have come also from her older sister, Ekaterina, married to another well-to-do Irkutsk fur merchant.[37] Even at age thirteen Natalia might have been quite aware of the discussions concerning exploration and trade in the North Pacific that no doubt were parlor talk in her childhood home, and certainly she provided her husband with significant connections both in Okhotsk seafaring circles and among prominent Siberian trading families.

Throughout her marriage Natalia Shelikhova would gladly share the dangers and hardships of her husband's active life. She demonstrated an adventurous spirit that may have owed something to the inspiration of Empress Catherine. And, as Aleksandr Andreevich would come to appreciate, she was

GRIGORII SHELIKHOV. This ambitious Siberian merchant prince is portrayed in a manner that illustrates his grandiose style. Baranov's employer and friend, Shelikhov hoped unsuccessfully to gain generous Crown support for his North American colonization project. His 1791 account of his voyage to America gained him the cognomen of "the Russian Columbus."

totally committed to her husband and to the success of his enterprises. Following her husband's death at a fairly young age, Madam Shelikhova proved herself an active, talented woman quite capable of managing the family's complex business interests.[38]

By the time the Baranov family reached Irkutsk, Grigorii Shelikhov was established as one of the most successful and farsighted Siberian merchants in the North Pacific fur business. He had become acutely aware of the dangers created by the unrestrained rivalry between separate fur companies. They all preyed on the same diminishing populations of fur seals and sea otters, and they all exploited in the same heedless fashion the Native peoples of the Aleutian Islands and adjacent territories. These problems could only be solved, Shelikhov concluded, by enlisting the imperial government in a plan that went far beyond strictly commercial calculations.

As a Russian patriot, he wanted to promote the expansion of imperial authority into the vaguely known North American regions. The explorers Vitus Bering and Aleksei Chirikov had established a first Russian claim to these lands by right of discovery during the 1740s. If an assertion of Russian sovereignty would halt the incursions of merchant traders from other nations, an exercise of national power in the North Pacific would bring advantages both for the Crown and for the Siberian fur trading nabobs.

Although others may have considered similar projects at an earlier date, in 1781 Shelikhov and his partner Ivan Golikov embarked on a sweeping geopolitical strategy to establish a Russian presence throughout the lands rimming the North Pacific. They advocated the creation of a Crown-authorized company monopoly to manage a cohesive, integrated Pacific Rim trading network, backed by government ships and Crown subsidies. With bases in Okhotsk and Kamchatka, according to their plan, authorized merchants would extend Russian trade from the northern Kurile Islands to Japan and southern China and from the Aleutian Islands eastward to encompass all of maritime Alaska and America's northwest coast, possibly extending as far south as Vancouver Island or even to the ports of Spanish California.

Modeled loosely on the British East India Company and the French South Seas Company, the proposed organization would combine the business interests of all the Irkutsk merchants with the territorial interests of the Russian Crown. To be most effective, Shelikhov understood, this grand enterprise would demand a series of permanent overseas posts to serve as bases for hunting and trading. These outposts of empire would be administrative centers for governing the lands and peoples to be brought under Russian sovereignty. A regular schedule of voyages between these posts and Okhotsk could keep the hunting detachments supplied and carry the annual fur returns to Siberia. Such a monopoly would end the destructive competition between Siberian trading companies. Equally important, it would provide incontestable proof of Russia's territorial claims in the North Pacific, thus blocking the incursions of traders from other nations.

In imagining this project, Shelikhov very likely was aided by the geographic expertise of Navigator Aleksei Kozhevin, his father-in-law. Kozhevin was the first Russian mapmaker to see the North Pacific maps drawn by Captain James Cook's third expedition. In April and May 1779, following Cook's tragic death in the Hawaiian Islands, his expedition's two ships under Captains Charles Clerke and John Gore spent six weeks at Petropavlovsk (St. Peter and St. Paul Harbor) in Kamchatka, where Kozhevin then happened to be located. During their stay, the English officers turned over a copy of their journals and maps to the local commander as a safety measure, with the understanding that he would send these documents to St. Petersburg for forwarding to London.

While Cook's ships remained in port, Kozhevin met the English officers and completed a Mercator map of the North Pacific and Bering Sea that combined data from the Cook expedition with information from Russian mariners.[39] Given their common interests, it is inconceivable that Kozhevin would not have shared this highly valuable information with Grigorii Shelikhov and equally inconceivable that Shelikhov would not have hoped to capitalize on it while preparing the proposal he subsequently made to the empress and her councilors.

Shelikhov's plan ran directly counter to the antimonopoly, free trade principles embraced by Catherine, the result of her deep admiration for the liberal economic doctrines of Voltaire and the French philosophes. Nonetheless, when Shelikhov and Golikov returned to Irkutsk from St. Petersburg in August 1781, they formed the American Northeastern, Northern, and Kurile Company—the Northeastern Company for short—as a partnership that also included Golikov's cousin, military captain Mikhail Golikov.[40]

The company's total capital was set at 70,000 rubles; Ivan Golikov contributed 35,000 rubles and Mikhail Golikov 20,000 rubles, while Shelikhov's stake was 15,000 rubles. As a distinctive business innovation, setting it apart from all other Russian fur companies, the charter for the Northeastern Company specified a fixed ten-year period for its operations. It provided that the company would establish permanent settlements in North America and that it would conduct explorations for new territories to be added to the domains of the imperial government. In short, Shelikhov and the Golikovs anticipated that their private concern would serve both the commercial interests of its backers and the imperial interests of the Russian Crown.

To carry out his business plan, Shelikhov embarked for North America in 1783 with three small ships carrying 192 officers and men. Also aboard were

Natalia Alekseevna and their daughter Anna, then three years old. When they returned in 1786, the family included an infant son born in America. By that time Shelikhov had built a company headquarters settlement at Three Saints Bay on Kodiak Island, east of the Aleutians and just south of the mainland Alaska Peninsula. This was the start for the first permanent Russian colony in North America.

After his return, Shelikhov, accompanied still by his wife, journeyed once more to St. Petersburg, where the senior Golikov was waiting. The two men reported their accomplishments and put before the empress and her advisors their plans for an expanded North American colony. In a written account that greatly exaggerated the success of his expedition and the strength of his Kodiak Island settlement, Shelikhov made extravagant requests for direct Crown support. Not only did he seek a trade monopoly in North America for the company, but he planned to ask the empress to grant him the services of a hundred soldiers and a government loan of five hundred thousand rubles for twenty years—a figure the two partners scaled down to two hundred thousand rubles after they reached St. Petersburg. He also requested a government ship at Okhotsk for company use, permission to trade with the English, and the right to trade on any island his men should discover and claim for the Russian empire.[41]

Despite enthusiastic support for their requests from the Siberian governor-general and the Irkutsk chamber of commerce, Shelikhov and Golikov failed to secure royal subsidies and assistance.[42] The empress, while expressing her appreciation for their deeds, declared that "Her Imperial Majesty does not consider it beneficial to grant them exclusive rights for these voyages and trade because such exclusive permission would be contrary to Her Majesty's policies concerning the elimination of all sorts of monopolies." Nor, because of other, more pressing needs for troops, could Her Majesty supply them with the military detachment and artillery they had requested.

Catherine limited her government's support to a gift of a silver sash and a gold medal to each partner, accompanied by a citation recognizing their "outstanding merit and zeal for Us and for the Fatherland."[43] While the sashes and medals were a gratifying reward, the partners were left to finance future overseas exploration and colony building on their own with private resources.

Behind Shelikhov's request for trading rights with the English was another business venture that soon involved Aleksandr Baranov. On the way back from Kodiak Island in 1786, Shelikhov met at Petropavlovsk Captain William Peters, the master of an English merchant ship sailing in the service of the British East India Company. The two men made a deal. They agreed that if Peters would return the following summer with a cargo selected specifically for the Russian trade, Shelikhov would buy it all in exchange for North Pacific furs.[44]

In anticipation, Shelikhov concluded an arrangement with Baranov the following June by which Baranov invested enough funds—very likely the money that he had borrowed four months earlier from another Irkutsk merchant—for a one-third partnership in this enterprise. The two men expected to make their profits within a year or two, when all the English cargo would have been sold.[45] But the deal ended with a disaster; Captain Peters shipwrecked and perished on Bering Island, with only two crewmen surviving.[46]

Despite this disappointment, by the end of 1787 Baranov and Shelikhov had become closely linked. During Shelikhov's frequent absences from Irkutsk, Aleksandr Andreevich looked after his affairs in the Siberian capital and kept him posted on significant events. Their surviving correspondence suggests that Baranov was in financial trouble and that Shelikhov had come to his aid. "I would like to express my humble gratitude for your friendly behavior toward me," Baranov wrote in December 1787, when Shelikhov and Natalia Alekseevna were in St. Petersburg. Along with a report on business matters, Baranov assured Shelikhov that the couple's children were fine. "I can inform you about myself," he added, "only that I am healthy and I am trying to put in order my upset affairs."[47]

A year later, in another detailed business report, Baranov explained that his problems were due to losses in the wine trade resulting from dealings with Shelikhov's partners the Golikovs. "That is why," he wrote, "I feel total disorder in my business." He ended with a plaintive observation. "In other times," Baranov stated, "I would not say a word, but I have now discovered the most extreme level of ingratitude, which you know about."[48]

Among other topics that figured largely in Baranov's letters to Shelikhov was the progress of the Billings Expedition, a well-funded government exploring project meant to survey the geography, Native peoples, and natural history of the extreme North Pacific and Bering Sea—in a sense, the Russian empire's extravagant response to Captain James Cook's third expedition. Authorized by the empress in 1785, the expedition was commanded by a young British-born naval captain, Joseph Billings, who had sailed with Cook.

The entire command and all the expedition's supplies came from St. Petersburg overland to Irkutsk and by July 1786 reached Okhotsk. There Billings's officers supervised the construction of two large vessels and various smaller craft.[49] Meanwhile, Billings and his second in command, Russian Navy lieutenant Gavrill Sarychev, spent two summer seasons with the expedition scientists, sailing along the Siberian coastline of the Arctic Ocean in small boats. After spending the winter of 1788–89 at Yakutsk, Billings returned to Okhotsk in late June 1789 to oversee the launching of his newly completed ships, the *Slava Rossii* (*Glory of Russia*) and the smaller *Dobroe Namerenie* (*Good Intent*). But a week after the expedition started for the open sea, the *Dobroe Namerenie* ran aground and was lost. In the *Slava Rossii* Billings and his men traveled to Kamchatka, where they wintered at Petropavlovsk while constructing another ship with the iron fittings salvaged from the wreck, planning to depart for America in the spring of 1790.

Relying on news that reached Irkutsk from Okhotsk and Petropavlovsk, Baranov kept Shelikhov informed of Billings's Arctic seacoast explorations, contrasting the expedition's limited results with Shelikhov's great deeds at Kodiak Island.[50] More critically, he alerted Shelikhov to the trouble that Billings was causing. M. S. Britiukov, a minor Russian official at Okhotsk, had told many stories about Shelikhov's barbaric treatment of Native peoples on Kodiak and adjacent islands.[51] On this basis, the overzealous Billings ordered Shelikhov's arrest and sent a bill of particulars to the Admiralty in St. Petersburg.

As Baranov related, the new Siberian governor-general, Ivan Pil, branded Britiukov's charges a lie. Pil even gave a full copy of the accusatory document to Aleksandr Andreevich for Shelikhov's benefit. Baranov assured Shelikhov that he had written to all his influential friends in St. Petersburg in order "to destroy the slanders of Billings in the Admiralty College" and to ask their help "in justifying the right."[52]

For the time being, Baranov and other Shelikhov partisans were able to blunt the criticism against him, but in time these charges would return to become more troublesome, amplified by the reports of other Russian visitors to America's shores.

✳ ✳ ✳

Baranov's relationship with Grigorii Shelikhov was not restricted to business affairs. These two ambitious men, approximately the same age, came to like and trust each other, each appreciating the personal qualities of the other. Their relationship soon encompassed myriad personal ties. Shelikhov's sister-in-law, for example, the wealthy widow Ekaterina Golenishcheva, was godmother both for Shelikhov's children and for the stepchildren adopted by the Baranovs in Irkutsk. In 1788 Aleksandr Andreevich himself served as godfather for Aleksandra, the fourth daughter born to Shelikhov and Natalia Alekseevna.[53] Later the same year he served as a host and tour guide in Irkutsk for Anna, the oldest Shelikhov daughter, while her parents were in St. Petersburg.[54] During Shelikhov's absences from Irkutsk, Baranov acted as an advisor and trusted friend to Natalia Alekseevna, even though in July 1789 she complained to her husband that she did not appreciate the restrictions Aleksandr Andreevich placed on her travels after she had again become pregnant.[55]

In the spring and summer of 1788, while Shelikhov remained in St. Petersburg with his wife and Golikov, Baranov undertook another job on his behalf. He began supervising the renovation of the Shelikhov house in Irkutsk. Apparently, it had suffered severe damage during the couple's absence, and now Shelikhov planned to combine the repair work with various structural improvements. Aleksandr Andreevich repeatedly assured his friend that the work was going well, providing details of the improvements and keeping a watchful eye on the workmen. At one point he paid the craftsmen fifty rubles from his own funds in order to speed the job. He also sent regular reports on the well-being of the Shelikhov household. These messages included news about some of the fifteen Native youngsters from Kodiak Island who had come to Irkutsk with the Shelikhovs in 1786 and who now were being schooled at the merchant's expense.

Sometime in 1788 Shelikhov asked Baranov to take a post as resident chief manager in Alaska for the Northeastern Company. The appointment would require Baranov to travel to Shelikhov's newly founded settlement on Kodiak Island where he would supervise the company's hunting and trading business. Aleksandr Andreevich refused Shelikhov's offer, as he told Kiril Khlebnikov many years later, "because of his [own] complex trade undertakings." Shelikhov repeated his proposition two or three times in 1788 and 1789, only to meet with the same response. But the two men remained in close contact, so Shelikhov was well aware of Baranov's situation as his fortunes again rose and, as chance would have it, soon fell.[56]

* * *

Independent of his dealings with Shelikhov, another aspect of Aleksandr Andreevich's "complex trade undertakings" in the late 1780s was an expansion of his operations into Siberia's farthest northeastern region as a trader to the Chukchi people. Of this venture he reported to the Irkutsk town authorities: "My business will be carried out in the Okhotsk Oblast' for trading activities and the formation of the company, which is being established to conduct trade with the *Chukotka* people along the Anadyr River."[57]

Baranov was moving into an area visited by very few Russians. Bordered by the Arctic Ocean on the north and the Bering Sea on the southeast, the Chukchi Peninsula is a wide, treeless tundra region. The Chukchi were then the most difficult of all Siberian Natives from a Russian point of view. Cossack bands had first contacted the nomadic reindeer Chukchi along the southward-flowing Anadyr River and the northward-flowing Aniui River, the western districts of their hunting and herding territories, in the mid-seventeenth century.[58] While willing to trade on a limited basis, for more than a century the reindeer Chukchi successfully fought off Cossack plundering expeditions trying to collect iasak and pominki. Chukchi resistance to Russian aggression led to prolonged small-scale warfare during the 1750s and 1760s.

Even when peace returned, the reindeer Chukchi were difficult trading clients. Mistrustful and hot tempered, they customarily carried out any trade with other Native peoples at knifepoint. They were no less cautious in dealing with the Russians. Although Russian merchants would not sell them firearms, Chukchi fighters proved formidable in battle. Iron-tipped spears and iron knives, axes, and arrows were their main weapons, while they protected themselves with ingeniously fashioned iron armor they got from the neighboring Koryak people.[59]

Despite its difficulties and dangers, the Chukchi trade offered opportunities for profit that must have been highly appealing to the Baranov brothers. The reindeer Chukchi could bring to market a small quantity of sable pelts, while red foxes, beavers, martens, and wolverines were still relatively abundant in their territory. Red fox skins were in fact the common standard of value in the Chukchi trade; all other items were priced according to their equivalent value in red fox pelts.

Along the shores of the Arctic Ocean and Bering Sea lived the maritime Chukchi: sea hunters who would barter highly valued walrus tusks, seal skins, and polar bear pelts, some of which they secured on trips across the Bering Strait to hunt and to trade with the Yupik peoples of far western Alaska. The maritime Chukchi customarily exchanged these items with the reindeer Chukchi, and they would travel hundreds of miles by dogsled to get Russian goods such as tobacco, iron for tools and weapons, and brandy or vodka.

Although details are lacking, Aleksandr Baranov's Siberian business included a trading site along the northernmost coast of the Sea of Okhotsk near the mouth of the Ishigak River, where the Anadyr and Telquap reindeer

Chukchi came south to trade. Farther north, he located a substantial post at a small settlement named Anadyrsk on the Anadyr River, in the heart of reindeer Chukchi country. Here the Baranov brothers built up a trade with a large stock of goods and a group of employees headed by a resident trader. Even farther north, close to the East Siberian Sea of the Arctic Ocean, the Russian commander at the town of Zashiversk on the Indigirka River took a force eastward to the Aniui River in 1788, built a fort, and entered into negotiations with the western reindeer Chukchi. The result was the founding of an annual Aniui fair at the fort site. This event became a major commercial nexus for relations between the Russians and the Chukchi people for more than a century. Since Aleksandr Baranov was already the licensed trader at Zashiversk, it is altogether likely that he and Petr were responsible for promoting this expansion of Russian authority and even more likely that the Baranov brothers enjoyed a privileged role under official patronage during the early years of business at the Aniui Fair.[60]

* * *

Aleksandr Baranov's business required him often to be away from Irkutsk. Nonetheless, he became a familiar figure among the city's leading merchants. Not long after his arrival, he bought an aging wooden house with outbuildings located close to the river in the Kharalampievskaia church parish, the oldest part of the city. On the site he built a new stone house and added service structures, fat rendering and candle-making buildings, and barns for his horses and cattle. To maintain their household, the Baranovs not only hired servants but added to the serving staff by indenture contracts with young men they took into the household, who came mainly from the families of Irkutsk guild workers and bourgeois.[61]

A city census during the early 1780s included Aleksandr Baranov as a homeowner.[62] He also leased from the municipal authority the meadowland hay fields on both sides of the lower Taltsy River where the Taltsinsk glass factory was located.[63] In 1787, in keeping with his apparent prosperity and his success in gaining the respect of his peers in the Siberian business world, he was elected to the Free Economic Society, an organization analogous to a local chamber of commerce in the modern United States.

Aleksandr Andreevich was careful to keep his legal status properly arranged with the Irkutsk city authorities. Identified as a Kargopol' resident, he lived in Irkutsk with a renewable one-year passport while declaring that he would remain as a temporary, nonresident inhabitant. He seemed to anticipate a return to Kargopol' once he had made his fortune in Siberia.

On city records he listed himself as a guest merchant. His name appeared high on the roster of Irkutsk nonresident businessmen. Further clarifying his status, in 1785 he declared that he owned capital in the second guild in the amount of 5,100 rubles, the minimum required for guild membership. Every year thereafter he declared this same figure as his second guild capital and paid one percent of this sum, 51 rubles, to the guild. He paid an additional annual fee of 100 rubles for use of the city marketplace and for a military exemption fee. His other yearly payments included 50 rubles for the use of the city's common lands to raise hay and 137 rubles, 36 kopecks for support of the Irkutsk city council.[64]

Unlike local residents, merchants registered in other Russian cities were generally not taxed by the local government for service obligations or personal duties. But the Irkutsk authorities demanded additional fees from the outsiders. In October 1788 Baranov petitioned the Irkutsk municipal duma, the city's ruling council, for a more favorable fee policy. He was in effect being required to pay a double burden, he said, because "my relatives in Kargopol' are paying duties for trade and I don't have any trade there, but possess a house."[65] Subsequently, he joined with eleven others, all from northern Russia, to present a specific proposal to the magistrate of the Irkutsk guberniia. Nonresident merchants, they argued, "should pay annually 160 rubles each, instead of [being obliged for] services and material [money] duties."[66] Judging from the record of Baranov's continued annual payments to local officials, neither his individual petition nor this group proposal did anything to lessen his expenses for living and doing business in Irkutsk.

At the request of the Irkutsk duma, at the end of 1789 Aleksandr Andreevich set forth his claims for consideration as a member of the local business fraternity. "In Irkutsk," he wrote, "I have my own house and a glass factory shared together with Mr. Court Advisor Kirill Efstaf'evich Laksman." A month later, on February 5, 1790, he wrote: "I have lived in Irkutsk as a nonresident merchant on the basis of one-year passports. . . . Now I am sending my wife back to my home city of Kargopol' while I will start in May to collect alcohol taxes in the whole Yakutsk Oblast'." To avoid double taxation he needed a copy of his most recent tax records from the Irkutsk city officials before his wife's departure. "These records," he declared, "will be taken [to Kargopol'] by my wife to add to the proof that I have already paid" the Irkutsk local taxes.[67]

The Baranovs' decision to separate in 1790, with Matreona returning to Kargopol', indicates a growing estrangement in the marriage. While Baranov was often absent on business, his young wife devoted herself to a number of foundling infants taken into their household. Childless when they settled in Irkutsk, they added five newborns to their family between 1783 and 1789. The first was a daughter, who died in May 1783.[68] Shortly thereafter they adopted a son, who was the first of the Baranov children to have Grigorii Shelikhov's sister-in-law, the wealthy widow Golenishcheva, as godmother.[69] During the following year they took in a girl named Afanasiia.[70] As recorded in the Kharalampievskaia church register: "On December 1, 1787 infant Appolonii was abandoned to the household of the Kargopol' merchant Aleksandr Andreevich Baranov. His [god]father is Sergeant of the Nerchinsk mining team Ivan Rodionov, the [god]mother—Baranov's wife, Matreona Aleksandrovna."[71] A little more than a year later, in early January 1789, one more infant daughter came into the Baranov home.[72] Of the five children, only Afanasiia and Appolonii survived infancy, mute testimony to the perils of parenthood in that age and place.

Presumably, the care of the household and its small children occupied Matreona while her husband looked after his diverse business matters. The couples' separation in 1790 may have seemed a normal turn of affairs, not surprising to their friends. If there were troubles in the marriage, they went unnoted in the documentary record. But we may suspect a moral judgment of sorts in another terse entry concerning the Baranovs in the church register: "Never came to confession."[73]

Always a responsible person, Aleksandr Andreevich would continue to provide adequate support to his absent wife during the following years and to safeguard her financial interests in the case of his death. But whatever emotional bonds may once have joined the couple were severed by the time they went their separate ways. A trader and merchant, a businessman apparently with many different profitable concerns in Siberia, Aleksandr Baranov was henceforth free to pursue his best opportunities wherever they might take him, unhindered by family duties.

III

MOVING TO AMERICA

━━━━━━━━━━━━━━━━✳━━━━━━━━━━━━━━━━

In 1790 Aleksandr Baranov set sail for Kodiak Island to become resident chief manager of the Northeastern Company, the most prosperous of Russia's Siberian-based fur businesses in the North Pacific. On the way he and his men were shipwrecked, stranding them for the winter on Unalaska Island. When he reached Three Saints Harbor the following July, he found the Russian company workers in rebellion against company owner Shelikhov and, like Kodiak's Alutiiq people, suspicious of the new manager.

━━━━━━━━━━━━━━━━✳━━━━━━━━━━━━━━━━

IN FEBRUARY 1790, WHEN ALEKSANDR ANDREEVICH INFORMED the Irkutsk duma about his entry into the Chukchi trade and his wife's imminent departure for Kargopol', apparently he still intended to remain in Siberia. But at that point his fortunes were falling drastically. Despite his earlier success, a cycle of troubles struck his varied enterprises, beginning with his difficulties in the wine trade with the Golikovs in 1788 and continuing in 1789 and 1790. He also suffered heavy trading losses, due in part to the temporary closure of the Kiakhta market by the Chinese emperor.

On a quick trip to Yakutsk in the winter of 1789–90, Baranov found his alcohol tax farming franchise likewise in disarray. From Yakutsk he traveled to Okhotsk, where he expected to meet his agent in the Chukchi trade with a report on the season's profits. He learned instead that the Chukchi had attacked the Anadyrsk trading station, killed Baranov's manager and his employees, and plundered his stores. In the space of a few months, he found himself reduced from prosperity to a far less affluent status, with heavy ongoing expenses, large unpaid debts, and his capital reserves dwindling.

Even before he learned the full extent of this appalling series of setbacks, by late May 1790 Aleksandr Andreevich had finally decided to accept a

renewed offer from his friend Grigorii Shelikhov to become the Northeastern Company's chief manager. The evidence is found in a contract he made
at Irkutsk on May 20 with Ivan Kuskov, a deeply indebted townsman from
Tot'ma in northern Russia, not far from Baranov's hometown. Kuskov agreed
to enter Baranov's service "in a commerce position" and "to go with him from
here to Yakutsk and Okhotsk and from Okhotsk to the American shore" on a
"sea-voyage for the fur-hunting company of Golikov and Shelikhov."

In return, Baranov agreed to support Kuskov, pay him 100 rubles annually, provide him one full participatory share in the company's profits, and
pay a debt of 1,690 rubles owed by Kuskov to a Tot'ma merchant. With a debt
this large, it is likely that his agreement to enter Baranov's service was for
Kuskov an alternative to court proceedings that might very well have landed
him in prison. Kuskov, as events would prove, was a hard man; but his warm,
trusting relationship with Baranov endured for the rest of their lives together,
nearly thirty years, and grew stronger with each passing year.[1]

With his decision to sail to America, Aleksandr Andreevich made a career
change that would reshape his life far more profoundly than he possibly could
have anticipated. The circumstances suggest that he expected to remain in
this new post only a few years before returning to his Siberian business interests. He kept intact his position in the Chukchi trade, which his brother,
Petr, continued to supervise on his behalf.[2] He also kept his interest in the
Taltsinsk glass factory until the death of his partner Kirill Laksman in 1796,
when Laksman's widow become the primary owner of the business.[3] But
the opportunity to repair his fortunes in the North Pacific fur business now
convinced him to venture into the new and for him unknown world of Russia's infant overseas empire.

* * *

The change in Baranov's career did not proceed altogether smoothly. After
returning to Irkutsk, he was occupied with putting his own damaged business affairs in order while overseeing Shelikhov's preparations for a major
reinforcement of the Kodiak Island colony. He was at Yakutsk in mid-June,
organizing a supply train for Okhotsk and finding it necessary to pay nearly
three hundred rubles from his own depleted funds because Shelikhov had
not left the money needed. "I have to send many things from here," he wrote
Shelikhov, "and each carriage costs 15–17 rubles. I hoped [in vain] that you
did not leave me without assistance, following the rules of friendship and
mutual assistance." But his grievances against Shelikhov had other sources
as well. Rather than help him settle his debts in Irkutsk, he complained,

Shelikhov had left him "to be a victim of those [among his creditors] who were angry."

These problems, added to the strain of his business reverses, were enough to threaten the good feelings between Baranov and his friend. "Your cold attitude toward me seems strange," he said, "and your comments are not consistent with the favor you have [previously] expressed toward me." Shelikhov, Aleksandr Andreevich remarked, had already taken care of his own business, leaving him to struggle. "I have no money to send my belongings to Okhotsk, and have to be occupied here for some time." And yet he was looking forward to assuming his new position. "As soon as I carry out and complete all my business here," he assured Shelikhov, "I will be in Okhotsk quickly and [expect] to hear from you yourself [at that point]."[4]

Two months later, on August 18, 1790, Baranov and Shelikhov signed at Okhotsk an agreement that fixed the terms of Baranov's service to the Northeastern Company and outlined his immediate tasks. Baranov would become the company's resident chief manager under a partnership arrangement, receiving at the outset ten ownership shares, a very substantial stake. In addition, he would be rewarded by a good part of the annual fur returns when the yearly cargoes of peltry were shipped to Siberia. Following the general custom in the fur business, these returns were to be divided into a total of 210 shares. Fifteen shares would be set aside for Baranov, while ordinary company employees would each receive a portion of thirty half shares designated for the workforce. If he traded with merchants from other nations, Aleksandr Andreevich would receive one-tenth of the profits. If such a trade proved highly profitable, or if a new land with rich fur resources were discovered, Baranov would receive a further reward of one-fourth of the profit for his heirs. The contract also stipulated that he could leave the job at any time. When Baranov wanted to resign as chief manager, he needed only to notify Shelikhov, who would provide a replacement.

The contract carried still other guarantees apparently designed to persuade Aleksandr Andreevich to accept the position. It read:

> If despite all precautions the vessel is wrecked, or my life is threatened in some other way when going from Okhotsk, my partner Shelikhov, my wife, and my two young children are to be paid. My stepchildren—my son Appolonii, who is ill in Yakutsk, and my daughter Afanasiia, who was sent to Kargopol' with my wife—are to receive a onetime payment in the amount of one thousand [rubles] and the property that is with me is to be returned

to them if it is not destroyed under some circumstances. If the vessel
is wrecked and I happen to be at some uninhabited island or unknown
part of the mainland and cannot return home, or if I'm taken prisoner
by some unknown European or barbarian people, then during my stay at
those places without any trade, 2,000 [rubles] per year are to paid [to my
account], and my children and wife are to receive an additional 300 rubles
per year until I return.

This was an exceptional and very generous insurance policy for Baranov and
his dependents.

Various articles in the contract described the new chief manager's duties
in a general way. The company, the agreement said, had 192 people in its
service—the same number Shelikhov had taken to America in 1783—and
the contract guaranteed that exactly this many workers would remain in
the colony under Aleksandr Andreevich's supervision, assuring him enough
men to make the business successful. "The ship prepared for the voyage to
America, entirely loaded with food, goods, rigging, and people as well," the
contract read, "will be managed by me [Baranov] except for navigation (for
there's a special navigator). On this ship I should sail to the places in America
where the Company has settlements, to the major harbor near the mainland
in Kyktak [Kodiak] Island where the Company's main settlement and a shop
are located. I will do my utmost to reach that territory this fall." The first
priority, Baranov agreed, would be to take care of the vessel. "If, God forbid,
something is damaged, it should be repaired."[5]

Once in America, Aleksandr Andreevich also agreed, he would avoid
wasting the company's resources. He would feed the men by fishing and
hunting rather than feasting them with the company's food stores. In addition, "I should keep the workers busy, provide fresh and healthy food, and
keep them from idleness, weakness, and lazy behavior." Above all, "I am to
start profitable commercial activity." He would prepare a list of the Russian
settlements, take charge of the existing inventory of company property from
the acting chief manager, write a report, and arrange a proper distribution of
the cargo he was taking to the colony.

One provision would benefit the company's workforce: "The workers are
to be given their freedom. Those who wish are to be sent home, and only vol-
unteers shall remain." Baranov pledged to keep accurate records that would
give every employee a fair and just accounting of his financial status. "An
account book of incoming and outgoing goods, a book of American goods

sold or given to the workers for exchange, and a book of payments [to the workers] are to be arranged so that everybody's account is made clear. Two registers will be kept for recording accidents and the behavior of the workers, keeping track alike of their previous good and disreputable actions."

In other provisions, Baranov agreed to prevent quarrels, fights, discord, and offenses and to maintain peace and harmony in company settlements. Also high on the contract agenda was a series of proposed explorations that Shelikhov wanted Aleksandr Andreevich to undertake, principally to search for new fur producing territories. To carry out his many responsibilities, the contract allowed Baranov two assistants, who he would support at his own expense. One was Ivan Kuskov. The other he expected to choose in America from among the diligent and intelligent local workers. The final clause of the contract was in effect a ritual statement of good intent by both Aleksandr Baranov and Grigorii Shelikhov: "All the terms mentioned in the contract are to be followed by both parties without violations, totally and consistently."

Although in later years some specific provisions might be disregarded on both sides, obviously the business and personal relationship between the two men rested on a broad foundation of mutual trust and goodwill. Shelikhov was anxious to have Baranov take over his company colony and increase the profitability of his North American ventures. The agreement was generous to a fault, assuring Baranov that he could easily restore his tattered financial affairs if good money could still be made in the North American fur business, as both men assumed to be the case.[6]

At the same time he was completing the contract with Shelikhov, Aleksandr Andreevich received a series of special instructions from the acting commandant at Irkutsk, Collegiate Assessor Ivan Kokh. A first directive was for Baranov to investigate reports of foreign ships visiting Alaskan waters, especially at Kenai Bay (Cook Inlet). Kokh ordered him to keep a special journal "about everything of interest," including new island discoveries and their Native inhabitants, and to keep the government fully informed by frequently forwarding reports to "give a clear picture of conditions in the colonies, and of our settlements there." Otherwise, Kokh said, a lack of information might prevent the government from sending necessary reinforcements to Baranov. "The more detailed and exact your reports are," he wrote, "the more they will be appreciated."[7]

In two additional edicts, Commandant Kokh was specific about his concern for Russia's territorial claims in North America. In one labeled "Most Secret," he instructed Baranov to display five imperial crests at strategic locations, each to be accompanied by a metal plate buried in the ground near the display site. The location of each site should be clearly identified with maps and described by the degrees of longitude and latitude.[8] The final edict informed Baranov that the King of Sweden, then at war with Russia, intended to attack the shores of Kamchatka and other places by means of an English privateer under the Swedish flag, commanded by Captain John Henry Cox.[9] Kokh advised Baranov to resist this enemy within reason, recognizing that his unarmed trading ship would not be able to withstand a concerted attack by an English warship.

On August 19, 1790, the day after he and Shelikhov signed their agreement, Aleksandr Andreevich Baranov boarded ship and sailed for North America, accompanied by his new assistant Ivan Kuskov. He had arranged for his family to return to Kargopol', made ample provision for their relocation expenses and upkeep, and assured them against calamity with the insurance written into his contract with Shelikhov. We cannot know what expectations Baranov had at this point for his marriage to Matreona and for the future of his two surviving adoptive children, then ages six and three. But in fact when he departed from Okhotsk on that summer day and headed toward the open sea, with the Siberian coast gradually sinking from sight beneath the horizon, he would never see them—or Russia—again.

＊　＊　＊

Shrewd management and audacity had made the Golikov-Shelikhov partnership the largest fur-hunting and trading business in the North Pacific. By founding a permanent colony on Kodiak Island, Grigorii Shelikhov had given the firm a strong advantage over its rivals. A temporary closure of the Kiakhta fur market in 1785 harmed most Siberian businesses, but Shelikhov prospered by sending North Pacific furs to European Russia and western Europe. "Past profits accumulated in this trade," said historian Vasilii N. Berkh, "enabled many company organizers and investors to retire and enjoy their success in peace. Others who had no luck had to quit the trade."[10]

When Baranov became the Northeastern Company's chief manager, only three rivals remained. Two limited their fur hunting and trading to the Aleutian Islands, now ignored by Shelikhov's company because the sea otters were gone. The troublesome third competitor was a firm led by the well-known Yakutsk merchant Pavel Lebedev-Lastochkin. Its activities were centered in Kenai Sound and Chugach Bay (Prince William Sound) on the Alaskan mainland east of Kodiak Island, where its unruly workforce directly challenged Baranov's men.

Like all Russians going to North America, Baranov had to risk one of the world's most dangerous sea journeys before he could start his new job. The hazards began at Okhotsk, the main Russian port on the Pacific. The site was woefully bad for a seaport, with the town perched precariously atop a sandy spit between the sea and the mouth of the shallow Okhota River. Its anchorage was along an open shoreline, a roadstead rather than a harbor, with no protection from the brisk southeastern gales common to the region. Ice halted all shipping during the winter. At the waterfront, all loading and unloading relied on small skiffs, a clumsy, inconvenient arrangement. Once a ship lifted anchor, in bad weather it might take weeks to reach the open ocean. Yet for lack of a better place Okhotsk would remain Russia's only significant Pacific seaport until the end of the nineteenth century.[11]

The poor sailing qualities of Russia's North Pacific merchant fleet were notorious. Local shipbuilding traditions favored sturdy, strongly built vessels, able to withstand rough seas and hard usage. The standard design was the galiot, a ketch-like small ship with two short, square-rigged masts carrying narrow sails, awkward to maneuver and incapable of sailing close to the wind. Working in primitive shipyards near Okhotsk, the shipbuilders had few tools and lacked marine supplies. Rigging, rope, cable, canvas, iron, and provisions all had to come seventeen hundred miles from Irkutsk or the far greater distance from European Russia. Okhotsk craftsmen had to call on their ingenuity to overcome the lack of proper gear. The results were seldom good. Navy lieutenant Gavriil Davydov, an acerbic critic during his 1802 visit, wrote that Okhotsk ships had always been built by untrained men "in the worst possible way" and then "loaded and armed in the same way."[12]

Aleksandr Andreevich took with him fifty-two new contract employees. Traditionally called promyshlenniks (hunters) by the Russians, these men would work at every sort of task needed to sustain the company. The party sailed for America aboard the galiot *Tri Sviatitelia* (*Three Saints*), a company-owned ship commanded by the experienced skipper Dmitrii Bocharov.[13]

We have Baranov's own description of his troubles getting the ship properly outfitted. "Formerly all owners of seagoing vessels," he told naval historian Berkh, "tried to build them very high, figuring they would have more room for crews and cargo. Most of these vessels had galiot-type rigging with short, heavy masts, and narrow sails in order to economize on canvas." Most remarkably, he explained, "the rudders were of amazing design with blades at least 1 1/2 sazhen [ten and a half feet] long. Putting out to sea in such a ship, the navigators soon found that it had no speed at all. Believing that a long rudder contributes to the speed of the ship, they added frequently to its length."

While Baranov was getting ready to depart, a clerk of the Golikov-She-likhov Company approached to ask his permission "to take eight bottles of French brandy to the shipwright." "Why do you want to give him such a hand-some present, brother? He gets a stipulated pay." The reply was astounding: "This, my dear sir, is unavoidable; for two weeks now I have been asking him to build the galiot . . . at least an arshin [two and one-half feet] higher, but he refuses and I think a present will help in this case a great deal." "Naturally," concluded Baranov, "I put this blockhead out of my room, but by doing so I offended all the Company's employees. Only the shipwright, a man skilled in his trade, approved my action."[14] As a youngster, Aleksandr Andreevich obviously had learned a great deal from experts in the Kargopol' shipyards.

A shortage of experienced sailors and competent shipmasters added to the perils of North Pacific voyages. While some men were veterans of voy-ages between the White Sea and the Arctic Sea, promyshlenniks recruited in Siberia rarely had been aboard any sailing vessel or even seen saltwater before they were pressed into seamen's duties on their way to North America. Most skippers were hesitant to sail out of the sight of land. Their caution lengthened voyages while adding to the risk of shipwreck.

Contrary winds, swift currents, and blankets of impenetrable fog, along with sudden, severe storms, hidden shoals, and rocky coasts with steep tides and few safe havens—these were all causes for worry. Because of the threat of storms, the sailing season was short, beginning in late May and ending in October. No matter where the wind took them, navigators looked for a secure winter harbor before November. The lack of good charts in Baranov's time made every voyage even more an exercise in guesswork and chance.

The *Tri Sviatitelia* was the same ship that in 1783, with Gerasim Izmailov as captain, had taken Grigorii Shelikhov, his family, and his pioneer work-force to Kodiak Island. After its return in 1786, with Izmailov still in com-mand and Bocharov as second officer, the ship had safely explored the Gulf of Alaska from the Kenai Peninsula around Chugach Sound and as far south as Lituya Bay, burying several metal plates to prove Russia's title to the region.[15] These successful voyages seemed to bode well for future expeditions.

Baranov's journey was not blessed by similar good fortune. A few days after leaving port, Captain Bocharov discovered that some of the ship's water barrels were empty and the rest were leaking badly.[16] Everyone went on a sharply reduced water ration, limited to four cups per person per day. Even so, the lack of water became critical. Once they passed through the Kurile Straits, Baranov and Bocharov decided to alter course and head for Unalaska Island—one of the Fox Islands, as the Russians called the eastern Aleutians— six hundred miles closer than Kodiak Island.[17]

Captain Bocharov brought the *Tri Sviatitelia* through Umnak Pass and coasted off the western cape of Unalaska in late September. Here he sent ashore a skin-covered ship's boat—a lightweight craft called a *baidara* by the Russians—for freshwater.[18] The crew returned with one barrel of water and news that another Russian trading ship was anchored at Captain's Bay (modern Dutch Harbor) on the north side of the island. The ship was the *Aleksandr Nevskii*, commanded by the experienced skipper Potap Zaikov.[19] Baranov learned also that the Billings expedition had visited three months earlier with two ships. Commander Billings had ordered the Aleut Fox Islanders not to obey the Russian fur hunters or supply them with food.[20] Worried about his own command, Billings had told them to gather food for his return journey, promising to pay well when he again called at Unalaska. For this reason, as Baranov told Shelikhov, Zaikov's hunters were going hungry. The Aleuts "would not obey them in anything and are not feeding them, and [they have] nothing to pay [the Aleuts] with because of their lengthy voyage."[21]

Captain Bocharov took the *Tri Sviatitelia* a short distance along the island's north shore and entered Koshigin Bay (modern Kashega Bay).[22] The site had a freshwater stream, but the anchorage lacked protection from northern and northwestern winds. Two days later the crewmen had repaired and filled the water barrels and readied the ship to sail the next morning. That evening a violent gale struck. "It was a storm with heavy rain," Baranov later told Shelikhov, "and the wind was so strong that it was hard to stay on our legs."[23] Helpless on the windward shore, the *Tri Sviatitelia* dragged its anchors and went aground. Through a long, tempest-filled night, "heavy waves broke one after another on deck, the hatches were ripped away, and the ship began to fill with water."[24]

The storm continued furiously through the next day. As wind and waves raged, the men hastily unloaded whatever they could reach and ferried it ashore with the ship's three baidaras, rowing through the surf on a rising tide. At one point Baranov and his boat crew rescued Captain Bocharov and Ivan Kuskov, "who were not able to reach the baidara in time." Before long all three baidaras had wrecked. Violent waves breached the sides of the *Tri Sviatitelia* and much of the remaining cargo sank into the sea. In the face of such destruction, Baranov later told historian Kiril Khlebnikov, "the only course was to save the crew."

Once safely ashore, everyone huddled into makeshift shelters as the storm continued day and night for a week. On October 6 the battered hull of the *Tri Sviatitelia* finally capsized and broke apart.[25] "A small part of the cargo survived," Baranov reported, but "part of the things turned wet." His sea chest "with clothes, tea, some sugar and vodka was saved, although other [items], including pieces of hard candy, provisions, other things" were lost. "But all our people have survived and all are healthy."[26] Marooned by the destruction of their ship, the Russians had only their muzzle-loading muskets and the few goods they had managed to bring ashore between themselves and utter destitution.

Baranov's sober calmness and presence of mind in the face of danger, qualities that would often be called on during his American career, greatly aided the *Tri Sviatitelia*'s men. Forty-three years old at the time of this calamity, Aleksandr Andreevich was already well past his physical prime. Yet in the following weeks and months he showed resourcefulness, leadership, and a hardihood that earned the enduring respect of all who shared his predicament.

His essential tactic for survival, emulating generations of Siberian hunters and traders before him, was to establish good relations with Unalaska's Aleut peoples, who proved friendly despite their orders from Commander Billings. By making generous gifts to the Fox Islanders from his salvaged cargo, Baranov gained their help and advice about the island and its resources. This practice—going native in order to sustain lives and preserve health—over the years became a distinctive feature of Baranov's rule in Russian North America. Adaptable himself and willing to learn from the land's indigenous people, Aleksandr Andreevich would not allow the men under his command to suffer and perish just because of a stubborn insistence—shown by far too many other European colonists in alien lands—on clinging to the lifestyles, customs, and dietary tastes of their homeland.

For the rest of October the Russians endured such bad weather they could not dry their clothes "and the people were exhausted." For shelter they built Siberian-style yurts and large earth-covered dugouts modeled on Aleut dwellings, commonly called *barabaras*.[27] Alarmed by stories from Zaikov's men about the Billings expedition and also the visit of a foreign ship, Aleksandr Andreevich wanted to reach the company colony on Kodiak Island as

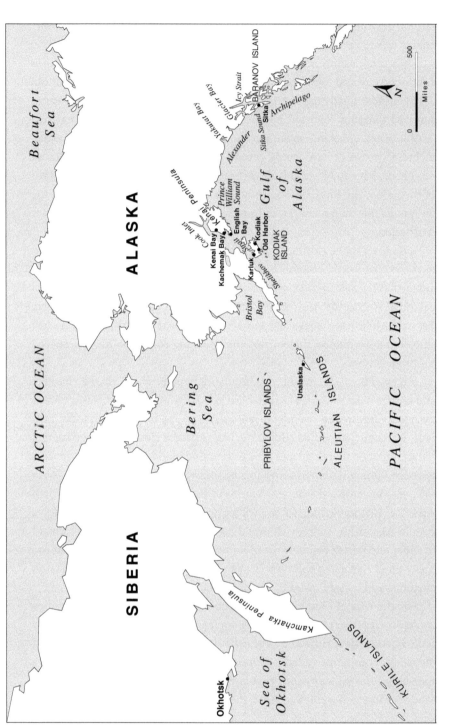

MAP 3. North Pacific Maritime Region

soon as possible. Within weeks he sent out promyshlennik Aleksandr Molev in a repaired baidara with a crew of Fox Islanders. But a larger Native force attacked Molev and his men long before they reached their destination. Five Fox Island Aleuts died and the survivors found a safe haven on Unga Island, the largest of the Shumagin group. They remained at this uninhabited refuge until Baranov himself came to their rescue in the spring.[28]

Conserving their few food stores from the wrecked ship, the Russians ate mostly what they could gather from their surroundings. During their first week on the island, Baranov told historian Khlebnikov in 1818, they killed three sea lions "and after that wanted for nothing." Storms kept everyone inside for two months, he recalled, but on every fine day they would go out with their muskets, "which provided us with a plentiful supply of food." Along with sea lion and seal meat, they made meals of "various grasses, roots, whale meat and crabs." They traded with the Aleuts for dried salmon, which they came to regard as a delicacy.[29]

Yet Baranov's letter to Shelikhov in April 1791 reported that because the weather prevented both Russians and Aleuts from going to sea, they did suffer a food shortage that winter. "But somehow," he vaguely explained, "with great difficulty, we all held out." He organized excursions to various parts of the island for gathering roots. He sent out a senior promyshlennik, Vasilii Medvednikov, on a deer-hunting expedition to nearby Umnak Island in a repaired baidara. The result was a small supply of dried venison.[30] For Christmas they cooked up a thin broth with rye flour from the ship and shared it equally among all the men. "Misfortune," Khlebnikov wrote, "is a great leveler of men."[31]

During the winter Baranov lived "in a state of great boredom, especially when the weather was bad." On one fair-weather ramble he fell into a snare set for foxes and injured himself, "but not seriously."[32] He later boasted of his success in boiling briny seawater for salt, which turned out "as white as snow," and they "salted with it sometimes fishes, sometimes flesh of sea dogs [seals] and hogs [sea lions]." Not abandoning traditional religious observances, everyone "fasted a true Lent" during the holy season. Immediately following Lent, "a piece of whale was thrown on shore," and they "had this [on] Monday the very [first] flesh day." So fully did the Russians adapt their tastes to Unalaska's resources that in April Aleksandr Andreevich claimed, "I am already accustomed not to [make] mention either of bread or of biscuits"—strong testimony indeed for any Russian. In addition, by their hunting and trapping, his men secured 509 pelts of red and silver foxes. Baranov also gathered rock samples that he hoped would prove valuable for their minerals.[33]

As spring approached the men built three sailing baidaras to carry them away from Koshigin Bay. The largest, about thirty-eight feet long, became Aleksandr Andreevich's personal craft. He planned to sail directly for Kodiak Island with seventeen men. Although Captain Bocharov had hoped to take a second baidara back to Okhotsk, Baranov insisted that with this and a third, smaller skin boat he must explore the north coast of Alaska's western peninsula with a party of twenty-six men.[34]

All three vessels were ready for sea by mid-March, but continued stormy weather kept them from leaving until late April. With the weather improving at last, they set sail together on April 24 or 25, leaving seven men behind at Koshigin Bay to hunt and guard the salvaged remnants of the *Tri Sviatitelia*'s cargo and rigging.[35] Presumably, each baidara carried a store of dried or salted fish and other foodstuffs set aside during the previous months.

Two days eastward along the rocky north shore of Unalaska, Baranov's mini-fleet reached Captain's Bay, a well-sheltered extension of Unalaska Bay. Here they found Captain Zaikov and his hunters preparing to return to Okhotsk.[36] Zaikov agreed to take Baranov's written report to Shelikhov, along with the fox pelts and rocks. From him Baranov bought another large baidara, which he added to Bocharov's command. The smaller craft he left at Captain's Bay with six men, who were ordered to remain for trading and hunting. Now shorthanded, he told Shelikhov: "I will take Aleuts with me from any place I can." He also bartered his two best rifles with Zaikov for vodka and tobacco, the items most highly valued by Aleksandr Andreevich and his compatriots.[37]

The three baidaras left together from Captain's Bay on April 28. Because of more bad weather they only reached Cook Harbor. On this short voyage, high seas soaked their newly purchased tobacco. As a result, Baranov temporarily gave up smoking, "only sniffing" to alleviate his nicotine craving.

Storms kept them ashore for another two weeks. The weather finally cleared in mid-May. The expedition moved eastward along the coasts of Akutan and Unimak Islands as far as Isannakh Strait (modern False Pass). This narrow five-mile-long waterway separates eastern Unimak Island from the westernmost tip of the Alaska Peninsula. Here the command divided. With his two baidaras Captain Bocharov headed along the peninsula's northern coast. Baranov turned southeast, navigated the swift tidal currents of the strait, and sailed toward Kodiak Island.[38]

Aleksandr Andreevich was ill when he left Koshigin Bay and he remained feverish for nearly the entire journey, yet he and his crewmen kept going to take advantage of uncommonly good weather and sea conditions. Like the Native peoples who were the Russians' mentors in Alaskan travel, they probably navigated from headland to headland and put ashore every evening, hauling their hide-covered baidara onto land. There they would build a fire, make a quick meal, and settle down to sleep, using the overturned boat as their sole protection from the elements.

Heading eastward from Isannakh Strait, Baranov must have reached Molev and his Fox Islanders on Unga Island within a week. Crowding these men into their baidara, the Russians continued along the southern coast of the Alaska Peninsula, then crossed Shelikhov Strait to reach the northwestern corner of Kodiak Island. They probably paused and resupplied themselves at Karluk, a substantial Native village at the mouth of the salmon-rich Karluk River, where Shelikhov had settled a small Russian outpost.[39] On June 27, two months after leaving Koshigin Bay, they arrived at Three Saints Harbor, bringing the first news of the *Tri Sviatitelia* disaster to the company's headquarters colony.[40]

Three months later, as winter drew closer, Captain Bocharov also landed at Three Saints with his two baidaras and all his men. They had their own story of adventure and hardship. After parting from Baranov, they had proceeded along the peninsula's northern shore into Bristol Bay, mapping the coast as they went. From the head of the bay they moved upstream on the Kvichak River to Lake Iliamna, where they charted the southwestern shore of this key inland waterway.[41] Rather than continue farther north, as originally ordered, here Bocharov cut short his survey because his baidaras had begun to leak badly. With the two boats barely useable, his command turned south in early August and started overland, carrying their baidaras across the mountain range that extends along the peninsula. With three days' heavy work they reached saltwater again at Shelikhov Strait, paused to repair their boats, and crossed to Kodiak Island on August 27. It took them two more weeks to navigate around the island, mapping as they went. On September 11 Bocharov's expedition finally came ashore at the company settlement.

* * *

Although Baranov had started for North America with no precise administrative blueprint, during his storm-enforced idleness on Unalaska he thought a great deal about the company's future. Before leaving Unalaska he wrote Shelikhov about his plans. As a top priority, he believed the company colony needed a Russian Orthodox priest "of good morality." "Send a wise priest," Aleksandr Andreevich advised, "a humble man and not superstitious or hypocritical." After this cleric had learned the Native language, he "would fortify them [the Natives] with better success in labors and sociality, by preaching the eternal word and by his manner of living truly Christian." The company would benefit directly from this missionary's work, Baranov said, since "we could make with the natives friendly conversions without giving them any mortification."

To get the Alutiiq people, the natives of Kodiak Island, to work for the company voluntarily, Baranov intended to make a generous use of trade goods as presents. Building on his experience with the Fox Island Aleuts, he told Shelikhov: "I want to gain the goodwill of these wild Americans by making them gifts, even in the most dangerous undertakings."[42] Since the chief director would not approve squandering the company's resources, Aleksandr Andreevich promised that he personally would take all the financial risk. "If such a plan is rewarded," he wrote, "then I can turn it to the good of the Company, claiming back only the cost of the articles involved; if the plan fails then the loss will be mine." Without expecting immediate success, he anticipated that his gift-based diplomacy might eventually secure a lasting peace and alliance with the Alaska Natives. "Time only, I hope, will attach them to us."[43]

While spending the winter with Captain Bocharov, Baranov had learned much about those places in North America the captain had previously visited. He told Shelikhov that the best site to build a ship to replace the lost *Tri Sviatitelia* would be somewhere on Chugach Sound. Such an expansion of company settlement to the Alaskan mainland would help establish friendly relations with the Chugach Alutiiq peoples, he said, "which may be profitable to the company."

Naively confident, Baranov expected that a Russian presence would somehow appeal to the Chugach. "We shall not interfere with them nor give them the slightest reason for bitterness, and after a while I hope simply to gain their support." Once the ship was built, he added, "I want to follow the Northwest Coast [southward] until I reach the first European settlement and only then to turn [back] north." Thus the new chief manager hoped to implement right away the expansionist aims of the Golikov-Shelikhov partners.

In a melodramatic flourish, Baranov ended his first report from North America by expressing great hopes, along with a very Russian sense of resignation if the future should bring setbacks. "Such is my plan at the moment," he wrote, "but its execution is dependent on Providence. My first steps here were visited with misfortune by a cruel fate, but perhaps the end of my endeavors will be crowned with generous good fortune, or perhaps I shall fall under the burden of Fate's blows." His final words emphasized both his sense of duty and his loyalty to his employer. "Privation and boredom I can bear with patience," he assured Shelikhov, "and I shall not rant at Providence, especially when I sacrifice to friendship."[44]

Baranov had come to America with the understanding that Shelikhov and his partners trusted his judgment and business experience. Farther than ever from the Crown authorities at St. Petersburg and now a very great distance from Irkutsk and even Okhotsk, with no reliable communication linking him to his employers, he needed to manage the company colony with little supervision from the homeland.

In the months and years to come, Aleksandr Andreevich would have cause enough to rant at Providence. His optimistic plans and grand ambitions often would be thwarted by misfortunes of every sort, most of them beyond his power to avoid. Though sometimes discouraged, he never despaired for the colony or lost confidence in his own ability to overcome the blows that fate sent his way. A forceful, highly capable leader for this singular Russian experiment in overseas empire building, Aleksandr Baranov would find his true calling as Russian America's long-term ruler.

IV

TAKING COMMAND

✻

Baranov's first months at Three Saints Harbor were spent under the tutelage
of Evstratii Delarov, his predecessor, who acquainted the incoming chief
manager with the demands of the job and the traits of the company's Rus-
sian and Alutiiq workers. After Delarov's departure, Aleksandr Andreevich
began moving his headquarters to Chiniak Bay, the site of modern Kodiak.
Seeking new sea otter hunting territories, he started a vigorous effort to
extend Northeastern Company operations into the mainland territories of
the Chugach Alutiiqs and, at greater hazard, the Tlingit people of south-
eastern Alaska.

✻

DESPITE HIS MANY YEARS OF EXPERIENCE AS A MERCHANT
trader in northern Russia and Siberia, Aleksandr Baranov was a novice
in the North Pacific fur business. He had received basic instructions from
Grigorii Shelikhov before he left Okhotsk, and he must have learned more
from Captain Bocharov during their winter together at Koshigin Bay. But for
the most part, it was all new to him. Fortunately, Evstratii Delarov, the man
he was replacing at Three Saints Harbor, proved to be an admirable mentor.

Six years older than Baranov, Delarov was a Macedonian Greek who had
moved to eastern Siberia and entered the North Pacific fur trade as a young
man. During an adventurous career he had been a chief trader and partner
with various merchant investors, making at least ten voyages to the Kurile
Islands and into the North Pacific. In 1783 he was one of the first Russians
to trade with the Alutiiq villagers living on Chugach Sound. After Shelikhov
returned to Irkutsk in 1787 (and Baranov turned down Shelikhov's early job
offers), Delarov agreed to replace the ailing interim chief manager Konstantin
Samoilov. But by 1791 he was anxious to return to Siberia.[1]

[66]

Since Delarov had worked his way up in the fur business, he understood the concerns of the company's contract employees, the promyshlenniks, and he was a highly popular leader. When the Billings expedition stopped at Three Saints Harbor in 1790, the workers made it a point to tell Dr. Martin Sauer, the expedition's English physician, that Delarov had earned their gratitude. "Every one, native and Russian," Sauer recorded, "spoke highly in his favor, and acknowledged several indulgences received at his hands."[2]

At the time of Baranov's arrival, however, these same workers were angry at Shelikhov. To appreciate their grievances, it is necessary to understand that they were working as contract employees with a unique position in Russian society, marginal to the class structure. Most came from a rural peasant background, though former townsmen could also be found in their ranks. A great number were illiterate. A good many had compelling reasons for moving beyond reach of the homeland's laws. Some were escaped serfs; others were criminal exiles or their sons. A substantial number, variously estimated from thirty to sixty percent, were Russo-Siberians, with a Russian father and a Native Siberian mother. Nearly all were impoverished when they entered the company's service. Quite a few, like Ivan Kuskov, were fleeing debts. Free men in theory, they all had been prodded by one set of circumstances or another to seek their fortune in America, despite the hazards.

Though as a group they were called promyshlenniks, hunters, they worked in various occupations, some as hunters or fur traders, others as carpenters or blacksmiths or sailors. A few had become crew chiefs (*baidarshchiks*), assigned to supervise a Native hunting crew from a specific village during the annual sea otter hunts. A smaller number were expedition leaders (*partovshchiks*), responsible for overseeing as many as a dozen village crews on these hunting sorties.

Before coming to America they had each signed a labor contract that gave them no wages but instead one-half of a "general share" (*valovye pai*) of the company's profits during their term of service, which might be one or two years or longer for expeditions to the North Pacific. The other half of each share was set aside for the company owners, to repay their outlay for the ship, provisions, trade goods, and management expenses. It was customary in the North Pacific fur business that every voyage, no matter its length, was organized as a separate business enterprise, conducted by a single company that would be dissolved after the voyage ended. The contract employees would be present then; they could look after their half-share interest when the company manager marketed the fur returns and calculated the amount due to each man for his half share. In effect, this system placed on the workers a large part of the business risk while giving them in return a small bit of the prospective profits. As a contract worker, each promyshlennik became a petty capitalist, investing his time and labor and risking every sort of danger while hoping to better his lot in life; but the value of his half share would depend on the joint hunting and trading success of all.[3]

Because they intended to establish a permanent colony in America, Shelikhov and his partners, the two Golikovs, chartered the Northeastern Company for a fixed ten-year term. Because of this novel arrangement, the workers who remained on Kodiak Island after Shelikhov left had trusted him to sell all their furs on their behalf and make a fair distribution of the profits. Opportunities for management abuse were glaringly evident, particularly in the absence of an impartial audit. Even if the company owners and managers were scrupulously honest, any hint of irregularities could stir the suspicions of the distant promyshlenniks.

They placed their grievances before Baranov within a day or two of his arrival. In detail, they described the ways in which Shelikhov had defrauded them. First, the prices they had to pay the company for provisions in America were exorbitant, far higher than Okhotsk prices. Second, Shelikhov had stolen the profits on the fur returns due to men who had died or left the colony, rather than divide the money among the remaining men according to their original agreement. Third, they claimed that Shelikhov had pocketed the part of their profits meant to pay for shipping their furs to Okhotsk, then deliberately guided his ship to Kamchatka where market prices were far lower. Fourth, they insisted that they had sent with Shelikhov only the best-quality sea otter pelts, but Shelikhov's accounting had classified them as third-rate skins, sold for a much lower price. As a result of these grievances, the promyshlenniks told Baranov, they had joined together and decided no longer to listen to Shelikhov, not to obey his orders, and to give no more sea otter pelts to him or his company managers.[4]

Over the years Shelikhov had not established a sterling reputation for fair dealing. Yet in this case he was less guilty of fraud than the men at Three Saints Harbor imagined. Bad weather and careless ship handling had made him end his homeward voyage at Petropavlovsk, leaving him stranded and forced to make a wearisome overland trek to reach Irkutsk. True, he had sold the furs for a sum substantially lower than anyone had expected, but he could not rightly be blamed for plotting against the interests of the workers still on Kodiak Island. Skewed stories about Shelikhov's reckoning of accounts had preceded Baranov to America. Along with the company store's high prices, it was these inaccurate reports, fed by rumor and groundless supposition, that provoked the promyshlenniks' rebellion.

* * *

The men impressed both Delarov and Baranov with the justice of their cause. Like Delarov, Baranov would attempt during the coming months to soothe the promyshlenniks and improve their situation within the limits of his authority, even as he tried to make some adjustments. Immediately he wrote to Shelikhov. "As a friend," he said, he was informing Shelikhov about the workers' complaints and their actions. Moreover, he added, Delarov "was annoyed himself by your calculation." In particular, he urged Shelikhov to lower the price of supplies for the workers.[5] But at best, it would take a year or two before any instructions from Siberia could reach the new chief manager. Meanwhile, he was left to handle this workers' revolt as best he could.

Since very few company ships reached America during the next decade, even the grievance over the company's high prices for supplies faded in importance. Rather than purchase goods or foodstuffs imported from Russia, the company men found it necessary to adopt a lifestyle based on Russian America's local resources. Yet the underlying economic issues for the promyshlenniks, focused on the value of their half shares, remained a source of difficulty throughout Aleksandr Andreevich's career in America.

As Baranov quickly realized, successful management of the promyshlenniks involved a great deal more than toting up debits and credits in a ledger. The bookkeeping itself, a mind-numbing chore, gave the chief manager direct contact with the men, allowing him to become familiar with each person's circumstances, talents, and character. It was not in his nature to set himself apart, aloof from the workers. He liked to move about, watching everything, and setting an example by his enthusiastic approach to whatever job was at hand. He was quick to take off his coat, roll up his sleeves, and work up a sweat alongside the men. In the small Three Saints community, as later in other company settlements, the promyshlenniks' barracks was the center of daily—and nightly—social life. Aleksandr Andreevich was no stranger in these quarters. He liked a good time. On any occasion for singing and dancing, he was almost certain to be there with the men, vigorously taking part. Like many Russian men, he loved to sing in a group with others, and at some point the chief manager even composed an anthem celebrating the great accomplishments of the Russian fur hunters in North America.

Very soon after reaching Three Saints, Baranov acquired a young female consort, beginning a long-enduring relationship. As much as anything else, this central feature of his personal life linked him with the Russian and Russo-Siberian promyshlenniks, who nearly all shared their lodging with one or more Native women—a potential cause of male Alutiiq resentment toward the promyshlenniks and Baranov himself but also, as in Siberia, a basis for cross-cultural amity that would weave a web of family relationships extending through Alutiiq society.

Not a prude and not a moral reformer, Aleksandr Andreevich easily accepted the casual disregard of Russian middle-class propriety found in this isolated outpost. That made it easier for the workers under his command to accept his orders. But even though he was an affable person, anyone who tested him would discover that the new chief manager could demand strict obedience when he thought it necessary. Backing him at every point was his assistant Ivan Kuskov, a person no one, Russian or Native, would ever want to cross.

*   *   *

Among the challenges facing Baranov in America, it was especially important for him to sustain good relations with the Kodiak Alutiiqs. Numbering more than six thousand at the time of Baranov's arrival, they were usually called Aleuts by the Russians, who sometimes qualified their terminology to distinguish between Fox Island Aleuts and Kodiak Aleuts, recognizing the great differences in language and culture that set these two groups apart. Lacking regular shipments of trade goods from Siberia, Baranov had to find a secure, low-cost way to maintain control over the Kodiak Alutiiqs other than the gift-based diplomacy he had originally envisioned. The most active men were needed for sea otter hunting and sometimes for whale hunting or halibut fishing. The elderly men and teenage boys were useful in hunting seabirds, foxes, and squirrels. Just as important were the roles of Alutiiq women of every age in food gathering, preservation, and preparation and in housekeeping. Their skilled garment making was needed to keep everyone, Russians and Natives, adequately clothed. With less than two hundred Russian workers when Baranov arrived, the existence of the company colony depended completely on the labor of the Alutiiqs, willing or not.

Right away Aleksandr Andreevich learned that he must distinguish between different groups within Alutiiq society. Most privileged were the *amanaty* (ahm-a-náh-tee), the adolescent youngsters from each village being held as hostages at Three Saints Harbor. Typically, they were the nephews of high-ranking men, the village headmen called *toions* (tóy-ahnz) by the Russians. They were the future Alutiiq leaders. Baranov, like Delarov, understood that these young men needed to be made comfortable and treated with respect. Living in the company's headquarters settlement, they might often be visited by family members and others from their home villages, who wanted assurance of their well-being.

Hostage-taking was a practice imported from Siberia into the Aleutian Islands by the first Russian and Russo-Siberian fur hunters. The early promyshlenniks had enforced their demands for furs by seizing control of Aleut wives and children in their home communities until the men delivered enough pelts. During Shelikhov's two years on Kodiak Island, the practice became somewhat more humane. Among the forty Natives who accompanied Shelikhov on his 1787 return voyage to Okhotsk were both Fox Island Aleut and Kodiak Alutiiq amanaty. Those remaining at Three Saints Harbor when Baranov arrived were serving as unofficial cultural intermediaries, interpreting Russian ways to the Alutiiqs and Alutiiq ways to the Russians.

The lessons Baranov learned about supervising the amanaty are seen in his 1797 instructions to Ivan Kuskov, who was taking over a new company settlement on Chugach Sound. Kuskov should give special attention to the Chugach amanaty, Aleksandr Andreevich directed, protect them, "look after them yourself, so that they are well cared for, fed enough, and on Thursdays each week a *banya* [steam bath] should be prepared just for their use, and they are to be washed and have their hair combed." Neither the cooks nor the promyshlenniks should shout at them, Baranov said. If they do something improper, "then politely explain that to them via interpreter and prevent them from doing that." Teach them Christianity, Baranov said, "and allow them always to worship according to their own will and inclinations, so that their residence among us will be pleasant and fair, and their fathers can feel comfortable." In addition, there should be servant girls to look after the youngest, to wash them, repair their clothes, and keep their living quarters clean. From time to time the amanaty barracks should be purified by smoke from a burning spruce bough.[6] In this fashion, the chief manager hoped to build a cordial relationship between the Russians and the young hostages for the benefit of all concerned.

The able-bodied Alutiiq village hunters and their families were the group most critical for the company's success. With compulsory iasak collection abolished, the villagers in theory were at liberty to trade with the Russians or not as they chose.[7] But according to the labor system devised by Shelikhov, the fur company demanded that they all embark on annual expeditions to hunt sea otters, with each settlement providing a set number of hunters (partovshchiks) with their skin-covered *baidarkas*, the light, highly maneuverable one-, two-, or three-person crafts that were ubiquitous among the Aleut and Alutiiq peoples in maritime Alaska. By 1792 the villagers from the south side of Kodiak Island would gather at Three Saints Harbor in April, while those from the island's north side would rendezvous with this party at the Aleksandrovskaia fort located at English Bay on the Kenai Peninsula, near the entrance to Kenai Bay. Paddling southward, they would be joined by Chugach Alutiiqs. The united party would pause at Nuchek (English) Island on the western salient of Chugach Sound to be assigned their hunting territories.

Under the supervision of Russian crew chiefs and usually two Russian expedition leaders, the partovshchiks followed a set routine. Each day, on a rotating basis, the men from one village would find food for the entire group: fish, seals, drift whales, birds, or, in times of scarcity, mollusks, sea urchins, mussels, and even kelp. Sea otters killed for their pelts would add to the hunters' moveable feast. Each village group formed a squad led by their toion. When they reached a place where sea otters were plentiful, the village squads hunted separately. During these early years, hunting expeditions would muster up to 800 baidarkas carrying as many as 1,600 men. By 1799 the number had declined to 500 baidarkas, and in 1804 only about 300 baidarkas—fewer than 600 men—made the journey to the mainland.[8] These declining numbers indicate starkly the fatal dangers faced by all the village hunters.

Some hunters' wives accompanied these expeditions. They took care of every sort of domestic chore, gathering food and fuel, preparing meals, and serving as seamstresses for the upkeep of everyone's clothes. They may also have handled the messy task of skinning the sea otters, scraping and drying the pelts, and keeping them packed until they could be delivered to a company official and stored for shipment to Okhotsk.

These hunting expeditions ended by the middle of September. Before returning to their villages for the winter, the hunters would stop at company headquarters to barter for their households. In return for the skins tallied to their credit, they might get tobacco, sugar or hard candy, black tea, steel knives and choppers, patterned yard goods from China, small seed beads for adorning finely made clothing, larger coral and blue glass beads that became jewelry, and other domestic items like those traveling peddlers took from village to village in northern Russia. But first they had to pay back their debts for any goods they had previously bought on credit. When supply ships failed to arrive regularly, the chief manager found it difficult to compensate the Alutiiq partovshchiks and their families for the sacrifices they made in service to the Russians.

After the hunt, young single men without their own baidarkas might continue working for the company during the winter, trapping foxes and land otters. They were paid with tobacco and, if they needed one, a bird-skin parka. The standard rate of exchange by 1804 was five fox skins or land otter pelts for one parka.

Baidarka owners during the winter months would hunt seals and walruses for their hides as well as their meat. Their wives and daughters would laboriously process and cure the hides to remove the hair, making the waterproof leather (*lavtak*) used to cover a new baidarka or repair an old one. It took the cured hides of ten seals to make one two-person baidarka and perhaps twice as many for the larger three-person baidarkas built to haul the Russians. If a hunter needed additional lavtak hides beyond the number of animals he had killed, he could buy them from the company on credit.

The company drafted older men and youngsters, twelve to fifteen years old, for bird-hunting parties. Puffins were their main prey, caught by snares on high cliffs and rocky outcrops where the birds nested in huge numbers. The hunters' climbing, sometimes aided by ladders, was dangerous, risking fatal injuries. They worked in small groups, paddling to islets and offshore rocks mainly along the southern coast of the Alaska Peninsula. Russian supervisors set a quota, expecting each hunter to deliver enough dried puffin skins with feathers attached to make seven parkas, with each parka requiring the skins of thirty-five birds. The hunters lived principally on the eggs they gathered in their climbing and the meat of the birds they snared and killed.

This puffin hunt came to an end by mid-July, when the birds left their nests after raising their young. Once the hunters delivered their catch, the Russians portioned out the dried skins to the Alutiiq village women and serving women at the company settlement, who sewed them into parkas that would later be exchanged by Baranov's storekeeper for sea otter pelts and fox furs.

All these labor-intensive tasks demanded that the Kodiak Alutiiqs forgo many of their traditional domestic tasks in order to serve the fur business. It was one of the chief manager's most demanding jobs, as Baranov quickly learned, to oversee the accounts for the village hunters as well as for the promyshlenniks. Each man had a separate ledger sheet on which the manager recorded all credit purchases from the company storehouse and the individual's share of hunting returns. When trade goods and provisions from Russia were scarce, the colony storekeeper ran a barter system heavily weighted in the company's favor. Paying the Alutiiqs mainly with bird skin parkas made by the labor of Native men and women, the Northeastern Company was not operating a market-based trading enterprise. Its fur business and the colony's very survival depended on Native labor in a command economy, with the Russians doing the commanding. It became Baranov's policy, however, to cloak his exercise of authority over the Alutiiq village hunters, so far as possible, with an appearance of genial, benevolent paternalism—learned most likely from Evstratii Delarov.

The company's domination was most complete over the *kaiurs* (káy-yurz), as the Russians called the men and women captives who had formerly been held as servants or slaves in Alutiiq village society.[9] Many of them had voluntarily joined Shelikhov and his men during the Russian invasion of Kodiak Island. Others came under company control by order of Shelikhov and his successors. Because of the high death rate among the kaiurs, company officials began to punish Alutiiq islanders for minor offenses by consigning them to forced servitude. This practice grew under Baranov's administration. By the first decade of the nineteenth century it was common for each Russian promyshlennik to have one or two *kaiury* (males) working for him. A similar number of *kaiurki* (females) lived in the company barracks, working as servants and in many instances providing sexual companionship for their Russian masters.

The kaiurs became an indispensable labor force, doing the most demanding work. They were a class of workers without rights, lacking any pretense of legal status. Company officials never mentioned them in reports to the authorities at Okhotsk or Irkutsk and certainly not to the imperial officials in St. Petersburg. Baranov in his 1797 instructions to Ivan Kuskov for managing the Chugach Sound settlement provided a brief statement of his own principles for looking after this most abused group in the company's workforce. "Keep *kaiury* and *kaiurki* in decent order," he wrote, "so that they always have enough food, have shoes, and have homes quite sheltered from bitter weather and rains. Make note of the diligent and hardworking, and send those who are lazy to do the unpleasant jobs."[10]

Most visitors who described their experiences in Russian America in later years took no notice of these workers. Whether from upper-class bias or simply because of different concerns, these writers gave little attention to the kaiury who paddled their baidarkas and the kaiurki who prepared their food and set it on the table. Fortunately two visitors, Hieromonk Gideon and navy lieutenant Gavriil Davydov, did provide a fragmentary record to help reconstruct the role of the kaiurs during the Baranov era.

Simply put, the kaiurs performed the most onerous and tedious tasks to ease the lives of the Russian promyshlenniks and their superiors. Hieromonk Gideon described a seasonal round of labor for the kaiurs, beginning in March with their building fish weirs and seining to capture the salmon that came into the streams on their annual spawning runs. Killing the fish, cleaning, filleting, and drying the salmon sides on racks, then storing them was a task for women. The men chopped wood and carried it by hand to the settlement or transported it in their baidarkas from distant locations. Through the summer both men and women cut and dried hay, used as winter fodder for the Russian cattle. The men traveled to outlying hunting posts to trap foxes in the fall. During the winter they delivered food, principally dried salmon, to the headquarters settlement. According to Father Gideon, other duties for the kaiurs included salt production, brick making, and the collection of spruce sap.[11] In some respects these tasks resembled the labors of independent serfs in northern Russia, except that they were carried out under company orders with no prospect of benefits beyond bare subsistence for these least-protected workers.

Lieutenant Davydov reported that kaiury usually paddled the large three-person baidarkas on distant hunting expeditions, while a Russian hunter or baidarshchik rode as a passenger in the middle seat. On longer journeys, he said, frequently the kaiury paddlers began to bleed from the nose and ears while trying to keep up with the smaller, lighter two-person baidarkas. After two such trips, Davydov added, many of these exhausted men "fall into a fever and are completely without strength."[12] By the time of his 1804 visit, kaiurs were being impressed for life service from every Native society under Russian control. Alutiiq kaiurs were being sent to all company posts, large and small. "Towards the winter," he added, "they are allowed back to the villages so that they do not have to be clothed and fed." As we might expect, "they were always glad to return to their villages in order to escape the unending work."[13]

Kaiurki were responsible for food gathering and cooking duties. These included the unpleasant task of rendering whale blubber for the lamp oil that provided the main source of light and heat in Russian and Alutiiq living quarters. For sheer drudgery, nothing was harder than their endless round of processing bird skins and mammal gut, using their teeth as tools, and sewing these materials into feather parkas and the waterproof gut parkas called *kamleikas*. They also were skilled in working seal and walrus hides and fashioning them into baidara and baidarka covers. A small number of kaiurki worked in the kitchens and served at the tables for company officers and their guests. The standard payment for all their work was one bird-skin parka, one long shirt, and one pair of boots per year, hardly enough to keep them decently clothed.

At the company headquarters and in scattered outposts, the sexual availability of the kaiurki may have offered some of them opportunities to negotiate better working conditions. In 1795 Archimandrite Ioasaf, head of the newly arrived Russian Orthodox spiritual mission, reported that about a hundred girls were then living with the promyshlenniks in the company barracks, with every man keeping one girl or several. In Father Ioasaf's view, they were living a depraved life, with "gatherings and parties and dancing on holidays and sometimes on weekdays too."[14] While some of these women were the daughters of Alutiiq villagers, apparently more were kaiurki.

The most favored must have enjoyed the privileges of their special relationship with a Russian mate, gaining trade goods and other perquisites through intimate bargaining. Among the promyshlenniks, as Baranov knew very well, bartering with one another for these women was a common practice.[15] A practical person, the new chief manager adopted a policy of easy tolerance for the kaiur system, including the trade in women, as a way to keep his Native workforce fully staffed and to maintain the morale and productivity of his Russian and Russo-Siberian contract workers. No official ever took notice that these benefits came at the expense of the Alutiiq villagers, left further impoverished by the loss of the kaiurs, male and female, from their traditional domestic economy.

✳ ✳ ✳

Before Baranov's arrival, Delarov had dispatched his promyshlenniks and Kodiak partovshchiks for the 1791 season. Most went eastward toward the mainland, where they hunted for sea otter along the southern shores of the Kenai Peninsula. While hunting in Kachemak Bay and Chugach Sound, they established peaceful relations with other Alutiiq groups living on the mainland. When they returned at the end of summer, their reports encouraged Baranov to plan a similar expedition the following year. The new chief manager's top priority was to extend the Russian reach into better fur-producing territories. The only way Aleksandr Andreevich could prosper in his American career was by gaining access for his hunters and traders to ever more sea otters, fur seals, and Arctic foxes, the three most highly prized fur-bearing mammals in North Pacific maritime districts.

Among these creatures, sea otters were far and away in greatest demand. Their pelts brought the highest prices, and their populations were the most vulnerable. One of the smallest marine mammals, sea otters are found in shallow coastal waters usually within two-thirds of a mile of shore. Adult males weigh from fifty to one hundred pounds, measuring from four to five feet in length. Adult females weigh at most seventy-five pounds and are no more than four and a half feet long. They live mainly along rocky coastlines with thick kelp forests and barrier reefs, in areas protected from ocean winds.

Sea otters forage by diving to the ocean floor, where they gather sea urchins, clams and mussels, crabs and other marine crustaceans, and small fish. Amazingly, to stay healthy each adult must eat daily an amount equal to at least a quarter of its body weight. Once females are three or four years old, they may give birth to a single pup each year or, typically, every other year. Responsibility for raising the young is exclusive to the mothers, who are devoted to nurturing and training their pups. Even so, pup mortality is high; only twenty-five percent of the young survive their first winter.[16] Thus sea otter population growth may be less than fifteen percent per year. Any greater rate of human predation places the species' survival in peril.

Naturalists estimate the entire original sea otter population at 150,000 to 300,000, spread from northern Japan through the Kurile Islands, Kamchatka, the Aleutian Islands, southwestern and southeastern Alaska, and British Columbia. The California sea otter is a separate subspecies, distinguishable from the northern animal by slight differences in skull and tooth structure.

What made all sea otters highly valued was their thick, lustrous fur, the densest pelt grown by any mammal. Long, water-resistant guard hairs overlay the short underfur, which completely protects the animal's skin from the ocean's cold. While their fur is usually deep brown with silver-gray speckles, the color among individual animals can range from a light grayish-brown to nearly black. Asian and European purchasers usually preferred the darker shades. Since the animals shed and replace their hair gradually rather than during a specific molting season, their pelts are in prime condition year-round. Yet because of weather conditions, organized hunts were practical in Alaskan waters only during the spring and summer seasons.

Around Kodiak Island as in the Aleutians, Aleksandr Andreevich at his arrival found that sea otter populations were already drastically reduced. Working for the Russians, Aleut and Alutiiq hunters, using skills practiced from childhood, could slaughter these defenseless creatures with deadly efficiency. Hunting teams in baidarkas surrounded their prey and attacked them at short range with light spears or arrows from their throwing sticks. When an alarmed or wounded animal dived from view, hunters had only to wait a few minutes before a lack of air forced it to surface again. Adults and independent sea otter juveniles foraged alone but tended to rest together in large single-sex groups called rafts, typically containing ten to a hundred or more animals that often entangled themselves in kelp to keep from drifting out to sea. The discovery of a floating sea otter raft would draw hunting crews together to kill every animal possible, juveniles and pups as well as adults, heedless of the consequences for the future of the species.[17]

Preparing the pelts for market was simple. The hunters or their wives skinned the animals, scraped the underside of each hide to remove clinging shreds of flesh, lightly dried them over a fire, and bundled the skins in bales. At company headquarters the Russians stored these bales in a shed until they could be put aboard ship for the voyage to Okhotsk. New to the business, Baranov in 1792 tried to improve these practices by washing the furs from his first season's hunt before shipping them to Siberia. At the first opportunity Shelikhov sent him orders not to do so.[18] The sea otter pelts, dense and soft with natural oils, could only be damaged by this treatment. In the hands of Siberian merchants such as Shelikhov and the Golikovs, most of these pelts would find their way to Chinese or western European purchasers

In future years Baranov would make sporadic gestures toward a policy of reducing and regulating the rate of sea otter slaughter, a policy we might term conservation today. But realistically, such steps could not be effective. The sea otter population was finite and market demand infinite. Competitors, both Russian fur-hunting companies and Native peoples trading with seagoing merchants from other nations, were sure to destroy any sea otter populations not taken by the Northeastern Company men and their Alutiiq hunting partners. Baranov faced what has been called the fisherman's dilemma: any effort he made toward conserving sea otter populations would only work for the advantage of his company's rivals. With no superior authority willing or able to impose an international hunting ban, the destruction of these animals was inevitable unless the market for their skins disappeared.[19]

* * *

The weather on Kodiak Island is more moderate than what Baranov had known in northeastern Siberia. Summer temperatures average in the fifties and winter temperatures in the mid-thirties. But as he had already seen at

Unalaska, abundant rain and wind are conditions of life throughout maritime Alaska. Annual rainfall at Three Saints Harbor is about eighty inches, with monthly averages from at least four to more than nine inches. During the summer, mist and thick fog banks often blanket the coastline. Stiff gales sweep the island throughout the winter. Even without wind or fog, wet clothes, soggy supplies, clammy housing, waterlogged travel, and working and sleeping in the damp were normal. The line between wet and dry, like the zone between daylight and darkness on overcast winter days, was inexact.

At the time of Baranov's arrival, the company's headquarters site offered scant protection. Chosen by Shelikhov in 1784, this place had previously been the location of an Alutiiq winter village, but it was far from ideal for the Russians. A steep mountain barrier shielded it from prevailing northwest winds; yet this barrier also meant that seagoing vessels could not enter or leave the inner lagoon under sail power. Visiting ships needed to anchor far outside the harbor or rely on a lengthy, laborious tow by baidaras and baidarkas to reach the settlement. When Captain Joseph Billings arrived aboard the *Slava Rossii* in July 1790, he and his officers found that rocky outcrops and encircling sand spits made this a difficult anchorage. Moreover, the surrounding mountains cut off the settlement from the rest of the island. The area lacked timber for building and burning, and it had no nearby streams with annual salmon runs, both major disabilities for the future of Russian settlement.

Still more daunting, the site was vulnerable to natural disasters. In July 1788, two years after Shelikhov's departure, a major earthquake and tsunami struck the harbor. According to Vasilii Merkul'ev, the colony's storekeeper, the shaking was so strong that no one could stand on their feet and "some thought the earth would collapse." Two enormous waves surged over the low-lying settlement, so that "every man was looking for a place to save his life."[20] While there were no casualties, these tsunamis destroyed some Russian dwellings, damaged all others, swept away much of the company's merchandise, and entirely carried off the sparse vegetation as well as the soil from a garden plot that the Shelikhovs had cultivated. Rushing water also broke the lines mooring the company's two small ships then in the harbor, the *Sv. Simeon* (*St. Simon*) and *Sv. Mikhail* (*St. Michael*), hurling them onto shore where they came to rest atop damaged buildings. For at least two weeks aftershocks continued daily, causing landslides from the mountains and an alarming subsidence of the shoreline.[21] Two more large earthquakes shook the site during the next three years.

As a result the Three Saints site was left, as Merkul'ev said, closer to the sea. Captain Billings in his expedition journal described the location as he saw it shortly before Baranov's arrival. "The Country low & at high water over-flowed to a considerable distance. The village is built on a Rock that projects into the Sea, a lake on each side with rivulets into the Sea, a Situation prob-ably thought to keep them from Attacks, as it is only accessible by Water."[22]

Dr. Sauer, Captain Billings's inquisitive English physician, spent days ashore during the expedition's weeklong visit. According to his description, the colony contained five houses "built in Russian fashion" and a barracks divided into apartments on either side of a central passageway. This building had various rooms given over to company operations, and here too was the chief manager's residence. Another building housed the young hostages who lived with the Russians. In addition, Sauer listed storehouses, warehouses, a rope walk, a smithy, a carpenter's shop, and a cooperage among company facilities. Several Russian workers had with them their Native wives—illus-trating that intermarriage already was well established in this company settle-ment—and they were raising gardens of cabbages and potatoes. He described the two vessels still stranded onshore as galiots of about eighty tons each. Although they lacked rigging, they were armed and well guarded, serving as protection for the harbor and the settlement.[23]

Sitting close to tidewater at low elevation, this cluster of buildings, hap-hazardly arranged, did not make a good impression on the new chief man-ager. "Our old harbor," he wrote Shelikhov a year later, "has become hopeless as a place for men to live in. After the earthquakes, the ground settled and became so low that there are regular straits between the buildings, and dur-ing extremely high tides there is very little dry ground left."[24]

The only practical solution would be relocating to a site with better har-bor facilities and adequate space for a new company town. Because of the complete destruction of Kodiak Island's sea otter population, it would be an advantage also to move closer to the remaining hunting territories on the Alaskan mainland. The lack of shipping was a more urgent immediate problem. That first winter on Kodiak Island, Baranov and the men he had brought with him joined Delarov and his workers in refloating and rerigging the *Sv. Mikhail*. By May 1792 the ship was ready to return to Okhotsk with Delarov and a cargo of furs. Once it departed, leaving Baranov now fully in charge, the new chief manager made it a top priority to find a better location for the Northeastern Company's American headquarters.

* * *

After a winter confined to the overcrowded little settlement at Three Saints Harbor, Baranov must have welcomed the opportunity to be away, back on the water. As soon as the weather allowed, sailing in a baidara with a small crew, he surveyed Kodiak Island's southeastern coast in search of a better location. He found it on Chiniak Bay, some fifty miles distant at the island's eastern end. With a sheltered anchorage, the inner bay is screened from the open sea by small islands. Freshwater streams—including the seasonally salmon-rich Buskin River—and an ample supply of timber were close at hand. Here he ordered the establishment of a new headquarters settlement at what he named Pavlovskaia Harbor, the modern St. Paul Harbor, honoring Prince Paul, Catherine II's heir apparent.

It would be the work of a season to transfer company property and erect the first wooden structures for the new post, which grew in time to become the modern city of Kodiak. But the task was delayed by one of the common tragedies of life in maritime Alaska. While Baranov was preparing to take a large hunting and exploring expedition eastward to the Alaskan mainland, he ordered a small contingent to stay behind and carry out the move to the Pavlovskaia site during the summer. In April fifteen of these men—eight Russians and seven Alutiiqs—along with a few Alutiiq women sailed a new baidara to Alitok at the far western end of Kodiak Island, intending to bring back furs and provisions. On the return trip the frail boat was heavily laden, carrying at least two additional passengers, fur returns from the winter hunt at Alitok, and a cargo of dried salmon. At Cape Iakhtash, the island's extreme southwestern point, a strong current apparently threw the baidara onto a reef. There were no survivors.

Because of this misfortune, Baranov abandoned his plan to move the colony's headquarters immediately. Instead, he ordered the foreman of the greatly reduced workforce remaining at Three Saints to transfer the company's goods to Pavlovskaia "as fast as the opportunity will allow." Because of the ever-present danger of earthquakes and tsunamis, he also directed that a clearing be made on a hill behind the new settlement as a place of safety.[25]

When Shelikhov learned of the move, he wrote from Okhotsk to thank his chief manager. "Pray God," he said, "that this new place will be quiet and more profitable than the old." He also expressed his satisfaction that the planning and construction were under Baranov's supervision.[26] Despite the hazards, Three Saints Harbor was not completely abandoned by the company. In time the town of Old Harbor (Nuniaq in the Alutiiq language) developed just to the north of the former Russian post.[27]

Descriptions of the Pavlovskaia settlement are lacking for its early years. Few ships, either Russian or others, visited Baranov's headquarters during the 1790s. Wartime conditions in Europe, a shortage of company ships, and the extreme hazards of North Pacific navigation, accompanied by a series of business reorganizations, disrupted Shelikhov's plan to keep the colony supplied by regular voyages. In 1802, nine years after the settlement's founding, navy lieutenant Gavriil Davydov arrived from Okhotsk aboard the *Sv. Elizaveta* (*St. Elizabeth*), only the second Russian vessel to reach Kodiak Island in five years. Sea weary, the young lieutenant described with appreciation the sight of "a pleasant shoreline" with "a small valley surrounded by fir tree groves whose constant greenery gave a happy aspect to this part of the island." The harbor entrance, he said, was no wider than fifty sazhens, slightly more than a hundred yards, which separated the mainland from a small island. On the headland overlooking the harbor, Davydov noted, was "a kind of fortified structure." When the *Sv. Elizaveta* dropped anchor in thirty feet of water, the shore was so close that his sailors ran mooring lines from the ship's stern to the shoreline.[28] Then as now, in other words, it was what deepwater sailors might call a snug anchorage.

By this time Baranov was living in his own house, where he entertained Davydov and his fellow officers with generous hospitality.[29] Uninterested in the details of hunting and trading operations, the lieutenant wrote no description of the company's commercial structures, nor did he document living conditions for the Russian workmen. His own lodgings onshore he characterized only as "a little house" built on a cliff, with windows that looked out over the bay. One additional feature of the settlement he mentioned was a large, round, wooden building called a *kazhim* that sheltered the company's Native employees. An empty space—a kind of open courtyard—was left in the middle of this structure, Davydov explained, "so that various tasks may be carried out, and around this space small huts are built for the Americans to live in."[30]

Two years later, in 1804, newly arrived company clerk N. I. Korobitsyn prepared a detailed inventory of the Pavlovskaia Harbor establishment, systematically listing twenty-three separate structures. A central building close to the harbor shoreline was Baranov's home and office.[31] Korobitsyn described a large barracks for the Russian workers, a company workshop and houses, storerooms for company-owned provisions, a kitchen and cook-

THE HARBOR OF ST. PAUL. This view of Pavlovskaia, the modern town of Kodiak, shows the site in 1805, a decade after its founding by Baranov and his men. Drawn by a shipboard artist, perhaps Captain Yuri Lisiansky himself, it was published in 1814 as an illustration in Lisiansky's book *Voyage Round the World*, which appeared in an English translation that same year.

house for servants, and separate houses for the tinker and smithy. He also listed a construction shed for small boats, a rigging loft and cooper's work-shop, and a blacksmith and locksmith's workshop. In addition, the settlement included a clerk's house, a company guesthouse for visiting officials, another house for the local manager, and four additional houses for the use of com-pany employees. He mentioned as well a barracks for Native employees and a private residence for the "Company elder"—presumably the headman for the residential Alutiiq workforce. Toward the end of his list were three structures built for the Russian Orthodox mission since the clergymen had arrived in 1794: a wooden church called the Church of the Resurrection, a house for the clerical mission, and a house for the clergy-staffed school and its offices. Filling out Korobitsyn's inventory was a public bathhouse and a shed for the beef cattle brought to Kodiak Island by the Russians. On the outskirts were a small orchard and a freshwater pond from which a stream flowed through the settlement.[32] For this company town, Baranov had supervised the construction of a well-planned, conveniently arranged community at his Kodiak Island headquarters.

* * *

As he took command, the new chief manager's most important project was to extend the Russian reach into better fur-producing territories, following up on the expeditions sent to Kenai Bay and Chugach Sound by Delarov. From Kodiak Island, Kenai Bay was the nearest mainland location with abundant sea otter stocks. Bordering the Kenai Peninsula on the northwest, from Pavlovskaia Harbor it is reached by a continuous sea voyage approximately one hundred miles eastward across open water. In 1785 Shelikhov had sent there a large party of Russians, Fox Islanders, and Kodiak Alutiiqs to explore, establish good relations with the Kenai Alutiiq and Taniana Indian people, and obtain furs. They returned unharmed, bringing back a large cargo of peltry and twenty Native youngsters as hostages from various Kenai communities.[33] The same year a hunting crew sent by the Lebedev-Lastochkin Company (with Shelikhov included as a minority investor) had also arrived on Kenai Bay and built a post they named Nikolaevsk at the mouth of the Kenai River.

In 1789 Delarov had resumed the initiative for the Northeastern Company. At English Bay, the nearest approach point from Kodiak Island, his men built a small post named Aleksandrovsk to serve as a wintertime base of operations.[34] The company's hunters made a profitable beginning, collecting three thousand sea otter pelts their first season and two thousand more in 1790. Then the returns declined sharply, partly because of conflict with hunters from the Lebedev-Lastochkin Company. Delarov and Baranov had no illusion as to the prime cause. The Kenai Bay sea otters too had been virtually hunted out, Baranov reported to Shelikhov after his first visit to that region.[35]

* * *

A few days after Delarov's departure for Okhotsk, the *Sv. Simeon* (*St. Simon*) under Captain Gerasim Izmailov arrived at Three Saints Harbor from Chugach Sound. Izmailov reported on his coastal explorations farther southward. He also brought alarming stories about the behavior of the Lebedev-Lastochkin men on Kenai Bay. Foreman Peter Kolomin had arrived there in 1787 with a small crew and taken over the Nikolaevsk post. Four years later, when Kolomin's surviving force numbered only twenty-seven men, a second expedition leader, Grigorii Konovalov, reinforced the Lebedev-Lastochkin contingent with sixty-two more Russians. With Kolomin's initial support, the newcomers built their own winter quarters close to Nikolaevsk. Then

Konovalov, a man with a violent temper, claimed control over the entire Lebedev-Lastochkin establishment. Kolomin resisted, so Konovalov and his hunters began to terrorize their rivals. They harshly mistreated Kolomin's allies among the Kenai Natives, stole supplies and peltry from Kolomin's people, preempted their hunting grounds, scared away all their Native workers, and threatened to destroy any who stood against them. Kolomin sent his antagonists a protest letter. In response, Konovalov declared: "It is just too bad that Kolomin didn't come [here] himself, because then I would have had him whipped with two ropes, put in irons, and sent back to Russia."[36]

Badly frightened, Kolomin fled to the Northeastern Company post at Three Saints Harbor. Then, after Konovalov actually tortured to death one of his own promyshlenniks, his workers turned against him and delivered him in shackles to Vasilii Malakhov, the Northeastern Company crew chief at Aleksandrovsk.[37] Malakhov hauled him, still shackled, to Delarov and Baranov at Three Saints Harbor. In May 1792 Konovalov sailed with Delarov and Malakhov aboard the *Sv. Mikhail*, with everyone expecting that he would face criminal charges before Lebedev-Lastochkin and his company's board of directors in Irkutsk.[38]

Captain Izmailov's information about Kenai affairs gave Baranov an urgent reason for his first trip to the Alaskan mainland. He sailed directly to Kenai Bay, where he found the situation still quite volatile. With Konovalov gone, the Lebedev-Lastochkin hunters were now united in trying "to do as much harm to our company as possible." These men meant to force the Northeastern Company to abandon Kenai Bay altogether, and they took possession of nearby Kachemak Bay by sending there a large crew. In these areas, Aleksandr Andreevich reported, "they made real slaves of the natives and forbade them to have any communication with us." They also intended to deny Baranov's men any access to Chugach Sound and adjoining territory on the southern side of the Kenai Peninsula. According to one story, they were waiting only for Malakhov's return from Okhotsk "to start hostilities with all their forces" against the company.[39]

Short of manpower and reluctant to begin open warfare with his Russian opposition, Aleksandr Andreevich was frustrated in this first effort to exercise a measure of general authority over other trading enterprises in maritime Alaska. "My plans and my diplomacy," he later said, "had no effect."[40] As events soon proved, Baranov's troubles with the Lebedev-Lastochkin company competitors were far from over. Even the violence-prone Konovalov would reappear to add to these difficulties.

Following a quick return to Three Saints Harbor, Baranov launched the large mainland hunting and exploring expedition that had been part of his planning since he first heard about Chugach Sound from Captain Bocharov two years earlier. In late May he set out with two baidaras and thirty Russians, accompanied by a Kodiak Alutiiq force of perhaps three hundred men in 150 baidarkas. He wanted to establish peaceful relations and trade with the Chugach Alutiiqs.[41] He also hoped to find a site for another winter camp that would help control access to Chugach Sound and adjacent hunting territories despite the efforts of the Lebedev-Lastochkin forces.

This venture, so he told Shelikhov the following year, was a great success. Along with their hunting, he and his men made a detailed survey of the Chugach Alutiiq settlements. They visited three major villages, took a census, and entered into cordial alliances, all "by humanitarian means and without the slightest bloodshed."[42] Aleksandr Andreevich also elicited from the Chugach headmen a promise to come and visit the Russians wherever he would decide to locate his winter fort.

Adopting the model of Shelikhov's relations with the Kodiak Alutiiqs, Baranov made it a central feature of his diplomacy with the Chugach to take teenage hostages to assure the good behavior of their home communities. These youngsters were in effect recruits who served their own society by agreeing to live with the Russians. At least twenty Chugach Alutiiq hostages joined Baranov's 1792 expedition.

✳ ✳ ✳

On Chugach Sound, Baranov first met a foreign trading ship, a two-masted English brig named the *Phoenix* under the command of Hugh Moore, an Irish-born Englishman.[43] The ship had come from Bengal by way of Canton, Manila, and Nootka Sound, with Captain Moore trading successfully for sea otter pelts on the coastal voyage northward from Vancouver Island. When Baranov met him, Moore was in the process of replacing his ship's masts, damaged during a recent storm. After some initial awkwardness because of Moore's fears when encountering Baranov's imposing baidarka flotilla, the two men became friends. During a spell of bad weather, Baranov spent five days aboard the *Phoenix* and took all his meals with Captain Moore. Once the weather moderated, Moore often came ashore and visited Baranov in his tent. "We talked about many things," Baranov summarized. Not the least of these must have been the growing number of British and American ships that were entering the Northwest Coast fur trade and impinging on Alaskan territory claimed by the Russians. Before his departure, Moore gave Baranov a unique gift: a young Bengali man named Richard, who became Baranov's personal servant and, because of his language skills, a valued interpreter. He later served as the boatswain on Baranov's small ship, the American-built *Olga*.[44] In return, Baranov presented Moore with a finely worked fox-skin jacket from the Fox Islands and his own recently gathered collection of Native "curios" from the Chugach people. When the two men parted, Moore honored Baranov with a salute from his ship's cannons, a gesture that the Kargopol' merchant's son deeply appreciated.[45]

This pleasant initial encounter with a trader from a rival nation may have done a great deal to shape Baranov's attitudes about future relations with such bold, enterprising merchant captains. Despite a fixed attitude of suspicion and hostility toward foreigners on the part of Russian government officials, Aleksandr Andreevich would find the British and New Englander shipmasters sailing the Northwest Coast personally a congenial group of men. At every opportunity he would make them welcome at his table, offer them the best food and drink he could manage, and relish the good company, the news, and the stimulating conversations they brought to Russian America. That these friendships would sometimes lead to mutually advantageous business agreements should be no surprise.

* * *

One experience in Chugach territory was truly threatening for Baranov and his men. In the latter part of June, shortly after Moore's departure, Aleksandr Andreevich sailed to Nuchek Island. There he met Captain Izmailov as he returned with the *Sv. Simeon* from further southward explorations. As he made camp the first evening at Nuchek, Baranov dispatched his baidara with its crew to search around adjacent islands for good fishing sites, something Nuchek lacked. Following their departure he counted sixteen Russians in his camp, along with a larger number of Kodiak Alutiiqs and some Chugach hostages, who assured the Russians that there was no danger since their own people were settled nearby.

Well before dawn, in deep darkness and with rain falling, a great many armed men crept up to the camp and slipped past the sentries. They were dressed for battle, wearing thick armor of hardwood layers bound with sinew and heavy capes of hardened moose hides and with their heads protected by stout wooden helmets carved into fanciful figures of monsters, as the Russians viewed them. They began their attack silently by stabbing Kodiak and Chugach Alutiiqs sleeping in the open and then stabbing at the Russians sheltered in their tents. Baranov and his men jumped up from their beds, grabbed their guns, and fired toward these dark figures. To their dismay, Aleksandr Andreevich later explained, "neither our buckshot nor our bullets could pierce their armor." In the dark, he said, "they seemed to us worse than devils."

The unidentified attackers, vastly outnumbering the Russians, showed remarkable discipline. They advanced in perfect order, following directions shouted out by one commanding voice. Fortunately, the Russians had brought ashore a small cannon, which Baranov put into action. After firing three shots, he wrote, "things began to go better." Although the cannon blasts hit nothing in the dark, the attackers started to retreat from the camp site, still moving in good order. Many of Baranov's Alutiiq allies meanwhile fled in terror, some being cut down as they tried to reach their baidarkas, while others made it to Captain Izmailov's ship, which was riding at anchor a short distance offshore.

For two more hours, until a hazy daybreak in the rain, the attackers kept up their siege on Baranov's camp. With Aleksandr Andreevich giving orders, the Russian guns managed to hold off the armored men surrounding them, whoever they were. With full light, just as the enemy force seemed to be preparing another assault, help came from Captain Izmailov, who sent ashore a ship's boat filled with armed sailors to rescue Baranov's beleaguered small command. After a sharp counterattack by the Russians, their foes abandoned the field and departed in six large wooden dugout canoes, which were, Baranov sardonically remarked, "full of a choice lot of barbarians."

When they were able to look about, the Russians found twelve of their attackers dead on the field, and they could see a trail of blood for nearly a mile where the wounded had retreated or been carried away by their companions. One Russian died in the first attack; another expired two weeks later from his wounds. Nine Kodiak Alutiiqs died during the battle and fifteen were left wounded. The attackers also took with them four Chugach hostages who had run from Baranov's camp into the arms of their foes, mistakenly assuming in the dark that their relatives had launched the attack. For his part, Aleksandr Andreevich had reason to be thankful. "God shielded me," he declared in his report to Shelikhov, "for although a spear ripped my shirt and arrows fell around me, I was unhurt."[46]

The identity of their foes did not long remain a mystery. Baranov's men had taken captive one badly wounded attacker, who told them that they were a combined force of Tlingits from Yakutat Bay allied with Eyaks from the

Cape St. Elias region farther south. Their war parties had originally come together, the captive said, to carry out a revenge strike on the Chugach Alutiiqs, who had raided the Tlingits the prior year. But when they learned that Baranov's men were instead a small Russian-led force, they had proceeded to attack "hoping for rich booty."[47] Before his death, the wounded man also revealed that ten additional large dugout canoes filled with Tlingit warriors were on their way from the Copper River area, intending to destroy the Chugach people and then advance northward to assault the Russians and Alutiiqs on Kenai Bay.

* * *

This violent confrontation with Tlingit and Eyak warriors brought the Russians and their Alutiiq allies into a conflict over territory and trading relations that would strongly shape Russian America's future. The Tlingit people occupied a resource-rich maritime region reaching from the southern shores of Chugach Sound to Yakutat Bay and southward along the coast and adjoining offshore islands as far as Dixon Entrance, opposite the northern cape of the Queen Charlotte Islands. Modern ethnographers tentatively place the combined Tlingit population in Baranov's time at ten thousand.[48] Quite distinct in ethnic origin and cultural traditions from the Alutiiqs, with a highly structured hierarchical system of territorial and clan-based social organization, the Tlingits viewed themselves as a powerful, aristocratic people, superior to all others.

Their social order was centered on the *kwáan*, a political and social unit that grouped matrilineal clans together within well-established home territories. Each kwáan was essentially sovereign within its own realm. Lacking a single overall authority, Tlingit society was knit together by strong bonds of language, custom, kinship, and shared history, all given focus by elaborate multiday ceremonial observances known as potlatches. Despite the sharp rivalries that flowed through their status-conscious, prestige-oriented economy, these bonds sustained a complex web of reciprocal obligations between individuals, families, clans, and moieties and between separate Tlingit communities. Though outbreaks of violence over infidelity or other types of domestic strife could lead to blood feuds, competition and cooperation among the Tlingits were usually kept in balance by a strong, shared code of morality and good behavior. With outsiders the Tlingits tended to be wary, weighing all encounters with an acute calculation of risks and rewards, ready to defend their territory and uphold their honor and prestige by warfare if necessary.

Generally tall and robust in comparison with Russians and Alutiiqs, Tlingit men from childhood learned to prize valor in warfare and skill in combat. Armed with spears, daggers, bows and arrows, and ceremonially decorated heavy clubs, well protected by their cleverly fashioned body armor and wooden helmets and visors, these were daunting foes. They were skilled in protecting their settlements with log palisades, favoring hilltop or cliff-top sites for defense. When making offensive raids, Tlingit war parties traveled in long, ornately decorated cedar dugout canoes and, as the Russians discovered, preferred to surprise their foes by attacking late at night or just at dawn. They were, in short, a formidable and proud people who were altogether unlikely to accept Russian domination.[49]

* * *

At the time Baranov and his compatriots arrived at Chugach Sound, the Tlingits and their neighbors to the south were rapidly gaining experience in trade with foreign shipmasters. While New Spain's viceroy had sent three expeditions to explore and lay claim to the Northwest Coast for the Spanish Crown during the previous few years, these were not trading ventures.[50] Following the third expedition of Captain James Cook, however, British and American merchant captains like Hugh Moore had begun sailing to Vancouver Island's Nootka Sound and northward into the Queen Charlotte Islands and adjacent Northwest Coast territories. There they met Native clients eager to exchange sea otter skins for a wide variety of European and American goods including iron tools and weapons, clothing and yard goods, and muskets and other firearms, along with high-potency brandy and rum—likely watered down and treated with additives such as pepper or tobacco leaves to assault and deceive the unsophisticated Native palate.

Skilled, shrewd merchant captains might make large fortunes by exchanging their Northwest Coast peltry in Canton for cargoes of Chinese goods to satisfy a growing demand in American and European upper-class households. Particularly for New England shipmasters and merchant investors—the so-called Boston men who had lost their access to British trading connections with the American victory in the War of Independence—the new triangular trade in Northwest Coast furs and Chinese staples and luxury items was a burgeoning profit opportunity.

The threat of this trade for Baranov was twofold. First, every sea otter skin gained by the Yankees or Britons was lost as a potentially valuable asset that might otherwise go to the Russians. Second, the goods that came into Native hands as a result, especially the firearms, lead, and gunpowder, constituted a threat to Russian expansion southward. The Haida of the Queen Charlotte Islands, the Eyak, and especially the Tlingit people were learning to rely on Anglo-American traders for weapons that enabled them to resist Russian and Alutiiq hunting incursions into their coastal waters.

Traditionally hostile to the Alutiiqs, Native communities all along Alaska's southeast coast might make common cause in opposing the territorial ambitions of the Russian-Alutiiq alliance under Baranov's command. Whether viewed as independent Native nations or as the military arm of an expanding Anglo-American system of seaborne commerce, by 1792 these Northwest Coast peoples were yearly adding firearms—small cannons as well as flintlock trade muskets and muzzle-loading rifles—to their military arsenals and increasing their ability to check Russian-Alutiiq encroachments. Moreover, their access to well-supplied British and New England trading vessels added to their considerable commercial savvy, making it highly unlikely that they could be recruited as Russian trading clients.

For Baranov there was no quick and easy solution to this problem. Indeed, the threat grew more acute with each passing year. Tlingit opposition and the annual arrival of British and Yankee trading ships in southeastern Alaska before long would force him to alter his commercial strategies for the Northeastern Company and its successor, the Russian-American Company. Yet retreat was the furthest thing from Aleksandr Andreevich's mind. The challenge posed by the Tlingits and less directly by the Eyaks and the Haida became instead a stimulus to develop a more innovative, far-reaching strategy for achieving his commercial goals.

* * *

Following the 1792 Nuchek battle, Baranov hurried northward to alert the company men at English Bay about the possible danger from the Copper River Tlingits. Then, in mid-July, he and his entire command returned to Kodiak Island for the winter. Four days after they reached Pavlovskaia Harbor, reinforcements arrived from Okhotsk aboard a trim new ship named the *Severo-vostochnyi Orel* (*Northeastern Eagle*), a vessel built at the Okhotsk yards under the supervision of James Shields.

The British-born Shields was a skilled shipwright who had come to Russia a few years earlier to join Empress Catherine II's army. After serving briefly as a second lieutenant in the Yekaterinburg Regiment under the command of the English colonel Samuel Bentham, he and four other British expatriates familiar with ship construction had agreed to work for Shelikhov.[51] Assisted by local laborers at Okhotsk, Shields and his assistants had completed the

Orel in the fall of 1791, late in the sailing season. At this point Shields agreed to take command of the ship for the Northeastern Company, sail to Russian America, and there establish a shipbuilding operation under Baranov's management. Because foul weather forced them to spend the winter at Kamchatka, Shields and his men reached Pavlovskaia the following July with a much-depleted inventory of supplies for the company's North American operations.

In a letter that Shields brought to Baranov, Shelikhov outlined his ambitions to start shipbuilding in Russian Alaska. "Herewith," he wrote, "we send you iron, rigging, and sails for one ship, which you will build with Shields' help." He also gave Aleksandr Andreevich a further charge. "Using him [Shields] to advantage, you should also begin two or three other ships of various sizes, bringing them to the point where you can finish them yourselves, without a shipbuilder's aid." While saying that Shields should return to Siberia by 1793, Shelikhov made a grand general promise of further assistance: "Everything you need for this [project] will be sent later." He ended with a final command, ostensibly meant to overcome the skilled labor problem in Russian America. "Teach the natives to be sail-makers, riggers, and blacksmiths," he blithely told Baranov.[52]

Despite his usual zeal for following Shelikhov's directives, Aleksandr Andreevich initially replied to the shipbuilding proposal with extreme skepticism. He was particularly dismayed by Shelikhov's orders about Shields. "These instructions." he wrote Shelikhov the following summer, "reached us at a time when we were busy building [at Pavlovskaia] a blacksmith shop, a warehouse, a store with living quarters, and a place to store the rigging." Kodiak Island, he explained, lacked the proper timber for ship construction. There were no larch (spruce) trees, and the local fir, as Shields told him, had too many knots and was far too brittle. Nor could they start a shipyard at a more favorable place on Chugach Sound during the winter. They lacked food there and the time to build living quarters. "Such an important affair as building a ship," Baranov said with some vexation, "cannot be left to careless hunters without the supervision of experienced men." If he had complied with Shelikhov's orders by returning Shields to Okhotsk right away, he wrote, "I would also have to send some of the men with him, at a time when we do not have enough hands, as not a few of the men are sick, unfit for work, or old."

For all these reasons, Aleksandr Andreevich kept Shields with him and waited before starting the shipbuilding project. Even though the contract

Shields had signed with Shelikhov specified only one year's service in North America, Baranov apparently persuaded the Englishman to stay longer— though perhaps not entirely of his own free choice. To mollify Shields, he encouraged him to explore for new islands and marine hunting grounds, promising to reward handsomely any discoveries made by the English seafarer.[53]

* * *

After spending the winter months with Shields at Pavlovskaia, Baranov by the spring of 1793 had experienced a change of heart about Shelikhov's project. He became an enthusiast for this first major experiment in Alaskan ship construction. To begin, he designated a protected shipyard location that he had seen the previous year on the north shore of Chugach Sound, a site he named Resurrection Harbor (Voskresenskaia gavan') on what came to be called Resurrection Bay, where the city of Seward now stands. He picked this place in part for tactical reasons. A Northeastern Company settlement there would block travel by Lebedev-Lastochkin's men across the shortest overland route between Kenai Bay and Chugach Sound, hindering their efforts to pre-empt control over the sound and its Native settlements. Baranov continued to avoid an armed confrontation with the Lebedev-Lastochkin crews, he later told Shelikhov, "not having enough strength to back me." But the site also had natural advantages: "plenty of fish in the creek [Bear Creek] and larch [Sitka spruce] trees for ship-building."[54]

In the late spring of 1793 Baranov sent Captain Bocharov to Resurrection Harbor in the *Sv. Simeon* with a cargo of provisions and nearly half his available workforce. He followed in June, sailing his own baidara. After making a brief further tour of exploration southward in the *Orel*, Shields and his four British companions joined him. Despite continued rainy weather, the construction crew began by laying down a sixty-eight-foot keel. But, as Baranov wrote Shelikhov, the shortage of shipbuilding supplies was severe. "We have only half a flask of pitch, not a pound of caulking, not a single nail, and not enough iron for such a big vessel." His workers were also hard-pressed to make sails for the ship. It had been necessary, he told Shelikhov, to use most of the canvas sent aboard the *Orel* for tents and sails for the company's baidaras. The old ones, he explained, had become so worn that it was difficult to make even ten pairs of pants from them for the Native workers, "and even these pants fell to pieces after they had been used for two days." In addition, the severe shortage of trade goods left the Russians scarcely able to pay the Chugach Alutiiqs for the food and furs they hunted. "They have almost quit taking beads," he said, "and want clothes, and I have nothing to give them but kamleia [parkas] made from the same canvas."[55]

Among other problems, Aleksandr Andreevich told Shelikhov, the worst was a severe shortage of good workers. Altogether, he reported in July, he had only 152 men left at Resurrection Harbor, and "out of this number about 15 are sick and old." Among those in poor health was their only blacksmith. The construction of a ship at such a great distance from Kodiak, he said, was a difficult matter and against the wishes of the men. "They grumble, and many of them," Baranov said, "accustomed to quiet and monotonous lives, want to go back." Food shortages at the construction site also worried Baranov, while wet and stormy weather made it necessary to finish their log barracks before proceeding with the ship. Because of an inadequate supply of Sitka spruce close to the shoreline—and with no draft animals to drag logs from upland locations—Baranov and Shields sent their men to nearby Greek Island (renamed Green Island by Captain George Vancouver) to cut and ship much of the needed timber.

When he reported his progress to Shelikhov, Aleksandr Andreevich added a postscript reflecting the continuing insecurity of his situation: "Please ship all the chain mail or armor you can. Guns with bayonets are very useful in time of danger; also we need more grenades for the cannons, and more cannons. Two of the old ones cannot be used. One burst when we tried it."[56] Surrounded by enemies and potential enemies, Native and Russian, with no military support and his Alutiiq allies as well as many of his own men not entirely reliable in battle, Baranov had good cause for his concern about armor, guns, grenades, and reliable cannons.

* * *

His insecurity may have been increased by the appearance of two British navy ships at Kenai Bay and Chugach Sound during the spring and early summer: the *Discovery* commanded by Captain George Vancouver and the *Chatham*, the *Discovery*'s consort, under the command of Lieutenant Peter Puget. These two ships were in the third year of an expedition ordered by the British Admiralty, with the principal goal of mapping the Northwest Coast from Kenai Bay southeast past Chugach Sound, Yakutat Bay, Icy Strait, and Sitka Sound to the southern tip of Sitka (Baranov) Island, thus completing the Alaskan coastal survey begun by Captain James Cook.

Coming from the Hawaiian Islands toward Kenai Bay—Cook Inlet on the English charts—Captain Vancouver guided the *Discovery* eastward past Kodiak Island in mid-April, staying well offshore due to stiff breezes and often thick, misty weather. He made no contact with either Russians or Kodiak Alutiiqs during this passage. The *Chatham* followed him a few days later, with Lieutenant Puget likewise not pausing to search for Russian settlements on Kodiak Island. After demonstrating beyond doubt that Kenai Bay did not lead to a supposed Northwest Passage through North America—an issue that had occupied armchair geographers for decades—Vancouver and Puget separately turned their ships toward Chugach Sound.

During Puget's weeks spent charting the southeastern shore of Kenai Bay, he had visited the Lebedev-Lastochkin post at Nikolaevsk, a place he found extremely unpleasant due to the noxious odors and foul condition of the Russian camp. He and Vancouver also met the Northeastern Company crew from Aleksandrovskaia led by Egor Purtov (identified as George Portoff in Vancouver's account), who was then preparing to lead the season's major hunting expedition to Chugach Sound. Although the lack of a common language hampered communication between Purtov and the English, Vancouver and Puget came to understand the conflict between the rival Russian groups and the role of Baranov as commander of the Northeastern Company's operations in Russian America. According to Purtov, Baranov would be pleased to visit the *Chatham*, but the uncertain progress of his survey prevented such an encounter. For his part, Purtov ingratiated himself with both captains by supplying their ships with freshly caught large halibut while they went about their surveying duties.[57]

Before Vancouver's departure from the Kenai region, while his ship was near Aleksandrovsk, Purtov carried to him a letter from Lieutenant Puget. He assured Vancouver again that Baranov wanted to visit him and would see the English commander aboard the *Discovery* that very afternoon, May 15. And, Purtov said, he would bring along an English interpreter. But Vancouver had already twice been disappointed by similar promises. Anxious to be on his way with the ebb tide, he began cruising slowly eastward and never caught sight of another ship.

When Baranov reported the British visit to Shelikhov the following year, he said that the officers had been eager to get information from the Russians "and wanted to see me, but I was detained at Kadiak on business and could not see them." He also remarked that "they were friendly and fair with our men."[58] According to Vancouver's account of his dealings with the Russians, it is clear that despite Purtov's claims, Baranov deliberately avoided a personal interview with the British naval officers.

* * *

Aleksandr Andreevich sailed from Resurrection Harbor back to Kodiak Island during the winter of 1793, leaving James Shields in charge of the shipyard settlement. When he returned the following May, he had first to deal with another incipient rebellion among the workers. Food was one problem. Russian in their taste, the newcomers from Siberia were unhappy with the customary Alaskan wintertime fare of dried salmon, dried salmon, and more dried salmon. Instead, they asked for flour every day, even though they each received two pounds of flour from the company's meager store each Sunday and on holidays. "When it came to food supplies," Baranov later told Shelikhov "the devil's influence was so strong that I could manage them only by well-meant advice and kindness, making only a pretense of being strict."[59]

The core difficulty remained the company's contract labor system, coupled with poor results from sea otter hunting and trading. Following Shelikhov's orders, Baranov was trying to accomplish a great deal with a small, partially disabled workforce. Since the pay of all the promyshlenniks depended on the annual fur returns, any diversion from hunting and trading obviously meant that fewer pelts would be sent to market, lowering the value of each worker's half-share interest in company profits. If he had first paid the men on Kodiak Island the paltry sums owed them, Baranov told Shelikhov, those who were free of debt would have quit and those who remained in debt would have started a mutiny. Many workers objected to their shipbuilding assignment at Resurrection Harbor because it would diminish even more their prospect for profits. They also gave other reasons, including the shortage of manpower, the threat from hostile Natives, and obstacles put up by Lebedev-Lastochkin's men. These grievances had festered among the men at Resurrection Harbor during Baranov's absence that winter.

"Though not without danger to myself," Baranov told Shelikhov in 1793, he stopped the trouble soon after his return. To quiet the dissident spirits among the promyshlenniks, a group that had sometimes received sympathy even from Shields, he relied on his rhetorical abilities, using a combination of flattery, bluster, threat, and sweet persuasion.[60] For Shelikhov's benefit—and in time the benefit of all historians of early Russian America—Baranov set down a synopsis of the speech he gave to the unhappy promyshlenniks on this occasion.[61] He declared that he was pleased to see all they had accomplished during the past seven months. But, he said, "my pleasure is imperfect." Some of the men had spoiled it, vexing Baranov by their meetings, conspiracies, and plots during his absence. They had divided into factions; some were bitter and had complaints against others. "I grieve," he went on, "that I have to manage such corrupt and depraved men." He reminded them all of the contract they had signed at Okhotsk when entering company service and their pledge to follow the rules and decisions made by the company partners. He invited them to examine again the terms of the contract, waving a copy for them to see—though he knew many would be unable to read it.

Aleksandr Andreevich said that he would investigate thoroughly to identify the instigators of sedition and revolt. If guilty, they would be banished from the company and shipped back to Okhotsk with a detailed report to the commandant there and the partners of the company. "Progress, success, and the welfare of the company," Baranov declaimed, "depend on unity." But here, he said, "we cannot stay a month without quarrels and causing injury to our comrades and superiors. We discuss and criticize every step of the administrators." He made his point with sarcasm: "Men who were herding pigs back home in the village or who spent all their time in a tavern feel here that they know everything, and are trying to be judge, and high-minded minister!"

The chief manager expected to hear a frank explanation and confession by the guilty of their "self-willed actions and plots." Those who repented their role could depend on him "to be humane and soft-hearted" when he investigated their guilt. And those who were not guilty "must not doubt [his] integrity." Indeed, all who had seen the deeds of the evildoers, he stated finally, were obliged to disclose them.

He had straightened things out on his return, he later assured Shelikhov, "but the scoundrels made an attempt on my life." Yet he declined to provide any details. "I would not deserve the position of manager if I could not stop troubles in my company," he said. Everything was stopped finally "with the use of some writing paper," Baranov summed up, "but the memory is sad."[62]

* * *

Another source of anxiety at Resurrection Harbor had been a wild rumor, perhaps started by Lebedev-Lastochkin's men, that Baranov and all the workers left at Pavlovskaia had been killed, leaving the Chugach Sound contingent on its own. Moreover, the Lebedev-Lastochkin's hunters had established a fort-like post on Greek Island, where Baranov and Shields needed to cut timber for their project. These rivals outnumbered Baranov's combined force on Kenai Bay and Chugach Sound, and they rejected his attempts at diplomacy. When he traveled to their outpost after his return, he reported, "I was met with cannons looking at me through embrasures," with all the Lebedev-Lastochkin promyshlenniks behind walls, armed and "cursing all they could." To avoid battle, Baranov restrained his anger and took recourse to legal proceedings, an action that at first displeased Shelikhov even though it was just what he himself would later recommend after the fact.

Once the crisis passed, Aleksandr Andreevich told Shelikhov, "with God's help, I finished the building of the ship and the rigging." He and Shields put aside their differences and worked together to complete this first Russian vessel built in North America. He had flattered himself, Aleksandr Andreevich later wrote, that the company directors would actually send him the supplies that Shelikhov had promised, "but the month of July arrived and nothing happened." Rather than abandon the project and shame the company, he said, he put himself to shame by forcing the hunters to start work without the necessary materials. Lacking steel fittings, they used "steel found in iron" by the company blacksmith. With this metal, the ailing blacksmith and his assistant fashioned nails and heavy hardware, including rudder hinges, bolts, windlasses, and anchors. They repaired and welded six hundred axes, since these tools broke often while the men were cutting the tall, tough spruce trees. Baranov congratulated himself on devising a caulking and paint substitute made from fir tree pitch mixed with ochre or iron ore and whale oil. For rigging, he and Shields made do with the defective material shipped from Okhotsk aboard the *Orel*, which they cautiously tested on a short trial trip and judged to be "strong enough" before they ventured a long voyage on the open ocean.[63] Historians are left to speculate whether these expedients may have contributed to the disaster that later overtook the ship somewhere at sea.

A contemporary drawing attributed to Shields portrays the early September launch of the vessel, which (like Captain Moore's brig) was named the *Feniks* (*Phoenix*). In the expert opinion of John Middleton, a specialist in Russian naval history, the *Feniks* as depicted by Shields was "a remarkably well-built state-of-the-art small frigate of 28 guns." Middleton adds that "it looks to be exactly what would be expected of a European naval vessel," particularly on comparison with an 1805 British Admiralty draft of a frigate designed for the Russian-American Company.[64] Company records describe the ship as a three-masted frigate with two decks, seventy-three feet long, a beam of twenty-three feet, and a depth of twelve and a half feet from the keelson to the deck, rated at 180 tons.[65] Flying from the stern is the Imperial Russian Navy's Andreevskii flag designed by Peter the Great, while the bowsprit displays the Jack also designed by Peter the Great for Russian warships. From the main mast flies the commission pennant, showing that a commissioned naval officer was in command.

As the design, the armaments, and the display of these flags attest, the *Feniks* was a military craft rather than a merchant vessel. Built in time of war amid shifting international alliances, it was a ship that might defend Russian interests in the North Pacific and protect the Northeastern Company's personnel and property from hostilities of any sort. To commemorate the launch, Baranov brewed "a bucket [*vedro*] of vodka" from berries and roots, with the addition of flour from the company's stores. "We all had drinks and I was drunk," he admitted to Shelikhov. "The men drank a glass or two, and some more and became intoxicated."[66]

A few days after the tipsy launch ceremony, Shields left for Kodiak Island aboard the *Feniks*. Baranov followed in his own baidara, making "a dangerous journey with lots of inconveniences" to Pavlovskaia Harbor. Left behind were a handful of men who continued shipbuilding efforts on a reduced scale. The result was the construction of two additional small vessels, the *Pegas* and the *Oleg*.[67] At Chiniak Bay, Lieutenant Shields soon set up another shipyard on Leisnoi (Woody) Island, within sight of Pavlovskaia Harbor. There he supervised construction of two more light, shallow-draft vessels, the *Del'fin* and the *Olga*, both launched in 1795. Each forty feet long, lacking substantial cargo space, these craft were not intended for hauling duty. Rather, Baranov relied on them for coastal exploration and, as needed, armed support for baidarka hunting expeditions. Replacing the baidaras he had previously used, the *Olga* became his personal craft that he often sailed—frequently as his own skipper—on excursions from Kodiak Island throughout southeastern Alaska.

Although Shields remained in the Northeastern Company colony until the spring of 1798, the completion of the *Del'fin* and the *Olga* brought a temporary end to the company's Alaskan shipbuilding efforts. Despite Shelikhov's abundant promises, a shortage of workers with the needed expertise and a lack of vital supplies terminated this brief, highly ambitious venture in economic diversification.

* * *

While Baranov and Shields were hard at work through the summer of 1794, Egor Purtov led the season's major exploring and hunting expedition farther southward along the coastal islands and bays into Tlingit homelands. On Baranov's orders, Purtov started from the Aleksandrovsk outpost in early May with at least 150 men, principally Kodiak Alutiiqs. They stopped briefly at Resurrection Harbor to repair baidarkas and recruit additional Chugach Alutiiqs. From stores aboard the *Orel*, Purtov reinforced his command with a few small cannon, guns, and ammunition. Leaving Chugach Sound with more than five hundred baidarkas, each carrying two or three men (including nine or ten Russians), they paddled to Icy Straits, Yakutat Bay, and Cape St. Elias. Despite stormy weather that cut short their explorations, they returned to Pavlovskaia Harbor toward the end of July with more than nine hundred sea otter pelts.

Baranov's instructions to Purtov had emphasized the need to avoid conflicts with the Tlingits and other Natives they might meet. When encountering the Tlingits, he said, Purtov and his men should explain to them their unjust behavior toward the Russians and Alutiiqs in the Nuchek attack the previous summer. Purtov should demand the return of the amanaty the Russians had lost during the battle "and possibly incline them [the Tlingits] to reconciliation" and submission to the authority of Her Imperial Majesty. Aleksandr Andreevich also cautioned Purtov to avoid any encounters with Lebedev-Lastochkin's people, since they were acting in a hostile manner "and do harm" to them. If they met foreigners on the way, they were "to behave politely."[68] Purtov was to make notes about all encounters, "act in a polite way," and avoid any annoyance to Russians and Natives throughout this expedition.

On his return, Purtov described his summer's excursion into territory previously little known by the Russians. He had met a group of Lebedev-Lastochkin hunters near Nuchek Island. Showing a letter that claimed all of Chugach Sound as their own territory, these men tried to stop Purtov from advancing southward. As instructed, he "answered politely" if somewhat mysteriously that he and his command were following the American coast "on a secret government mission" while also hunting sea otters and "had no intention of interfering with them and their men on Chugach Sound, whereas they were interfering" with him and his command.[69] Purtov's claims, backed by the overwhelming size of his command, were enough to avoid trouble for the time being.

Moving south of Chugach Sound, Purtov and his men kept peace with the Tlingits. They exchanged gifts, traded hostages, made a census of Tlingit settlements, and nominally claimed sovereignty on behalf of Catherine II's empire. One of the Russian promyshlenniks and a few of the Kodiak Alutiiqs were able to serve as interpreters in discussions with the Tlingit headmen. In their talks, the Yakutat Bay Tlingits affirmed that they had begun their attack at Nuchek by mistake, thinking they had found Chugach Alutiiqs. As the interpreter related, "When they came close to camp and saw that we were Russians," however, "they made up their minds to attack us just the same."[70] All Purtov's inquiries about the Chugach amanaty were met with the same reply: traded to people south of Yakutat Bay, they had died. Despite some awkwardness over the mutual exchange of hostages, requiring at one point a show of force at Yakutat Bay by Purtov's men in order to rescue their Russian interpreter, the expedition established the basis for cautious if not cordial trade relations between the Northeastern Company and Tlingit village leaders.

Purtov also reported about his further friendly contacts with Captain Vancouver and Lieutenant Puget at Yakutat Bay. When the Russian crew chief had come aboard the *Chatham* in mid-June, he learned that once more the British were in need of fresh fish. "We brought them about thirty halibuts," he told Baranov, "and they gave us a fine reception, with whiskey."[71] For more than a week the *Chatham* kept company with Purtov's command, moving about Yakutat Bay. By request of the commander, the Russians kept supplying the British with fresh halibut "for which," according to Purtov, "they thanked us in a most touching manner." When the *Chatham* put to sea again, Purtov also presented Lieutenant Puget with a female sea otter pelt and a three-person baidarka.[72]

From another foreign ship, a small British brig or schooner named the *Jackal* that had arrived in Yakutat Bay and anchored near the *Chatham*, Purtov was able to learn something about the current state of international relations. The captain, likely William Brown, told Purtov that the English and the Russians were on friendly terms. He also passed on the information that Russia had signed a peace treaty with Turkey and that China was now open to trade with some nations, "though he did not know just which ones."[73]

As he traveled farther south, Purtov had found more and more evidence of British and American trading activities with the Tlingits. Supplementing their own weapons and armor, these people owned many guns, with lead and powder, brought by foreign trading vessels that came every year to barter for sea otter skins. The Tlingits also asked the Russians for guns and ammunition. In keeping with fixed company policy and their own sense of self-preservation, Purtov and his men refused to sell their small supply of firearms. The presents they gave the Tlingit village leaders were beads, "various articles of copper, kettles, big and small rings, and plates of copper to be worn on the chest."[74] This commerce in household items and personal adornment, though at first brisk, would soon sate the Tlingit demand, while competing foreign traders continued to profit from the arms race they had helped create among the Tlingits and other Northwest Coast Native peoples.

Along with the furs he brought back to Pavlovskaia, Purtov had gathered much useful information. With Purtov's report in front of him, Baranov wrote to Shelikhov an extremely sympathetic account of the hardships such trips to distant territories imposed on the company's closest allies, the Alutiiq village hunters. Just the baidarka travel from Kodiak Island to Yakutat Bay and back was quite difficult and dangerous, he pointed out. "Imagine the poor natives making this journey both ways, 2,000 versts [ca. 1,325 miles]," Baranov said. "They must endure hunger on the way and often perish in stormy seas because this coast offers no adequate shelter." Traveling where the local people had not been subjugated to Russian rule, "they are always in constant danger of attack by the bloodthirsty inhabitants of these regions." For now, he concluded, "they endure it, but it takes courage and supervision by the Russians, and you can judge for yourself their state of mind."[75] Baranov suggested no immediate alternative to these long, hazardous baidarka voyages, yet his report displayed an acute awareness of the risks that the company's demands imposed on this indispensable Native workforce. Quite likely it was this concern that first set him thinking about moving the center of company operations once again, this time to some mainland site near the best sea otter hunting territory remaining in southeastern Alaska.

✳ ✳ ✳

With the fur returns from Purtov's expedition added to the pelts gathered at Pavlovskaia during the previous two years, Baranov could be pleased with the results of his administration to date. The cargo he sent to Siberia aboard the *Feniks* the following spring, 1795, would bring 276,550 rubles when sold in Okhotsk.[76] Since the Chinese emperor had just reopened the Kiakhta market, the arrival of this North American peltry proved a timely boon to the company, greatly improving the fortunes of the Shelikhov family and allied members of the Irkutsk merchant elite.

At this point, Aleksandr Baranov could rightly take pride in his accomplishments since starting for America five years earlier. From shipwreck to a rebellion among company promyshlenniks, battle with Tlingit warriors, and sharp conflicts with rival Russian traders, he had survived many challenges. After relocating the company's headquarters, his men and their Alutiiq allies had peacefully extended the Northeastern Company's hunting and trading operations. By increasing the fur returns from America, he had added to the Northeastern Company's wealth and improved his own fragile finances. Aided by James Shields, he had built five ships for company service that bolstered his efforts to manage the company's isolated, far-flung outposts while improving his contact with the Okhotsk market and his Irkutsk-based superiors. Above all, he had placed himself securely in command as the leading managerial figure in the fur business of Russian North America. But with this role, so he would discover during the next few years, came further problems, some anticipated and others totally unexpected.

V

CALAMITIES AND CATASTROPHES

---✳---

Despite Baranov's early successes, by 1794 daunting problems threatened the Northeastern Company's ambitious experiment in merchant-managed empire building. A discontented labor force, along with competition from rival Russian traders and aggressive Yankee shipmasters, endangered Aleksandr Baranov's administration. Then the news of Grigorii Shelikhov's death in Siberia shook the very foundations of the chief manager's authority. Physically hampered by two serious injuries, he soon experienced further major setbacks that led him to consider surrendering his post and returning to Russia.

---✳---

IN LATE SEPTEMBER 1794, TWO WEEKS AFTER BARANOV HAD returned from the Resurrection Harbor shipyard, the veteran captain Gerasim Izmailov arrived at Pavlovskaia with the *Tri Ierarkha* (*Three Hierarchs*). Recently built for the company, the vessel had departed from Okhotsk only six weeks earlier. It was a spacious three-masted cargo ship, sixty-three feet from stem to stern, with two decks. On this maiden voyage, blessed with good weather and smooth seas, the ship carried more than 230 tons of passengers, animals, and supplies.[1] Among the new arrivals were eight Russian Orthodox churchmen and two novices—all fresh from monastery life—sent to staff a spiritual mission, two company foremen, sixty-two promyshlenniks, and thirty settlers who had come from criminal exile in Siberia with their wives and children. Placed under company rule by order of the empress, these settlers were meant to be the founders of an agricultural colony under Baranov's general supervision. For their benefit, Izmailov's cargo included domestic cattle and chickens, seed grain, agricultural tools, and provisions meant to sustain the colonists until they could make themselves self-sufficient.[2]

A month behind the *Tri Ierarkha* came a second new Okhotsk-built company ship, the brig *Sv. Ekaterina* (*St. Catherine*), fifty-one feet long with a single deck, commanded by the experienced navigator Gavriil Pribylov.[3] Aboard were an additional fifty-nine promyshlenniks, two more foremen, five Aleuts or Kodiak Alutiiqs, and, at the start of the voyage, another small herd of cattle on the open deck.

Navigator Pribylov had first stopped at Unalaska to unload part of his cargo. Returning to sea on a course for Kodiak Island, the *Sv. Ekaterina* was struck by a fierce storm and caught by a severe riptide in Akutan Strait. Wind and high waves claimed the ship's two baidaras along with the main mast and fore topmast. Also swept into the sea were some of the cattle and cargo stored on deck.

For days Pribylov's damaged craft could only drift with the storm, but when the weather moderated, captain and crew regained control of the vessel. Baranov's men towed the *Sv. Ekaterina* into Pavlovskaia Harbor on October 24, with all on board unharmed and giving thanks to God for their survival.[4] Aleksandr Andreevich later complained that Pribylov had misappropriated some vodka consigned to the chief manager, swallowing a whole flask "without leaving a drop."[5] In the circumstances, Baranov's irritation was remarkably uncharitable.

Coming right after the launch of the *Feniks*, the arrival of these two ships marked the high point in Northeastern Company efforts to enlarge and strengthen its American colonial enterprise. Ironically, this boost in resources added to Aleksandr Baranov's immediate problems. The thirty settler families were ill prepared for American conditions and the tasks awaiting them. Heading each family was a convict. These men, farmers and craftsmen, had been sent into Siberian exile and were now forced across the North Pacific to a land totally strange to them. Furthermore, the addition of over 120 new contract employees required Baranov to integrate one-third more men, mostly inexperienced and likewise unaccustomed to the colony's hardships, into his workforce. And the ten monks in the missionary contingent, as described in the following two chapters, posed another distinctive series of challenges to the chief manager. Trouble might be expected.

Captain Izmailov delivered to Aleksandr Andreevich a lengthy dispatch from Grigorii Shelikhov and his Okhotsk office manager, Aleksei Polevoi.

Written in part as a response to Baranov's 1792 and 1793 reports, which had expressed deep skepticism about the Alaskan shipbuilding project and summarized his conflicts with the Lebedev-Lastochkin men, the Shelikhov-Polevoi letter showed little patience with Baranov's situation. Most painful to Baranov, wounding his pride in his accomplishments, were sharp complaints about various aspects of his performance as chief manager.

Because of the time lag in correspondence moving back and forth between Siberia and America, Shelikhov and Polevoi spoke of matters already one or two years in the past. They censured Aleksandr Andreevich for sending ships to Okhotsk too late in the season, staffed with unreliable officers and crewmen. They derided his handling of the Lebedev-Lastochkin workers and criticized his personal life, apparently relying on gossip about his drunkenness and his relationships with Alutiiq women that came from disgruntled former company employees.[6] They condemned his friendly behavior toward Captain Moore, the visiting English trader. And they scolded him for sending government officials negative information about the status of the company colony, including its shortage of manpower.

The Shelikhov-Polevoi letter also told Baranov that the errant Lebedev-Lastochkin foreman Grigorii Konovalov would be resuming his position at Kenai Bay. When he had been sent back to Okhotsk two years earlier, they said, "Konovalov . . . certainly spit on you." At a formal hearing, Pavel Lebedev-Lastochkin had demanded that his foreman be reinstated and his company repaid with new merchandise, demands that Shelikhov opposed. As a compromise, Shelikhov and Lebedev-Lastochkin had agreed that the archimandrite who headed the Orthodox mission should investigate the Konovalov case.[7]

Typical of the chief director's correspondence, this letter gave page after page of unrealistic instructions about developing the company's proposed agricultural colony, expressed in terms we might today call extreme micromanagement. Supervised by Ivan Polomoshnoi, another longtime Shelikhov associate, the exile families were to be settled in a new town that Baranov should help them build on the Alaskan mainland.[8] Shelikhov's main goal was the creation of a frontier showplace—"one that will look like a town instead of a village, even at the start"—for the benefit of foreign observers.

While the site selection would be left to Baranov's judgment, Shelikhov described the main features he wanted in this model company town. These included public squares for meetings and gatherings; short, wide streets; trees in front of the houses and in gardens; and all the houses of a uniform design and size, widely spaced to make the town look larger. Public buildings should be built "in the style of big cities." Further, "to give the place an air of importance and to impress foreigners and the [American] natives, it wouldn't be bad to dress the hunters in some coats of a military pattern and give them when needed some weapons to carry, such as, for instance, bayonets to be worn on the side." The chief director stressed that visitors should be able to see that "Russians live in an organized way" at this site. "Don't give them reason to think that Russians live in America in the same abominable way as in Okhotsk." In time, he airily predicted, "this small settlement will become a big city."[9]

Within this fantasy ideal community, Shelikhov envisioned a peaceful, trusting relationship between the Russians and the Native peoples whose territory the settlers would be invading. Yet he also gave exact attention to defensive arrangements, including the construction of high redoubts for artillery and a tall perimeter palisade extending along the most dangerous places. For show, this palisade should have a pair of "big strong gates," to be grandly named the Russian Gates, the Chugach Gates, or perhaps the Glory of Russia or the Glory of America. These gates must be kept locked, with people allowed to pass through only with permission from the chief manager or his local administrator. According to these instructions, Baranov would need to devise a system of guards who would exercise a strict surveillance over all residents: settlers, promyshlenniks, and Natives alike.

Shelikhov was obsessed with making this town into a grand display of Russian power. He told Baranov to build lofty turrets above some of the gun batteries and to place "a big Russian crest" on them. Also a merchant flag should fly over the wharf. "Everything must be impressive and look important," the chief director said, "especially when a foreign ship arrives." Aleksandr Andreevich's reports about the town, Shelikhov also said, would make Russians want to go there. Baranov should send a detailed description of the new settlement, separate from company correspondence, with a copy of the plans and even sketches of the buildings—in effect a promotional brochure. "Your achievements will become known," the chief director predicted, "and will create a sensation at the court."[10] Surely, it was Shelikhov who wanted most to create the sensation.

European troubles, Shelikhov and Polevoi's letter also said, had disrupted the company's hope to take furs to Canton. The French were forcing the whole world to fight them. But the company directors would not abandon their ambitions for opening a Cantonese trade because "supplies for Okhotsk and even more for America" were needed and at as low a cost as possible. To carry out their strategy, they urged Baranov to continue his shipbuilding efforts. Although the directors had been unable to provide him with the needed equipment and fittings this year, Shelikhov again promised that "in the next navigation season, we will supply you with everything necessary for that."[11]

Through the following winter and spring months, Baranov had ample time to mull over Shelikhov's criticism of his management. His response, sent to Okhotsk aboard the *Feniks* in 1795, is unique among his surviving writings. Businesslike in some parts, rambling and disjointed in others, it tells us more about Baranov's personal concerns and his living situation than any other document we have from his pen. Because of its length, it must have been the work of many evenings. And from its style, we may suspect that the chief manager wrote quite a few of these pages with a brandy bottle close by his elbow.

Baranov began with a frosty statement, declaring that he had read Shelikhov's letter "with extreme politeness, in spite of the fact that you consider me not as a friend, but as a lowly slave who serves only for his own interest and gain, and is not worthy of the important position of manager of the colonies."[12] He would answer every point, he promised, "following my rules of righteousness to which I have always adhered without fear of the strong and powerful of this world."

Regarding Shelikhov's sarcastic complaints about a dearth of furs and the times of their shipment, he responded in a similar tone. "Sea otters are not caught in the same way that humpback salmon are caught in Okhotsk," he wrote, "but over a distance of some 2,000 versts." The hunting at the older, closer sites, including both Kodiak Island and Kenai Bay, had been getting poorer "and now amounts to nothing," as the experience of the previous summer had shown. He certainly would have sent more sea otter pelts the previous year, he explained, "if I could, as I said, scoop them up as they do for humpback salmon." But thanks to Purtov's expedition southward into Tlingit territory, he now had more than sixteen sea otter pelts per company share that he was shipping back to Okhotsk. "I have decided not to send you any more disagreeable reports," he said, "without sending furs along." Exasperated, he threatened to leave the colony and return to Siberia. When God had helped him gather enough pelts, he wrote, "I intend to bring them myself, unless you change your rules and your attitude towards the men with whom I must work."

Clearly annoyed, Aleksandr Andreevich again explained his difficulties with the Russian workforce, his struggles to build the *Feniks* with inadequate supplies, and his continued hostile encounters with the Lebedev-Lastochkin hunters. He also challenged Shelikhov's claim that the colony had received enough trade goods. This might be true, Baranov wrote, if the sea otters were hunted still on a daily basis and the Natives would accept whatever the Russians wanted to give them. But, he pointed out, "we get all our skins here by regular trading, for sea otters and fox skins alike." The Russians needed to pay also for food supplies and had to give presents to newly pacified Natives. "You cannot compare this to former times, when you could sometimes settle with only nine bags of provisions," he said, "and did not have to force the [Russian] hunters to work because all the work was done by the natives who were working like asses." Now, he wanted Shelikhov to understand, "here everything is conducted differently."[13]

Among his other grievances, Baranov emphasized his disappointment with the newest group of employees sent from Okhotsk. "Send me some men who are really capable of doing things," he told Shelikhov, "instead of parasites who are shipped here just to make up the number." There were no more than eight carpenters left in the colony, he reported. Most of the hunters were new men. "The old timers either are filling in some position or other for the Company or are sick, or cowards, or the unfit."[14]

Baranov also resorted to sarcasm in commenting on the glaring mismatch between his resources and Shelikhov's ambition to create a showcase Alaskan company town out of nothing. "Your plans for the construction of settlements," he said, "seem to surpass human strength and especially the strength of our settlers. . . . I can rely only on the help of the Almighty and the prayers of the Holy Fathers in continuing the work of colonization."[15]

Aleksandr Andreevich defended himself against the slanders about his personal conduct. "You can judge by what has been accomplished," he declared, "whether I have spent my time in idleness and debauch or not." Shelikhov would not learn the truth, he said, by questioning the lazy idlers among the returned hunters who would say nothing good about the chief manager. If he would only ask those who had really performed worthwhile services for the company, he would hear a different story. "It is true," he allowed, "that we are having good, clean fun on some of the holidays. For example: we have music in the evening, and dancing with the Americans, six or eight couples dancing the kazach'ka, the contredanse, and others." These social occasions were instructive to the Americans, he claimed, and provided the musicians with lots of practice. The Native girls learned how to be sociable, and everyone got the exercise they needed in wintertime "as a preventive against scurvy." Of course, he added, "this pastime has been and is criticized."[16]

Regarding the stories about his drinking, Aleksandr Andreevich tried to convince Shelikhov that these tales were gross exaggerations. "It is not true," he wrote, "that we drink vodka all the time." Only he and Captain Izmailov had actually made any alcoholic concoctions; or if the hunters also made some, "it is done in such secrecy that I never hear of it." Only once or twice a year, when he returned from a tour of inspection or a long journey and found a barrel or two of wild raspberry and bilberry juice already prepared, did he brew up a batch. On his birthday he also made a bucket of vodka and treated everybody to it. And sometimes too on Christmas, he declared, he made a half bucket from snakeweed roots. "We get so used to living without it," Aleksandr Andreevich said, "we do not even think of it." He also explained that by making wine infused with mercury, highly regarded at the time as a treatment for syphilis, "I have rescued from death many who were perishing from venereal disease."[17] Twice while building the *Feniks* at Resurrection Harbor, he added, he had made a bucket of vodka from roots and berries. On the second occasion, at the launching, he freely admitted that he and some of the men had gotten drunk on this mixture. "If you call it vice," he concluded, "then it was vice." But he wanted to assure Shelikhov, "You should trust me in my zeal and loyalty for your benefits and glory." He had ignored all other opportunities for gain, Aleksandr Andreevich asserted somewhat ingenuously, to join Shelikhov and seek "what you are after, particularly the honor and glorious deeds."[18]

Baranov told Shelikhov, "For a long time now I have been keeping a girl," the daughter of an Alutiiq villager leader. He had taught her to sew and be a good housekeeper, and, he said, she could be trusted in business matters. But during his lengthy absence from Pavlovskaia the previous year she had "shown weakness"—that is, she had engaged in a brief sexual dalliance with another, younger man. In a rare moment of candor, Aleksandr Andreevich admitted his own culpability in matters of the flesh. "I sin too, sometimes from weakness, and sometimes from necessity, as I did during my long stay at Chugach when the Chugach people gave me a girl for a hostage." Because of this intimate tie, he further explained, "the Chugach became more attached to me and more confiding."[19]

The woman at Pavlovskaia was Anna Raskashchikova, who would remain with Baranov as his consort and later his wife for the rest of his life in Russian America. A local tradition identifies her as a native of Karluk, the village on the northwestern salient of Kodiak Island where Aleksandr Andreevich had likely made a landfall in 1791. Her father was Grigorii Raskashchikov, a headman who Baranov trusted to lead a reconnaissance expedition to the Bering Sea coastal region in 1794 or 1795. Anna was considerably younger, nearly thirty years junior to Aleksandr Andreevich, probably in her mid- or late teens when the relationship began. Their two children were born in 1797 and 1804. Despite their mutual infidelity during Baranov's absence at Chugach—apparently for her an isolated incident—she and Aleksandr Andreevich were a devoted couple, as visitors to their home would later attest.[20] Their companionable long-term liaison would be an example not only for the Russian promyshlenniks, but more particularly for other company officials who formed similar bonds over the years.

Baranov again tried to convince Shelikhov that the colony was short of workers. Counting Russians and Alutiiqs together, he wrote, 300 were busy with routine work, another 120 were working in the harbors, and about 35 were engaged in trapping. In all, "there are about 1,000 men on ships and baidaras." In addition, the Native hunters in baidarkas numbered 1,400, which included some men assigned to fish and trap for land furs. Altogether, there were "about 3,000 accounts," showing the magnitude of the bookkeeping chores that took so much of Aleksandr Andreevich's time. Behind these figures is the remarkable fact that never during Baranov's American career were there more than about five hundred Russians at work under his supervision. Already a problem in 1795, this shortage of manpower would only get worse as Aleksandr Andreevich stretched the company's operations southward during the next two decades.[21]

Like Baranov's earlier remarks, his 1795 response to Shelikhov and Polevoi showed his sensitivity to the hardships imposed on Native workers by the company's demands. Among the diminishing Alutiiq population, he said, "many are killed or drowned, too old or too young, or rotten from a disease [syphilis] well known here." Every year the Native hunting parties were getting smaller, and the villages were left "nearly abandoned" in summertime. "It seems to me that moving people from here is wrong," he said. The Billings expedition, he added, had forbidden the fur companies to take the American Natives away from their birthplaces. "You are playing politics," he cautioned

Shelikhov, "by asking me to hire them to leave their homes and face the unknown in new settlements."[22] Living with an Alutiiq woman and working daily with Aleut, Kodiak, and Chugach native people, Aleksandr Andreevich had gained an empathetic understanding of the human costs the fur business demanded from these new subjects of the Russian Crown. And yet he never would be able to conceive any alternatives to this perilous labor system that harshly exploited the Alutiiq villagers and kaiurs for the benefit of the company men and the profits he was making for absentee owners in Irkutsk and later St. Petersburg.

Although he did not mention it, Baranov might also have been reflecting on the hazards that long-distance travel imposed on the Russian promyshlenniks as well as the Alutiiq partovshchiks. The previous fall a baidara with fourteen contract workers had set out from Kenai Bay with a cargo of peltry. While sailing toward Pavlovskaia their small boat was struck by a gale. All had been lost: the boat, the men, and the cargo.[23] Such stark proof of the dangers of travel in the waters adjoining Kodiak Island and the mainland could never be far from Aleksandr Andreevich's thoughts when he was sailing his own small ship.

* * *

While explaining other features of his operations, Aleksandr Andreevich repeatedly mentioned his intent to resign. In concluding remarks to Shelikhov and Polevoi, he restated his sense of grievance and his desire to quit his post. "I will wait either for a change in your attitude toward the men and me," he wrote "or for the arrival of my successor who will be better than I am."[24] But despite his wounded feelings, he still wanted Shelikhov to understand that he remained devoted to the service of the company and personally dedicated to Shelikhov's interests. "You should trust me in my zeal and loyalty for your benefits and glory," he repeated, and "just act [toward] me without pretense and politics. . . . I ignored all [other opportunities for] gain [to join you and seek] what you are after, particularly the honor and glorious deeds."[25]

Probably because the *Feniks*'s sailing was delayed, Aleksandr Andreevich after affixing his signature filled more pages with short, defensive responses to Shelikhov's criticisms. He again mentioned the colony's food shortages, the heavy demands of his position, and how hard he had worked to make everything safe and in good order. He also explained his brief quarrel with James Shields, who had been angered because Baranov prevented him from returning to Okhotsk. Their differences were resolved when Aleksandr Andreevich promised Shields a reward of two shares in the company if he should discover a new island. As a result, the Englishman had been probing southward along the Alaskan coast and soon would sail north of Bristol Bay in search of hunting territories.

Near the end of Baranov's lengthy postscript, he wrote about his failing physical condition (at age forty-nine), restated his intent to resign, and again expressed a sense of outrage at his treatment by Shelikhov. He vowed his determination to continue acting according to his personal code of honor.

> I am afraid of losing something that I cherish more than anything else in the world—my good name. The time has come when I am getting old. The senses become dulled. I have to use a magnifying glass when I read and write at night time. My energy begins to dwindle and I do not feel myself strong enough to fulfill all the new important instructions nor do I feel that I have the ability. Besides I hear that you are giving men drinks, presents and collecting slander. My conscience is clear. I am not guilty of misappropriation of your or of the company's property, or of inefficiency. Even if you gather from a thousand Bocharovs and others like him all kinds of notes and proofs, I will right myself in the light of justice. There will always be enough men left alive who were with me to testify, and no amount of chicanery will make me guilty of evil intentions. By using diplomacy, you are trying to hide from me what is on your mind, but in vain. From your letters sent on the *Orel* I know that you intend to hurt me. These letters were written even before Bocharov's arrival. It is only the oath that I took to observe the interest of the Empire, honor, and instructions connected with the aims of the government, which have made me stay and spend my strength and energy. It was not our mutual agreement, many parts of which were broken by you. Nevertheless, however little I see of good will on your part, I will try to render you as many good turns and services as I can. And as till now I will never deviate from the rules of honor and integrity.[26]

Grigorii Shelikhov never saw this remarkable letter from his chief manager. On July 20, 1795, two weeks before Captain Izmailov reached Okhotsk with the *Feniks*, Shelikhov died in Irkutsk. According to a young relative, company bookkeeper Ivan Shelikhov, his death was not sudden. He expired after "suffering from a long and hard fever for a long time."[27] Persistent gossip circulated by business rivals alleged that this Siberian merchant prince had been poisoned by his young wife, Natalia. Some whispered instead that he had taken his own life because of financial problems.

Neither supposition has the least bit of credibility. Modern scholars agree that Shelikhov, though only forty-seven years old, died of natural causes. Historians Dawn Lea Black and Alexander Yu. Petrov present a persuasive case that the cause of his death was actually a fungal plague coming from infected grains, which killed not only Shelikhov but also his infant daughter.[28]

Presuming to represent the Golikov-Shelikhov Company directors, Ivan Shelikhov quickly wrote to assure Baranov that those now managing company affairs had complete confidence in the chief manager's "good personality and good qualities" and wanted him "to work at the same position with mutual understanding and trust in each other." But with the organization in a confused state following the chief director's death, no ship left for America during the 1796 sailing season, and so neither this letter announcing Grigorii Shelikhov's death nor any other recent news from Russia—and certainly no fresh supplies—reached Aleksandr Andreevich that year.

* * *

Isolated from Okhotsk after the 1794 arrival of the *Tri Ierarkha* and the *Sv. Ekaterina*, Baranov's most urgent task was now to do something about the thirty exiled settler families under Ivan Polomoshnoi's management, as well as the 123 new contract employees. At first all these people were crowded into the small new community at Pavlovskaia Harbor. From the start, a spirit of "sedition and revolt" was apparent among the settlers. They refused to take orders from Polomoshnoi. Against all company rules they began to trade furs with the Alutiiqs. They also threatened to loot the storehouse holding the provisions brought with them aboard the *Tri Ierarkha*, "shouting that [Shelikhov] had cheated them by promising them rations and that now they do not get them at all, or very little, and that they cannot get used to local food."[29] According to one report, the settlers told Polomoshnoi that they would kill him. It was part of their secret design, this report added, that as soon as they were being sent to a mainland settlement site and received guns to protect themselves, they would take over the ship and sail back to the Kurile Islands.[30]

This plot apparently developed while Baranov was away from Pavlovskaia for more than three months beginning in December 1794, sailing around Kodiak Island to conduct a census and compile a roll of the residents at all the Alutiiq villages.[31] When he returned in March, he found the settlers' rebellion well planned. "They had three guns with ammunition ready," said one account, "when the manager discovered the conspiracy." To halt the mutiny,

Baranov first attempted to appeal to the conscience of the malcontents. After this tactic failed, Aleksandr Andreevich later wrote, "I punished the ringleaders cruelly." These men "and other parasites," he explained, were sent to a distant outpost where the local supervisor "knows how to get along with them." The remaining settlers, originally crowded into the workers' barracks, now were forced to live "under the barracks" with guards always on duty. By the following spring, said Baranov, everything was quiet.[32] But he kept the exiles unarmed and guarded by a few of his own men even after they moved to the mainland to begin building their new settlement.

The location for this farming colony remained at issue until the summer of 1795. Sailing in June as skipper of the recently completed *Olga*, Baranov carried out an inspection of the company's trading outposts that took him to Kenai Bay, Chugach Sound, Nuchek Bay, and finally to Yakutat Bay, where he arrived in August. The margins of Kenai Bay and Chugach Sound were unsuited for farming; the rocky shorelines backed onto high, glaciated mountain ranges, with neither arable soil nor a moderate climate.

At Yakutat Bay, visited by Purtov's hunting expeditions the two previous years, Aleksandr Andreevich found what he thought was a suitable site.[33] With ceremonial pomp, he took formal possession in the presence of many Yakutat Tlingits. While his men stood on a height in military formation, Baranov made a speech and then raised an imperial flag and a crest of the Russian empire as symbols of sovereignty. Drums beat, Russian rifles fired salvo after salvo, and all the Russians and Alutiiqs reportedly joined in cheers of celebration. No one recorded the Tlingit reaction.

Departing from Yakutat Bay at the end of August, Baranov left behind thirty men, including Polomoshnoi and a few settlers, with instructions to begin building the colony. Although Polomoshnoi's subsequent report condemned the site, Baranov sent the *Tri Ierarkha* back there the following summer, 1796, with the remaining settlers and a force of thirty promyshlenniks headed by Stepan Larionov. With them went a cargo of cattle, seeds, tools, and provisions for the settlers' support until they could raise crops and care for their own needs. Polomoshnoi, despite his unpopularity, remained in charge.

Baranov soon arrived aboard the *Olga* to supervise construction. After being delayed for weeks by bad weather, Aleksandr Andreevich and approximately sixty men, settlers and promyshlenniks, worked together for two months to build sheds, warehouses, and the barracks that became the colony's first housing. He also established peaceful, cooperative relations with both the Yakutat Tlingits and nearby Eyaks, taking amanaty from both groups and giving them written assurances that the Russians would always treat them well.[34]

In the grandiose spirit of Grigorii Shelikhov's 1794 instructions, Baranov named the settlement Novo Rossiia, New Russia, following the precedent for colonies named New France, New England, and New Netherlands on the northeastern coast of North America a century and a half earlier. The exile families and promyshlenniks in New Russia—about eighty people in all—experienced many of the same challenges faced by their English and western European counterparts in the earliest days of these other settlements: a starving time, a high loss of life from disease, difficult relations with neighboring Native peoples, and sharp factional conflicts among the settlers themselves. In New Russia these challenges were not adequately met. Meanwhile, the company directors failed to strengthen the colony with fresh recruits or additional supplies from the homeland. Nor, in Baranov's absence, did a strong leader step forward to unite the colonists at New Russia with an effective program for survival.

When he left the settlement at the end of the 1796 summer season, Baranov gave Polomoshnoi instructions to complete the necessary buildings, begin gardening efforts, and stock up winter provisions by hunting and fishing. Judging by the chief manager's letter to Polomoshnoi written in April 1798, responding to two written reports from the previous summer, there had been only a string of failures in the intervening year and a half. "I am grieved by the unhappy events that happened at your place," Aleksandr Andreevich stated, "especially by the fate of men who perished ingloriously from laziness and disorder." Twenty of the male residents, thirteen promyshlenniks and seven settlers, had died from scurvy that first winter, "not counting the women and children."[35]

In his 1798 letter, Baranov ripped into Polomoshnoi for feuding with Stepan Larionov, who remained in charge of New Russia's promyshlenniks. "According to you," Aleksandr Andreevich wrote, "all your subordinates in the new establishment are worthless." "If it is so," he said, "the question will be asked: what worthy deeds were accomplished by the commander? We will leave it to time to show us the truth."[36] If Larionov was bad, Baranov told Polomoshnoi, he should replace him with someone else and do the same with those settlers who opposed him. "There are so few of them left alive that there is not much bossing to be done," he commented dryly. Because he could not come anytime soon to deal with the situation in person, Aleksandr

Andreevich told Polomoshnoi bluntly that he should do what he had been told: "Use your own judgment so as to get the best results for the State and the company."[37]

Unhappily, Polomoshnoi's judgment was quite poor. Subsequently summarizing the course of events at New Russia, Baranov wrote that the colony leader had "collected a great amount of chicanery in stacks of paper complaining about the settlers and mixing the hunters in their troubles." Based only on hearsay, "like old women's gossip," these charges reflected Polomoshnoi's utter incompetence in the position of trust that Shelikhov had bestowed on him. When Baranov again visited the settlement in 1799, he began a detailed investigation of Polomoshnoi's complaints. "To my surprise," he later said, "with the exception of one settler and his family who were related to Polomoshnoi, all the settlers, hunters, and natives complained" about the supposed colony leader. Faced with this united opposition, Polomoshnoi asked Baranov to halt the investigation. "He was so scared himself that he did not want to stay with the settlers," who were again threatening his life. "The cause of this," Baranov concluded, "was love of power and pride."[38]

In an attempt to set matters right, Aleksandr Andreevich kept Stepan Larionov in place as captain of the promyshlenniks and appointed a new man to take charge of the settlers. This was Nikolai Mukhin, formerly a merchant at Kursk, who had recently arrived in America as a company contract employee. But Mukhin could do little to repair the settlement's deteriorating situation. Farms failed, house construction lagged, and in their dire condition the colonists butchered and ate the cattle given them as breeding stock. At least thirty more died of disease. While some suffered from scurvy, most were lost in an epidemic most likely caused by an acute strain of influenza, taking hold in a population with little or no acquired immunity. Severe nausea and tightening in the chest, followed by death within twenty-four hours made this outbreak a horror for those struck down and terrifying for everyone else in this small community who witnessed its effects.[39]

By 1800 Baranov gave up his last faint hope for realizing Shelikhov's New Russia fantasy. Abandoning the site, he drafted a handful of hardy survivors for a new colonization project on Sitka Sound, farther south in Tlingit territory. All that remained at Yakutat was a fortified company outpost staffed by Russian and Alutiiq hunters whose survival depended precariously on maintaining the goodwill of the region's Yakutat Tlingit peoples. The New Russia colony had ended ingloriously as an expensive fiasco.

* * *

Aleksandr Baranov at long last learned about the deaths of Grigorii Shelikhov and Empress Catherine in mid-October 1797, when the *Feniks* returned to Pavlovskaia Harbor. Now under the command of navy sub-lieutenant Gavriil Talin, the ship delivered much-needed supplies. It also carried three other junior naval officers—two Russians and one German from Archangel—who, like Talin, had been assigned to serve as company skippers as a result of Natalia Shelikhova's entreaty to the government.

Among the many letters and instructions carried to Baranov aboard the *Feniks* was a short communiqué from the "Partners of the United Company," signed by Natalia Shelikhova, Ivan Golikov, Nikolai Myl'nikov, and ten other Irkutsk-based merchants. Though brief, the partners' letter informed Aleksandr Andreevich about a recent reorganization that had created the United American Company. Madam Shelikhova and her partners expressed great confidence in the chief manager's leadership and commercial skills. They urged him to stay on the job at least for the time being. "Thank God for everything" they said. "We are very glad to have you for a manager in the Northeast. We beg you to stay and to let us see our plans executed." But "if boredom or a conclusion that our plans are impractical make you quit your position and if you return to Okhotsk next year," the plan should be to turn over the chief manager's duties to Emel'ian Larionov. A former Irkutsk neighbor and comrade (and the older brother of Stepan Larionov at the Yakutat Bay post), Larionov was now on his way to Unalaska to become manager there as part of a collateral operation by another newly formed company that included Larionov and Evstratii Delarov as partners.[40]

Also aboard the *Feniks* were personal letters for Baranov from the new company's directors, including two from Natalia Shelikhova. She took her old friend, the godfather of her dead youngest daughter, deeply into her confidence. Although these letters have not survived, we can surmise their contents from Aleksandr Andreevich's subsequent summaries for his North American colleagues and his lengthy reply written the next year. Among developments at Irkutsk were the tidings that the three oldest Shelikhov daughters had married, making advantageous connections for the family. The eldest daughter, Anna, was now the wife of Nikolai Rezanov, who was presently serving in St. Petersburg as the head secretary of Russia's governing senate. The second daughter, Ekaterina, had wed a medical doctor in the Irkutsk region, while the third, Avdot'ia, had recently married, Natalia Shelikhova wrote, "our friend" Mikhail Buldakov, a thirty-year-old aspiring merchant from Velikiy Ustyug, another native of northern Russia.[41]

As she took firm command of her company's affairs, Natalia Alekseevna would make significant use of the influence and expertise of both Rezanov and Buldakov in achieving her goals. Bold and intelligent, apparently well schooled in business affairs by her late husband, the widow Shelikhova would prove herself highly capable in what was by custom the exclusively male realm of finance and trade. Over the next decade, she truly earned the historical sobriquet "Russia's first businesswoman."[42]

Among other items of information, the *Feniks* carried a directive for the Russian Orthodox mission chief, Archimandrite Ioasaf, to return briefly to Irkutsk for consecration as bishop of Kadiak and America. Although Baranov and Father Ioasaf had not always seen eye to eye, this promotion met with Aleksandr Andreevich's wholehearted approval. To honor him after this news arrived, the chief manager hosted a "friendly reception" at his own residence, undoubtedly inviting the ship's officers and other company dignitaries to attend. Some of the *Feniks*'s cargo had probably replenished Baranov's liquor cabinet, adding to the jollity of the occasion. While the affair was in progress, Aleksandr Andreevich stumbled and fell heavily on the staircase in his home, dislocating his hip. It was an extremely painful injury for which there was no adequate treatment and certainly no rapid recovery.

For three months the chief manager suffered terribly, unable to leave his bed. By the following January he was beginning to feel better, but then came another bad accident. While Aleksandr Andreevich was working at a table in his room, a servant girl entered with a samovar filled with boiling water for tea. She tripped and fell, spilling the scalding water on his injured leg. The result was severe. "Not only the skin but also the flesh was burnt deeply," Baranov recorded. Once again, as he explained to his old friend Emel'ian Larionov, he had to stay indoors and doctor himself. "Thanks to God," he wrote the following March, "the leg is getting better now, but I do not think I will be able to travel this summer."[43]

The *Feniks* also brought Baranov news about a host of personal business reverses back in Siberia. As he confided to Larionov, all his investments, "though they do not amount to much, are in bad shape." He described the calamities in some detail: 22,000 rubles lost in the death of one debtor; a 3,000 ruble deduction from his accounts in the company's Okhotsk office for an unexplained reason; a 7,000 ruble disparity between what he believed was the proper market value for furs that he had sent to Okhotsk on his own account and the amount allowed him at the company office. Furthermore, one of his Siberian partners had "shamelessly appropriated" another 3,000 rubles due at Irkutsk, leaving Baranov's brother, Petr, to pay that amount. The trading business with the Chukchi at Anadyrsk, involving another 9,000 rubles of his money, "is in such shape," he said, "that it not only gives no profit but I can hardly expect to get back even half of my original investment." His Anadyrsk partner, a Mr. Krechevtsov, was showing paper profits only, Baranov wrote, so "I would like to quit if I could get my money back." He bemoaned also the poor condition of the glass factory near Irkutsk, where Kirill Laksman and his partners had abandoned the enterprise. Aleksandr Andreevich hoped only to sell the factory permit for whatever he might get for it.

Besides these financial setbacks, he added, he still had to pay off an old debt in Siberia; support his wife, Matreona, living in Kargopol' with their two surviving adopted children; and satisfy the claims of various "unscrupulous men" including Lebedev-Lastochkin. "No matter how much money I have sent or will send from here," he lamented, "it becomes nothing." The outlook seemed quite bleak: "The money I hoped to make here is being lost due to malevolence," he told Larionov, "and if I stay here any longer I am liable to lose what is left."[44]

In these circumstances, Baranov confided to his friend a fond hope to leave America and return to Russia, where he might rehabilitate his fortune. But the company board of directors had sent no one to replace him, he said in despair: "And they are asking me to stay till they will find a reliable man, and that will never happen." He could not simply quit, he told Larionov, "because the company's business is connected with the interests of the State." He expected to wait at least until the arrival of another ship from Okhotsk. "In the meantime," he added in a rare expression of self-pity, "I have become old and am getting older. My health and senses become weaker and my ability to see to the interest of the company and the State duller." Even with his injuries healing, he could foresee little change for the better. "It would be wise," Baranov said, "to retire now so as not to end my life in turmoil and sin."[45] And yet, inexplicably, he did not ask Larionov to take over from him at Pavlovskaia Harbor, as the United American Company directors had indicated he might do.

Although he did not mention it in any of his correspondence at the time, while Baranov was suffering at home with his injuries and financial worries his sleep must have been interrupted at times by the cries of an infant. In 1797 Anna Grigor'evna gave birth to a son, Baranov's first child of record. Coming after years of a childless marriage to Matreona, his son's birth was a great moment for the aging chief manager. Christened Antipatr Aleksandrovich, the baby would grow into a fine young man under his father's gaze. In time he and his sister, Irina, born seven years later, must have eased Aleksandr Andreevich's dissatisfaction with his life in America. Through their early years the two children thrived under their mother's care. It is likely that in formal learning the two youngsters were guided by the clergymen who served as teachers in the Pavlovskaia mission school. They were raised in the Russian tradition, so far as the colony's resources allowed. Aleksandr Andreevich was determined that they should have a reputable social standing according to the criteria of the Russian homeland. To assure their future well-being became one of their father's fondest ambitions.

* * *

Baranov's expanded responsibilities under the new company structure added to his cares during the late 1790s. For a few years he was distracted by the continuing deterioration of the agricultural colony at Yakutat, as well as complications from the withdrawal of the last Lebedev-Lastochkin contingents from the Kenai and Chugach regions. Meanwhile, he was directing James Shields, Egor Purtov, and other company men in exploring maritime hunting territories as far south as the Queen Charlotte Islands. All the while he kept a wary eye on his English and American competitors in the seaborne fur trade and stayed alert to the rivalry between Great Britain and Spain over possession of Nootka Sound, the strategically key harbor on Vancouver Island's western coast. Explorations north of Bristol Bay, mainly carried out by Shields, discovered no untapped sea otter stocks. Aleksandr Andreevich became convinced that future profits required expansion southward by his small, inadequately supplied command. Only there, he concluded, could plentiful sea otter peltry still be gained by hunting and trade.

The shortage of shipping continued to be a major problem for the chief manager. Writing to Grigorii Shelikhov in May 1795, he said that once Shelikhov sent back the *Feniks* from Okhotsk, the company colony would "have enough ships: four big and two small." Yet two of the large ships, the *Orel* and the *Sv. Ekaterina*, were then not able to sail because of a lack of canvas and rigging materials.

The scarcity of good workers to man these ships and undertake other duties was also critical. "And where shall we get capable men?" he rhetorically asked. "From among those sent recently very few are capable of glorious deeds." Some of these newcomers were already so far in debt to the company because of their credit purchases that they were "in bondage" and still had no adequate clothes or footwear. "We will perish if we have to depend on such men," declared Baranov.

The company's lack of skilled shipmasters in North America soon proved disastrous. When the veteran skipper Gavriil Pribylov died in April 1796, Baranov placed the crew chief Vasilii Medvednikov in command of the *Tri Ierarkha* to make a short voyage to Yakutat Bay. On the return trip a violent storm caught the vessel and drove it ashore on Kamyshak Bay. Four people and a large part of the fur cargo were lost. Hoping that the ship could be repaired, refloated, and returned to service, the following summer Baranov sent a party headed by a ship's carpenter to work on the wreck. These efforts succeeded briefly, but as soon as the *Tri Ierarkha* was again on the water, another storm carried her once more onto a rocky coast. In 1798 the chief manager sent a second group to examine the wreckage. They found the ship now beyond salvage. Baranov's men burned the ruined hulk to reclaim all of the remaining iron they could retrieve.[46] And this loss of his largest cargo ship was only a small part of Baranov's marine transport problem.

* * *

Among the newcomers who Baranov would have called a person of no outstanding ability was Sub-Lieutenant Gavriil Talin, commander of the *Feniks* on her return voyage to Pavlovskaia in 1797. One of four new government-appointed skippers assigned to company service, he was a timid, recalcitrant navigator. Because he deemed himself a government man, not a company employee, Lieutenant Talin refused repeatedly to comply with Baranov's orders. No proper navy officer like himself, he claimed, could be forced to obey the commands of a mere merchant, no matter how high that merchant's standing might be. After elaborate, costly preparations, Baranov dispatched Talin with the *Orel* for southeastern coastal survey duties in 1798, directing him to map Sitka Sound. Instead, Talin went only to the New Russia settlement on Yakutat Bay, then sailed north to the company outpost at Nuchek Island, where he lingered a month—"for no reason whatsoever," according to Baranov—before returning to Pavlovskaia in September.[47]

The following year the chief manager again assigned Talin to command the *Orel* on another survey voyage in the same southerly direction. The results were calamitous. After venturing no farther south than Lituya Bay, in August the lieutenant reversed course to begin a leisurely cruise back to Kodiak Island. His first port of call was again the New Russia colony, where he arrived soon after Aleksandr Andreevich had made an inspection tour. Here Talin found Ivan Polomoshnoi deposed from his post by Baranov and fearful for his life because of settler hostility. He was anxious to leave. Talin took Polomoshnoi and four family members aboard the *Orel*, along with a substantial fur cargo from the Yakutat hunters, intending to deliver them to Pavlovskaia. Within a day or two, a storm blew the ship off course along the Chugach coast. Under inept helmsmanship, the *Orel* ran onto the rocks at Sukli (Montague) Island. Polomoshnoi and his family drowned in the wreck, the only casualties. The ship was a total loss, along with furs worth twenty-two thousand rubles by Baranov's estimate and additional cargo belonging to Yakutat settlers and the Polomoshnoi family.[48]

The worst was yet to come. During that same summer, 1799, Aleksandr Andreevich was awaiting the return of the *Feniks* from Okhotsk. The ship had set out from Pavlovskaia the previous year with a large cargo of furs and, among other passengers, Archimandrite Ioasaf on his way to Irkutsk. In late May, still quite early in the sailing season, a story reached Baranov that Alutiiq residents at Cape Chiniak, on the southern coast of Kodiak Island, had seen "an object much like a ship" far out at sea, The following day strong winds blew from the northeast and for the following three days a gale blew from the west. After the weather cleared Alutiiq bird hunters found a flagon of rum washed ashore at Shuiakh Island. They brought it to Baranov, "drinking it all the way" there. When the flagon came into his hands, the remaining rum, about three pints, was still good, not mixed with saltwater. Baranov found nothing on the damaged wrappings to identify its origin.

Over the next few days pieces of ship's timber washed ashore at Shuiakh. A large wooden beam, identified as Sitka spruce, complete with iron bolts, beached at Ugak Bay. More evidence in the form of ship's timbers came to Baranov from Ugak. This all proved, he wrote a year later, that a misfortune had occurred. "Probably our *Feniks*, carrying the transport, was wrecked." Baranov started an inquiry all along Kodiak Island's southern coast and at Chugach Sound from Nuchek Island northward to Kenai, hoping to find the wreckage and salvage anything that was left, "but no one there kn[ew] anything of a shipwreck." Aleksandr Andreevich was left with terrible doubt. "I do not know where to search now," he wrote. "The uncertainty troubles me," he added. "It is a great misfortune for all of us, not to mention the loss of Company money and of private capital."[49]

Ultimately, Baranov concluded that the wreckage from late May must have come from another, unknown vessel but that the *Feniks* had actually wrecked somewhere at sea in early November 1799. Under the command of James Shields, the ship had left Okhotsk in the fall, sailing directly for Kodiak

Island. On October 28 it had been seen off Umnak Island by local Russians and Aleuts. That was the last sighting.

As to the cause of the wreck, Aleksandr Andreevich speculated that some of the crew may have been disabled and died from an epidemic then raging in Okhotsk, perhaps a strain of bacterial pneumonia. Even Captain Shields himself, Baranov theorized, might have died from the disease. With no one else capable of handling the ship, the *Feniks* would have been "at the mercy of the unbridled effects of the waves and the winds," though reportedly the vessel was under full sail with a course set for Kodiak when last seen. Pieces of wreckage continued to wash ashore for more than a year in a wide swath of territory that extended along the mainland coast from Chugach Sound south to Sitka Sound and beyond, but no further definite information ever came to light regarding the ship's sad fate.[50]

Built with such great effort by Shields, Baranov, and their small, mostly unskilled workforce at Resurrection Harbor and launched with immense pride, this first ship built in Russian America had disappeared at sea with all hands. In addition to Captain Shields, among those who lost their lives were the new bishop, Father Ioasaf, and the missionary monks Father Makari and Father Stefan. Along with the crew, seventy new promyshlenniks were also aboard, bringing the total loss of lives to at least ninety men. The catastrophe was magnified by the destruction of a full cargo of provisions and trade goods badly needed in Russian America.

In the total absence of any sound evidence, company historian P. A. Tikhmenev reported the speculation that the crew might have been disabled by an epidemic disease.[51] It is also possible that the ship's ability to withstand severe weather had been compromised by the shipwrights' lack of proper iron fastenings and the brittle nature of the Sitka spruce used in her construction. But none of these theories can be maintained with any confidence. We can conclude only that disappearance of the *Feniks* was one of the many tragic losses at sea so prevalent in Russian America's early history.

Coming after the two earlier shipping disasters, the loss of the *Feniks* was a catastrophic blow to the company's fortunes and to the spiritual mission as well. Personally, the tragedy was particularly agonizing for Aleksandr Andreevich, not the least because of the death of his good friend Shields and also Father Ioasaf. It was significant in shaping a decisive change in Baranov's managerial strategies. He had briefly come to hope that the company's merchant fleet could be kept at full strength by his American shipyards. But without the *Feniks* and lacking the expertise of Shields and the supplies needed to build other vessels, he had to set aside at least temporarily his ambitions for building more ships in Alaska.

Aleksandr Andreevich realized quickly that he needed to find different means to keep the colony stocked with food and trade goods. He was, after all, a merchant. Like many another merchant, Baranov was acutely sensitive to the currents of supply and demand. If the lack of company shipping was going to keep his operation isolated from Russia, perhaps he could find other sources for the items that he, his men, and all others in Russian America needed to survive and perhaps prosper.

* * *

Still one more devastating calamity added to Baranov's managerial woes during the summer of 1799. In July a large party of Kodiak Alutiiqs with a few Russian crew chiefs began the return trip from Sitka Sound to Kodiak Island in their baidarkas. At the end of their first day's travel they stopped for the night on the beach at Khutsnov Strait. Following usual practice, the weary men made their evening meal on a plentiful supply of small black mussels exposed at low tide. Within twenty minutes a good many began to suffer nausea, dryness in the throat and mouth, cramps, and then convulsions, symptoms of paralytic shellfish poisoning. Quite sensibly, the Russian crew chiefs attempted to induce vomiting with a mixture of dried gunpowder, tobacco, and soap. This crude, desperate treatment brought relief in some cases, but within two hours at least one hundred men were dead. By one account, forty more died from other causes during this ill-fated expedition.[52]

When the survivors reached home, every Alutiiq village must have felt immense sorrow for this needless loss of lives. Coming so soon after another ten to twenty Alutiiq hunters drowned while returning from a Sitka expedition the previous year, this 1799 catastrophe emphasized dramatically the extreme hazards imposed on the Kodiak Islanders by such long-distance expeditions under company supervision—just as Baranov had pointed out to Shelikhov four years earlier. In an effort to express his sympathy in a traditional Alutiiq manner, Baranov sent an experienced Russian crew chief to all the Kodiak villages with tobacco and other gifts to the prominent men.[53] But this gesture, however well meant, could do little to ease the hearts of the sorrowful.

The following year a hunting party from Tugidak village, located on Tugidak Island off the extreme southwestern coast of Kodiak Island, was sent out in bad weather by a Russian hunter against the villagers' protests. The storm overwhelmed them. Sixty-four men in thirty-two baidarkas drowned that day.[54] And still it would be left to the chief manager, doing his duty to the new company and its stockholders, to try to convince the grieving brothers, sons, cousins, clan brothers, and comrades of all the dead Alutiiq village hunters to venture again and still again to the mainland coast on more such expeditions.

With his many other troubles, Baranov had no other good option. Yet, to Aleksandr Andreevich's extreme dismay, his management of the Alutiiq village hunters was soon threatened by a coterie of men opposed to him and eager to damage the RAC. Ironically, these were people he had earlier welcomed as his associates: navy sub-lieutenant Gavriil Talin, interpreter Osip Prianishnikov, and the four remaining monks of the spiritual mission.

VI

THE MISSIONARY MONKS
AND THE CHIEF MANAGER

The arrival of an eight-man Russian Orthodox spiritual mission in 1794 added vexing complications to Aleksandr Baranov's duties. Despite initial misunderstandings, the chief manager and Archimandrite Ioasaf, the mission head, in time formed a cordial relationship. But after the loss of Father Ioasaf and two of his colleagues at sea, along with the death of another in Alaska, the remaining four monks ceased all ecclesiastical outreach and began to accumulate grievances against Baranov.

IN A 1787 REQUEST TO THE GOVERNMENT FOR SPECIAL PRIVI-
leges for his company, Grigorii Shelikhov declared the need for Russian Orthodox clergy—two priests and one deacon—as missionaries in his newly founded American colony. Their purpose, he explained, would be "to educate people who have come into the Greek-Catholic faith, or who may desire to embrace it in the future."[1] In his first dispatch from Unalaska in 1790, Baranov urged the appointment of a priest to take charge of the colony's religious affairs. His reasons were pragmatic. A proper cleric, he wrote, could help reconcile America's Native peoples to Russian control and company rule. Shelikhov forwarded this proposal to Metropolitan Gavriil of St. Petersburg in April 1793, also requesting permission to build churches in the company's North American territory.

With approval from Empress Catherine II, head of the Russian Orthodox Church, the St. Petersburg metropolitan authorized the appointment of a single hieromonk qualified to teach Native converts to read and write Russian, with the understanding that some of these new Christians might then be ordained as priests. The governing senate endorsed this plan, providing that newly literate Native candidates for priesthood would be educated at the Irkutsk seminary with Golikov and Shelikhov paying the entire expense.[2] Six months later, in December 1793, by a process not documented, this modest initiative had grown into an ambitious undertaking to found an American spiritual mission staffed by eight monks ordained as priests to minister both to the Russians and to the Native peoples of Russian America.[3]

Accompanied by two novices, these eight new missionaries set out from Moscow in January 1794. After reaching Irkutsk in time to observe Easter week, they took the customary river route to Yakutsk, where they transferred their abundant baggage onto one hundred packhorses. The journey to Okhotsk was memorable for the abundance of bears seen by the clerics as they tried to control their skittish horses. They reached Siberia's Pacific seaport by mid-August, then sailed for Kodiak Island aboard the heavily loaded *Tri Ierarkha*.[4]

Led by Archimandrite Ioasaf, a well-educated, intellectually gifted priest's son then in his mid-thirties, the mission staff included hieromonks Juvenalii, Afanasii, and Makarii; hierodeacons Nektarii and Stefan (perhaps the younger brother of Juvenalii); and monks German and Ioasaf.[5] Significantly, Archimandrite Ioasaf and five of the other seven came from Valaam, northern Russia's oldest and most revered monastery, located in Russian Karelia on an island in Lake Ladoga, a short distance from Baranov's hometown. Historically a bastion of Eastern Orthodoxy against heathen invasions and subsequent Swedish Lutheran assaults, Valaam was well known for its demanding monastic life and its conservativism in spiritual matters. Its appeal was strikingly apparent in the career of Archimandrite Ioasaf. With his talents and education he might have joined any of the monasteries in St. Petersburg, where he would be positioned to enhance his status and ecclesiastical authority. Instead, "he chose the strict regime of hard work and privation offered at Valaam."[6]

For Father Ioasaf and his clerical colleagues, their life under Valaam's stern rules had prepared them for a disciplined and pious monastic career while instilling in some of them an ardent ambition to bring the Orthodox Christian gospel to North America. They were not schooled, however, in attitudes of tolerance and forbearance in dealing with parishioners, such as characterized the Orthodox regular clergy. Dedicated and keenly righteous, these monks were eager to battle sin and unlikely to overlook the failings and foibles either of North American Natives, with their polygamous traditions, or of the free-living, unchurched Russian company men.

* * *

Aleksandr Andreevich may have anticipated that he would find amiable companions among the missionary contingent. When the monks first reached Pavlovskaia, Baranov made appropriate gestures of welcome. "When Father Archimandrite arrived," he later told Shelikhov, "he found at my place his best sweet brandy."[7] For living quarters, Aleksandr Andreevich gave Father Ioasaf a comfortable room in his own home. The other mission members he sent to live in the overfull, noisy company barracks with the promyshlenniks (and their women), as well as the thirty newly arrived settler exiles and their families. For the monks, this situation was intolerable. "I deemed it better not to leave my brethren," Father Ioasaf later explained, so the entire group moved into a roughly constructed building next to the chief manager's house, which became a virtual monastic retreat where they would not be affronted day and night by the rough manners and imperfect morals of the exiled settlers or the Russian promyshlenniks and their Native consorts.[8]

Exactly what transpired during the first months that Archimandrite Ioasaf and his brethren lived in the crowded Pavlovskaia settlement is not clear, though for a good part of that time Baranov was absent on his census-taking tour around Kodiak Island. The main document in evidence is a single, long, strongly worded, very secret letter that Father Ioasaf sent to Grigorii Shelikhov in May 1795, urging Baranov's immediate removal. But even these pages and pages of complaints were not enough for the archimandrite to record fully his condemnation of the chief manager. "If I were to describe all his acts in detail," Father Ioasaf fumed, "it would fill a book."[9]

Aleksandr Andreevich, for his part, later insisted to Madam Shelikhova that he had treated the missionary monks with due consideration. "At first," he admitted, "it was really somewhat difficult to get along with all these clergymen." Father Ioasaf, he stated, might inform the company directors about "some of my blunders." When they arrived, Baranov explained, he had been sorely overworked, lacking time to distribute provisions. In this situation, he stated, "it was no wonder at all that sometimes I could be at fault." Even so, he claimed, "I insisted that my people should always do everything to please the clergymen." None of the clerics had shown him any sign of displeasure, he further declared. If they liked, some might abuse him behind his back, "but isn't it sinful?" "As for me," Aleksandr Andreevich insisted, "I feel no guilt at all."[10]

* * *

Weighing the evidence, it is apparent that Shelikhov, all too typically, had made generous promises to the archimandrite and his colleagues about the support they would receive in the company colony. They arrived at Pavlov-skaia expecting to be looked after, well housed and well fed, with virtually all their temporal needs met at company expense. No one had prepared them for the deprivations and hardships, from their perspective, that were normal in Russian America at that early date. These hardships were greatly intensified by the overflow of 1794 newcomers who required food and lodg-ing. Baranov in fact left the clerics to shift for themselves entirely in a time of scarcity, giving them no assistance in making the difficult adjustment to their living conditions at Pavlovskaia.

The missionaries were accustomed to an austere monk's life, but perhaps not to pinching hunger, numbing cold, and constant dampness, week after week, nor to managing unaided all the details of their own corporeal exis-tence. "From daybreak," said Father Ioasaf, "we have to think about food. We have to walk about five versts [three and a half miles] to find clams and mussels." Besides, the archimandrite continued, "we have to bring in the wood, make shirts and trousers and do our laundry; about a hundred girls and domestic servants are being kept in the harbor, but they are not for us."[11] Shelikhov's assurance to Baranov that the clergymen would be able to take care of their own needs was not at all confirmed by Father Ioasaf's resent-ment over the clerics' ill-treatment at the hands of Aleksandr Andreevich and other company officials.

In addition to these matters of personal comfort, the archimandrite had many broader criticisms to make about Baranov and his management of the company colony. He had no sympathy for what he saw as moral transgres-sions. The Russians in the colony, he declared, were living a depraved life. "Everyone openly keeps one girl or several," he wrote. Not only was the com-pany barracks full of women he called prostitutes, "but they have gatherings and parties and dancing on holidays and sometimes during the week too." The chief manager, he added, was the main offender, setting a poor example by living with a Native woman. Moreover, "his only pleasures are girls and dancing. That's the kind of Christian he is!"[12]

Besides these perceived moral lapses and the extreme scarcity of food in the crowded colony that first winter, the archimandrite's litany of grievances showed that a sharp ideological divide separated the two men. According to Father Ioasaf, Baranov demonstrated an attitude the archimandrite called "French free-thinking," which he shared with his good friend, the Englishman James Shields, and which these two allegedly spread to others. For Father Ioasaf and his colleagues, the doctrines of secular liberalism put forward by Voltaire and other writers of the French Enlightenment were anathema, even though Empress Catherine herself endorsed many of these views. The Valaam-trained missionaries regarded any criticism of their ultraconservative version of Orthodox Christianity as an assault on good order and a manifestation of atheism. Though he was by no means anticlerical in his personal beliefs, Aleksandr Baranov's rather casual attitude toward ritual observances, his sinful living arrangements while still married to his wife in Russia, and his sense of the missionaries' proper, marginal role in the company's operations at first marked him as a dangerous radical in the mind of the archimandrite.

The missionaries had expected Baranov to give top priority to the construction of a church and other buildings necessary for their duties. As Shelikhov had previously promised, Aleksandr Andreevich volunteered to build a small church, but little was accomplished over that hectic first winter. After returning to Pavlovskaia from his census-taking excursion around the island, he had to deal mainly with the rebellious settler exiles. By May, Father Ioasaf complained, the log walls for the church still were not ready. (Baranov at the same time explained to Shelikhov that during his absence, Captain Izmailov had taken to Unalaska a large load of timber—"more than enough lumber for the chapel"—without the chief manager's authorization.)[13] As for living quarters, Father Ioasaf stated, the log walls of their company-provided house lacked chinking, the windows were in disrepair, and the weather was very cold. "Thus we passed the whole winter," he told Shelikhov, presumably hungry, damp, and shivering.

The monks may also have anticipated that all company personnel from the chief manager down to the most humble worker would join in supporting their efforts to bring the word of God and their Orthodox ministry to unchurched Russian promyshlenniks and heathen American Natives. But Shelikhov had neglected to instruct his chief manager about this matter.

Given the multiple demands on his time and the settlement's limited resources, Baranov was unable to accommodate the missionaries as they had been led to anticipate. He did pledge a personal contribution of fifteen hundred rubles, no small sum, to assist the missionaries and the church. Yet the archimandrite cited various hearsay comments to the effect that Aleksandr Andreevich had prompted his men to scoff at church regulations and advised that they not marry. He also encouraged the promyshlenniks, claimed Father Ioasaf, to ridicule the archimandrite and his rules. He quoted the Russian hunters: "We are not such hypocrites that we do not see these regulations are made for fools." Quite plausibly some of these reports were brought by disgruntled employees with their own reasons for darkening Baranov's reputation. The archimandrite was more than willing to endorse these allegations after his difficult first months in Russian America.

The company workers' resistance to clerical guidance, according to Father Ioasaf's letter, had economic as well as social causes. "Mr. Baranov says a married man is a poor hunter," he reported; "some men who married lost all their credit [because of extravagant expenditures on their Native wives] and were obliged to leave the colony for Russia." But, the archimandrite argued, marriage would bring greater social stability to the colony. "In time," he argued, "when the hunters have children, they possibly will have no desire to go back to Russia." If they returned to the homeland with their families, however, "this export of children to Russia will be an evidence of the bad conduct of our hunters, and you [Shelikhov] will be blamed for it."[14] While Aleksandr Andreevich was himself encouraging a cross-cultural, biracial union of Russian men and Alutiiq women by his personal example, the archimandrite seemed affronted by the natural consequence of these conjugal relationships, whether consummated with or without clerical sanction. At the same time, the toleration of Alutiiq polygamy by company officials likewise concerned the monks.

* * *

For reasons that are not apparent, Father Ioasaf apparently believed it was his duty to report in secret to Shelikhov on every aspect of Baranov's administration, not simply those related to ecclesiastical affairs. He alleged that Baranov was openly critical of Shelikhov himself. Though providing few specifics, he called Aleksandr Andreevich an incompetent manager who should be replaced at once.

Among his strongest charges, the archimandrite relayed a story that Baranov had met during the previous summer (before the arrival of the spiritual mission) with English naval officers from the expedition led by Captain George Vancouver and "not only gave them all the particulars about our settlements, but even a list of all our hunters with their names." The English mariners, continued Father Ioasaf, gave Baranov presents and were kind to him, though "he behaved like a churl."[15] Of course this tale was scurrilous nonsense. Baranov had carefully avoided every possibility of a meeting with the English explorers. Who it was that passed this fable to the archimandrite we do not know, but his decision to relay it to Shelikhov was another ploy in Father Ioasaf's determined effort in May 1795 to discredit Baranov and bring about his removal.

The archimandrite's condemnation stemmed also from Baranov's failure to consult him and follow his advice. Father Ioasaf seemed to believe that despite his own comparative youth and utter lack of experience in commercial matters, he knew better than Aleksandr Andreevich how to manage the colony and its business. But he had found it impossible to talk with Baranov because "he has his own way about everything." The only remedy he could recommend was to replace Baranov with someone who would be willing to listen to the archimandrite's counsel. "With a straightforward man," he declared, "I could discuss things and we could have orderly management."[16]

Was Father Ioasaf only giving voice to the inherent conflict between secular and spiritual priorities that often appeared in the history of overseas colonization by Western nations? At the same time he was sending Shelikhov his catalog of complaints against Baranov, the archimandrite wrote to his superior at Valaam depicting a far less dire situation. "We live comfortably," he reported, and the Alutiiqs "like us and we them; they are a kind people, though poor."[17] This bland statement, obscuring much, seems akin to the short, totally favorable retrospect on Baranov's relations with the archimandrite that Aleksandr Andreevich later made to his company-authorized biographer.[18] Neither man, it would seem, was anxious to document their differences in public.

*   *   *

At the time of the holy father's departure for Irkutsk three years later, the chief manager provided another succinct summary of his relationship with Archimandrite Ioasaf and his attitude toward other mission members. During the struggle at Irkutsk for control of the North Pacific fur business after Grigorii Shelikhov's death, someone had charged that Shelikhov had told Baranov to deprive the clergymen of the food they needed. This accusation was "a shabby act," Aleksandr Andreevich wrote to the widow Shelikhova, and an outrageous slander on the late chief director. The missionaries "seem to have never suffered from lack of anything at all," he said. Shelikhov had told him only that they had enough food shipped with them from Okhotsk to last until a new cargo of provisions came from Siberia. "This is the truth," Baranov emphasized. "And should they be in need of anything, do you think I would be so stupid and crude as to refuse any of their requests?" The company directors should ask the Right Reverend himself about this matter, he suggested. "He would probably tell you it was he who accustomed the clergymen to eating locally-available meals and posed an example himself." Perhaps some of the other missionaries had complained, he continued, "since all of them, except His Right Reverend, are willful and rude people."[19]

* * *

Like Baranov's long 1795 defense of his management, Archimandrite Ioasaf's lengthy anti-Baranov diatribe only reached Irkutsk after Shelikhov's death. In the changed circumstances, the archimandrite's effort to have the chief manager removed had absolutely no effect on the company's interim directors. For these Russian investors, profits were the important matter, not the status of the Orthodox mission and certainly not the well-being of the Alutiiq people being exploited by the chief manager and his promyshlenniks.

In October 1797 the *Feniks* brought back to Kodiak Island the very dated news of Shelikhov's demise, the death of Empress Catherine, and the organization of the United American Company. With it came the directors' request that Baranov remain in America at least temporarily as the new company's chief manager. As previously noted, the ship also carried dispatches for Archimandrite Ioasaf, informing him about his elevation to become bishop of Kadiak and America and ordering him to travel to Irkutsk for investiture.

By this time the two men had been living side by side for nearly three years, off and on. Quite obviously, they had long since begun coming to terms. Certainly, Aleksandr Andreevich's help in building the Pavlovskaia church and his generous personal donations, along with smaller contributions by other company officials, must have helped mollify the archimandrite. Improvement in the missionaries' diet after the forced scarcities of their first American winter should also have boosted their morale. There was still no bread or beef, but the spring run of herring and then successive salmon runs, the occasional bounty of whale and seal meat, the harvest of sarana bulbs, ripe berries, and other plants, and soon the produce grown in their own mission garden enabled the monks to forgo a dreary dependency on shellfish.[20] And as their evangelical work progressed among the local Alutiiqs, the monks were able to call on Native converts to help in their daily tasks.

Apparently, the clerics did not really care much about improving their housing. When Father Gideon arrived in 1804 to inspect the condition of the American spiritual mission, he found his clerical colleagues living still in the same "rickety structure" between the public bathhouse and the chief manager's home that they had occupied since 1794. "In this ramshackle house of God," declared the Valaam Monastery's history of the spiritual mission, "with its roof leaking from the rain, was carried on the great work of enlightening the people with the light of the true faith."[21]

Along with Archimandrite Ioasaf's duties overseeing the spiritual mission's day-to-day activities, he took over the colony's school begun by Shelikhov. Here he instructed a few youngsters in the elementary subjects usually taught in church-run Russian schools. His pupils were a handful of young men, mostly the creole sons of Russian promyshlenniks and their Alutiiq wives, perhaps joined by a few of the amanaty. Despite—or perhaps because of—Aleksandr Andreevich's own lack of formal schooling, he was always concerned and financially generous in his support of education in Russian America. This may have been one of the mutual interests that improved relations between the well-educated archimandrite and the chief manager.

Although Aleksandr Andreevich was not immediately in a position to marry Anna Grigor'evna, the couple's obvious domestic harmony and Baranov's pride in their infant son must also have softened the archimandrite's attitude toward the chief manager's personal morality. So too, we may speculate, did Anna Grigor'evna's piety as a devout parishioner. When he was not away on business, Aleksandr Andreevich joined her in going to church regularly during these years, no doubt with the archimandrite's encouragement.

The relationship between Baranov and Father Ioasaf clearly had taken a sharp turn for the better by June 1796. Aleksandr Andreevich was then leaving Pavlovskaia for the summer, placing Ivan Kuskov in charge of the colony headquarters. In a letter of instruction, he directed Kuskov to provide any support necessary to the spiritual mission. He told his aide "to follow the demands of the Father Archimandrite, to be polite, and provide him services for any possible occasion." Most tellingly, Baranov told Kuskov that he should "ask his [Father Ioasaf's] prudent advice and follow his recommendations."[22] Thus, just over a year after the archimandrite had written so critically about his problems with the chief manager, Baranov showed a cordial, trusting attitude toward Father Ioasaf and ordered Kuskov to give him the utmost respect and support. Writing again a little more than a year later, the chief manager reported that relations with the spiritual mission had improved, though he still criticized the behavior of a few of the colony's other monks.[23]

During the winter of 1797–98, while Aleksandr Andreevich was confined to bed with hip and leg injuries, surely Father Ioasaf, his next-door neighbor, must have visited him often. Knowing by that time that Shelikhov was dead and that company affairs were being reorganized by people who trusted Baranov completely, they would have been foolish not to reconcile. With the archimandrite planning to return to Irkutsk the following summer, the two men must have had a great deal to discuss, chatting perhaps over a cup of tea or a small taste of sweet brandy. Whether company exploitation of the Alutiiq village hunters figured at all in these discussions is not a matter of record.

*   *   *

In June 1798, as he was preparing to depart, Father Ioasaf wrote a letter of instruction to Father German, who was taking charge of the mission's business affairs during his absence. These guidelines reflected a spirit of mutual cooperation between Baranov and the missionary monks. "Make sure that you do not go short of anything for long periods," Father Ioasaf advised, and if the monks needed anything, Father German should call upon Baranov. "If your request is just and he has plenty, I have every hope that he will not refuse you," said Father Ioasaf. He encouraged Father German to be generous in return. "If the company or the administrator himself needs to borrow something from you," he directed, "then you may let him have some of our surplus stores against a receipt."[24] Gone now were any traces of his earlier censure of Aleksandr Andreevich and his management.

At his departure Archimandrite Ioasaf divided responsibilities for the spiritual mission among the four clerics remaining at Pavlovskaia. These four—hieromonks Afanasii and Nektarii and monks German and Ioasaf—were all Valaam-trained, scantily educated, steeped in monastic ideals, and in the vigorous prime of life.[25] According to the archimandrite's assignments, Father Nektarii would manage the church itself, taking care of holy services and the church's "good order." The monks German and Ioasaf were to be responsible for "domestic economic duties," keeping the mission store and managing food supplies. Father Afanasii, who was illiterate and so unable to keep records, remained the mission gardener.[26] Assuming that he would soon be returning, the archimandrite did not name an interim mission director, though in time Father German would assume that role.

The apparent goodwill between the archimandrite and the chief manager by 1798 may be further shown by a far-fetched speculation circulated by Baranov's critics after Father Ioasaf had sailed for Siberia. This rumor claimed that Baranov himself would soon be taken to Russia for investigation and that Father Makarii rather than Father Ioasaf, newly invested as bishop, would be placed in charge of the spiritual mission.[27] The supposed reason was that the other missionaries had complained about the archimandrite's friendship with Baranov, using against him the evidence of Aleksandr Andreevich's generous donations to the Pavlovskaia church.

* * *

Immediately after arriving, two of the missionary monks focused their efforts on converting the Native Alaskans, beginning with the Kodiak Alutiiqs. During their first winter in America, hieromonks Makarii and Juvenalii traveled about the island on a crash campaign of mass conversions. Father Makarii preached and baptized on the south side of the island, Father Juvenalii on the north. By spring 1795 the two clergymen claimed that they had baptized altogether more than seven thousand Natives—all the island's village inhabitants. Fathers Makarii and Juvenalii also said they had celebrated more than two thousand weddings among the villagers, a sign of their success in ending polygamy.[28]

These two young monks, observed Father German, "are always so fervent, almost like madmen, wanting to rush off in all directions."[29] They were anxious to extend their evangelical efforts to all the Aleutian and Alaskan mainland territory under Russian sway. Father German witnessed a heated discussion between the two as they disputed which region each would go to next. Father Juvenalii made the most forceful and sweeping demand. "Aliaska," the Alaskan mainland, "really belongs to my area," he asserted, "so I would ask you [Father Makarii] not to interfere there." He planned to take the next company ship to Yakutat. There he would begin preaching from the south, travel north along the coast to Chugach Sound, cross the mountains to Kenai Bay, and from there move onto Alaska's western peninsula. Father Makarii was saddened by this extreme claim, according to Father German, and still sought a right to evangelize Alaska as well as all the Aleutian Islands. "You may have the whole of southern America if you like," he reportedly told Father Juvenalii; "there's enough there for the rest of your life."[30] But in the end Father Juvenalii won the dispute, a victory with fateful consequences.

Curiously, the archimandrite had nothing to do with this argument. While he was anxious at first to advise the chief manager about company management, Father Ioasaf may have found it hard to control these two ardent missionaries. Both Father Makarii and Father Juvenalii rushed ahead on their separate, self-directed missionary excursions apparently without consulting him.[31]

Father Makarii's ambitions took him first to Unalaska aboard the *Feniks* in May 1795, then to Unga and adjacent islands. On Unalaska, despite opposition from some Russian fur traders, he found the Aleuts eager for baptism. They had been living for decades in the company of promyshlenniks, who introduced them to the fundamentals of Russian Orthodox belief and ritual forms. According to the testimony of Father Ioann Veniaminov, who arrived a generation later and served as the priest on Unalaska for more than fifteen years, Father Makarii traveled with only one Russian servant, "but the very Aleuts whom he baptized . . . transported him, fed and sheltered him, and all without seeking any reward or anything in return." Father Veniaminov summed up the accomplishments of his predecessor among the Aleut people.

> Father Makarii, partly because time was short and partly because he had
> no good interpreters, could not convey to them the Christian truth apart
> from a general concept of God, His Omnipotence, mercy, and so forth.
> Nevertheless the Aleuts remained Christians or, at least, as soon as they
> were baptized they not only abandoned completely their pagan beliefs and
> destroyed all the idols and masks, which were used at the rituals and rites,
> but even the songs which might remind them in any way of their former
> beliefs, so that when I arrived amongst them, however much I looked . . . I
> could find nothing of this kind. Even their very superstitions, which are
> alien to anyone who has a true Evangelical faith, were abandoned by many,
> and . . . lost their force.[32]

During his evangelical tour in the Aleutians, Father Makarii became alarmed by Native reports of the abusive treatment the Aleuts had suffered in earlier years from Russian hunting crews, particularly Shelikhov's men.[33] As part of their spiritual baggage, the mission members had brought with them to North America a unique, long-established monastic tradition, tracing to medieval Byzantium: Russian Orthodox monks had a right and obligation to intercede with even the highest secular authorities on behalf of the poorest and most oppressed members of society.[34] Set apart by their holy status and ascetic lifeway, they were enveloped by a spiritual aura that sanctified their role as representatives of the downtrodden. It was this tradition that, in retrospect, might explain why Metropolitan Gavrill sent the monks from Valaam to North America rather than regular clergy. And, certainly, it was this tradition that influenced Father Makarii to become an ardent advocate for the Aleut people who had borne the heaviest burden of grief at the hands of promyshlenniks and various fur company officials.

Seeking redress for these many wrongs, in late June 1796 Father Makarii sailed for Okhotsk aboard a ship owned by the Kiselev company, the Aleutian-based archrival of the Golikov-Shelikhov organization.[35] With him went six Aleuts and a letter of grievance signed by other village leaders. After various misadventures, including the death by disease of four of his Aleut companions, the hieromonk arrived at St. Petersburg with the surviving two in May 1798.

Although Emperor Paul I granted them an audience, the new imperial administration was indifferent to their cause. Within weeks the emperor censured Father Makarii for leaving his post without authorization, ordering him to do penance to Archimandrite Ioasaf and return to his proper duties in North America. He also told his officials to give clothing and a few presents to the Aleuts and send them back to Unalaska.[36]

They never made it. Both died suddenly in Irkutsk shortly before they were to sail aboard a company ship. Father Makarii, pardoned meanwhile by the emperor at the request of the Aleuts, also set out for the return trip across Siberia and the Pacific to North America. He reached Okhotsk in 1799, just in time to join Father Ioasaf, newly consecrated as bishop, on the ill-fated last voyage of the *Feniks*.[37] His death at sea ended all missionary activities at Unalaska and the other Aleutian islands until the arrival of Father Veniaminov in the 1820s.

* * *

At the same time Father Makarii set out for the Aleutians, Father Juvenalii sailed eastward to Nuchek Island and Chugach Sound. After baptizing an estimated seven hundred Chugach Alutiiqs, he traveled north to Kenai Bay, then westward to Lake Iliamna. From there, accompanied by a Native assistant, he headed toward the Bering Sea, where he meant to investigate persistent rumors that an old Russian settlement was located in the Bristol Bay region. Somewhere on their travels Father Juvenalii and his assistant were killed, though the details long remained elusive.

Five years later, in 1800, Baranov reported a vague account that their deaths had occurred either near Lake Iliamna or on Bristol Bay. This tale was retold with various embellishments by company officials, the remaining Russian Orthodox mission members, and succinctly by P. A. Tikhmenev in his 1861 history of the RAC.[38]

A generation later the truth about Father Juvenalii's death was confounded by a fraud perpetrated on the distinguished pioneer historian of Alaska, Hubert Howe Bancroft. His monumental *History of Alaska* relied on a fake document, the supposed diary of Father Juvenalii. It was actually a forgery manufactured by Bancroft's trusted Russian researcher and writer, a sometime San Francisco journalist who called himself Ivan Petrov.[39]

According to Petrov's preposterous fiction, the Iliamna men had murdered Father Juvenalii because he would not submit to the sexual advances of the local girls.

The likely truth about Father Juvenalii's end has awaited the modern investigation of Father Michael Oleksa. Father Oleksa examined the sparse documentary record in the light of an oral tradition among the Yupik people at Quinhagak village, located at the mouth of the Kanetok River where it flows into the Bering Sea. The earliest European traders to visit this region, Native accounts agree, were viewed with fear, and so they were killed. The first Russian priest to arrive at Quinhagak, as one respected elder told Father Oleksa, appeared with a second person in a small boat—not a baidarka— which Father Oleksa interprets as possibly a canoe such as those built by the Athabascan people of the Lake Iliamna and Kenai Bay region. Frightened by the arrival of these strangers, the account continues, Yupik hunters killed the priest immediately. His companion dove into the water and amazed the non-swimming Yupiks with his skill in remaining underwater for long periods, swimming "like a seal." The hunters chased him some distance, then captured and killed him as well. A village shaman removed a heavy pectoral cross from around the dead priest's neck and donned it himself, but he later discarded it because the cross had strong mystic properties that blocked the shaman's own powers. In the future, this shaman advised, the Yupiks should welcome anyone else who came in similar attire, since these people surely possessed superior influence with the spirit world.[40]

Because of the details in this traditional account about the boat of the strangers and the swimming ability of the priest's companion, Father Oleksa concludes that Father Juvenalii and his Native assistant had likely traveled downstream from the Lake Iliamna / Lake Clark district to the Bristol Bay region, perhaps by an ancient portage route that connects Kenai Bay to Bristol Bay by way of Lake Iliamna and the Kvichak River. In Yupik eyes, Father Juvenalii and his companion would have appeared as outsiders and potentially dangerous. As Father Oleksa's research makes clear, the Quinhagak Yupik tradition testifies that it was not misadventure (or conflicting moralities) but a deliberate homicide that created Russian Alaska's first two Christian Orthodox martyrs.

* * *

The 1798 departure of Archimandrite Ioasaf and Father Stefan for Okhotsk left the ecclesiastical establishment on Kodiak Island at half strength, staffed with only four Valaam-trained monks led by Father German. All evangelical outreach came to a halt in Russian America. The monks stayed in the Pavlovskaia area throughout their American careers. They learned little of the Alutiiq language. None of them ventured to the New Russia settlement, where Shelikhov had originally expected them to settle, nor did they visit the outlying Kodiak Alutiiq villages.

At Pavlovskaia they conducted church services and ran the training school for Alutiiq and creole boys. They settled once more into a monastic lifestyle, shunning the worldly society of the chief manager and the company men around them. But for more than a year after the archimandrite's departure, relations between Baranov and the four remaining monks to all appearances remained tranquil.

Then, abruptly, Father Afanasii initiated a dispute with Aleksandr Andreevich that totally disrupted the peace of the company settlement. The following events threatened to undermine Baranov's authority and the fur company's command over the Alutiiq village hunters. The most severe conflict ever to disturb the internal tranquility of Russian America, this schism and its emotional legacy have tended ever since to color historical interpretations of the Baranov era.

VII

GOVERNMENT MEN, MONKS, AND THE ALUTIIQ REBELLION

Following the untimely deaths of the newly consecrated bishop, Father Ioasaf, and three of his colleagues, the remaining four Orthodox clergymen let two fractious officials, a navy lieutenant and an interpreter for the spiritual mission, lead them into a bitter dispute with Baranov about his authority and control over the company's Alutiiq village hunters. When many of these villagers refused to join any more expeditions to the mainland, Aleksandr Andreevich had this rebellion forcefully repressed. He also upheld his authority over the rebellious officials and the most contentious of the monks, restoring peace to the company colony. Within a few years two highly placed visitors, one clerical and the other imperial, fully sustained the chief manager and sharply censured his antagonists.

BARANOV'S WORST MANAGEMENT TROUBLES BEGAN IN 1798, directly following the departure of Archimandrite Ioasaf. The instigator-in-chief was Sub-Lieutenant Gavriil Talin, a junior Russian navy officer who had arrived at Pavlovskaia as skipper of the *Feniks* the previous year. His assignment to Russian America, virtually a sentence of exile from the imperial navy, evidently angered Talin. A timid navigator, deficient in seamanship and apparently a heavy drinker, he devised an argument to justify his repeated failures to carry out Chief Manager Baranov's instructions.

He was a government official, Talin claimed, not an employee of the fur company. For this reason, he declared, it was totally incompatible with his dignity to take any orders or instructions from a mere merchant such as Aleksandr Baranov.[1]

Echoing Talin's claim of independence was Osip Prianishnikov, a trader from Tobolsk married to an Alutiiq woman. Prianishnikov had come from Siberia with the Russian Orthodox missionaries as their Alutiiq interpreter. Like Talin, Prianishnikov objected to Baranov's authority over the Russian workers and the control he and his men exercised over the Kodiak Alutiiqs. And he was in a unique position to influence the four monks remaining at Pavlovskaia to his point of view.

The clash between Baranov and Talin began when the chief manager placed the veteran captain Bocharov in charge of the *Feniks* and assigned Lieutenant Talin instead to command the smaller *Orel* on a surveying voyage south of Yakutat Bay. Both that summer and again the following year, the lieutenant failed to carry out Aleksandr Andreevich's orders. In a 1799 encounter at Sitka Sound, he threatened to seize Baranov and have him whipped if he so much as set foot aboard Talin's ship. Baranov avoided a direct confrontation on this occasion and so, he wrote, "saved us both from things we might be sorry about."[2]

When Baranov returned to Pavlovskaia from Sitka Sound in the early summer of 1800, he left behind a small Russian and Alutiiq crew at a new company outpost named St. Michael, as described in Chapter 9. Once again he found distressing problems waiting at the headquarters settlement. Most serious was a dispute over the fate of two Native men from the Lake Iliamna district who had confessed to murdering two Russian promyshlenniks the previous fall. Sent to Pavlovskaia as prisoners, they had been set free during Baranov's absence at the urgent demand of interpreter Prianishnikov and the monks. Lieutenant Talin meanwhile had lost the *Orel*, shipwrecked beyond salvage. With no command and no duties, he also took a role in the effort to gain freedom for the Iliamna criminals. But when Aleksandr Andreevich reappeared, the chief manager immediately took the two guilty men back into captivity and sent them to supplement his work force at the Sitka Sound outpost.

This collision set the scene for further challenges to Baranov's authority by Lieutenant Talin, joined by the monks. Rumors reached Pavlovskaia that because of the tragic recent deaths of so many of their relatives and comrades, some Alutiiq village men were reluctant to venture again on the long hunting trips to the mainland. A few Russian promyshlenniks were perhaps likewise growing hesitant to carry out the orders of the chief manager.

Trouble erupted on the last day of 1800. Work had stopped this day, Baranov said, "so that the men could merrily see the Old Year go and could meet the New Year according to the Russian custom." In the morning Baranov went to the barracks to investigate the hunters' complaints about one of their rebellious fellows, "a depraved and restless individual." Aleksandr Andreevich ordered the man to appear before him. As soon as he arrived, in rushed interpreter Prianishnikov and Father German, followed by an irate Lieutenant Talin.

As Baranov told the story, Talin shouted: "What kind of meeting is this? Who called it and why?" By his own account, Baranov replied calmly that he and the men had called it to discuss some company business matters and that he was about to make a decision regarding one of the hunters. At that, he recounted, "all of them shouted at once that I, a private citizen, could not judge matters without them, government employees." Still talking mildly, or so later he claimed, Aleksandr Andreevich described the basis of his authority and cited the pledge that all promyshlenniks had signed that they would obey the chief manager's orders. "Having been chief manager for ten years I did not know of any other way or procedure."

He asked the intruders whether they had any government orders or orders from the company's head office. If so, he said, he would like to see these orders, and he promised to comply strictly with them the moment they were put before him. "They only repeated time and again," Baranov wrote, "that they had such orders but were under no obligation to show them to anyone and that it was enough that they were government employees and officers." These statements "caused an even greater hub-bub, and all the monks came running." The clerics, Aleksandr Andreevich added, "shouted, scolded, and threatened us all with the whip and fetters, but in vain." Because they could produce no written instructions "permitting them to get mixed up in our affairs," in the end, says Baranov's account, "they all left, ashamed."[3]

This New Year's Eve shouting match was only a beginning. The next morning, following church services, a few men including the company clerk and several workers gathered at Baranov's house. They were drinking tea and no doubt discussing the previous day's events when Father Afanasii ran in "very excited" and shouted that Baranov must not send out the Alutiiq bird-hunting crews this year. Further, "all the people on the island had to take the oath of allegiance [to the new emperor, Paul I,] right away."

After politely giving the cleric a cup of tea, Baranov answered that since the bird hunters would not be leaving until May, there was lots of time. "To gather people for taking the oath of allegiance right away," he said, "was inconvenient for the hunters and islanders to come from different settlements in such cold and stormy weather as we had this winter." Moreover, because it was not the islanders' custom to bring their own food when coming to Pavlovskaia, "we all were liable to undergo a period of starvation if they were called." The oath of allegiance, Baranov assured Father Afanasii, could be taken in the springtime when the Alutiiqs gathered before going on the annual hunt, when there would be plenty of food at the settlement.

As he recorded it, the chief manager's response did nothing to calm the monk. "Suddenly he called me a traitor to the Emperor and accused me of interfering with the people taking the oath."[4] Baranov's account admitted that he was "sorely vexed, being called such a name." He asked Father Afanasii whether he had an official pronouncement or an order from Archimandrite Ioasaf. If taking the oath was such an urgent matter, he inquired, why had the government expedition—the 1797 *Feniks* expedition with its four naval officers—done nothing about it? For that matter, why had Archimandrite Ioasaf not previously instructed the Kodiak Alutiiqs to swear the oath? And why must it be done right now, in the winter, without waiting for Father Ioasaf to return as bishop?

Admitting again that he did not have an imperial order, Father Afanasii gave Aleksandr Andreevich a curt reply. He claimed that the manifesto at the time of Emperor Paul's accession must apply to all loyal subjects and that he and the other clerics considered the Alutiiq islanders to be included. It was none of Baranov's business, he said, why the archimandrite had ignored the matter, but the monks had decided now to administer the oath themselves. He ended with a threat that seemed to echo Lieutenant Talin's previous outbursts: "They would consider everyone who opposed them a traitor and would see that they were punished with a whip."[5]

At this, Baranov later said, he laughed and asked Father Afanasii to leave his house peacefully. On his way out, the hieromonk made one further declaration. All those who lived with unmarried girls and had children by them—like Baranov of course—henceforth should not be admitted to the church, according to the ecclesiastical statute. Aleksandr Andreevich was absolutely sure there was nothing of the kind in the statute issued by the emperor. But to avoid being abused by the wrath of the priests in God's temple, he quit going to church after this New Year's Day set-to with Father Afanasii.

What Baranov's account of this encounter did not mention, perhaps because the chief manager did not fully recognize it, was the underlying reason for Father Afanasii's demanding that the Alutiiq villagers all take the oath of allegiance to the new emperor. This was not simply a way to harass and embarrass Aleksandr Andreevich. It was part of a larger strategy to undercut the fur company's heavy-handed exercise of authority over Alaska's Native peoples. Once the villagers took the oath, according to this reasoning, they would be unquestionably the subjects of the Russian Crown; in theory, their primary fealty would be to the emperor's government and to the government men—including the clerics—who represented the government in Russian America. Like Lieutenant Talin, Father Afanasii and his colleagues considered themselves independent of company rule, and they hoped to establish through the oath a similar independence on behalf of the mistreated Alutiiq villagers. Motivated by their sincere hope to end the fur company's abusive management of the Alutiiq people, Father Afanasii and his clerical colleagues now emerged as champions of Alutiiq liberty and the villagers' freedom from Baranov's control.

The clerics' version of these events is in substantial agreement with Baranov's account, but it makes no mention of the chief manager's earlier problems with Lieutenant Talin. Yet the circumstances strongly suggest that with their sincere concern for the abused Alutiiqs, Father Afanasii and his colleagues were to some degree being manipulated by this self-styled government official in an effort to discredit Baranov and cripple the company's management. In this way, Talin and Prianishnikov must have convinced the clerics that they might make their ministry a source of earthly deliverance as well as eternal salvation for Native Alaskans.

* * *

In the aftermath of the New Year's Day confrontation, the monks discontinued religious services altogether during Lent, and they would not even promise services during Easter week. At the same time, Baranov wrote, "they entice people as much as they can not to recognize my authority but to join them and to ruin the company's gains and aims." So far, he said, only three company workers—at least one of them an Alutiiq or creole—had sided openly with the monks. But "God only knows" what might be the thoughts of the rest of them, wrote the chief manager. "I cannot penetrate into the depth of their souls." Most significant of all, according to Aleksandr Andreevich, the monks had "promised the islanders independence and freedom to live according to their old custom if they would take the oath of allegiance."

As spring approached, the headmen of five villages, including those that had lost the most men to shellfish poisoning and mischance at sea the previous year, came to Pavlovskaia. They were there to announce their decision not to join the annual mainland hunting party then being organized. First they went to tell Baranov, who tried to change their minds by contrasting their previous primitive, barbaric way of life, as he called it, with the benefits they had gained from the Russian presence. The village leaders were not swayed. "They would not listen to me and the priests took them to church and made them take the oath of allegiance," Baranov recounted. Exactly what that oath meant, so he claimed, the islanders did not know and could not explain; but perhaps they understood full well following their discussion with the clerics. Then, without again seeing the chief manager or any company employees, "and without settling their accounts and debts," these men returned to their baidarkas and made ready to go back to their villages. Their behavior, Aleksandr Andreevich declared, was that of former times, "full of cold arrogance and independence."[6]

According to the cleric's memory of these events, the Alutiiq leaders were "very bitter and desperate" when they came to see the monks "and dared inform the missionaries that they did not want to go on this expedition because many of their relatives had died . . . and some of their villages were deserted." In defying Baranov, the villagers feared for their lives. They had each brought along a new parka. In case they died, they said, they hoped the monks would bury them in their new clothes "to bear witness to this killing of the innocents." The clergy and the two "officers" present at this meeting, Lieutenant Talin and interpreter Prianishnikov, "were horrified and tried to talk them into forbearance, assuring them that His Imperial Majesty would be favorably disposed."

When the Alutiiqs had calmed somewhat, the clerics raised the matter of the oath of allegiance. All the assembled Native leaders "readily agreed to this and promised to obey in all things." Together the monks, the villagers, and the two "government men" set off for the church—located on a cape overlooking the harbor, some distance from the missionaries' residence—where Hieromonk Afanasii administered the oath of allegiance.[7]

Here was the ultimate challenge to Baranov's authority and his managerial skill. He saw the actions of the Alutiiq headmen as "clear evidence of revolt," which indeed it was. With only a short time left before the hunting crews needed to depart for the mainland, Aleksandr Andreevich was convinced "that if this state of affairs became known in our remote establishments at Kenai, Chugach, Yakutat, and at Sitka, disastrous and bloody events were bound to result; the Russians would be exterminated, all our settlements destroyed, the company would cease to exist and with it any advantage to our Country, and it would be hard to restore the region to its present state again even in fifteen years." From Baranov's perspective, the precipitous action of a few dissatisfied, headstrong men—the two "government officers" and their clerical allies—threatened to destroy Russian America under his management. Strong measures were demanded.

The Alutiiq visitors were just getting back into their baidarkas when Ivan Kuskov and a squad of promyshlenniks arrived and seized one of the prominent headmen—who happened to be Father German's godson. They took their captive away to the company barracks and shackled him in solitary confinement in a room without a sliver of light showing. Carrying their muskets, Kuskov and his men then returned to the shore, climbed into a baidara, and started after the others. But with paddles splashing the other Alutiiq leaders had all hurried out of the harbor, beyond the grasp of Kuskov's strong-arm crew.[8]

This demonstration of naked force, like his earlier public display of anger, in Baranov's opinion had a good effect. Alutiiq villagers quit coming together to Pavlovskaia to meet with the clerics and no longer refused to have anything to do with the company. The captive sent word to his village to gather hostages. Baranov demanded that hostages must now be brought to Pavlovskaia from all the villages on the southern part of the island, something he had never before required. Meanwhile, the monks, he reported, "became very excited, and running back and forth to the barracks and to me they called us robbers, traitors, mutineers, and all the insulting names that they could think of, shouting that we would not escape the whip and forced labor."[9]

* * *

Under the guise of administering the oath of allegiance to Emperor Paul, the monks were now fully embarked on a campaign, as they believed, to liberate the islanders from the company's oppressive rule. They sent messages to all Kodiak villages, urging the villagers "to declare their independence and freedom." If they did so, they said, "the natives would not have to work in the company's hunting crew but could hunt for themselves and sell skins to who they pleased at Irkutsk prices." But with the fur company fully in command of Russian America and controlling all the shipping to and from the colony, the prospect for such commercial free trade was altogether chimerical.

Talin and Prianishnikov also asserted "that they personally had a right to buy as many furs as they could as well as the company, and that they were going to do so." Apparently, the navy lieutenant and the interpreter hoped to profit personally from the crisis they had instigated. When Baranov told Prianishnikov that he was disrupting the company's interests and the interests of the whole community, the interpreter merely made a written memorandum of the chief manager's statement and "all the ideas and propositions of the rascals everywhere in the villages on the island." Furthermore, Baranov said, the monks and the officers "were intercepting the natives on the trails when they were on their way here to persuade them in their ways of thought."[10]

Aleksandr Andreevich learned that one particularly troublesome person, a "rebel" who had visited other villages "inciting revolt," was secretly coming to Pavlovskaia at night and talking with the monks. To capture him, Baranov ordered guards to watch for the man and seize him when he tried to leave. The clerics somehow found out about this plan—suggesting that at least one of Baranov's household servants was informing the monks about Aleksandr Andreevich's confidential discussions. To foil the chief manager, Father Afanasii dressed in the wanted man's clothes and in the dark went down to the shore to climb into his baidarka. The guards fell for the ruse. They seized the monk, but then immediately realized their error and "freed him without any molestation."

At this point, according to Baranov, "a real riot started." The other clerics ran to the scene, "with the skirts of their cassocks tucked high and with their shirt sleeves rolled up as if ready for a prize fight, cursing and shouting." In describing these events to his friend Emel'ian Larionov, Baranov reported that he confronted them: "I . . . also did some shouting and told them frankly that if they did not stop inciting rebellion I would have to use extreme and disagreeable measures: either I would build a high fence around their residence and allow them to go nowhere except to perform church services or I would deport the principal instigators to you on Unalashka."[11]

The clerics' account of this encounter confirms Father Afanasii's costumed trickery and Baranov's exhibition of hot anger. This night he appeared "in a towering rage," cursing loudly and "calling Afanasii a runaway state serf" while labeling all the monks as well as Lieutenant Talin and interpreter Prianishnikov as rebels. When Father German asked Baranov to state the reason for his objections in decent language, he began yelling about "some kind of oath" being used "to turn the Americans against" them. At the height of his anger, according to a later version, Baranov threatened to have the clerics clamped in irons and taken away to Unalaska. Or, he added, their quarters would be locked and boarded up so that no one could get to them, and the monks would in effect be imprisoned within their old house. "This made everyone greatly afraid," the monks' account summarized. "They all expected at any moment to be seized by the hunters on Baranov's orders and dragged off or beaten." They scarcely dared go either to their house or the church, which were both surrounded by armed promyshlenniks. But finally they retreated to the house and the safety of its closed doors.[12]

From Baranov's perspective, this latest display of temper may also have served a useful purpose. Intimidated by his threats, the clerics gave ground. But even then "they did not improve their conduct," according to the chief manager. For more than a year the clergymen quit performing any church services, saying they were too frightened by Baranov and his company men to venture out. They did, however, quietly conduct services in their house. Moreover, Aleksandr Andreevich told Larionov, "during the night they prowl around and seize our servants, taking them under their protection and marry them in the bathhouses." In this way, he continued, they managed to marry not only servant girls "but even some who were bought—married them no matter to whom."[13] "From all this," he wrote Larionov, "you can see in what a peaceful and pleasant state are affairs here with these restless fellows."

* * *

Aleksandr Baranov simply could not imagine that independence from company rule might benefit the Alutiiqs. "Their freedom," he wrote, "consists in robbery and everlasting bloody barbarism."[14] Yet because of the crisis caused by the resistance of the village hunters to his demands for their continued services, Baranov abruptly abandoned his long-standing policy of amiable paternalism. He ordered Ivan Kuskov and a squad of promyshlenniks to crush Native resistance against company authority.

Kuskov's actions as Baranov's assistant were in themselves barbaric, with consequences that have ever after cast a dark shadow on the reputation of both men. Taking a baidara carrying a cannon and with every man armed, Kuskov and his men first set out for Tugidak, the southwestern island village that had lost many men in the drowning catastrophe brought on by Russian orders the previous year. Understandably, Tugidak's leaders were prominent in the protest against joining another hunting expedition. When they reached the village, the first Russian to come ashore was Mikhail Kondakov, an experienced crew chief well known to the Alutiiqs. According to the clerics' later account, Kondakov at once began "cursing foully," making sneering remarks about the monks, and mocking the oath of allegiance. Then Kuskov and his promyshlenniks landed, carrying iron shackles and threatening to beat anyone who refused to join the company's mainland hunting expedition. According to one cleric, "They went on to commit shameless acts against the islanders, too shameful to mention."[15]

Kuskov and his squad next went ashore at another village on the western cape of Kodiak Island. They brought leg irons and neck yokes, and they
brought also birches for whipping the young men, rope ends for lashing the
thirty-year-olds, and canes to beat the old men. With their flintlock rifles
cocked, they assembled the villagers and reportedly told them: "If you don't
want to go on the expedition just say so now . . . and we'll shoot."[16]

Moving to nearby Sitkinak Island, where the villages of Ubaguik and Ikuk
had lost forty men by drowning and other causes during the 1798 expedition
and more in 1799, Kuskov and his crew repeated their display of force. The
Russians fired their cannon, came ashore with rifles ready, and spread out
before the villagers all the iron shackles, manacles, and neck yokes and their
assortment of whips and lashes. "Anyone who doesn't want to go with us,"
they loudly announced, "should choose one of these." At this, one foolishly
brave villager began to protest. The Russians seized him, locked him in irons,
and flogged him "until he was hoarse from screaming and could hardly say
'I'll go!'"[17]

This fierce, deplorable campaign of intimidation was a success. Willing or
not, the Alutiiq village hunters joined the year's mainland expedition and the
survivors would continue to do the same each following year. Moreover, the
islanders were now afraid of making any further visits to talk with the monks
at Pavlovskaia. For their part, the clerics were themselves too frightened to
minister to the Kodiak Alutiiqs. Hence, a later clerical investigator reported,
"the success of the Religious Mission did not come up to expectations."[18] For
at least another year, he said, Baranov continued in many ways to oppress the
monks—primarily because of their defense of Alutiiq liberty.

Included in the bill of particulars was an 1802 dispute over access to the
Pavlovskaia church and its bell tower that led to one more heated public clash
between an enraged Baranov and Father Afanasii. During this incident the
chief manager shouted that he would put Afanasii into a baidarka and set him
adrift. Then, after grabbing Father Afanasii by the chest, Aleksandr Andreevich threatened to hang him from the bell tower. At this, the monk finally
handed over the key to the church. For Baranov, this last angry outburst had
also achieved its desired effect.

In retrospect, the bell tower affair can be likened to the final rumblings of
a thunderstorm passing over Kodiak Island, with its energy already waning.
During the next few years, despite everyone's vivid memories of the earlier
conflict, the relationship between Baranov and the monks substantially mel-
lowed. Abetting that process was the disappearance of both Lieutenant Talin

and interpreter Prianishnikov, the two principal troublemakers, who simply fade from the documentary record. Historian Richard A. Pierce surmises that Talin soon returned to Russia. It is quite likely that his friend and accomplice, interpreter Prianishnikov, accompanied him.[19]

* * *

In May 1802 news at last reached Pavlovskaia Harbor in roundabout fashion about the 1799 formation of the Russian-American Company, with Baranov included as a shareholder and his managerial role strengthened. Another item in this report was the violent death of Emperor Paul I and the accession of his heir as Aleksandr I. Most surprising and gratifying to Aleksandr Andreevich was the information that shortly before Emperor Paul was murdered, he had conferred on Baranov a gold medal and band of Vladimir. This honor was signified by a parchment document and the actual large medal and ribbon to wear on his chest for every ceremonial occasion. As an act of gratitude, the chief manager made a personal donation of two thousand rubles to Father German's Pavlovskaia school.

By the end of that summer Baranov had forwarded to the clerics some correspondence and other papers that he had seized earlier. In mid-September he authorized them to hold a memorial service for the dead monarch, then a vigil and Te Deum for the health and well-being of Emperor Aleksandr. He also asked the churchmen to administer "to all of us" an oath of allegiance to the new emperor, which everyone would sing according to a specified ritual.[20]

The monks resumed church services, apparently terrified no longer by Aleksandr Andreevich's volatile temper. He in turn sent the four clerics peace offerings: two pounds of tea, four pounds of sugar, a barrel of whale fat, a cask of whale meat, and a barrel of berries mixed with fat—a preserved fruit mixture that locals considered a great delicacy. Later, in return for conducting memorial services on behalf of fallen Russians and Alutiiqs at a battle in Sitka Sound, described in Chapter 9, he gave the monks a letter of credit for five hundred rubles worth of goods from the company store. This gift was followed by a five hundred ruble personal donation from Baranov and other company men, to be directed to the upkeep of the church and the needs of the ecclesiastical brothers.[21]

If there had ever been a real question about the extent of Aleksandr Andreevich's authority, by the middle of 1802 it was absolutely clear to everyone in Russian America that under the RAC charter he represented the imperial government as well as the company's merchant shareholders and directors. The RAC's main office was being relocated from Irkutsk to St. Petersburg, reflecting a new order of priorities that gave precedence to the interests of Russia's ruling elite in company affairs. It remained true, as Baranov had once observed to Madam Shelikhova, that St. Petersburg cared mainly about the money—the flow of profits secured by Baranov and his Russian and Alutiiq workers from fur hunting and trade along the maritime margins of the North Pacific—with no more than a minor, passing concern for the spiritual labors of the few monks remaining on Kodiak Island.

* * *

If vindication was needed for Aleksandr Andreevich's conduct in dealing with the cantankerous government officials and uncooperative monks, it soon came from investigations by two highly placed official visitors. In July 1804 a new clergyman, Cathedral Hieromonk Gideon, reached Pavlovskaia aboard the British-built navy ship *Neva*, one of two vessels sent to Russian America from the Kronstadt naval base near St. Petersburg on a historic first round-the-world voyage.[22] Coming from the prestigious Aleksandr Nevskii Monastery in St. Petersburg, Father Gideon was well educated, proficient in French, and able to teach rhetoric, philosophy, and mathematics. From Metropolitan Amvrosii and the Holy Ruling Synod of the Russian Orthodox Church he had received an assignment to scrutinize the condition of the American spiritual mission. His reports would be directed both to the synod and to the father superior at Valaam Monastery, and they would also be forwarded to the emperor.

When Father Gideon came ashore, Baranov was away from Pavlovskaia, dealing with the RAC's Tlingit foes on Sitka Sound. In his absence Ivan Banner was managing the Kodiak district. Although Banner had earned a reputation for cordial hospitality, Father Gideon did not find him congenial. Banner recognized Father Gideon as the new de facto head of the spiritual mission. But soon the men clashed over the future of two talented creole boys who Father Gideon wanted to keep in Pavlovskaia to serve the church, rather than see them sent off to Russia aboard a navy ship.[23]

In his first report, Father Gideon wrote a lengthy description of the clerics' dispute with Chief Manager Baranov four years earlier.[24] He told the story from the monks' perspective, though he gave Aleksandr Andreevich ample credit for his subsequent generosity to the clergymen, their school, and their church. After Baranov's victorious return from Sitka Sound in 1806, however, Father Gideon found him a helpful and likable person. The learned, well-traveled mission supervisor grew sympathetic toward Aleksandr Andreevich.

As had apparently been true earlier for Archimandrite Ioasaf, Father Gideon developed a deep appreciation for Baranov's character and abilities—and for the daunting challenges that he had been facing in Russian America—once he came to know the man and gained a fuller understanding of the local situation.

Father Gideon soon learned firsthand the regrettable shortcomings of some of the clerics who had once roundly condemned Baranov. In late October 1805 he tried to sail to Sitka Sound aboard the *Sv. Elizaveta* to meet the chief manager. After more than a month of fierce storms, fog, freezing cold, driving slush, and still more contrary winds, with a sick skipper and a crew hardly able to manage the sails, the ship ran aground at night while trying to return to Pavlovskaia. Following three more weeks of great suffering, the holy father at last reached the company settlement in a baidarka. There, he said, "I suffered aggravations no less than before." The cause of those aggravations was Ivan Banner, who showed an "insulting manner" to the clergyman and rejected his recommendations for improving the school teaching staff. But also "some members of the [RAC] office," he thought, were "disturbing [exciting?] the clerics Hieromonk Afanasii and Hierodeacon Nektarii, who had been very rude to me following the wreck of the vessel." In their behavior he saw evidence of collusion. "Well," Father Gideon remarked, "the senior officials here egg them on in this."[25]

A year later, in 1805, another government ship brought to Pavlovskaia an even more highly placed visitor, Natalia Shelikhova's son-in-law Nikolai Rezanov. Now bearing the title chamberlain of the imperial court, Rezanov had come from St. Petersburg as a special envoy from the sovereign and the RAC main office, carrying documents that identified him as a crown plenipotentiary. Of course, Rezanov had been influential at court in securing the RAC charter. Indeed, during his lengthy North American tour of duty he claimed exclusive credit for being the RAC's creator. A widower since 1802, he was now on an extended official excursion that had already taken him to Okhotsk, Kamchatka, the Kurile Islands, Japan, and Unalaska.[26] Despite his total failure in a yearlong effort to open trade relations with Japan's rigidly traditionalist, isolationist Meiji government, Rezanov was an extremely talented man: small in stature but brimming with big ideas and large ambitions—as well as a highly elevated sense of his own self-worth. Above all, he was eager to reform the RAC's North American operations and make the company an effective Crown agent in advancing Russian power and prestige all around the Pacific Rim.

NIKOLAI PETROVICH Rezanov. A skilled politician in the Russian court and the son-in-law of Grigorii Shelikhov, Rezanov arrived in North America in 1805 on an extended inspection tour of the RAC's overseas colony. Originally skeptical, he became impressed by Baranov's unique suitability for his position as the RAC's chief manager. His expedition to San Francisco Bay in 1806 opened a surreptitious, mutually beneficial trade with the Hispanic Californians.

Rezanov was not a deeply spiritual person and was even somewhat anti-clerical in his attitude toward the holy fathers in Russian America. Yet he intended to examine the condition of the Orthodox mission and the history of Baranov's conflict with the resident monks. In this task, he became Father Gideon's companion and adjunct. Among first matters, Rezanov was skeptical about the evangelical campaign waged by Father Makarii and Father Juvenalii. With their great enthusiasm, he wrote, they had been merely "bathing" Americans at the baptismal font—an insulting term—while doing nothing to develop their mentality or enlist them in the government's goals for the colony.[27] These goals, as he interpreted them, included improving agriculture and raising the level of training for young Alutiiq and creole students so they could be integrated into the RAC's skilled workforce.

Like Father Gideon, Rezanov was impressed with the chief manager's financial support for the mission's school program. To help meet the expense of boarding students at Pavlovskaia, he reported, Baranov had generously earmarked the annual profit on five shares of company stock—presumably from his personal holding—for the students' benefit. Since the RAC directors had earlier given fifteen shares to the late Archimandrite Ioasaf, Rezanov pointed out, those shares should now be transferred to the mission school, making a full twenty shares that could be dedicated to funding the students.[28]

Chamberlain Rezanov came down hard on the four remaining members of the spiritual mission. "Having little to do," he wrote, "they try to take part in the civil government of the country, calling themselves government representatives." The monks were not the only ones guilty. "The restless officers use them as their tools against the Manager." The result, Rezanov declared, was grief, and "there is danger of our losing the whole country."[29] As his prime example, he cited the oath of allegiance controversy. If Baranov had not halted the monks' ill-considered demands, Rezanov said, a winter gathering of several thousand Alutiiqs at Pavlovskaia "would have killed everybody from starvation alone."

While endorsing Aleksandr Andreevich's views so completely, Rezanov apparently also enjoyed Father Gideon's support and confidence. Both men were disappointed that the monks had made no progress in mastering the Alutiiq language. In Father Gideon's presence and presumably with his approval, Rezanov called together the four clerics, drew himself up tall, and delivered a stern message: "If any of them took another step without getting the Manager's approval, or if they meddled in civil affairs, I would order such criminals deported to Russia, where for disrupting the peace of the community such people would be defrocked and severely punished to make an example of them."

Faced with this blazing wrath from the highest official ever to reach Russian America, the churchmen expressed total contrition in dramatic style. According to Rezanov: "They cried, rolled at my feet and told me that it was the government employees who had told them what to do. They promised me to behave, so that the manager would have nothing but praise for them in the future."[30] This admonishment he made privately, Rezanov added, solely in Father Gideon's company. In public, he said, "I have always shown respect for their dignity."

From that point, Rezanov said, the monks' behavior improved remarkably. They now understood their mistakes and were doing their best to help in agriculture and education. With encouragement from Father Gideon as well as Rezanov himself, Hierodeacon Nektarii—who had earlier begged Father Gideon to recommend his return to Russia as soon as possible—took over direction of a newly reorganized Kodiak Russian-American school. The first class began with thirty students enrolled in the rudimentary study of reading, writing, and the Orthodox short catechism.[31] Thirty advanced students were challenged by a curriculum including Russian grammar, arithmetic, sacred and profane history, geography, and that era's clerical version of the sciences. All pupils supplemented their academic work with lessons in farming and domestic crafts: "how to prepare the vegetable plots and plant and sow vegetables, how to cut and harvest various types of grasses, roots, and how to fish" according to Russian methods. A few also took lessons in shoemaking and leatherworking.[32]

Father German, formerly head of the Pavlovskaia church school, now shifted responsibilities. He took charge of twenty boys to be specially trained in farming, moving with these young men to nearby Leisnoi Island in the summer. There they sowed wheat, planted potatoes and other vegetables, and learned how to make preserves of mushrooms and berries. During the winter they returned to the school in Pavlovskaia for the same elementary instruction that the first class was receiving under Father Nektarii's supervision. "In this way," Chamberlain Rezanov wrote to the RAC's St. Petersburg headquarters, "I will make ready for you the first twenty families of agricultural settlers and think that after they get used to work these boys will become reliable and literate farmers."[33]

Rezanov's reports directly addressed the bad conduct toward Baranov and his aides by Lieutenant Talin and the other officers who had refused to cooperate with Aleksandr Andreevich. The RAC's main office, Rezanov urged, must convince the emperor to expand further the chief manager's power and authority. As it was, he said, every commander of a ship or dock-yard believed that he was independent of Baranov's orders. These arrogant characters, he pointedly remarked, would not obey the chief manager except in the presence of a regular army force, and maybe not even then "because alcohol vapors interfere with clear thinking."[34]

The officers led a dissipated life, he said, some of them owing the company more than a year's salary for the enormous quantity of vodka they drank and charged to their store accounts. "Ask for the accounts from Kamchatsk, Okhotsk, and Kadiak and all you will see in them will be vodka." They might easily save more than half their income, but "they drink two or three bottles of vodka every day and of course in this case any salary would be insuffi-cient."[35] The only remedy he could suggest, surprisingly, was for the company to recruit RAC ship captains from among foreigners, no longer relying on the sodden Russian navy men.

Rezanov's detailed reports from North America, along with his stern actions in dealing with the clerics at Pavlovskaia, provided a strong endorse-ment for Aleksandr Andreevich. Father Gideon apparently shared this appraisal. In 1807, while preparing to return to Russia, the cleric wrote Baranov to thank him for various kindnesses and, among other matters, to share his own highly critical view of Father Afanasii. Saying that he was handing over the direction of the religious mission to Father German, the departing priest revealed that both Father Nektarii and Father Afanasii had records of misbehavior and disrespect toward their clerical superiors. "Since Hieromonk Afanasii does not have any capability for authority, and since he has little wit and cannot read or write," Father Gideon wrote, Archimandrite Ioasaf had previously left instructions that he should be harshly punished for insubordination. "He should not be allowed to become rebellious as has often happened," the archimandrite had directed. "In such cases he should be attached to a chain and left there until he reforms himself and asks for-giveness for his sins." The truth of Father Ioasaf's concerns, had been fully confirmed, Father Gideon went on to tell Baranov, by Afanasii's "stubborn, self-willed insubordinate and brazen behavior since I have been here."[36]

Father German's appointment as head of the mission, Father Gideon was careful to explain, came with the authority to manage the affairs of all the other missionaries as he saw fit and "decisively to resist their whims and fancies." With total confidence in Father German's "great qualities and [the] rare mind of this enlightened, experienced, industrious, and most honorable father," his clerical friend assured Baranov "that his eagerness, watchfulness, and insight will allow nothing to get past." He hoped that the chief manager would feel the same way toward Father German and do all he could "to ward off any unpleasantness which might arise."

Even more noteworthy was this statement Father Gideon made to Baranov: "I have very often heard the devoted and peace-loving Elder's humility, quietness and humble wisdom praised highly by Your Honor, as a man of experience and worthy of great honor, a man who has spent the whole of his life as an object of praise because of his many labors for the good of the Fatherland." This statement of admiration from Baranov, Father Gideon concluded, "is more important for Father German than any other praise."[37]

Two hundred years after the events they record, a critical reading of these documents might suggest to skeptical historians that Father Gideon was indulging in a bit of hopeful hyperbole as he tried to soothe relations between Baranov and Father German. Were these former adversaries really lavishing one another with such praise by 1807? Consider the circumstances. Father Gideon was leaving behind at Pavlovskaia a careworn, rather tattered remnant of the ten-man spiritual mission that Aleksandr Andreevich had welcomed thirteen years earlier. With Father Nektarii also sailing back to Russia at the same time, the mission force was being reduced to only three men.

Of these three, Father Afanasii would soon be assigned to live in relative isolation on Leisnoi Island, where he conducted services and administered sacraments until leaving the colony in 1825. For the time being, Father German bore entire responsibility for maintaining the Pavlovskaia church and the Russian-American school at the harbor settlement, assisted quietly by the junior Father Ioasaf. Quite understandably, Father Gideon may have meant to consolidate a cordial relationship between Aleksandr Andreevich and Father German, hoping to promote a new attitude of warm good feelings between the chief manager and the remaining priests.

But such skepticism may be unwarranted. Father Gideon could have been recording nothing more than the literal truth. In either case, his departure signified closure to the dispute that had once totally disrupted the Russian company community at Pavlovskaia and threatened an end to the RAC's North Pacific fur business. Years later, when Baranov finally was allowed to resign his post and sail away from America, he arranged for his wife, Anna

Grigor'evna, to live on Leisnoi Island under Father German's care. That fact too is testimony to the respect that had developed between the veteran monk and the veteran chief manager.

* * *

Despite this halting reconciliation between the RAC officers and the clerics, it must also be recognized, any remaining concerns for the safety and well-being of the Kodiak Alutiiq people dropped from view. Father Afanasii's attempted challenge to Baranov's authority had cut short any last trace of evangelical activity by the churchmen. More than ever, they acted like monks, not missionaries. Apparently, they even abandoned their efforts to abolish plural marriages and other cultural practices they found abhorrent.

Even so, the original directive from the metropolitan for them to train Native converts and prepare them to enter the Russian Orthodox priesthood did not go ignored. Talented Alutiiq and creole youth were mentored into responsible church positions, beginning a transitional process that would see educated Natives become steadily more important in Alaskan church affairs. But totally ignored, fortunately for the clerics, was Shelikhov's plan to have them accompany the agricultural colonists to the mainland and attend to the spiritual needs of New Russia's shrinking community of exile families.[38]

Writing from Sitka Sound in 1806, Rezanov, like Baranov before him, explained to the RAC board of directors the dilemma of the Kodiak Alutiiq people. Think of the situation they were in, he urged. On Kodiak Island the sea otters were long since exterminated. Yet these people, by trading with the Russians, had developed "new tastes, and with them new wants." Not having the means at home to satisfy these acquired tastes and wants, they went willingly, he said, under Russian direction to the mainland, leaving their homes and families for a season or more at a time and were "exposed to danger." But Rezanov blatantly fudged the facts by omitting any mention of the Alutiiq rebellion and its brutal repression, something he must have known about.

To mitigate part of the company's labor problem, Rezanov said he favored moving some Kodiak Alutiiqs permanently to the RAC's new Sitka Sound establishment if they were willing. Yet realistically, he had to admit, in the face of continued Tlingit enmity, this too was impractical. "Our number [here at Sitka] is so small that it is hard to defend even ourselves."[39]

Lacking any other reliable source of workers, the RAC and its chief manager were handcuffed to a long-established style of Native exploitation. No matter how sensitive they might be to the Alutiiq villagers' predicament,

Baranov and Rezanov could do virtually nothing to relieve the difficulties and dangers imposed on them by Russian company rule.

For their part, the few surviving Russian Orthodox clergy could do little more than take care of their own needs, lead holy services, and teach at Pavlovskaia while praying for the good health of a distant sovereign and the forgiveness of a distant deity. That was enough. After Father Gideon's visit, apparently no churchman ever again spoke in public about the concept of sanctioning Alutiiq independence from RAC management.

And yet Father German kept alive the monastic tradition of advocating for the poor and abused. In late December 1818, a month after Baranov's final departure from Russian America, the cleric wrote to navy lieutenant Simeon Ianovskii, then serving as the interim RAC governor of the colony, to introduce himself and proffer his congratulations on Ianovskii's taking office. Saying that he was "the most humble servant of the local peoples and their nursemaid," Father German implored Ianovskii, while standing before him "with bloody tears," to "be a father and protector" to the people. In highly figurative terms, the monk pleaded, "Wipe away the tears of our defenseless orphans, soothe the sorrows of aching hearts, let us know what joy is like!" Ianovskii might determine for himself "the full breadth and scope of the people's sorrows," added Father German. "We wait expectantly to see what kindness the Creator will place in your heart on behalf of the poor." But, he also said, "we await more . . . in the expectation from our new master of new kindness, new joys, and new life for this area."[40]

During his two-year term of office, Lieutenant Ianovskii (who had married Baranov's daughter, Irina) formed a close personal and spiritual connection with Father German.[41] But there was little even he could do to relieve the suffering of the Alutiiq people. Since the scarcity of sea otters had brought an end to all hunting expeditions by that time, the Kodiak Island economy was reduced to an impoverished subsistence level. And since Lieutenant Ianovskii and the naval officers who would succeed him as RAC administrators had no interest in making Russian America return a commercial profit, company policy from that time forward was largely neglectful of the surviving Alutiiq people.

Looking toward the future, Kodiak and Chugach Alutiiqs in time found that their best long-term strategy for survival was one of personal accommodation with the Russian newcomers and acculturation to their ways. Their interaction with the Russians was marked by a significantly large percentage of intermarriages and a general embrace of the Russian Orthodox religion. These processes came to sustain an innovative, unique blending of cultural traits and practices that have continued to preserve Alutiiq identity and values ever since the Baranov era.

VIII

THE RUSSIAN-AMERICAN COMPANY

The widow Natalia Shelikhova, with the aid of her two influential sons-in-law, successfully preserved the Shelikhov family fortune after her husband's death despite initial opposition from rival Irkutsk merchants. With adroit political maneuvering in St. Petersburg, she then led a merchant coalition to secure Crown approval for formation of the Russian-American Company in 1799. The directors of this chartered imperial monopoly were pleased to retain Aleksandr Baranov as the new company's chief manager in North America, with authority that made him the virtual viceroy of Russia's overseas empire. Highly honored by both Emperor Paul I and Emperor Aleksandr I, Baranov came to enjoy a position of dignity and personal distinction that drew the admiration of prominent visitors to Russian Alaska.

G RIGORII SHELIKHOV'S AMBITION TO BRING UNDER SINGLE management—his own—the bitterly competitive Russian fur rush into the North Pacific had gone unrealized during his lifetime. After his unexpected death in 1795, the widow Shelikhova deftly managed to gain control of his fortune, aided by personal and business allies. With a superb knowledge of the family's business and exquisite political skills, she then made further attempts to influence the St. Petersburg administration on behalf of her company and her family.

Madam Shelikhova proved particularly effective in gaining male sympathy by flattery while bemoaning her plight as a grieving widow and the frail protector of her fatherless children. Deploying these wiles, late in 1795 she appealed to Prince Platon Zubov, the dashing young favorite of the aging empress, imploring him to intervene with the Crown on her behalf. She described in detail Grigorii Shelikhov's accomplishments and the status of Golikov-Shelikhov Company affairs while praising Baranov's management in North America. Now, Madam Shelikhova said, she badly needed more navigators and generous government support for the company's agricultural colony.

She also appealed for Crown officials to negotiate with England the southern boundary of Russian possessions in North America. She urged a settlement that would protect the company's rightful trading and hunting preserves and future agricultural districts from British incursions. Only by fixing the boundary south of Lituya Bay, she said, could Russian America hope to raise the grain crops necessary for a growing Russian population. Like her husband before her, the widow Shelikhova advocated an expansion of Russia's overseas activities that would go far beyond the fur business. She hoped to create a settler colony populated by families who would transplant their lives and risk their small fortunes by bringing Russian culture—including farming practices and dietary styles—from the homeland.[1]

The death of the empress and the accession of her son as Paul I in 1796 led to Prince Zubov's rapid downfall. Madam Shelikhova then turned for help to her two talented, highly capable sons-in-law, St. Petersburg politician and court official Nikolai Rezanov and Velikiy Ustyug merchant Mikhail Buldakov. Rezanov had come to Irkutsk, where his father was a well-known jurist, with the 1794 spiritual mission. There he met Anna Shelikhova, the oldest Shelikhov daughter. Early the following year, shortly before Grigorii Shelikhov's death, the couple married.

Lacking details about their courtship and marriage, we can only surmise that it was a satisfactory match, carefully arranged. Despite the fact that Rezanov was twice the age of Anna, her parents must have approved this linkage with the scion of an important family who already had made his way into the ranks of Russia's lesser nobility. At one time a member of Prince Zubov's entourage, Rezanov's later rapid advance at the court of Paul I made him an ideal agent to represent the Shelikhov family interests in the new imperial regime.[2]

Madam Shelikhova's younger daughter Avdot'ia married Mikhail Buldakov in 1797, when the bride was no more than fourteen and the groom was thirty-one. This marriage too, like Rezanov's union with Anna, was a conventional arrangement, advantageous to all parties. Buldakov, much like Shelikhov and Baranov, apparently had come to Irkutsk from northern Russia in the 1780s and prospered in the fur business.[3] As a consequence of their marriages, both Rezanov and Buldakov, only a few years younger than their mother-in-law, became significant company shareholders through their teenage wives' inheritances, and both cooperated with the widow Shelikhova to accomplish the business and political maneuvers that led toward the creation of the Russian-American Company.

Madam Shelikhova asserted her control over the Golikov-Shelikhov Company as the majority stockholder in late 1795. After further commercial and political skirmishes following the death of the empress, she presided over a 1797 merger between this firm and the Irkutsk Commercial Company of Myl'nikov and Associates, a newly founded organization that represented the interests of her family's main rivals in the Irkutsk business community. A year later, after incorporating a few other merchants including Evstratii Delarov and Emel'ian Larionov, this organization became known as the United American Company. Because Pavel Lebedev-Lastochkin and the Kiselev brothers were withdrawing from North American operations, this consolidation meant that for the first time all the Irkutsk-based commerce in America could be coordinated and carried out with a concern for the shared interests of the Irkutsk merchants and, incidentally, the distant imperial Crown.

The final step, the capstone in building this business edifice, would be securing Crown approval for a chartered monopoly, along with enhanced support from Paul I's government. At this point Rezanov and Buldakov called on all their influential connections in St. Petersburg to gain the official backing necessary for the Shelikhov family agenda. They proposed placing the United American Company's monopoly under royal authority. Prince Aleksei Kurakin, a prominent aristocrat, served as a public spokesman for this plan. In August 1797 he delivered to the emperor a lengthy report with a cumbersome, prosaic title: "On the Harmfulness of Many Companies in America and the Advantages of Uniting Them in One, with an Explanation of the Means for This." Many parts of the prince's report, historian Mary E. Wheeler observes, read as though they were written by Shelikhov himself.[4] Most likely, Rezanov was the actual ghost author.

The emperor approved this awkwardly titled report at once, and Prince Kurakin sent it on to the Commerce College, the government's highest deliberative agency for economic affairs. This body delayed, asking for more information and questioning the intent of the Irkutsk merchants to form a state-authorized, Crown-backed commercial alliance. Doing its work thoroughly, the agency also questioned the adequacy of the company's stock provisions, raising doubts that the proposed capital fund of 740,000 rubles would be sufficient for all the firm's operations. Some of these concerns were allayed in the fall of 1798, when the Commerce College executive received from Irkutsk the formal "Act of the United Company" signed by Natalia Shelikhova, Ivan Golikov, Nikolai Myl'nikov, and seventeen other reputable merchants—nearly the same roster of directors who had requested Baranov to remain in North America as chief manager. In addition to a capital fund fixed now at 742,000 rubles, divided into 724 shares, the United American Company had borrowed 400,000 rubles from Golikov and Natalia Shelikhova with a provision that no profits would be paid to shareholders until this debt was retired.

The imperial bureaucracy, headed by men who wore gorgeous uniforms and displayed finely calibrated aristocratic manners, was not a well-oiled, smoothly functioning apparatus. The Commerce College at last reported the results of its deliberations in January 1798. This document called for a few changes in the provisions for stock sales, principally to make it easier for other investors, Russians and certain resident foreigners, to buy into the chartered company. Stockholder representation and voting rights were other areas of concern. The report would restrict board membership to investors who owned at least twenty-five shares. Only those who owned at least ten shares would be eligible to vote, and only shareholders who were physically present at the time of balloting would have their votes counted. It also recommended that the firm should be renamed the Russian-American Company, with its governing board obliged to report directly to the Commerce College.

Taking up these recommendations the following July, the Imperial State Council approved most of them, adding a few further changes desired by the emperor. Among these was a provision to give an advantaged investment status to new shareholders who were not part of the Irkutsk cadre of merchant owners. The company name, Paul I now proposed, should be "the Russian-American Company under Our Supreme Protection—for the enjoyment of the privileges granted to it for twenty years." During its twenty-year charter, the company by royal fiat would have an exclusive right to do business—hunting and trading, settling, and sending ships to conduct trade with cooperative, friendly nations—in all North Pacific maritime regions above fifty-five degrees north latitude that were not already occupied by other powers. Moreover, the RAC directors would be directly under the authority of the emperor, not the Commerce College.[5]

After the state council incorporated these changes, the emperor issued an edict ordering the governing senate to prepare the RAC charter for his signature. Final approval came at the end of December 1799, when Paul I placed his elaborate official scrawl and seal on the final document. The deed was done. Madam Shelikhova and her daughters, along with their husbands and heirs, were assured of their Siberian and North American trading fortunes into the distant future. The RAC with Baranov as its first American chief manager would enjoy a position of unchallenged supremacy in Russia's overseas fur business, with a patent for expansion that could be liberally interpreted. And because it had suited the young government of Paul I, Russia's St. Petersburg officials were now to become directly involved in advancing and maintaining the monarch's claims to an overseas empire that had been gained for the Crown by Irkutsk merchant initiative during the previous half century.[6]

* * *

In the midst of these negotiations, the emperor and the governing senate also granted the Shelikhov family an exceptional honor and privilege. In November 1798 Paul I bestowed on Natalia Shelikhova and her children a "merit of nobility of our Empire," elevating them from the merchant class into noble status. This action, the emperor declared, came in recognition of the services of the late citizen Shelikhov, "who gave his life and property in annexing to our Scepter the peoples inhabiting North America" and laying there "the foundation for the Greek-Catholic Christian Faith and for various trades useful to the State." The widow Shelikhova deserved the honor as well because she had "shared with him the hardships of his travel." By the same act the emperor also specifically directed that Madam Shelikhova and her children be left "the liberty to continue their trade as before." The governing senate added its approval the following February, as the emperor had ordered, and dispatched notification in proper form to the Irkutsk guberniia administration and Siberian local officials.[7]

The rise from provincial merchant status into the St. Petersburg nobility—usually deeply scornful of unlanded merchants—was a huge climb, rarely made in the society of imperial Russia. Lacking documentary evidence, historians may well suspect that it was the experienced climber and political rope puller Nikolai Rezanov who boosted the widow Shelikhova and her progeny—including of course his own young wife—on this dizzying ascent.

When the emperor signed the RAC charter, he also agreed to appoint an agent of the Shelikhov family as one of the four members of the board of directors. This appointee became Mikhail Buldakov, designated as the "first director"—in effect the chairman of the RAC board, which in 1800 moved the company's main office from Irkutsk to St. Petersburg by order of the emperor.[8]

At nearly the same time, Rezanov, newly bereaved by the death of his young wife, Anna, began making plans for a North Pacific expedition from St. Petersburg aboard a navy warship. This venture would become a multiyear inspection tour of RAC operations as well as a mission to Japan. As warrant for the trip, he cited his dual capacity as Crown plenipotentiary and an agent of the RAC board of directors, fashioning himself as the emperor's personal representative in realms scarcely known to any of Russia's autocratic rulers.

* * *

Isolated in America, Baranov did not learn of the RAC's formation until May 1802, when Ivan Banner arrived by baidarka from Unalaska. A former trader in northeast Siberia linked with the Baranov brothers and then a provincial police chief, Banner had entered the company's service just recently. As a first task, he took charge of a proposed colonizing expedition intended to establish a trading station north of the Bering Strait. When he reached Unalaska, however, Banner had his assignment changed by local manager and company director Emel'ian Larionov, who sent him to Pavlovskaia to become Baranov's understudy, expecting that Banner might take the chief manager's place when Aleksandr Andreevich retired.[9]

Along with intelligence of the RAC's creation, Banner brought to Pavlovskaia news that Emperor Paul was dead, the victim of a palace coup, and his son had taken the throne as Emperor Aleksandr I. In addition, Banner delivered to Baranov his first great honor: a gold medal and band of Vladimir from the late Paul I, bestowed on him for his services to the Crown.

This day of triumph, as Aleksandr Andreevich rightly regarded it, was duly celebrated. "In the barracks," Baranov recalled for historian Khlebnikov, "they sang the 'hours' and prayers, and then the Imperial parchment was read, also the acts enforcing privileges, etc. to general rejoicing, and then I placed around my aging neck my Monarch's sign of excellence—about which no one knew in advance." As a "weak imitation of such generosity" and his "spiritual gratitude" for this gift from the monarch, Aleksandr Andreevich subscribed an additional two thousand rubles to the Pavlovskaia school, run at this time by Father German. And for this feast day, in a gesture hearkening back to countless generations of tradition in northern Russia, the newly decorated chief manager had an elderly ram slaughtered and roasted.[10] Beyond doubt, Baranov's imperial decoration immensely fortified his position. Wearing his imperial gold medallion and bright band, no longer could he be scorned as a mere provincial merchant's son.

* * *

A far greater honor was ahead. Natalia Shelikhova, with a style quite different from her late husband's personal glory seeking, did not ignore the men most responsible for the American achievements, the profits, and the territorial gains that together made possible her enhanced lifestyle in Irkutsk and her courtly status at St. Petersburg. In 1799, while the RAC charter was being prepared for Emperor Paul I's signature, she petitioned the Crown through the Irkutsk military governor to award noble rank to Aleksandr Baranov, James Shields, and company office manager Ivan Zelinski.

By the time this request came to the attention of the Crown administration, following the accession of Aleksandr I, everyone knew that Shields was dead. The young new emperor apparently passed over Zelinski, who would serve as manager of the RAC's main office in St. Petersburg until 1824. But in August 1802, responding to Madam Shelikhova's appeal, the emperor granted to Baranov the rank of collegiate counselor, which automatically brought entry into the ranks of the nobility for him and his children.[11]

Word of this astounding promotion did not reach Aleksandr Andreevich until March 1804. According to Rezanov, who was with the chief manager in Pavlovskaia at the time—and who probably had a crucial role in securing this recognition for him—when Baranov learned of his newly acquired title and privileges, "he wept from gratitude because he felt that the Monarch appreciated the exploits achieved in remote countries."[12] The emperor's action came as a validation of his career and a reward for all the miseries and dangers he had experienced in Russian America. Forever after, the title collegiate counselor warmed his inner being against all chills.

A year later Aleksandr Andreevich wrote the emperor an effusive letter to express his gratitude. Preserved in the archival publication of company historian P. A. Tikhmenev, this formal but highly emotional document deserves quotation in full.

> Most Gracious Sovereign,
>
> Being born in the merchant class and educated almost by nature alone, being devoid of necessary learning and knowledge of the sciences, I could never hope to acquire the distinction that your Imperial Majesty, on representation by the American Company, has bestowed upon me. Now that

your generosity has willed that, allow me, Mighty Sovereign, the temerity to fall at your feet and express my supreme gratitude, from the bottom of my heart, for such an incomparable favor. I beg you to be lenient when I express my sorrow that my health, weakened by advancing years and labors, does not allow me to continue to labor and to merit more of your Grace's [favor]. My strength, health and ability have become exhausted by my fifteen years stay here and I am forced to seek retirement and quiet. It is only left for me, with all Russia, to pray to the Supreme Being to grant your Imperial Majesty prosperity and precious health. This I will consider my duty until the end of my days, Most Gracious Sovereign.

I am the loyal subject of Your Imperial Majesty, Manager of the American Company on the American Coast,

Aleksandr Baranov[13]

For the rest of his life Aleksandr Andreevich would proudly sign his letters, orders, and reports with the title collegiate counselor.

That same year Baranov was promoted, 1802, the RAC main office in St. Petersburg placed the Unalashka District directly under his supervision, making him chief manager for Russia's entire North American empire. His old friend Emel'ian Larionov, once considered a potential replacement for Aleksandr Andreevich, remained at Unalaska as district manager. Larionov reluctantly stayed in this position until, in 1806, he suffered a brief period of derangement and died. His Russian-born widow and teenage daughter, living in reduced circumstances, were unable to leave for Siberia until a year later. Their rescue came finally through the concern and generosity of Yankee shipmaster John D'Wolf, Baranov's friend, who ransomed them from an obdurate new local manager with a keg of brandy.[14]

* * *

Baranov first began telling Grigorii Shelikhov and others about his intent to retire and return to Russia as early as 1795. We see such statements more often during his conflict with Lieutenant Talin, interpreter Prianishnikov, and the Pavlovskaia monks, in part because he was venting his frustrations in letters to his friend Larionov at Unalaska. By the time this crisis passed, it had become habitual for Aleksandr Andreevich to talk and write of resignation as though the matter was settled and he was only waiting for a replacement.

At the same time, he invariably cited the reasons that ostensibly were forcing him to remain at his post: his duty to Shelikhov, then to Madam

Shelikhova and the company directors, and his important role in advancing the goals of the imperial Crown. As the years went by, Baranov's display of ambivalence about retirement became evidently a psychological game he was playing with himself.

Rezanov recognized Aleksandr Andreevich's conflicted attitude when he wrote that the chief manager must be kept in office "notwithstanding his daily resignation."[15] At that time, in November 1805, Aleksandr Andreevich had recovered from the wounds received in battle against the Tlingits the previous year, though he had taken to carrying a heavy cane to help him get about. Now fifty-nine, he was suffering the physical effects of advancing years and extraordinary exertions. He had worked hard all his adult life, exposing himself to exhaustion and physical danger, traveling often in baidarkas or open boats, living in tents and leaky shacks, and enduring every sort of weather in a climate lacking warmth. His strength and resilience were remarkable, but surely on cold, wet, stormy mornings his personal inventory of aches and pains must have argued for an easier life.

Whatever his reasons for wanting to leave Russian America, Baranov always found other reasons that allowed him to vacillate and remain. One of the strongest was his genuine desire to serve the Russian nation as well as his employers. The terms *glory* and *honor* appear frequently in his letters. These were not empty ideals for Aleksandr Baranov. He wrote and spoke with conviction about his responsibilities to the emperor and to the Russian Crown. When granted high recognition by the emperor for his loyal service, as Rezanov witnessed, he was genuinely and deeply moved.

Not long after Rezanov brought him the surprising news of his honors, Aleksandr Andreevich reflected poignantly on his situation to one of his friends: "I should retire but God knows when I will be replaced. If the plenipotentiary representative of the company—the General [Rezanov]—will not accept my resignation I foresee that I will have to end my life here, because there are in view so many profits and advantages for our Country that even the most energetic executive possessing an active mind cannot accomplish everything that has to be done even in fifty years' time." But, he said, he was now hardly able to meet any longer the demands of his office. "My faculties, both of mind and body, become weaker. I am tired from constant labors and even the honors bestowed on me by the Monarch become a burden when I think at my age my end is near."[16]

Personal concerns also must have had a significant bearing on his decision to remain in America. The education and training of his son Antipatr was quite important to him. In 1804, at the same time Baranov was risking his life during the Tlingit conflict on Sitka Sound, Anna Grigor'evna gave birth to a daughter. The baby was baptized Irina. She too apparently became a darling child for her father as the years advanced. In 1814, when she was ten years old, he wrote that Irina was being taught reading and writing, not common accomplishments for a Russian girl at that time and certainly a distinction for a creole young woman. The fact that Baranov's rank as collegiate counselor gave his two Alaska-born children an elite standing in Russian society was not lost on their father. As they grew, he showed himself interested in their advancement and anxious that they not remain in America, but attain respectable, suitable positions in Russia's upper-class circles.

At some point during these years Baranov learned that he had become legally a widower. His Russian wife, Matreona, died at her Kargopol' home in 1805 or 1806. Although no Kodiak Island church records survive from this period, it is certain that Aleksandr Andreevich wed Anna Grigor'evna soon after he received this news. By formalizing their status as an established couple in the eyes of church authorities, Baranov removed any taint of illegitimacy on the reputation of his young children.

* * *

Both at Pavlovskaia and later at New Archangel, various official visitors commented on the settled domesticity of the Baranov home and the tidy arrangements they found there under the management of Anna Grigor'evna. Lieutenant Gavriil Davydov, a young navy officer employed by the RAC, recorded his impressions of the Baranov household when he arrived at Pavlovskaia aboard the company ship *Sv. Elizaveta* in November 1802. As soon as the vessel dropped anchor, despite foul weather a three-man baidarka came alongside, bringing the ship's officers a gift from Baranov: "a fish-and-goose pie," which, Davydov wrote, "we were very glad to receive."[17] Once their ship was securely moored, Baranov came aboard to greet them and offer his hospitality. He and the officers set off for the chief manager's home. "There we found everything simple and clean," Davydov recorded. Since a British merchant ship had recently called at Pavlovskaia, "Baranov had bought from them many goods and household utensils, and consequently gave [Davydov and his men] a very decent meal, at least for local conditions."[18]

The following May, shortly before sailing back to Okhotsk, the lieutenant reported another social visit with Aleksandr Andreevich, whom he had come to know quite well. "Today," May 24, "was Trinity Day," Davydov wrote in his journal, "and in the morning we went to church. We spent the evening with Baranov. We sang, danced, and were very merry and eventually dispersed at two in the morning."[19] We can only sympathize with Anna Grigor'evna and the servants who were obliged to clean up after these roistering men finally called it a night.

A few observers left records of the impression made on them by Aleksandr Andreevich during the period of his conflict with the Sitka Tlingits. Lieutenant Davydov set down his vivid first view of the general manager. Physically, the tall young officer wrote, "Baranov is shorter than average, fair-haired, well-built with very prominent features erased neither by his labors nor by his age, although he is now fifty-six." His history and his character gained Davydov's admiration. "He had already been in America for twelve years, in the company of wild and primitive people, surrounded by constant danger . . . [and] struggling with the deep-rooted depravity of the Russians living here, working constantly, in need of many things, often hungry, and at the same time almost without anyone who could work with him with the same energy." All his labors, the obstacles, sorrows, deprivations, and failures, judged Davydov, "had not blighted the spirit of this rare man, although it had naturally an influence on him and thereby made him rather somber in manner." He was not very talkative "and seemed like a dry stick until you come to know him, but on the other hand he always explained matters with enthusiasm, especially when he knows his subject well." After Baranov's recent problems with Sub-Lieutenant Talin, we should not be surprised at his initial reserve when welcoming this new batch of aristocratic naval officers. Once they became well acquainted, however, Davydov observed that "he will do anything for his friends and he likes to entertain foreigners with all that he has and is always ready to help the poor."

According to the young officer, Baranov's qualities were widely esteemed both by the Russian promyshlenniks and by American Natives. "He is not interested merely in amassing wealth at other people's expense, but will willingly share his own just salary with absent friends who are in need," Davydov declared. "His firmness of spirit and constant presence of mind are the reason why the savages respect him without loving him, and the fame of the name of Baranov resounds amongst all the savage peoples who live on the northwest coast of America, even as far [south] as the Strait of Juan de Fuca. Even those Natives who live in isolated areas," according to Davydov, "sometimes come to see him and are amazed that such wide-ranging schemes can be undertaken by such a small man."[20]

It is from Lieutenant Davydov that we learn about Sargach, a large dog that protected the chief manager's Pavlovskaia home when he was away. The Alutiiqs referred to this animal as Baranov's son, Davydov wrote, because they could see how devoted the dog was to his master. An elderly Chugach man, following Alutiiq custom between mutual friends, asked Baranov's permission to exchange names with Sargach. "And so the old man began to call himself Sargach and brought his friend fish and other things to eat, and tried to please him in every way." One day, however, he came visiting while Baranov was absent. "The dog flew at him, knocked him down, and stood growling at his throat, in spite of all the man's protestations of tender friendship." Some promyshlenniks nearby came to the old man's rescue. Even then, the lieutenant related, the feelings of the Chugach did not change, "and he was very upset when the dog died."[21] This story tells us something about the precautions Aleksandr Andreevich took to assure the safety of his family and his American household. It illustrates as well the unusual informality of his dealings with local people on occasion.

Lieutenant Davydov in his account of the *Sv. Elizaveta*'s six-month layover at Pavlovskaia emphasized Baranov's pleasure and relief at the ship's unexpected arrival. Built at Okhotsk for the RAC, the vessel carried a large cargo of supplies and a healthy crew, two things that reassured the Russian residents at Pavlovskaia that they were not completely forgotten in their homeland. No other ship had come from Okhotsk during the previous five years except the galiot *Aleksandr Nevskii*, which appeared a month before the *Elizaveta*'s arrival. This earlier ship, having wintered on Atkha Island, reached Pavlovskaia with an empty hold. It was manned by only a few feeble or sick men, having lost fifteen crewmen to epidemic disease during the voyage.[22] Since the Kodiak Alutiiqs had seen no other company ships from Okhotsk for five years, according to Davydov, they were starting to believe fanciful stories that all the Russians in Russia has already come to them, and so they would only have to kill those who remained in Alaska "to free themselves forever from their authority."[23]

Some of the young Alutiiq men who were taken to Siberia by Shelikhov had returned with reports about the huge numbers and great wealth of the Russians living across the sea. But, Davydov learned, these youngsters were not believed. Older Alutiiqs scoffed at such tales and said the travelers had been shown things that could not and did not actually exist. Given the unsettled state of relations with the mainland Native peoples from Iliamna and Kenai southward to Yakutat and Sitka Sound, it might seem quite plausible that Russia's capacity to maintain its outposts in North America had been exhausted.

The coming of the *Elizaveta* proved otherwise. As Davydov explained, "Our arrival in America was of the greatest importance to the company's affairs," the more so "since there were sixteen thousand sea otter pelts and other furs lying in the company storehouses on Kad'iak."[24] Baranov had been unwilling to entrust such a rich cargo to some inexperienced skipper to take to Okhotsk, but he feared meanwhile that his wealth of peltry might fall into the hands of "some sea pirate" if left longer at Pavlovskaia. Hence Aleksandr Andreevich was very glad for the opportunity to ship this cargo—with an estimated value of at least 1.2 million rubles—aboard the *Elizaveta* with these experienced officers.[25]

Two years after the *Elizaveta*'s departure, in late May 1805 the RAC ship *Maria* arrived at Pavlovskaia Harbor with Dr. Georg H. von Langsdorff accompanying Crown plenipotentiary Nikolai Rezanov. A distinguished medical doctor, naturalist, and ethnographer from a German baronial family, Langsdorff was traveling as Rezanov's personal physician.[26] Since both men were anxious to meet Baranov, in August they sailed for Sitka Sound, where the chief manager was then directing construction of a new RAC settlement. Subsequently, Langsdorff recorded his appreciative appraisal of Aleksandr Andreevich, colored somewhat by the doctor's upper-class bias. "He has a most extensive local knowledge of the countries under his jurisdiction," the German savant wrote, "and since the greater part of the Promuschleniks and inferior officers of the settlements are Siberian criminals, malefactors, and adventurers of differing kinds, not a little credit is due to his vigilance and address, that he has been able in any degree to put a bridle upon them."

Langsdorff admired Baranov's ceaseless energy in traveling from place to place, "always carrying on some project for the general good." He sympathized with Aleksandr Andreevich's enforced isolation and the adjustments in lifestyle forced on him. "For several years," he wrote, Baranov had "remained in this miserable part of the world almost entirely neglected, without receiving any support or intelligence from the head-quarters of the Company in Russia. Pursued by hunger and thirst, he and his companions had sometimes no other resource left but to live like the Aleutians on sea-dogs [seals], fish, and muscles [mussels], yet in the midst of this wretchedness he built boats, erected new settlements, enlarged the fur-trade, and extended the territories and domains of the Company." Not a young man when he came to America, Langsdorff said, Baranov "continued in this sort of banishment" for many years. "Now, as a most upright and faithful steward grown grey in the service of the Company, to whose advantage his health and the best years of his life have been sacrificed," in Langsdorff's estimation, "he has a truly just and urgent claim upon their [the company directors'] gratitude to afford him the means of a tranquil and happy retirement."[27]

The German physician made no effort to disguise his class prejudices even while excusing Aleksandr Andreevich for certain uncouth, rough ways. "His long abode among so rude and uncivilized a race," Langsdorff argued, "his daily intercourse with a dissolute and licentious rabble, with rogues and cheats, and the necessity he has been under of having recourse to severity and harshness in order to insure his own safety and that of the Company, have indeed somewhat blunted his finer feelings, and rendered him less alive than he probably once was to the voice of compassion and philanthropy."

The problems he observed in Russian America, Langsdorff declared in his pedantic style, were the consequence of circumstances, not of any failure by the chief manager: "The weakness of his declining years, the shameful conduct of the people under him, the great extent of the colonies under his care, and their distance from the fountain-head in the mother-country, the want of regular institutions and a regular administration of justice, these are, according to my opinion, the principal causes of a great many abuses, which even the most upright man cannot wholly counteract."[28] Baranov's only real fault, suggested Langsdorff, might be too great a partiality toward men in whom he had confidence and who had aided him—surely a remark aimed at Ivan Kuskov and Ivan Banner. Aleksandr Andreevich's "goodness and forbearance," Langsdorff wrote, were frequently abused, with results harmful to the interests of the RAC and prejudicial both to the Alutiiqs and to the Russian promyshlenniks.

The New England merchant captain John D'Wolf arrived at Sitka Sound with his ship *Juno*, heavily laden with trade goods and scarce provisions, at nearly the same time as Rezanov and Langsdorff. D'Wolf negotiated an agreement with Rezanov and Baranov to trade the *Juno* and the goods in its well-filled hold for sea otter pelts, accepting as well cash drafts payable in St. Petersburg and a smaller ship to take his first mate and ship's clerk along with his furs to Canton.[29] While waiting for the sailing season to reopen the following spring, Captain D'Wolf spent the winter in New Archangel sharing living quarters with Langsdorff and venturing out on short local excursions with his new friend.

Concerning Baranov, D'Wolf's brief observations largely echoed the views of the German physician. Because of the kind treatment he had received from Aleksandr Andreevich, he wrote, "I was indicted to form a very favorable opinion of him." During the years he had spent in North America, the New Englander said, Baranov had been "excluded, as it were, from all civilized society, except that of a few of his fellow adventurers." Overall, "he possessed a strong mind, easy manners and deportment, and was apparently well fitted for the place he filled." Moreover, added D'Wolf, "he commanded the greatest respect from the Indians, who regarded him with mingled feelings of love and fear."[30]

Rezanov had a great deal more to say about Aleksandr Andreevich, and what he stated could not be regarded as idle observations. His words would have great weight within decision-making circles at St. Petersburg. When he reached North America, Rezanov had been predisposed to recommend Baranov's immediate replacement by a younger, more energetic man. During their months together, watching the chief manager in action and sharing long discussions with him, he changed his mind.

In the conclusion to a detailed 1805 report about his inspection of Russian America, Rezanov wrote that he wanted the St. Petersburg authorities to understand that he was not prejudiced in favor of the chief manager. Yet, like many others new to the local scene, Rezanov had gained greater and greater appreciation for the strength, abilities, and good sense of Aleksandr Baranov the longer he was in his company. Any idea that Baranov could soon be allowed to end his service with the RAC should be discarded, Rezanov informed the company directors: "I will tell you that the loss of this man will be not only a loss to the company but to all our Country, and you may believe me . . . that with the loss of Baranov you will be deprived of the means of executing all the vast projects toward which his labors have blazed a wide trail."[31]

After reviewing a list of the chief manager's most praiseworthy deeds, Rezanov drove home the point that Aleksandr Andreevich should be retained, adequately reinforced in his authority, and protected from insults as he went about his duties. Despite a few faults shown by Baranov, his removal now would be very painful to the company "because not only does he have a rare knowledge of the Country, but there is no other man who can get along with the hunters as well as he can." Perhaps when Russia's overseas territories had been reorganized (along lines Rezanov was advocating), then "Mr. Baranov, not belittling his great virtues and achievements, will hardly be sufficient to govern the country." His great age and his "exhausted strength" might make him unequal to such activity, Rezanov supposed. With Aleksandr Andreevich having been cast by fate in "a mass of violent spirits," to win their love and obedience, "he was forced to feign their way of life to some degree," adopting behavior "alien to his mind and heart."

If the RAC were to have a major reorganization, Rezanov said, new times would require new men, cut from different cloth than the aging merchant's son raised in Russia's provincial northland. Meanwhile, despite his age and physical infirmities, Aleksandr Baranov remained the indispensable leader for Russian America. Though very often desperate from grief and sickness, "he is in his element when he is seeking glory and fame." His success is his sole recompense, Rezanov concluded, "but nevertheless his countrymen must be just to him, so as not to be criticized by later generations."[32]

The news he had received by way of Unalaska in March 1804—the news that Emperor Aleksandr I had conferred upon him the rank of collegiate counselor—arrived at an extremely difficult time for Aleksandr Andreevich. He had been brought low by the destruction of a first RAC post on Sitka Sound, Fort Mikhailovskii, two years earlier, with almost all the garrison killed. He was obsessed with the need to reestablish the Russian position and avenge the death of his men at the hands of the Sitka Tlingits. Yet due to the company's long neglect, he lacked the resources of military manpower, armaments, supplies, and ships to assure victory. His situation was precarious, and his personal morale nearing an all-time low. Then he received this totally astounding gift of noble status from the monarch. Baranov shed tears of gratitude, according to the account in Khlebnikov's biography, and "he cried with fervor, 'I have been rewarded, but Sitka is lost! No! I cannot live! I shall go—and I shall either die or make it another of the territories of my most August Patron!'"[33]

Though we lack independent eyewitness verification for this scene, the account is plausible in portraying the dramatic fervor that Aleksandr Andreevich brought to his most emotional moments. And it is more than plausible in capturing his determination to regain RAC control over the homeland of the Sitka Tlingits, no matter how poor the odds. Fortunately for the future of the RAC—and unfortunately for the continued security of the Sitka Tlingits—timely reinforcement from northern Russia then altered the balance of power to favor the imperial and commercial ambitions represented in America by Aleksandr Baranov and his men.

IX

THE SITKA SOUND WAR

In the ongoing quest for sea otters, Baranov led his Russian promyshlen-
niks and Alutiiq hunters into the Tlingit homelands around Sitka Sound.
After enduring a series of insults, aggrieved Sitka Tlingits and their allies
destroyed a poorly defended Russian post, Fort Mikhailovskii, in 1802. Two
years later a visiting Russian naval ship backed Aleksandr Andreevich and
his men in their attack on a Sitka Tlingit stronghold. The battle ended
with the Natives' stealthy retreat but no surrender. Baranov directed con-
struction nearby of the settlement named New Archangel. Even though this
place later became the RAC's American headquarters, the Sitka Tlingits
maintained their independence and asserted their enduring right to the
rest of their homeland.

PURSUING GRIGORII SHELIKHOV'S AMBITION TO EXTEND A RUS-
sian presence southward along the Alaskan coastline, Baranov by 1799
had fastened his eyes on Sitka Sound. Here, he believed, he and his men
should build a fort as a base for their maritime hunting operations. After
Shelikhov's death, his widow, Natalia Shelikhova, strongly supported this
plan. Like Madam Shelikhova, the chief manager invoked the cause of imperial glory and the honor of the Crown to justify this effort to advance the
borders of Russian America. But in truth it was a commercial imperative
alone that drove his hazardous campaign to invade and occupy portions of
the Tlingit homeland.

Aleksandr Baranov was a trader, not a fighter. He hoped to gain access to
southeastern Alaska's peltry by peaceful means, relying on diplomacy with
gifts, trade, and an attitude he termed politeness. But he had nothing to offer
the Tlingits in trade that they could not get more readily at lower cost from
visiting Yankee and British merchant captains. Because of the Northeastern

Company's disarray after Shelikhov's death and the tightfisted penury of the company's directors, Russian America suffered a chronic shortage of personnel, ships, guns, supplies, and trade goods. This situation did not soon improve following the formation of the Russian-American Company. Aleksandr Andreevich was left to improvise a program of commercial expansion as best he could, isolated in Alaska with none of the resources of imperial power at his command. Rather than trade with the Tlingits, he felt himself forced to undertake the invasion of Tlingit waters with his large Russian and Alutiiq hunting expeditions, despite the dangers.

In 1793 and 1794 the mainland excursions led by Egor Purtov had made the Russians and their Alutiiq allies a threatening presence among the Yakutat Tlingits. During a 1794 conference between Purtov and local Tlingit headmen, Lieutenant Peter Puget observed that the Russians really had nothing to exchange with the Tlingits for sea otter pelts. An outbreak of hostilities between Purtov's hunters and the Yakutat Tlingits led to tense negotiations over captives taken on both sides. This affair ended with a mutual exchange of hostages on terms of wary mistrust.[1]

Farther south, the situation was similar. Russian promyshlenniks and Alutiiq partovshchiks in 1795 began extending their activities around the Alexander Archipelago and into Sitka Sound. Here too Baranov's men were a sizable alien force. Unable to compete for the Tlingit trade, Baranov and his promyshlenniks depended on their Alutiiq hunting crews to raid all the sea otter herds they could find. The Tlingits were thus made marginal to the Russian-Alutiiq alliances' predatory assault on the sea otter population in Tlingit waters, despite Native protests. This conduct struck the Tlingits as virtually a form of piracy, damaging to their trading economy and inflicting a grievous insult to their honor.

As the Russians saw it, Baranov's men had no real alternative to this freebooting style of expansion. Once the hunting around Kodiak Island and Kenai Bay had become so poor that "it did not amount to anything," Aleksandr Andreevich later wrote, "the benevolent Creator led us against our expectations to find other places that are just as good if not better than the old ones."[2] To the Russian mind in the age of Baranov, exemplified by the chief manager, free, independent Native peoples like the Tlingits, beyond the borders of European dominion, were backward barbarians, possessing no rights and entitled to no consideration until they submitted to the absolute authority of Russia's imperial monarch. And God, the benevolent Creator, they might claim, was blessing the RAC's colonial ambitions.

In August 1795, while the main Russian and Alutiiq hunting expedition carried out an exploratory probe along the shores of the Alexander Archipelago, Baranov spent a few weeks at Yakutat in search of the best site for the New Russia agricultural colony. He left there some thirty men, exile settlers and hunters, under the nominal supervision of the ineffectual Ivan Polomoshnoi. The following year Aleksandr Andreevich returned with the remaining exile families and all the supplies, equipment, and livestock meant to make their colony self-sustaining. The subsequent failure of this project owed little to Tlingit opposition. It was enough for the Yakutat Natives simply to stand back at a safe distance while the quarrelsome, faction-ridden, disease-weakened Russians proved less and less able to survive amid the bounteous resources of the Tlingits' watery homeland.

In the fall of 1796, after supervising construction at New Russia, Baranov for the first time took the *Olga* and its small crew farther southeast along the coast, where company hunters led by Purtov had already carried out one successful hunting expedition. Despite heavy storms, Aleksandr Andreevich probed Cross Sound, Lynn Canal, and the shores of Sitka (now Baranov) Island before returning to Pavlovskaia in late October. Meanwhile, James Shields surveyed the Alexander Archipelago from the deck of his newly constructed small ship, the *Del'fin*.[3]

These voyages brought the Russians for the first time in direct contact with the Sitka Tlingits headed by the Kiks.ádi ḵwáan, a Raven moiety clan identified with the Sitka area. Though bad weather prevented a landing on Sitka Island, Shields did conduct some trade. In Cross Sound he heard Tlingit complaints about the ruthless behavior of Captain Henry Barber, a grasping English merchant trader who then commanded the heavily armed brig *Arthur*. Barber had taken one Tlingit headman captive and held him hostage until his people delivered enough peltry to buy his freedom. Such tactics were typical for Captain Barber, who would not hesitate to play off the Tlingits and the Russians against one another.

*   *   *

During the next two years Baranov's hip and leg injuries kept him from revisiting the coastal region south of Chugach Bay. He returned in the summer of 1799, sailing first to New Russia and then continuing to Sitka Sound, where he meant to build a fort despite a climate even rainier than at Pavlovskaia. He had sent ahead a flotilla of 350 baidarkas and two ships: the *Orel* under Lieutenant Talin and the *Ekaterina* commanded by the German captain Podgash, which carried tools and building materials. Following a hot-tempered exchange with Talin, who soon departed northward on his ship's ill-fated final voyage, he began negotiations with the Kiks.ádi headmen for the right to locate a post somewhere on the sound.

He coveted the location of the main Kiks.ádi village on Sitka Sound, known as Noow Tlein ("Big Fort") to the Tlingits and now called Castle Hill, but there was no way he might be allowed to displace the resident community there. What he settled for was an uninhabited site called Gajaa Héen by the Tlingits, now known as Old Sitka, seven miles north along Starrigavan Bay near the modern Sitka ferry terminal. First scouted by Vasilii Medvednikov, this location had a creek and calm harbor, though it was rather too hilly in Baranov's estimation.

Securing the right to occupy this site was a true negotiation. Aleksandr Andreevich needed to win the favor of the Kiks.ádi leaders, and he had very few resources for bargaining. As he told Emel'ian Larionov the following summer, "Being without company goods, I gave most of my clothes to the natives of Sitka as presents, seeking their friendship when looking for a place for a settlement."[4] He may have also assured the Sitka people that the Russians and Alutiiqs would be on their best behavior, as he had done earlier with the Yakutat Tlingits. In any case, on Starrigavan Bay surrounded by the well-armed Native peoples, Baranov fully realized that he and his men were in a vulnerable, precarious position; their security depended on maintaining the goodwill of the Kiks.ádis and other neighboring Tlingit clans.

Aleksandr Andreevich named this post New Archangel, but because Saint Michael was its patron saint, it came generally to be known as Fort Mikhailovskii. Construction began in mid-July, with help from the crew of the *Ekaterina*. After the year's main baidarka expedition departed, some fifty Alutiiqs remained there, mainly to fish and hunt. The first building constructed was a large log shed to store supplies and foodstuffs. Next was a small temporary bathhouse. Giving up his ripped tent, Baranov lived in this log shack during the rainiest months, "suffering from the effects of smoke and a leaky roof," with his bed often standing in water. The largest project was a two-story barracks with a cellar for storing provisions.

Completion of the manager's house in mid-February at last allowed Aleksandr Andreevich a dry roof over his head. The men also built an eight-cornered kazhim enclosure for the Alutiiq workers, who put up their huts or yurts within. Other structures included a temporary blacksmith shop, a kitchen, and a cattle shed, as well as a section of palisaded wall for the fort with a sentry box.

The work went slowly, since usually only twenty men at a time were felling trees and putting up these buildings while ten or more stood guard. The workforce included six Alutiiq women, who kept busy cleaning fish, repairing baidarkas and baidaras, and making waterproof hooded kamleikas for both the Russians and the Alutiiqs. During the winter, Baranov reported, "with God's help, about 50 sea lions and about 150 seals were shot." Even so, there was a food shortage in November and December, but by March food was plentiful due to the seasonal arrival of halibut and bountiful herring schools in the bay.[5]

* * *

At Fort Mikhailovskii, Baranov gained a new appreciation for the danger caused by British and American shipmasters dealing in arms with the Northwest Coast Natives. Two merchant trading vessels had been in the area shortly before his arrival, another arrived in July, one more came the following February, and a month later two more appeared on the scene. Three of these ships stopped at the Kiks.ádi Noow Tlein settlement to trade. There, "before our very eyes," the chief manager wrote, "they bartered about two thousand sea otters."

The prices these seagoing merchants paid, competing with one another as well as the Russians, he thought quite high. Always a businessman, he quoted the value of sea otter pelts in barter for heavy woolen cloth, flannel-lined blanket coats, knives, scissors, beads, and other items. For one skin, Baranov said, the foreign traders would give one gun—a muzzle-loading musket—with ten cartridges, powder, and lead. With prices this favorable for the Tlingits, we can better understand their concern about the hundreds of animals being taken from their waters cost-free by Baranov's hunters.

After visiting some of these foreign ships, Aleksandr Andreevich reported that the British were complaining about the Boston men who were forcing them out of this trade. The Americans, he explained, were very familiar with the Natives, since the same ships appeared every two or three years. About six ships came from New England every year because of the profits they could make in a triangular trade, selling sea otter pelts in Canton in exchange for tea, silks, and other cloth, which were in great demand in the American republic. Even if the price for skins in China was not high, only twenty or thirty dollars each, Baranov reasoned, "they get big profits in selling goods brought home from Canton that are readily sold for cash."[6]

Baranov had vigorous discussions with the Yankee shipmasters about their gun trade. It was dangerous to the traders themselves, he argued, but still more harmful to the Russians. He told the traders about the peace treaties between the Russian court and the government of the infant United States that should have halted these incursions, but they paid no attention. "We are traders," he quoted them as saying, "sailing more than fifteen thousand nautical miles in search of profits, and no one has told us that such trading is prohibited."[7] Despite Baranov's objections, they carried on their trade openly, not only for muskets and pistols but for heavier armaments. While visiting nearby Tlingit villages, Baranov related, he saw four one-pounder cannons, and he heard that there were more of larger size in other settlements.

Aleksandr Andreevich also reported that the Americans were polite. They invited the Russians to visit them and often came to visit Fort Mikhailovskii in return. Looking over the Russians' construction, they said that within two years' time it would be impossible for them to do anything more here. "They wondered at our fortitude and endurance," Baranov added, "and above all at our ability to exist on local food, and to drink only water." But one may wonder whether any of these visitors might have encouraged their Native clients to force the RAC people to leave. Later evidence strongly suggested such was the case.

Perhaps such encouragement was not really necessary. Baranov reported that he and his men had to endure many insults from Tlingits living in the Sitka vicinity "and still more from rascals who were from distant villages." These people "did not expect us to settle permanently." Three times during the winter the Russians discovered that some groups visiting inside their camp, coming to dance in the new barracks building, had brought spears and daggers with them. "But we were always on guard," Baranov said, "and when we saw they had spears, sent them out of our settlement in shame."

They had another nasty challenge during Easter week. Baranov sent an Alutiiq female interpreter to a nearby Kiks.ádi village to invite its residents to come see a Russian parade in honor of the emperor. The woman was beaten and robbed by visitors to the village. Although the local Tlingits did visit Fort Mikhailovskii for the ceremony, Baranov decided that a bold deed was needed "to show them we were not afraid of them." Three days later he took twenty-one men and, as he related, "went bravely with two cannons into the middle of their village, where we were surrounded by more than 300 of them, armed with guns. We marched straight to the dwelling where we had been told the offenders were waiting for us, and ready to offer armed resistance." Baranov's men fired two volleys as a demonstration of their armed power. At that, "all but a few old men took fright, ran away and hid."

These "Sitka braves," according to Baranov, "had boasted that they were ready for a fight but in reality they became afraid and finally tried to get rid of us by offering us food and a few presents." As for himself, he wrote, "I was very glad that the incident was liquidated without bloodshed, offering them no reason for revenge, which is in their nature." On Sitka Sound, the chief manager concluded, "our strength is very inadequate and this makes us use diplomacy with them and be lenient."[8] The brazen action of Baranov and his men that day was grand imperialist theater. But if he truly believed the Kiks.ádis would pass off this incident just because there was no bloodshed, Aleksandr Andreevich totally failed to understand the power of insult among the Tlingits.

A few days after this Easter week episode, Baranov made ready to return to Pavlovskaia. He was leaving Fort Mikhailovskii in charge of Vasilii Medvednikov, previously the leader of the expedition that had established New Russia. For Medvednikov's guidance Baranov wrote a long letter of instruction. Much of the document concerned building projects, feeding his workers, and personnel management. Yet the central theme was the settlement's security. There appeared to be no immediate dangers, he said, nor should any develop unless the Tlingits were provoked by the Russians or the Alutiiq hunters. "Provocation must be avoided," he warned, "especially in view of our weakness, and we must patiently bear the minor annoyances caused by the roughness and ignorance of [the Tlingit] people. The Russians and the [Alutiiq hunters] . . . must often be reminded of this so that they keep their coarse prejudices in check as much as possible and remember the consequences which often followed minor incidents during the winter."[9]

These cautions reflected Aleksandr Andreevich's analysis of the root cause for Russian difficulties with the Sitka Tlingits: "We must hope that time will improve their opinion of us and order will tame them," he told Medvednikov, "because these people being used to natural freedom since the creation of the world have never thought of, nor know how to submit to the will of others and can bear no slight without retaliation. They are either vindictive by nature or because of the barbaric customs inculcated into them, as I had every chance to learn during the past winter." It was important for Medvednikov to keep this in mind, he wrote, "as well as their uncontrollable greed, covetousness, and ingratitude."

In other words, according to the chief manager's reasoning, the Tlingits were inherently guilty for refusing to accept Russian domination. They lacked a civilized understanding, Baranov might say, of their duty to serve the Russians and the interests of the RAC. Yet he also urged Medvednikov to show special favors to certain eminent Tlingits whom he named, particularly among the Kiks.ádis, "considering that our occupation of their lands deserves more than a little gratitude on our side."[10] It was a logically conflicted position, balancing on a thin line between Baranov's imperialist assumptions and his realistic assessment of RAC weakness in the Tlingits' home territory.

Unfortunately for Baranov's hopes, Medvednikov did not fully heed the chief manager's warnings, nor did he exercise sternly enough his authority to police the conduct of the Russians and Alutiiqs at Fort Mikhailovskii. For over two years, while his workforce remained fairly large, all seemed safe. Then he let lapse his concern for security. On at least three occasions during the spring of 1802 he received warnings that trouble might be expected, apparently relayed by Tlingit women living in the settlement with Russian mates. But he took no precautions. Instead, he let about half his local Alutiiq hunting crew leave the post, joining a large expedition heading north toward Yakutat Bay under Ivan Kuskov's supervision. This proved to be a fatal mistake.

* * *

Throughout Russian America, Sunday was a holiday. One Sunday in mid-June 1802, the people at Fort Mikhailovskii were spending their time in various casual tasks. By midday four men were out hunting sea lions for meat and hides. Two were fishing from baidarkas nearby. Alutiiq marksman Vasilei Kochesov and a companion had taken a large baidarka to hunt for deer or other game along the shoreline close to the fort. During the early afternoon promyshlennik Abram Plotnikov was at the creek caring for calves from the post's small cattle herd. One of his comrades was at the fish traps. Elsewhere within the compound, some twenty Russians and maybe as many as forty Alutiiqs, including women and children, were tending to their own interests, none of them with any unusual sense of concern for their safety. Manager Medvednikov, despite the weakness of his forces, had posted no guards outside the gates or in the gun towers atop the barracks. Just outside the gate, the post's blacksmith might have served as a sentinel, but he was instead preoccupied with pounding out knives, little aware of his surroundings.

There is where the attack began. From the forest rushed a group of Tlingits led by K'alyáan (Kotlian), military leader of the Sitka Kiks.ádis. All were clad in armor and protective wooden headpieces—K'alyáan wearing a raven helmet—and armed with knives, guns, and spears. They overwhelmed the blacksmith before he could sound an alarm. K'alyáan seized the blacksmith's heavy hammer, a war trophy that would become his weapon of choice. Perhaps earlier than planned, a flotilla of large Tlingit dugout canoes appeared at the shorefront. The paddlers jumped ashore and joined scores of attackers running from the woods to break through the gate and begin a slaughter of everyone inside the fort. The attackers took directions from the strong voice of K'alyáan's uncle, Shk'awulyeil (Skautlet or Mikhail), headman of the Sitka Kiks.ádis, who commanded the attacking force from his vista atop a nearby hill.

Caught totally by surprise, many men and women inside the fort rushed into the barracks structure and locked themselves behind its stout log walls. Here, surrounded on all sides by an overwhelming number of enemies, they made a desperate stand. Medvednikov and perhaps six other Russians held the upper floor, while evidently twice as many remained below, shooting back at their besiegers.

The day before the attack two older Tlingit men, both honored warriors in their early years, had gathered together great bundles of pitch-filled wooden splints, veritable torches, which they carried into the Russian fort on their backs. Younger warriors tried to discourage these elders, saying they were too old to fight. "No," they replied, "we have our way of fighting." Taking careful aim, the old men threw rocks at the barracks' upper-story windows, breaking them open. Then they lit their pitch torches and lobbed them through the windows, setting all ablaze. With remaining pieces of the pitch wood they set fire to the stockade itself. Younger attackers began torching the other buildings—storage sheds, the cattle barn, the cook shed, the bathhouse, the empty sentry box—along with a nearly completed ship under construction on the beach.

At the barracks stronghold, as flames began to envelope the second story, Tlingit fighters broke the heavy shutters over the bottom-story windows and started firing their guns through these openings. They also smashed down the outside door leading from the back porch, hacked a small hole through the inside main door, and shot directly into the crowded room, killing one Russian and wounding three others. One of the wounded defenders began firing a cannon at the door, blowing away a few attackers and keeping the rest from rushing inside. When cannon shot began to run short, his companions started cutting a hole through the ceiling to reach ammunition stored above. But as soon as they broke through, a sheet of flame swept from the second floor into the lower story. As the fire spread, the Alutiiq women ran down into the cellar to hide. Soon the attackers made their way into the barracks, killed the remaining defenders on the first floor, then pulled the women from the cellar and forced them into the street. There they were divided up among their captors and taken to nearby canoes for transport to the Tlingit villages.

Outside the fort as the attack began, Abram Plotnikov fled into the forest, where he managed to hide in a hollow tree. From there Plotnikov witnessed the burning of the barracks. As the flames rose, he saw two comrades jump from the second story to the ground below. They were immediately swarmed by the Tlingits and their bodies hoisted on spears. One was beheaded at once, a fate that befell almost every Russian and Alutiiq male casualty before the carnage ended. As the whole barracks structure began to go up in flames, the attackers looted the stored bales of sea otter skins and company supplies, throwing these goods from the second story balcony and loading them into their canoes on the beach.

The captive women in the canoes also saw the battle's end. On the street, said one of these witnesses, the Tlingits "were stabbing everybody, and burning the buildings. They divided the company's supplies, furs, and us girls among themselves and so it was all over."[11]

Like Plotnikov, a few other Russians and Alutiiqs were able to evade capture and death amid the confusion of battle. They too hid in the forest and waited in hope of rescue. Plotnikov stayed close to the ashes of Fort Mikhailovskii, returning secretly every night to "weep over the fate of my comrades who had perished there." He remained in this pitiful condition for eight days, he later said, wandering about without food until a foreign ship appeared and sent an armed whaleboat to his rescue.[12]

Less fortunate was the Alutiiq marksman Vasilei Kochesov, known to the Tlingits as Gidák, and his companion. Returning from their hunt late in the day, they saw the burning ruins and fled in their baidarka from Tlingits chasing them with large dugout canoes. They paddled first toward the open sea, but a storm on the ocean forced them to turn back. The Tlingits were right behind them, according to a Kiks.ádi oral historian, but did not paddle very fast to catch up. "They want[ed] them to feel the sting of being chased and disliked until they are worn out."[13] At length the two Alutiiqs came ashore at the base of a small cliff that protected them from Tlingit gunfire. Kochesov's accurate fire was deadly to at least one overly brave pursuer. Yet soon his gunpowder supply ran out, making it possible for the Tlingits to rush his position and take the two men prisoner. Carried to a Kiks.ádi village on a small island close to Fort Mikhailovskii, they were made to suffer agonizing torture before death liberated them.[14]

* * *

At Pavlovskaia, Baranov had been in an elated mood during the early summer of 1802. In May his old friend Ivan Banner arrived by baidarka from Unalaska, bringing him the first news about the formation of the Russian-American Company and the accession of Emperor Aleksandr I, and putting into his hands the gold medal and band of Vladimir granted him by the late emperor Paul I. This euphoria came to a crashing halt on July 24. Captain Henry Barber came into the harbor with his heavily armed merchant ship the *Unicorn*, bringing a report about the disaster at Fort Mikhailovskii.

Aboard the *Unicorn* were twenty-eight survivors of the Tlingit attack gathered by Barber: three Russians, five Alutiiq men, seventeen women, and three children.[15] Some of these people his men had found hiding from the Tlingits. Others had been rescued by different trading ships, whose captains passed them on to Barber for delivery at Pavlovskaia. Still others Barber had forced the Kiks.ádis to hand over by his well-practiced strong-arm tactics. He had lured both K'alyáan and Shk'awulyeil onto his ship, seized them, put them in irons, and refused to free them until they delivered the captive women to him. As part of his ransom scheme, he had also taken from the Kiks.ádis many bales of sea otter pelts plundered from the burning Russian barracks, although he did not bother to inform Aleksandr Andreevich about this detail.[16]

In return for the survivors aboard the *Unicorn*, Barber demanded from Baranov fifty thousand rubles in cash or sea otter pelts, payable at his own valuation. The situation was dangerous. With twenty guns, Barber's ship was better armed than the company headquarters, and his crew perhaps more able fighters than Baranov's promyshlenniks and Alutiiq hunters. In the company warehouses at Pavlovskaia was a great treasure in sea otter peltry and seal skins, stored to await safe delivery to Okhotsk. Yet, despite the risk of open hostilities, the chief manager refused to submit to Captain Barber's extortion, particularly after he learned from some of the refugees the true story about their rescue.

The captain's demands and his "warlike threats," according to Baranov's first biographer, put the chief manager "in a tight corner." Yet he rejected Barber's "shameless demands" and took what defensive measures he could to fend off an attack. At length the two men agreed on a price of ten thousand rubles in furs, paid mostly in furs other than sea otter: fox, river beavers, and beaver tails. Only after Aleksandr Andreevich delivered this ransom did the English captain send his prisoners ashore.

Baranov then took the opportunity to barter with Barber for another twenty-seven thousand rubles worth of goods, including several cannons, fifty rifles, and a large supply of ammunition. It was far better for the RAC forces to have these armaments, he must have realized, than for them to come into Tlingit hands. The two men would continue to deal with one another on friendly terms in the future, although distant RAC officials long harbored a suspicion that the English mariner had been complicit in urging the Tlingits to expel the Russians from Sitka Sound.[17] While this suspicion was apparently baseless, one Yankee captain—William Cunningham of the *Globe*—had encouraged the southern Tlingits to join with the Kiks.ádis in ousting the Russians and their Alutiiq hunters.

* * *

The Tlingits' 1802 destruction of Fort Mikhailovskii and the massacre of most of its people was a devastating blow to Aleksandr Baranov's ambition to establish RAC suzerainty over southeastern Alaska. More than two hundred years later many details of the attack remain uncertain, yet the central story is fairly clear.[18] The attacking force, led by the Sitka Kiks.ádis, numbered at least six hundred and maybe far more. Later rumors spoke of a meeting at Angoon of various clans from Yakutat, Dry Bay, Angoon, and Kake and possibly Haida villages as well. Though the truth of these stories cannot now be verified, Baranov was convinced that these peoples had come together in a coalition intended to drive the Russians from their homeland.[19]

The defenders were no more than two dozen Russians and perhaps four times that many Alutiiqs, including women and children. Involved on both sides were a few American sailors who had deserted their ships, maybe as many as five working for the RAC and seven living with the Tlingits. In addition to the twenty-eight survivors who Baranov ransomed from Captain Barber, fragmentary data indicate that a significant number of Alutiiq women and children remained in Tlingit hands until 1804, when they were returned to the Russians as part of truce negotiations that year. Two young Aleut creoles, according to Kiks.ádi sources, lived with the Tlingits the rest of their lives.

Calculation of the numbers engaged in this battle and the numbers killed, wounded, and captured are complicated by other Tlingit attacks on Russian and Alutiiq forces that same summer. Led by Ivan Kuskov, the season's main hunting party faced the hostility of the Yakutat Tlingits on an excursion southward toward the Alexander Archipelago. After fighting off one major attack, Kuskov's men patched up a truce with their foes. Low on ammunition, this party then returned to Yakutat Bay, where Kuskov strengthened the garrison's defenses and sent warnings to the other Russian outposts to the north. He also dispatched six three-person baidarkas southward to alert the Fort Mikhailovskii people about their danger. This party returned two weeks later, after having lost one baidarka and its men to the Tlingits, and reported the horrifying news: they had seen the fort's smoldering ruins and evidence of the massacre that had befallen its residents.

The hunting party that had set out from Sitka Sound shortly before the Tlingit assault numbered about two hundred men. Headed by Ivan Urbanov, this group apparently intended to join with Kuskov's main expedition. After just a few days travel, however, they were attacked at Dry Bay near Kake by an overwhelming force of Tlingits, who struck them in the middle of the night as they slept in the open. According to historian Kiril Khlebnikov's statistical record of "Unfortunate Events during Mr. Baranov's Time," the casualties totaled 165 Alutiiqs, a figure that apparently also includes the Alutiiq death toll during the destruction of Fort Mikhailovskii.[20] It is highly likely that the attackers were part of the force that struck the RAC fort just a few days later.

* * *

These hostilities had many causes, some immediate, others more remote. Together they blended into a perfect storm of Tlingit hostility toward the Russian promyshlenniks and Alutiiq hunters who had invaded their homelands under Baranov's supervision. Russian accounts describe a few specific cases of injustices toward Tlingits, including the murder of a high-ranking couple and their children and the harsh imprisonment of another young man, the nephew of a headman, for a trifling offense. They also acknowledge the provocation caused by Alutiiq hunters who had plundered Tlingit grave sites and stolen Tlingit winter food stores, as the Yakutat leaders complained about to Kuskov.[21] But these same accounts place much of the blame on British and Yankee merchant traders for instigating the Tlingit uprising, thus deflecting guilt away from Baranov's men.

The long-preserved Tlingit oral tradition, by contrast, details incident after incident of bad behavior by the Russians and Alutiiqs, usually all identified simply as Russians. Among the accounts are the forcible sexual abuse of Tlingit women and violence toward their husbands, the imprisonment of a respected shaman, and deliberately degrading insults to friendly Tlingit individuals. Also included are descriptions of the scorn heaped on Kiks.ádi leaders by other Tlingit groups at a distance and the crude, earthy language they used to ridicule the Sitkans for submitting to the Russians. This peer pressure may have had a decisive influence in determining the Kiks.ádis to take the initiative in planning to strike the undermanned Russian establishment at Fort Mikhailovskii.[22]

What may be deduced from all these sources is that Tlingit fighting men came together under Kiks.ádi leadership, unifying to rid themselves of the RAC invaders. One eminent keeper of the Kiks.ádi oral tradition a generation ago expressed in poetic form the underpinnings for his people's uprising against the Russians:

> When
> a Tlingit
> is abused
> he has enough patience to endure for a while.
> He might even plead
> to be left alone.
> But if they continue
> doing this
> he never forgets it as long as he lives.
> There will be a time when
> he will avenge.
> This is what happened.[23]

From this perspective, the armed struggle that began so dramatically at Fort Mikhailovskii and Yakutat in 1802 was not simply a war over territory and over sea otter peltry. Neither was it merely the outcome of foreign shipmasters' unrestrained trade in firearms and ammunition with the Tlingits. Nor did it stem just from Baranov's effort to extend Russian sovereignty over an indigenous population, as some authors writing from a Eurocentric point of view have emphasized. To some degree, all these factors were involved. But in addition, the Sitka Sound war strongly expressed the Tlingit people's determination to preserve their autonomy, the independence of their homeland, the safety of their women from assault, their control over the fur trade in their own country, and, above all, their prideful self-respect.

∗ ∗ ∗

The destruction of Fort Mikhailovskii and the resulting loss of RAC access to the sea otter–rich waters of the Alexander Strait made Baranov heartsick. He simply could not accept this reversal. While mourning all those killed in the

1802 hostilities, he resolved to win back what had been lost, no matter how great the cost or the danger to his men. As interpreted by his first biographer, his reasons were lofty: "He desired to preserve the Nation's fame in the eyes of the foreign traders, to keep the trust placed in him by the Government and the Company, and, by expanding trade and hunting, to make them yield profits, and thus render new services to the Fatherland."[24]

In the terms of our age, it is more apt to say that Aleksandr Andreevich and the RAC directors were facing in maritime Alaska the predicament of turbulent frontiers.[25] Baranov and his men coveted more territory than they could control. Their fighting strength lagged far behind their commercial ambitions, and the chief manager's ability to rule over the RAC's far-flung commercial borderland was curtailed by a lack of support from both the company directors and the imperial government. Yet he was determined to fight his way back so his men could regain access to the wealth in sea otters that swam in Tlingit waters. His resources were puny, but Baranov's aspirations remained immense.

As previously described, two ships from Okhotsk arrived at Pavlovskaia toward the end of the 1802 sailing season, bringing reinforcements to Russian America. In mid-September the RAC galiot *Aleksandr Nevskii* come into port. The commander was Navigator Efim Petrov, who had been reassigned from the imperial navy to serve as a company skipper. At the beginning of November the brig *Sv. Elizaveta* appeared, commanded by navy lieutenant Gavriil Davydov.

The coming of these vessels, especially the larger, better-supplied *Elizaveta*, relieved Aleksandr Andreevich's worries about the precarious situation of Russian America. Their appearance showed the Kodiak Islanders and other American Native peoples that Baranov's men were not the only Russians left in the world, thus easing the threat of a general uprising against the RAC. Although the *Elizaveta* returned to Okhotsk in 1803, bearing an immense cargo of sea otter peltry and other furs, the additional men and supplies the ship had delivered to America, supplemented by the armaments purchased from Captain Barber, gave Baranov a conviction that he could muster a large enough force to avenge the loss of Fort Mikhailovskii and reestablish a Russian post on Sitka Sound.

Following Ivan Kuskov's advice, the general manager delayed his invasion plans from the late summer of 1803 until the following year. In April 1804 he left Pavlovskaia with the *Ekaterina* and the *Aleksandr Nevskii*, accompanying an Alutiiq force in three hundred baidarkas. When he reached Yakutat Bay toward the end of May, he found that Kuskov and his men had constructed there two additional small ships, the *Ermak* and the *Rostislav*.

While sending the *Ekaterina* and the *Aleksandr Nevskii* southward toward Sitka Sound by the customary coastal route, Baranov took command of the *Ermak* to lead the Alutiiq hunters and the *Rostislav* in search of a better-protected inland water route. After reaching the entrance to Cross Sound, he turned his expedition eastward, moved past Glacier Bay to the north, and reached the head of Icy Strait.

Despite a forbidding wall of ice and an intensely thick blanket of fog hiding the rocky shoreline, Baranov headed southward into the strait. Moving with the current between high cliffs and towering icebergs, the two small ships lost the wind. Then, alarmingly, the current strengthened, carrying the entire command southward through fog so dense that Baranov's sailors could not see the accompanying vessel, the surrounding baidarkas, or the icebergs and rock cliffs pressing in on them. The southward moving current, flowing virtually like a river, carried them helplessly, blindly, through the enshrouding whiteness. Sails hung motionless from the mast. Beneath them the bottom was too deep to anchor. The current was too swift for the use of a towline. "Nothing remained," he later told his biographer, "but to seek the mercy of Almighty Providence."

As best they could, the *Ermak*'s crew used long poles to push their frail craft away from the looming high mountains of ice and rock cliffs. Then, just as they appeared to be safely through the most constricted passage, the current sharply reversed. Back they went on this ebbing tide, moving silently again toward the head of the strait. It was, Baranov recalled years later, "like going into the mouth of Hell."

Altogether, this terrifying ordeal lasted twelve hours. Finally, the entire fleet moved clear of the ice and fog. They found refuge and anchored in a small harbor—likely Spasski Bay. Surveying the damage, Baranov found his force surprisingly intact. Ice had carried away the *Ermak*'s dinghy, destroyed the tiller of the *Rostislav*, and crushed one three-person baidarka, but everyone was safe.

The two small company ships remained at anchor for three days while contrary winds blew up the strait. Then a change in weather enabled Aleksandr Andreevich to attempt the same passage once again. With the fog dispersed and a following current, both ships and all the hunters' baidarkas easily passed by the great masses of ice, shot through a narrow passage that another seafarer would describe as like going down a waterfall, reached the open waters of Khutsnov (Chatham) Strait, and entered Chilkat Sound (Lynn Canal): a daylong journey. Pridefully, Baranov later pointed out that not even the intrepid Tlingits had previously used this route.[26]

As they continued together toward Sea Otter Bay, the Russians and their Alutiiq hunters found an abundance of animals and no threat of interference by the local Tlingits, who all fled their villages before Baranov and his men appeared. Protected by the guns of the Russian ships, the hunters made a great haul. They killed sixteen hundred sea otters, with no effort to leave a breeding stock for the future. At Baranov's command, the Alutiiqs troubled none of the abandoned villages except for two that were the farthest south. These people had reputedly been responsible for the deadly attack on the Urbanov party two years earlier. Baranov's men burned their wooden clan houses and ceremonial lodges, leaving nothing but ashes.

Aleksandr Andreevich and his command reached a Sitka Sound rendezvous point with his two ships and the Alutiiq baidarka fleet in mid-September, followed four days later by a smaller hunting party under Ivan Kuskov. The *Ekaterina* and *Aleksandr Nevskii* were waiting for them. So too was a Russian navy ship, the *Neva*, commanded by Captain-Lieutenant Yuri Lisiansky.

Though only thirty-one years old, Lisiansky was a highly experienced, battle-tested officer. After service with the British navy, in 1802 he had joined with his close friend and fellow officer I. F. Kruzenshtern to promote a round-the-world voyage with two British-built ships, renamed the *Neva* and the *Nadezhda*. After departing from Russia's Baltic Sea navy headquarters at Kronstadt, they had sailed across the Atlantic, rounded Cape Horn, and cruised the southern Pacific's island territories.[27] While Kruzenshtern headed for Kamchatka, Lisiansky learned of the Tlingit destruction of Fort Mikhailovskii during a visit to Hawaii in June 1804. This news prompted him to leave at once for Kodiak Island, then to continue toward Sitka Sound. He had arrived there a month ahead of Baranov and his expedition of Russian and Alutiiq hunters.

When Baranov met with Captain Lisiansky, they agreed on an aggressive policy. They would exact from the Sitka Tlingits not only the return of the Fort Mikhailovskii site but also the surrender of the Kiks.ádi main village location, the prominent Noow Tlein hilltop on Sitka Harbor. Confident in their military advantage, the two commanders immediately started a campaign to dispossess the Kiks.ádis and their Tlingit neighbors. They would attempt to secure their goal through diplomacy, they agreed, but fully expected that they would need to fight.

* * *

The Kiks.ádi elders believed the same. Urged by a shaman to prepare for the reappearance of the Russians, a year earlier the Sitka villagers had built a very strong, ingeniously designed fort structure—called Shis'gi Noow—alongside Indian River, near the shoreline about two miles south of their Noow Tlein site. It was formed of sturdy logs about ten feet long, set on end and placed tightly side by side, with each lower end firmly planted in a deep trench and the upper end slanted back at a twenty-degree angle. These log walls were braced with heavy timber scaffolding on the interior side, with lighter timbers placed horizontally on both the inside and outside. As the Kiks.ádis intended, the angling of the braced log walls would lessen the impact of the Russian ships' cannonballs, causing them to glance away harmlessly.

The fort's overall dimensions were roughly 195 by 120 feet, shaped in an irregular square with a longer side facing the bay and a shorter side backing onto forest. Within these heavy walls were fourteen wooden structures: a ceremonial lodge and clan houses, all partially sunk in the ground so that cannon shot would sail overhead without reaching them. These buildings provided housing for a community estimated at eight hundred people. It was a secure fortification, yet it must have been a terrifying experience to be inside the fort while being bombarded hour after hour by the heavy guns on the *Neva* and the RAC ships.

On September 29 the full Russian and Alutiiq force reached Sitka Harbor, carried out a careful reconnaissance, disembarked, and took possession of the deserted Noow Tlein hilltop site. By midday they had brought ashore several small cannons and two larger fieldpieces, mounting them in a defensive position atop the rise the Russians would later call Castle Hill. According to Captain Lisiansky, it was he who named this location New Archangel (Novo-Arkhangel'sk), the name it would continue to carry throughout the history of Russian America.[28]

Every Tlingit account of the 1804 hostilities describes an episode that is ignored in the Russian sources. While Baranov was supervising the takeover of Castle Hill, some Alutiiq hunters and Russian promyshlenniks came ashore and camped alongside Indian River below the Shis'gi Noow fort. The Kiks.ádi war leader K'alyáan thought about how to strike these enemies. He had some young men go into the forest upstream and cut down tree branches and limbs. Every afternoon about the same time they would toss some of these cuttings into the river.

On the first few days that this tangle of greenery came floating downstream, the Russians and Alutiiqs jumped up to investigate. But repeatedly finding nothing, they relaxed their guard. This gave K'alyáan his opportunity. One afternoon he drifted down hidden amid the debris, swam close to shore, and jumped out in front of a group who were eating. He was wearing his Raven helmet and carrying a knife in one hand. In the other was the heavy Russian blacksmith hammer he had taken as a trophy. He rushed toward the surprised men using his sea lion call: "huh-huh-huh-huh-huh." One man he stabbed with his dagger. Then he raised the Russian hammer.

Tlingit historian Andrew P. Johnson recorded the oral tradition of this fight.

> He was a very powerful man,
> trained for strength
> as well as a warrior.
> The blacksmith hammer wasn't anything in his hand.
> He swung it back and forth
> smashing the heads of his enemy.

One Russian rushed at him with a broad hand ax. As K'alyáan dodged, the ax scratched the beak of the Raven helmet, leaving a mark that can be seen today. K'alyáan killed this man too with his hammer.

> The Russians and Aleuts [Alutiiqs] begin to run
> towards the forest.
> They were so excited, not knowing what to do.
> they were caught off guard. They didn't even come near
> to their guns.
> The Tlingits that [had] stationed themselves [hidden] in a semi-circle
> all jumped up and encircled the Russians.
> The killing took place
> until [just a] few of the Russians
> made it to their boats
> and went off to sea
> [to] the war vessels that were anchored.

That night, as Johnson also describes, to complete the humiliation of their enemies, the Tlingit women completely stripped the bodies of all the dead Russians and Alutiiqs.

Next morning
it looked like
a lot of dead halibut
white on the beach,
the dead bodies.[29]

After Baranov and his men took over the Noow Tlein village site, Captain Lisiansky made preparations for a siege of the Shis'gi Noow fort. Under his supervision the *Neva* and the three company ships anchored in a line before the fort, though they were forced to remain some two hundred yards offshore because of the shallow bottom in that part of the bay—another element of the Kiks.ádis' planning for their fort site.

Soon after taking their position, the Russians caught sight of a Tlingit dugout canoe moving between small islands across the bay. Captain Lisiansky sent his ship's launch in pursuit. After the sailors fired a few shots, the canoe blew up in spectacular fashion, killing most of its crew.

According to Tlingit accounts, these men had been bringing a large quantity of gunpowder from a secure cache on a nearby island. Once the Russians began their pursuit, one young Tlingit opened a powder keg and loaded his flintlock musket, meaning to demonstrate his valor. When he then fired back at the Russian boat, a spark fell into the keg and everything blew sky-high. The Russians pulled from the water six survivors, four badly wounded. This destruction of their reserve powder supply proved a critical loss to the Tlingits. During the next two days the Kiks.ádi elders entered into a negotiation of sorts with Baranov and Lisiansky. The Russian demands were severe: they wanted a guarantee for the permanent possession of their newly fortified Castle Hill location and the surrender of two leading men as hostages. Failing this, Lisiansky warned, "their former treachery would be punished by [the Russians] with the utmost severity."[30]

On the morning of October 1, as Lisiansky phrased it, "we carried this menace into execution." First, as one last gesture toward reconciliation, the captain hoisted a white flag aboard his ship. The Kiks.ádis responded by showing their own white flag from the fort, a reciprocal gesture appropriate in Tlingit culture, but it is doubtful that they understood the meaning

THE SITKA SOUND WAR   [199]

of this symbol to the Russians. When no one came from the fort to offer submission, Lisiansky ordered the ships to begin firing. Only then did he discover that the fort's walls were so sturdy and cleverly made that shot from his cannon could not penetrate from their offshore anchorage.[31] The Tlingits returned fire from the fort with their own small cannons. The gunners were accurate enough to cause Lisiansky concern over the damage being done to the *Neva*'s rigging.

To remain on the offensive, Captain Lisiansky sent ashore two of his ship's boats with armed sailors under Lieutenant Pavel Arbuzov. On the beach they destroyed a great many Tlingit dugout canoes, including a few large enough to carry sixty men. They also burned a shed near the beach that Lisiansky thought might contain supplies. Taking a four-pound cannon from one of the boats, Arbuzov then began advancing toward the fort.

At this point Aleksandr Baranov, who had been observing from the deck of the *Neva*, rushed into action with his men in their baidarkas. Landing with about 150 promyshlenniks and Alutiiq hunters and taking along two small fieldpieces of his own, he joined Lieutenant Arbuzov onshore. By now the day was well advanced. Met with only an occasional musket shot from the fort, Baranov and Arbuzov began a frontal assault even though darkness was quickly falling. As they neared the fort's walls, however, the Kiks. ádi warriors massed inside "fired on them with an order and execution that surprised" them.

Baranov's men were unprepared for such disciplined fire. After the first volley the Alutiiqs turned and fled back toward their baidarkas, abandoning the two fieldpieces they had been pulling along. So too did most of the Russian promyshlenniks. The Tlingits, well protected by their body armor and headgear, rushed out of the fort in pursuit. The sailors from the *Neva* briefly held their ground, then slowly retired, managing to take along both the guns while Captain Lisiansky covered their retreat with cannon fire.

Toting up the casualties, Lisiansky counted two sailors killed and ten wounded, along with Lieutenant Arbuzov and three noncommissioned officers. Baranov's casualty list totaled three sailors, three promyshlenniks, and four Alutiiqs killed, with two sailors, nine promyshlenniks, and six Alutiiqs wounded. In all, the chief manager said, there were ten dead and twenty-four wounded. Baranov himself was one of the seriously injured. Though he may have had the protection of a chain mail vest, he suffered a painful gunshot wound in his right arm, disabling him at the very time he was attempting to lead the attack against the walls of the Tlingit fort.

As Captain Lisiansky later admitted, this fight, which included the sight of one of the dead Russian sailors lifted high on Tlingit spears, "disquieted us considerably." Hearing no victory celebration songs from the fort, the Russians comforted themselves with the thought that their enemy had suffered perhaps even more than they themselves had; yet it afforded them "but slender consolation." Baranov put the blame squarely on the Alutiiqs who had fled first from the field. Lisiansky in turn pointed to Baranov's impatience, wanting to end the affair too quickly, which had caused him to trust the bravery of his people, Russian and Alutiiq, "who had never been engaged in warfare of this kind before."[32]

The morning after this precipitous, mismanaged attack Aleksandr Andreevich, suffering from his wound, turned over the entire military and diplomatic operation to Captain Lisiansky. Consequently, the younger man later wrote, "I resorted to the plan I wished at first should have been adopted, that of annoying the enemy from the ships, and I instantly ordered a brisk discharge of guns on the fort."[33] Following this bombardment, the Kiks.ádis made a peace offer, proposing to release to the Russians all the Alutiiq people they had taken prisoners during the past few years—including women and children captured at Fort Mikhailovskii—and to provide as hostages "some of their best families." Lisiansky accepted the offer, but added a further stipulation: none of the remaining Tlingit canoes should leave their shoreside location until all these peace conditions were completely satisfied. In effect, he wanted to keep the Tlingits landlocked and blockaded, unable to use the only ready means of travel from place to place in their homeland.

As a first sign of agreement, that evening the Kiks.ádis sent a young man to Lisiansky as a hostage. This fellow proved most cooperative. When questioned, he told the Russian captain all he wanted to know about the strength of the force inside Shis'gi Noow fort, with details about their muskets and cannons, their meager ammunition supply, and their provisions. It was clear that a shortage of gunpowder had become critical for the Kiks.ádis.

During the following two days more hostages arrived, yet Lisiansky was vexed to see the Kiks.ádis venturing outside the fort to scavenge Russian cannonballs that were lying about. To discourage this behavior, the captain occasionally had his men fire again on the Tlingit stronghold. He learned from newer hostages that some Kiks.ádi elders were still "ill-disposed," unwilling to make peace with the Russians. He particularly demanded hostages from this hostile faction.

Another person the Tlingits surrendered to the Russians, a young Alutiiq woman from Kodiak Island, told Captain Lisiansky that the Kiks.ádis had sent an embassy to their former allies the Hoonah, asking for assistance. Following this report, Lisiansky demanded an immediate surrender of the fort. He received what he deemed to be evasive replies. Through one afternoon and all the next day, the captain pressed his demands. At length he began once more firing at the fort, since he thought the Tlingits were only stalling until reinforcements could arrive. He also ordered his men to build a raft that they could use to carry some of his big guns closer to the fort. Simultaneously, he kept up his diplomatic pressure, hoping to get a peaceful evacuation of the Kiks.ádi bastion.

Finally, late on the fourth evening after his siege had begun, Lisiansky and his crew heard in the dark the Tlingits crying out loudly, as he wrote, "oo, oo, oo!" This was the agreed upon signal that the inhabitants would finally leave Shis'gi Noow fort. On hearing the sound, the Alutiiqs burst into their own song, expressing happiness that they were now free from danger.

Expecting to see the Tlingits depart in their remaining dugouts when morning arrived, the Russians were greatly surprised to find the fort had been abandoned. At first light that morning the Kiks.ádi community had quietly slipped away, leaving behind only two or three old women and a boy. Lisiansky judged that the Tlingit elders had not trusted the Russians to allow their people to depart peacefully. "They had therefore preferred running into the woods, leaving many things behind, which, from their haste, they had not been able to take away."[34] These spoils included a substantial store of provisions and twenty to thirty large dugout canoes, many quite new.

After allowing the promyshlenniks and the Alutiiq hunters to plunder the food and other supplies remaining in the fort, Baranov had some logs dragged to Castle Hill for his own use and ordered everything else burned to the ground. Neither he nor Captain Lisiansky showed any wish to chase after the Kiks.ádis. They had simply vanished into the forest so far as the Russians were concerned, and that was fine. While keeping guards posted against the possibility of another surprise attack, Aleksandr Andreevich was not interested in negotiating further for any part of the Tlingit homeland. He and his men continued to hold the Castle Hill site simply by the fact of their physical occupation.

*   *   *

The decision to leave the Shis'gi Noow fort on foot, setting out silently into the forest with only the tools and supplies they could carry on their backs, was critical for the Sitka Kiks.ádis. Known to modern Tlingits as the Kiks.ádi Survival March, from their perspective this was a strategic retreat from the Indian River battlefield. By disappearing, they got away from the Russian cannons. By not surrendering, the Kiks.ádi warriors prevented their women and children from becoming slaves to the Russians, as they viewed it; remained strong to fight another day; and preserved the honor of the Sitka Kiks.ádi people.[35] Their withdrawal had no taint of defeat.

Well planned, the march took place in fairly short, easy stages. The goal was to move everyone to the opposite side of Sitka Island, then to cross Peril Strait to Chichagov Island, where they might resettle until the time was right to return to the Sitka location. The exodus from Shis'gi Noow began secretly while Lisiansky was trying to force the Tlingits to surrender. First a group of elderly people and their young grandchildren left the fort and moved northward toward Gajaa Héen, the Old Sitka site, a walk of ten miles or so. They were followed soon by a party of young mothers and their infant children. At first light the following day the main body of men and women moved out. They organized themselves into separate house groups that proceeded one after another, keeping in touch with those ahead and those behind. Trailing everyone else was a rearguard of warriors to protect the Kiks.ádi community from possible pursuit by RAC forces.

Their route led over at least one low-lying mountain ridge, but for the most part they moved through the forest and along rivers and rocky seashore beaches. Late-season salmon and other fish, shellfish, and berries, along with various plants, fed them. Even so, the hardships of the journey resulted in some deaths on the way, mostly among the very youngest and the very oldest.

When they reached Peril Strait, the Kiks.ádis camped and gathered wood for a huge bonfire. Waiting until a clear night, they lit the fire and periodically caused it to flare up as a signal for the Kootznahoo Tlingits in their village, nine miles across the water. The Kootznahoo investigated, then arrived to ferry all the Kiks.ádis across the strait. There the displaced Sitkans took over an abandoned village site and made it their new temporary home.

Before leaving Shis'gi Noow fort, the younger Kiks.ádi house leaders had made a plan to impose a blockade that would prevent all Native groups, Tlingits and others, from dealing with the Russians. Their new location on Peril Strait helped them put this plan into effect. Baranov and his men were isolated at their New Archangel outpost. Not only were they unable to trade for furs, but at first they found it impossible to barter with the local Natives for game or fish.

Making the situation worse, it remained dangerous for the RAC workers, Russian or Alutiiq, to go hunting or fishing at any distance from their Castle Hill stronghold. This Kiks.ádi tactic left the Russians now unable to make any commercial gains from their Sitka Sound location, and it made the survival of the RAC garrison difficult because of recurrent food shortages. Baranov's long-standing policy of having his people live off the land became virtually impossible. The absence of a sea otter supply and the difficulty of supplying the Sitka establishment left this newest RAC garrison in an extremely tenuous situation.

Meanwhile the relocated Kiks.ádis continued to hunt sea otters and trade with the foreign shipmasters who came into their waters. Beginning in 1805, Yankee merchant captains brought their ships into Peril Strait for this trade, carrying household items to the Tlingits and replenishing their supply of guns and gunpowder. Despite the Russian presence, it was business as usual for these Northwest Coast sea traders.

✳   ✳   ✳

The Sitka Sound war had no clear victors. In 1804 Baranov, with the vital armed assistance of Lieutenant Lisiansky and his sailors, avenged the 1802 destruction of Fort Mikhailovskii, but the subsequent Tlingit blockade kept the RAC hunters from further access to the sea otter resources of the Alexander Archipelago.

Perhaps in hope of gaining a more favorable resolution, in 1805 Baranov initiated peace negotiations with the relocated Kiks.ádis. The evidence on this point, however, is a bit muddled. Baranov himself left no documentary record of the episode. His contemporary biographer, Khlebnikov, also failed to mention the matter. The single piece of Russian direct documentation comes from the eyewitness account of Captain Yuri Lisiansky, who says that after spending the winter in Pavlovskaia, he returned to New Archangel with the *Neva* in July 1805, bringing along three hostages taken the previous year: one Sitkan youth and two men from another "tribe." Consequently, Lisiansky continues, Baranov sent an interpreter to the new Kiks.ádi settlement on Peril Strait, inviting a parley. As Lisiansky relates, this emissary soon returned with the message that the Kiks.ádi headmen "wished for further assurance of good intentions on our part, before they would venture to come to the [Russian] fort." To provide this assurance, Baranov sent back the interpreter with presents "and a message of invitation couched in the civilest terms."[36]

Thus convinced, says Lisiansky, a Kiks.ádi ambassador accompanied by a large party came with the interpreter to New Archangel, arriving in five cedar dugouts with much ceremonial display, including a great deal of singing and dancing, on the afternoon of August 16.[37] The following day the Tlingits visited the *Neva*, where Lisiansky turned over the Sitkan hostage, who proved

TLINGIT DANCERS AT NEW ARCHANGEL. These costumed dancers, garbed in cloth robes they obtained from American merchant traders, are holding eagle tail feathers. Their outfits are decorated with ermine skins, a sign of wealth, and some dancers have their heads powdered with eagle down feathers. The sitting women sing to accompany the dancers. This view appeared in Georg H. von Langsdorff's *Voyages and Travels in Various Parts of the World*, volume 2, published in London in 1814. The artist is unknown.

to be the ambassador's eldest son, and discussed the destruction of Fort Mikhailovskii with the older man. Eager for peace, the ambassador claimed to have opposed his peoples' war plans from the start and then to have gone to live among the Chilkat at the time of the 1802 attack.

Later in the day this embassy, with further ceremonial flourishes including much more dancing and singing, went ashore to visit Baranov. The general manager treated the guests with great honor. He gifted the ambassador with a red cape or cloak trimmed in ermine and presented each of his male companions with a blue cape—all made of heavy wool we may assume. He also distributed pewter medals among the group, "as tokens of peace and amity with their country." After these ceremonies, the entire party moved to Baranov's house for entertainment and a grand feast, which the Tlingits enjoyed with so much gusto, Lisiansky says, "that in the evening they were carried to their apartments in a state of perfect inebriety."[38]

The next morning the Kiks.ádi delegation made their departure. Before they left, Lisiansky reports, Aleksandr Andreevich presented the ambassador with one more symbol of peace: a copper plaque bearing the Russian coat of arms, affixed atop a long pole and ornamented with eagle feathers and ribbons, meant to be prominently displayed in the ambassador's village. Baranov also officially released the young Sitkan hostage to his father, who promised to send a younger son to live among the Russians in the place of his oldest boy. Making their farewell, the embassy members "set off as they came," says Lisiansky, "singing."[39]

The Kiks.ádi recollection of these events adds pertinent details to the narrative, explaining in particular the preliminary peace negotiations that led to the Sitka peace ceremony witnessed by Lieutenant Lisiansky. According to Andrew P. Johnson, the Kiks.ádi oral historian, after the Survival March and their relocation across Peril Strait, the Sitkans were able to rearm themselves with more guns and ammunition by calling on their relatives' clans at Hoonah, Angoon, and other nearby villages, and their new fort was very strong. "There were enough young men—young warriors—we don't need any help," they said. In this confident frame of mind, they received an Alutiiq messenger from Baranov trying to make peace. But the message from Baranov was that he had conquered the Tlingit people "and therefore the whole Alaska—Southeastern Alaska—belongs to him by right." The Kiks.ádis responded, in Johnson's telling:

> They fired shots
> Into the water right near their boat.
> Water splashed in their faces.
> They fled the place, back to Sitka.[40]

A second party came from the Russians with a similar message, saying that Baranov was to dictate the peace treaty. As Johnson relates,

> But the Kiks.ádis
> wouldn't give in.

Why should we?

We [had] only retreated.

And we're plenty strong enough.

And to show them we are well prepared

a lot of shots were fired

into the water right by their boat.

Water splashed into their boats

and into their faces.

They fled back to Sitka

To report that the Kiks.ádis were well armed.

The peace treaty was to be dictated by the Kiks.ádis.

A third time, says Johnson's account, Baranov sent an Alutiiq interpreter to the Kiks.ádis to discuss a peace. This time the messenger convinced the village's headmen that he had "the heart of Wanáanák' [Baranov] to talk" and that Baranov "was ready to have Kiks.ádis dictate the peace treaty." The terms, recorded by Johnson, were all encompassing:

You shall not touch the land

That belonged to our great uncles. . . .

You shall not touch the salmon streams,

the trees,

the rivers,

the salmon in the sea,

all the resources of Alaska—

Southeastern Alaska.

If you are in need of any of these things,

you shall buy it from us.

You are not to cut any trees

or kill any game,

unless you get permission from us.

Baranov knew then, as Andrew P. Johnson emphasized, that "he wasn't dealing with just a handful of people, the Kiks.ádis of Sitka, but the whole of Southeastern Alaska. He had no right of claiming anything." With this understanding, affirms the Kiks.ádi tradition, Baranov agreed to a peace treaty that fixed precise boundaries around the Russian territory, taking in the largest part of present downtown Sitka as "land given to the Russian government free of charge."[41]

THE HARBOR OF NEW ARCHANGEL IN SITKA OR NORFOLK SOUND.
This 1805 view of Baranov's newly established post at New Archangel, modern
Sitka, shows the ample harbor facilities that made this site ideal as a center for
trade with the merchant captains of many nations. Yuri Lisiansky, captain of the
Russian navy ship *Neva*, may be the artist. It appeared in Lisiansky's account of his
travels, *Voyage Round the World*, published in St. Petersburg and London in 1814.

* * *

Over the next few years some of the Kiks.ádis—led, surprisingly, by the military chieftain K'alyáan—moved back to the Sitka area and settled in a small
village adjacent to Baranov's well-fortified New Archangel location. Aleksandr Andreevich and K'alyáan even resumed a friendship that had begun
during negotiations for the Fort Mikhailovskii site.

Trade between the Tlingits and the Russians during the following decades
remained quite limited, involving only small quantities of fish and deer meat
in exchange for items that Baranov and his successors mainly obtained
from visiting foreign merchant ships. New Archangel was located on a better harbor than Pavlovskaia, convenient alike for RAC ships and merchant

vessels from other countries. At least seventeen American ships visited the Russian establishment on Sitka Sound from 1801 through 1809, delivering cargoes worth approximately five hundred thousand rubles.[42] Yet, without the subsidy of a profitable sea otter trade, it was expensive to maintain, difficult to provision, and in a situation that demanded constant caution in dealing with the Russians' Tlingit neighbors. Its benefits as a port just barely offset its shortcomings as a business and commercial center for Russian America. But Baranov liked the place. Ensconced in his official residence and headquarters, he was very proud of his role in securing the Sitka site for the Russian empire and the RAC.

From the Tlingit perspective, the loss of the Noow Tlein village site harmed their prestige. Yet, since they retained their trading relationships with Yankee and British merchant adventurers, it caused them no commercial injury. They had effectively countered the RAC's attempt to plunder a treasure in sea otter peltry from their waters. And the success of their secretive escape from the Russian naval bombardment of the Indian River fort gave them a new reason for pride. In retrospect, as one descendent of the participants has written, the history of this escape and the Kiks.ádi Survival March came to be seen as "a story of Tlingit courage, bravery, dedication, loyalty, honor, and endurance in defense of the Kiks.ádi homeland."[43]

Despite the loss of life and the injuries on both sides, and despite an enduring ill will between the RAC people and some of the Kiks.ádis, the Russians gained very little from this series of armed clashes. Baranov and the RAC authorities who succeeded him had always to keep in mind their problems dealing with the Tlingits, among them the continuing need to restrain Russian promyshlenniks and Alutiiq partovshchiks from unfriendly acts toward the Sitka Kiks.ádis. While there were no more full-scale hostilities, occasional small episodes of violence showed that the underlying clash of cultures was far from resolved.

*　*　*

Almost as an encore to the 1802 destruction of Fort Mikhailovskii and the Sitka Sound war, in October 1805—about the same time as Baranov's ratification of the peace with the Sitka Tlingits at New Archangel—the Yakutat Tlingits ended the Russian and Alutiiq occupation of their homeland by a concerted strike on the Russian fort. According to the sparse documentation, contained in two secondhand reports the following year by Nikolai Rezanov, the attack on the post was led by Native workers for the Russians, who had reportedly been bribed by the Akoi Tlingits. The fort was captured and burned, while all the people—Russians and Alutiiqs—were killed except eight men, two women, and three boys, who had been working in a hayfield away from the fort at the time of the attack. These few survivors, according to Rezanov's account, were then "held as prisoners by the Ugaliagmuts, who demand[ed] a ransom which will be sent from Kadiak."[44]

In an earlier, first account, Rezanov wrote to the RAC board of directors that the Yakutat Tlingits had massacred all the Russians, forty altogether counting women and children. At the fort, the attackers had captured heavy armaments, two three-pound brass cannons, two one-pound cannons of cast iron, a smaller "unicorn" gun of a half-pound caliber, along with ammunition and a substantial supply of gunpowder. When he received this news at Pavlovskaia, Rezanov added, local manager Ivan Banner had sent a baidara to notify all the villages on Kodiak Island to take precautions, and he dispatched another baidara to Chugach Sound with ten men to strengthen the company posts. This was all that Banner could do, Rezanov said, "but you must admit that it is not real reinforcement and will only increase the number of victims." There was a lesson to be learned, Chamberlain Rezanov added: "We have to deal with thousands, children's toys are out of place and you see, My Dear Sirs, that without a garrison and good ships, our establishments will always be in danger."[45]

Adding to this same report apparently a few days later, Rezanov said that the unpleasant news from Yakutat had inspired "the old man," Baranov, "exhausted though he is with labors and illness," to make still another sacrifice for his country. He meant to start out to recapture the Yakutat fort site, taking the small ship *Rostislav*, with four cannons and only twenty-five men. More men could not be spared, Rezanov explained, and no more ships were available. "Unless I can talk him out of it," he concluded, "they will weigh anchor in five days."[46]

Presumably, Baranov was finally convinced to give up this plan for an undermanned punitive expedition against the Yakutat villagers and their neighbors. Neither in Khlebnikov's biography nor in any other surviving document is there further mention of these events. Apparently, the chief manager had to reconcile himself to the loss of the Yakutat fort, recognizing that the sea otter resources of that district had become negligible. It was clear, as Rezanov emphasized in his reports to the authorities back in St. Petersburg, that the Russian and Alutiiq invasion of southeastern Alaska had provoked a strong hostile reaction from the Tlingit clans and other people of the region. New Archangel, well fortified, could stand as a lone center of

Russian power along that coast, maintaining access to Sitka Sound for the Russians and all those mariners from other nations who would come to deal with the RAC. But, from Baranov's perspective, lacking sufficient military and naval support, the Tlingit blockade could not be broken. If there was a feasible alternative, it would have to come by reaching farther away, hoping to find elsewhere new opportunities for trade and profits.

X

BEYOND ALASKA

---

*Beginning in the fall of 1803, Baranov entered into a series of agreements
with New England-based merchant captains to carry RAC hunting crews
south to coastal California. There they found virtually untouched sea
otter populations. These hunting voyages prompted attempts to open trade
with California's Spanish residents. Despite opposition by Spain's rulers,
a surreptitious trade of mission-grown foodstuffs for manufactured goods
helped ease shortages in both Spanish California and Russian Alaska. From
these beginnings grew Baranov's project to plant a new RAC outpost, Fort
Ross, on the northern California coast. At the same time he entered into
a long-distance commercial courtship with Hawaii's principal ruler, King
Kamehameha I.*

I N LATE OCTOBER 1803 THE MASSACHUSETTS TRADING SHIP
O'Cain slipped away from Kodiak Island's Pavlovskaia Harbor, edged past
the headlands into open water, and set a course southward toward Spanish
California. If the weather was typical for that time of year, the day would have
been cool and overcast, with a steady wind from the northwest to fill the
sails and rain squalls to drench everyone on deck. At the helm was Captain
Joseph O'Cain, an American-born Irishman who had made four previous
trading voyages from New England to the Pacific coast of North America.
Along with his small American crew, crowded onto the ship were forty Alutiiq partovshchiks with their two- and three-person baidarkas stowed on
deck. Also aboard were two RAC crew chiefs, Afanasii Shvetsov and Timofei
Tarakanov, assigned by Baranov to supervise the Alutiiq hunters and serve
as intermediaries with Captain O'Cain and his sailors.

The *O'Cain's* 1803 voyage to Spanish California, coming at the same time
that the Louisiana Purchase and the Lewis and Clark expedition were bring-

ing the United States into the American Far West, was not meant to expand Russia's Pacific empire. It was instead a short-term, expedient response on the chief manager's part to relieve a desperate situation. Unchecked hunting had destroyed Alaska's sea otter stocks everywhere north of Lituya Bay. The powerful, well-armed Yakutat and Sitka Tlingits were blocking Russian access to the waters of southeastern Alaska. Even before the 1805 peace that concluded the Sitka Sound war, Aleksandr Andreevich desperately needed to find other sea otter hunting grounds. Yet, as he was acutely aware, the RAC lacked the sturdy vessels, competent sailors and navigators, and military strength to overcome the Tlingit blockade.

Fortuitously for Baranov, Captain O'Cain had arrived at Pavlovskaia during the late summer of 1803, bringing a cargo of goods that he sold to Aleksandr Andreevich. Learning of the Russian's dilemma, made more critical by the destruction of Fort Mikhailovskii the previous year, O'Cain described a newly discovered sea otter breeding area at an island off the coast of Baja California. He may have known, moreover, that an abundance of sea otters, virtually untouched by the Spanish, could be found all along the central and southern California coastline. He and Baranov agreed on an arrangement that would open these waters to the Russians. The Yankee ship would carry Alutiiq hunters and their Russian supervisors to California to hunt during the winter. On their return to Kodiak, the two men would divide the fur catch equally, half for the RAC and half for O'Cain and his shipowners, the Winship brothers of Brighton, Massachusetts.

Spain's imperial policy prohibited contact and commerce with foreigners in its overseas colonies. Yet O'Cain also knew that California's small, isolated cadre of military officials and missionaries usually welcomed the opportunity for surreptitious trade with visiting Yankee and British shipmasters. Official cooperation was virtually assured if these arrangements were accompanied by appropriate gifts from the merchant captains.[1]

Baranov agreed to this sea otter–hunting partnership without consulting St. Petersburg. For the chief manager, the venture was ideal: a low-cost, low-risk exploratory project, with Shvetsov and Tarakanov assigned to supervise the hunt and safeguard the RAC's interests. The trip would be far less hazardous for the Alutiiq partovshchiks than a hunting excursion into Tlingit territory. And there was the incidental benefit of leaving Alaska to spend the winter months in southern California's comparatively dry, balmy climate. As for Captain O'Cain, he and the Winships gained a half share in the services of the world's most skilled sea otter hunting crews, starting a venture in which at first they faced no competition.

From Pavlovskaia Harbor the *O'Cain* sailed directly to San Diego, then continued south to Baja California's San Quintín Bay. Claiming falsely that his ship had been badly storm damaged, Captain O'Cain received official permission to remain a few days to make repairs and secure supplies, already a customary ruse. He actually stayed three months, anchoring in San Quintín Bay while Tarakanov, Shvetsov, and the Alutiiq partovshchiks ranged along the coast between Mission Rosario and Santo Domingo. A catastrophe for the sea otters, this hunting voyage was an outstanding success for the RAC and for Captain O'Cain and the Winships. The *O'Cain* returned to Kodiak in June 1804 with no casualties, bringing eleven hundred sea otter skins that were worth more than seventy thousand dollars in trade at Canton.[2]

Baranov and Captain O'Cain added to their partnership a voyage to Canton, which was the Chinese empire's major marketing center for trade with other nations. To protect the interests of their Kiakhta merchants, China's imperial authorities had closed this port to Russian traders. But since the *O'Cain* flew an American flag, the RAC's sea otter pelts could be marketed there just as though they belonged to Captain O'Cain and his partners. So long as the captain paid *cumshaw*, the duties and fees that included a customary amount of bribery in the Chinese way of doing business, no one objected to this shrewd evasion of imperial regulations.

The profits from this joint venture heartened Baranov at a low period in the RAC's history. Like Joseph O'Cain and the Winship family, he was encouraged to undertake similar operations regularly during the next few years. Cooperation with the Americans gave the chief manager a way to bypass the Tlingit barrier and advance Russian sea otter hunting and trade well south of Alaska. Undertaken by Aleksandr Andreevich on his own initiative, such dealings with foreigners could not be approved by the Russian high authorities in St. Petersburg any more than by Spain's rulers in Madrid. But amid the worldwide military and diplomatic clashes during this era of Napoleonic Wars, it was easy and convenient for all Europe to ignore such distant, seemingly inconsequential events.

* * *

Following Baranov's 1804 success in securing the Kiks.ádi village location on Sitka Sound and starting to build there the strongly fortified New Archangel post, the chief manager began transferring the RAC's American headquarters to this site, a change completed by 1808. Though it placed his center of operations in the heartland of the still powerful Tlingit clans, this relocation made sense; it took advantage of Sitka Sound's large, well-protected harbor area with its vastly better access for both Russian and foreign merchant ships.

Yet it had one extreme drawback: the problem keeping the RAC's Russian and Alutiiq workers fed. Continued Tlingit enmity made it dangerous for Baranov's men to hunt deer or other game in the surrounding countryside or even to fish at any distance from their fort. And in times of shortage, the demands made by the officers and crews of visiting Russian ships placed a further critical strain on Baranov's slim stock of provisions.

In late August 1805 the arrival of the RAC ship *Sv. Mariia Magdalina* (*St. Mary Magdalene*) ushered in a season of severe hardship. On board was Nikolai Rezanov, now a chamberlain in Emperor Aleksandr I's government and a correspondent for the RAC's board of directors, authorized to report directly to the emperor. Recently bereaved by the death of his young wife, Anna, Madam Shelikhova's oldest daughter, Rezanov was conducting a leisurely inspection tour of the company's operations. Although he arrived thinking that younger, more vigorous men should take charge of the RAC, during his stay at New Archangel he came to admire Aleksandr Baranov. Within weeks he concluded that Baranov's continuation in office was indispensable for the well-being of Russian America.

To ease the immediate food crisis, he and Baranov purchased the Yankee ship *Juno* from John D'Wolf, its captain and owner, with D'Wolf's full cargo of foodstuffs and trade goods.[3] But this was merely a stopgap measure. Hoping to secure a supply of grain, beef, and other provisions, Rezanov decided to take the *Juno* to Spanish California. Traveling with him would be his personal physician and friend, the German naturalist and savant Dr. Georg H. von Langsdorff, who shared Rezanov's avid interest in foreign lands and peoples.

Under the command of navy lieutenant Nikolai Khvostov, the *Juno* departed from Sitka Sound in February 1806. The crew numbered thirty-three men, all badly disabled by scurvy. On the way south, Lieutenant Khvostov tried to enter the Columbia River. Chamberlain Rezanov hoped to find in that region a site for a new Russian post to preempt British or American trading and occupation of the lower Columbia basin. Had Lieutenant Khvostov succeeded in crossing the dangerous bar at the river's mouth, the Russians might conceivably have met Meriwether Lewis and William Clark's expedition, which left its winter encampment on the lower Columbia to head back toward St. Louis in mid-March 1806. But a winter storm and the incapacity of the ailing ship's company frustrated the Russian attempt.

With its weakened crew "pale and half-dead" according to Rezanov, the *Juno* arrived in San Francisco Bay in late March. California's Spanish officials welcomed the Russians most cordially. They had been instructed by Madrid to expect a visit from two Russian ships, the *Nadezhda* and *Neva* on their round-the-world voyage, and to extend every courtesy and assistance to the visitors. Rezanov explained the circumstances that brought him to San Francisco in a different ship and told Governor José Arrillaga that the emperor had given him command over all of Russian America. This assertion, he later explained to his superiors in St. Petersburg, he made "solely to lend weight" to his statements in the eyes of the Spaniards and, he said, "to put our business on the best course."[4]

While his original goal was simply to trade the *Juno*'s cargo of various manufactured goods from Russia and New England for wheat and other food supplies, the chamberlain now conceived a far more ambitious plan for establishing long-term commercial ties with the Californians. Like other foreign observers in this era, he was struck by the military weakness and the poverty of California's Spanish inhabitants. And he marveled at the abundant grain fields and prolific cattle herds at the Franciscan missions.

After lengthy discussions with Governor Arrillaga, Rezanov sent to St. Petersburg an extremely detailed outline of the mutual benefits that could be derived from a regular exchange—two ships a year, he projected—with an elaborate listing of potential trade items, prices, and exchange values. "This will assure Your Highness," he wrote to the Russian minister of commerce, "that in the whole world there could be no other trade more useful to us than the California trade."[5]

During a six-week stay, Rezanov lived ashore in the household of Don José Argüello, commandant of the San Francisco presidio and a good friend of the elderly Governor Arrillaga. His efforts to ingratiate himself led him to an intense romantic involvement with Maria Concepción, the family's lovely, headstrong teenage daughter. The dashing middle-aged Russian widower convinced the impressionable young lady that life with him in St. Petersburg's high society would be far more glamorous than her isolated, boring existence in California. Despite initial parental objection to the match, the couple negotiated a betrothal agreement with her family, assisted by an obliging Franciscan missionary. After returning to Alaska, so they planned, Rezanov would travel to St. Petersburg, Madrid, and Rome to secure approval for their marriage from the highest religious and imperial authorities, then return to claim his bride.

There may be some question about the sincerity of the chamberlain's professions of love, but beyond doubt he left California fully committed to the prospect of marrying into the Argüello family. As Langsdorff observed,

Rezanov had resolved "to sacrifice himself by this marriage to the welfare, as he hoped, of the two countries of Spain and Russia."[6] Since Doña Concepción was reputedly the most attractive young woman in the entire province, a dark-eyed beauty with a slender form, presumably the sacrifice would not have been too great.

When the *Juno* departed from San Francisco Bay in May 1806, all those on board had been restored to good health by their California diet, and the ship's hold was filled with a cargo of wheat; smaller amounts of flour, peas, beans, and maize (Indian corn); a few casks of salted beef; and a sampling of salt, soap, tallow, and other mission-made products. The whole, according to Langsdorff, represented a trade worth twenty-four thousand Spanish dollars. The ship's arrival back in New Archangel was greeted with great cheer. During the *Juno*'s absence, Langsdorff learned, ten men had died miserably of scurvy, and the baidarka paddlers who met them "looked like living skeletons . . . so starved and thin, and formed a striking contrast with the plump, well-fed sailors" coming from San Francisco.[7]

If proof were needed, the appearance of the *Juno*'s crew must have been for Baranov and others a living demonstration of the benefits Russian America might gain from a California connection. Yet Chamberlain Rezanov's grandiose proposal for reorganizing all trans-Pacific trade under RAC management would never be given serious consideration in either Madrid or St. Petersburg. Even Langsdorff believed that his friend's scheme was impractical: in part due to the company's extreme lack of ships and sailors, and in part because Russian Alaska's people also lacked the sort of manufactures and luxury goods that were most wanted by the missionaries and settlers in Spanish California.[8]

It is possible that Rezanov might have enlisted support for his plan, even during wartime, had he lived to present them in the two imperial capitals. After returning from California, he sailed from New Archangel to Okhotsk as soon as possible. He then quickly headed onward to Irkutsk but apparently tarried there for some months. Only when the winter travel season was well along did he depart on the Great Post Road toward St. Petersburg. In March 1807, after falling into an icy river from a riding accident, this haughty, politically adroit personage, Madam Shelikhova's closest ally and Aleksandr Baranov's firm new friend, contracted a fever and died at Krasnoyarsk, age forty-three.[9]

✳ ✳ ✳

While the *Juno* was still in California, the Winship brothers reached New Archangel with three ships including the *O'Cain*, now under the command of Jonathan Winship, Jr., formerly the first mate. Baranov eagerly entered into new agreements with these enterprising Yankee shipmasters, supplying them with Russian-led Alutiiq hunting crews under the same terms negotiated for the *O'Cain*'s first partnership voyage. After the *Juno*'s return from San Francisco, a fourth Winship-owned vessel, the *Peacock* commanded by Captain Oliver Kimball, a Winship brother-in-law, also arrived at the Russian headquarters. Kimball too was keen to contract for an RAC hunting crew. If Timofei Tarakanov had been aboard the *Juno* on its voyage to San Francisco, as seems quite likely, he must have been back in New Archangel only a few days before Baranov assigned him to head the partovshchiks he put aboard the *Peacock* for a return to California.[10]

Because the Spaniards had captured three of his sailors near Mission San Juan Capistrano before he reached Alaska, Captain Kimball was anxious that Tarakanov and his hunters should avoid contact with the Spanish. After first anchoring in Trinidad Bay on California's isolated north coast, Kimball made Bodega Bay his base of operations during the spring of 1807. From this secure harbor, about fifty sea miles north of San Francisco Bay, Tarakanov and his men raided northern California's sea otter populations from the Mendocino coast southward to the Farallon Islands.

Spanish records indicate that Tarakanov's partovshchiks also entered San Francisco Bay. They worked their way cove by cove along the northern shore to avoid the Spanish presidio on the south. Exasperated by this incursion, the acting presidio commander, Luis Antonio Argüello, Doña Concepción's older brother, ordered his men to fire a cannon at five baidarkas as they were leaving the bay. This surprise attack created enough of a panic that the Alutiiq hunters abandoned two of their skin boats in their haste to escape.[11]

Two months later, in mid-May, Captain Kimball departed from Bodega Bay, sailed south to San Quintin Bay to meet with Captain Winship aboard the *O'Cain*, then returned to New Archangel in August 1807. Tarakanov's men came ashore with 753 prime adult sea otter skins, 258 yearling skins, and the pelts of 250 pups, worth approximately thirty thousand dollars in trade at Canton.[12] More important for the future, Tarakanov now impressed Chief Manager Baranov with his expert knowledge of the geography and resources of Bodega Bay and the adjacent coastline, including the land and sea access routes to San Francisco Bay.

* * *

Meanwhile, in roundabout fashion, the RAC had acquired another small ship, variously identified as a brig or a schooner. While hunting from the *O'Cain* near the island of Ceros off the Baja California coast, crew leader Pavl Slobodchikov quarreled violently with Captain Winship. He left the ship, taking his crew's half share of sea otter skins. For 150 of these skins he purchased there a small vessel built in Hawaii by Yankee craftsmen for King Kamehameha I, originally christened the *Tamana*. Subsequently, the craft had been bought by two Americans and sailed to Baja with a crew of three Hawaiians and three New Englanders. After making a deal with its American owners, Slobodchikov renamed the ship the *Sv. Nikolai* (*St. Nicholas*) and took it back to Hawaii.

He was cordially received by the king, who showed a strong interest in establishing a friendly relationship with Aleksandr Baranov. In exchange for sea otter furs, Kamehameha sold the Russians a cargo of foodstuffs. Before Slobodchikov's departure, the king also entrusted the Russian with a brightly colored ceremonial cape of red and yellow feathers to present to Baranov as a gift from one monarch to another. Slobodchikov reached New Archangel with the *Sv. Nikolai* in August 1807, the same month Tarakanov arrived aboard the *Peacock* and three months ahead of Captain Winship with the *O'Cain*.

That same year Baranov purchased another ship, the British brig *Myrtle*, which he renamed the *Kad'iak* and put into service with the *Sv. Nikolai* to carry hunting expeditions southward from New Archangel. These two ships sailed as escorts for Alutiiq partovshchiks in southern Tlingit territory during the first part of 1808. Emulating the tactics of the California hunts, this expedition returned in July with a cargo of seventeen hundred skins. The Tlingit clans and their Yankee trading partners must have regarded Baranov's new style of hunting with well-armed escort ships as an alarming disruption of their profitable commerce.

* * *

At this point, influenced by the reports from California hunting voyages and Rezanov's hopes for a trade in mission-grown foodstuffs, Baranov decided to locate an RAC post on Bodega Bay. Here his Russian and Alutiiq workers could have a year-round base for California sea otter hunting. His ship captains and company agents might also develop a covert trade in wheat, beef, and other goods available from the Franciscan missions, even if the crown authorities in Spain and Mexico remained opposed. Also with Rezanov's prompting, Baranov intended to have his men explore in detail the coastline near the mouth of the Columbia River—the area called New Albion by both the English and the Russians—to investigate possibilities for still another RAC post. Wartime conditions in Europe, he realized, were now keeping British, Spanish, and most American merchant ships away from the Pacific Coast. As a result, a window of opportunity had opened that might enable the RAC to increase its profits and widen its influence on North America's Pacific Rim, even without the sanction of Aleksandr I's government.

In the fall of 1808 Baranov sent south a two-ship expedition. The *Sv. Nikolai* was the earliest to depart. It was ideal for coastal exploration because of its small size and maneuverability. Its skipper was Navigator Nikolai Bulygin, a Russian navy officer who had been assigned to the RAC in 1801 and who brought along his wife, Anna Petrovna, most likely a young creole woman either from Kodiak Island or Sitka. Baranov designated Tarakanov as the supercargo, responsible for managing the ship's contingent of Russian and Alutiiq workers and conducting any trade with New Albion's Native peoples.[13]

Tarakanov and Bulygin had orders to make a detailed survey of the coastline from the Strait of Juan de Fuca southward to the mouth of the Columbia River, then to rendezvous with the expedition's second ship, the *Kad'iak*, commanded by Navigator Ivan Petrov and carrying expedition leader Ivan Kuskov. The two ships should then proceed together to California and establish a Russian post at Bodega Bay or some other suitable site north of San Francisco Bay. Because Tarakanov had already been there and could be trusted to guide local explorations, Baranov regarded him as essential to the expedition's success. "Try to be a good manager," Aleksandr Andreevich told him, "for I am determined to extend the period you will remain there and direct all those workers."[14] For Tarakanov, who had been born into serfdom in European Russia, this must have seemed an exalted assignment.

Aleksandr Andreevich emphasized in his instructions to Kuskov that his only objective should be "to hunt and to determine where all the most advantageous places are along the coast of Albion."[15] Under his command was a very substantial force: according to a Hispanic source, they numbered 40 Russians and 150 Alaskan "Indians," including 20 women.[16] After reaching northern California, Baranov directed, Kuskov might build a fortress for housing his people at Bodega Bay or elsewhere, but it should only be a temporary structure. Wherever they went, Kuskov and his workers should take great care in establishing and maintaining cordial relations with the Native peoples. If the expedition met any traders or others from the United States near the Columbia River, Baranov further instructed, Kuskov should try to determine whether their government was trying to establish colonial settlements there. Definitely, he should not enter any negotiations about occupation rights. "You are only to say that the Russians have the same right as other nationals to hunt marine animals and seek profits along all coasts and islands, from the port of New Archangel south to California, where other nations have not established claims in accordance with natural law."[17]

If by some chance Kuskov should have an opportunity to discuss matters with the acting commandant of the San Francisco presidio, Don Luis Argüello, Baranov told him first of all to inform the Argüello family about the death of Chamberlain Rezanov. (The chief manager had already given the same instructions to crew chief Afanasii Shvetsov, then sailing to California with Captain George W. Eayrs on the *Mercury*.)

Hoping to maintain cordial relations with the Hispanic Californios, Baranov also told Kuskov that he should send fitting gifts and ask the commandant to allow RAC hunting parties to operate in San Francisco Bay. He should offer to pay a small amount, one piaster in goods for each large sea otter. He could then go on to invite—or entice—Captain Argüello to approve further Russian trade for flour and other food supplies with the nearby Franciscan missions. "Above all," Baranov wrote, "you are to try, if you have a chance, to establish future mutually advantageous, amicable trade, and hunting relations, so we can freely supply them with our goods in exchange for their products."

Baranov's instructions left it to Kuskov to decide whether or not to leave a party of Russians and Alutiiqs in northern California when he returned to New Archangel the following year. He even opened the possibility that Kuskov himself might decide to stay there. Then, he wrote, "if these hunting opportunities and dangers come to an end, you should decide about our future course of action and when to return there with the entire party of hunters and with the vessels." With this delegation of responsibility, Aleksandr Andreevich in effect made Kuskov the manager of the RAC's northern California settlement project.

* * *

Unfortunately for the chief manager's plans, four weeks into the *Sv. Nikolai*'s voyage a combination of bad luck, faulty gear, and Captain Bulygin's poor judgment found the ship drifting dangerously toward the rugged New Albion coastline, its foreyard broken and all anchors lost. While the ill-trained crew stood by helplessly, high waves and a brisk northwest gale pushed the vessel toward a rocky, tree-lined shore. Fearing the worst, all hands piously invoked divine aid. As if in answer to their prayers, the *Sv. Nikolai* floated safely past looming rocks, drifted aground, heeled over, and settled firmly on a sandy, gently sloping beach.

Thus began a Russian-American epic of shipwreck and survival. The site of the wreck was Rialto Beach on the Olympic Peninsula in modern Washington State, just north of the mouth of the Hoh River, a location all but inaccessible for sailing ships. The *Sv. Nikolai*'s people were marooned in the rainiest region of the rainy Pacific Northwest coast just as winter set in, in an area covered by dense, virtually impenetrable rain forest and cut off from the interior by the snow-covered Olympic range. With minimal supplies and few tools except for an axe or two and their flintlock muskets, they were stranded entirely on their own, with no ready means to communicate their plight to any ships that might be sailing offshore. Moreover, as they quickly discovered, the rumored hostility of the region's Native peoples toward strangers was no unfounded seaman's tale.

A full account of the ensuing events has been published elsewhere.[18] Here it is enough to record that after first fighting with the local Hoh and Quileute tribesmen, Tarakanov and his companions—some by surrender, some by capture—came to live with the Hoh and Makah people, most in a servile status rather like kaiurs in Alutiiq society. In May 1808, eighteen months after the *Sv. Nikolai*'s shipwreck, Tarakanov and twelve other survivors were rescued by Yankee shipmaster Captain Thomas Brown aboard the *Lydia*. Already on friendly terms with Baranov, Captain Brown paid a substantial ransom to each of their Native masters for the RAC people and delivered them safely to Sitka. Baranov gladly repaid Brown for his expenses and services. Seven others including Captain Bulygin and his young wife had died either from battle injuries or from illness and misadventure during their captivity. One of the Alutiiq workers had been found living with the Chinook people on the Columbia River in 1809 by another Yankee sea captain, who also ransomed him and carried him to Baranov. A final expedition member, a creole apprentice, may also have been traded away to a Columbia River Chinook village and perhaps remained there; he subsequently disappears from the historical record.

The report brought back from the Olympic Peninsula by Tarakanov and his comrades must have convinced Baranov to abandon efforts to establish an RAC outpost in the Pacific Northwest. Meanwhile, after failing to connect with the *Sv. Nikolai* at Grays Harbor, Ivan Kuskov and Navigator Petrov had proceeded aboard the *Kad'iak* to Trinidad Bay. Stormy conditions and a lack of sea otters soon sent them farther south to Bodega Bay, which they reached in mid-December. There they anchored in the cove they called Tuli-atelivy Bay, later renamed Rumiantsev Bay in honor of the Russian minister of commerce. Here too their hunting success was hampered by continued stormy weather and a scarcity of sea otters. They remained, however, waiting through the winter and spring months for the expected appearance of the *Sv. Nikolai* while refitting their ship's rigging and sails and making other repairs.

Unexpectedly, in late December four crewmen deserted the expedition, apparently seeking refuge at one or another Spanish mission near the San Francisco presidio. Kuskov, who was not a popular leader, feared that others might follow, as they threatened from time to time. Feeling that he could not rely on many of his men, he abandoned the possibility of contacting the presidio commandant. He also decided not to sail farther south toward the Channel Islands or Baja because of what he supposed would be the danger from enemy ships cruising those waters.

Kuskov and skipper Petrov did take their partovshchiks north to Cape Mendocino, where they "proceeded at great risk along this shoreline, with its rocks, cliffs, and heavy surf, but there was nothing to hunt." Twice the entire party searched around Bodega Bay in their baidarkas for the deserters, with no luck. They also portaged overland to Point Bonita and hunted sea otters along the north shore of San Francisco Bay, where Tarakanov and his hunters had come under the presidio's cannon fire two years earlier.

The *Kad'iak* finally departed Bodega Bay and headed to New Archangel in August 1809, but contrary winds delayed its arrival until early October. The expedition brought back over 1,800 adult and yearling sea otter pelts and, in addition, nearly 500 more pup pelts and over 400 fur seal skins.[19] Despite all their problems, Kuskov and his Alutiiq hunters had made it quite a profitable voyage. In reporting to the chief manager, Kuskov described the attractive opportunities in northern California: its suitability for farming, for raising cattle, and for further sea otter hunting and the prospects for future trade with the Franciscan missionaries.

At this point Baranov proposed to the RAC main office in St. Petersburg that the company's officials seek permission from the imperial court to establish a northern California post, mainly for the purpose of growing wheat and other foodstuffs and starting their own cattle herds. Essentially, he hoped the Russians might emulate the success of the Franciscan missionary fathers

IVAN KUSKOV became Baranov's principal assistant before the two men journeyed to North America in 1790, and he continued to serve in that role until the chief manager's retirement in 1819. Not a genial man with his subordinates, he became the first manager of Fort Ross on the northern California coast in 1814–15. A Native artist painted this portrait at Fort Ross prior to Kuskov's return to New Archangel with his Tlingit wife in 1818.

by establishing an agricultural colony that would recruit both Alutiiqs and northern California Natives into a Russian-managed workforce.

* * *

While putting together the 1808 expedition to New Albion and northern California, Aleksandr Baranov also found an opportunity to respond to the friendly 1807 overture from Hawaii's King Kamehameha. The navy ship *Neva*, which had returned to Sitka Sound from St. Petersburg under the command of Lieutenant Leontii Hagemeister in September 1807, proceeded to Pavlovskaia to unload a large cargo of goods and munitions. The following summer Baranov took his entire household aboard the *Neva* and made the move to New Archangel, though he left the RAC's main American office at Kodiak for the time being.

As had been true after Rezanov's 1806 arrival aboard the *Sv. Mariia*, the food supply at New Archangel was inadequate to support the *Neva*'s large Russian crew, some seventy-five men. Captain Hagemeister agreed to relieve the situation by sailing for the Hawaiian Islands. In November 1808 he departed with sundry locally made goods, including hatchets and adzes as well as walrus tusks, which he meant to trade for foodstuffs and a cargo of salt that he would carry to Kamchatka. Traveling with him was Archibald Campbell, a marooned British sailor who had become Baranov's friend while recuperating at Pavlovskaia from injuries—including the amputation of both feet due to severe frostbite a year earlier. Campbell hoped to find in Hawaii, then as now the crossroads of the Pacific, a vessel to carry him back to England.

According to Campbell's account, Captain Hagemeister acted as the chief manager's emissary to King Kamehameha. On Baranov's behalf he presented the Hawaiian monarch with a scarlet wool cloak lavishly trimmed with ermine. No more appropriate for Hawaii's balmy climate than Kamehameha's feather cape had been for Alaska's wet and cold, this cloak was a similar high-status gift, symbolizing personal regard. In both cases, it was the thought that counted.

Did Baranov then have in mind a scheme to establish a Russian settlement in Hawaii? Archibald Campbell thought so, particularly since the *Neva* carried from New Archangel a prefabricated wooden house frame. After Campbell shared this surmise with one of his countrymen who was living on Maui, Captain Hagemeister somehow learned about his remark. He was not pleased. Hagemeister gave Campbell "a severe reprimand, for having, as he expressed it, betrayed their secrets." The captain warned the crippled sailor "to say nothing more on the subject in future; otherwise [he] should not be permitted to quit the ship."[20] Campbell also said that he did not know why the plan died. Even though the *Neva* remained in the islands several months, he heard nothing more about a possible Hawaiian RAC settlement.

Although some writers have claimed that Baranov was already scheming to extend Russian sovereignty to the Hawaiian Islands in 1808, this assertion is highly dubious. Despite Campbell's statement, the *Neva*'s visit may more accurately be seen as a speculative fact-finding expedition, similar in character to the Tarakanov and Kuskov first venture to New Albion. When Captain Hagemeister returned to New Archangel, he must have briefed Aleksandr Andreevich about not only the islands' resources but also their political situation, which was not at all favorable to meddling by the Russians or any other foreign power.

King Kamehameha I, a renowned warrior and empire builder, had consolidated control over all of Hawaii's major islands except for Kauai, the domain of his rival King Kaumualii. Kamehameha was supported by a cadre of trusted British and Bostonian advisors, mostly shipmasters interested in trade, and all intent on bolstering the independence of his realm. In particular, Captain Hagemeister learned, the Bostonians had spread a rumor that the Russians hoped to settle there. For King Kamehameha, this seemed no great threat. "Let the Russians come," he reportedly said. "We have lived without them, we can also live with them." According to Hagemeister, he would even be willing to sell part of the island of Molokai to the Russians, a move, the captain believed, that would be "well worth our attention in the future."[21]

King Kaumualii, however, hoped for active Russian support to prevent Kamehameha from invading his realm and punishing him for his family's history of opposition to a united Hawaiian kingdom. He tried to bargain with Captain Hagemeister or bribe him to gain Russian aid in his opposition to Kamehameha. The naval officer was too astute to become involved in any such effort. Later Hagemeister appeared to regret that the RAC and the imperial government ignored his suggestions about striking a bargain with Kamehameha in 1809, since "no one then paid any heed."[22] But he dismissed any consideration of doing business with Kaumualii. Unfortunately, as would later appear, another supposed representative of Baranov and the RAC proved all too susceptible to the blandishments of Kauai's rebel monarch.

* * *

Handicapped more than ever by a shortage of RAC ships and skilled sailors, Baranov entered into at least seven additional partnerships with New England merchant captains for sea otter hunting in California waters between 1808 and 1813. Most were with the Winship brothers and their associates and with the Dorr brothers of Boston. According to an abstract prepared by RAC historian Kiril Khlebnikov, the company's share of the returns from California hunts aboard American ships totaled more than seven thousand pelts.[23] An additional three thousand sea otter skins came from Ivan Kuskov's two

California voyages in 1808–9 and 1811. These were by far the RAC's largest profit-making operations during this period, bringing much higher returns than Baranov's trade in fur seal hides from the Pribylov Islands.

To govern these partnership voyages, the chief manager and the American shipmasters drew up contracts that detailed their business arrangements and mutual agreements about personnel issues. A surviving example is an 1808 contract between Baranov and Captain George W. Eayrs, commanding the *Mercury*.[24] The chief manager agreed to supply twenty-five Alutiiq hunters and two Russian crew chiefs, "steady men who know the work and how to keep accurate records," for a ten- to twelve-month joint hunting venture in the southern hunting grounds that only Eayrs "know[s] sufficiently well." During the outward and return voyages, the Russian crew chiefs would share the cabin table on an equal basis with the ship's officers. All the partovshchiks would carry their own food from Kodiak Island, but in case of shortage they would be provisioned from the ship's stores. Four Alutiiq wives would accompany the hunters since they were "greatly needed for mending and sewing new *baidarkas* and marine attire, camlets [capes], and so forth." At inhabited places, the hunting crews would never remain ashore without armed protection. On uninhabited islands with hunting opportunities, Captain Eayrs might leave them for a short time with the consent of the Russian crew chiefs. If any of the RAC people were captured by the Spanish, killed, or "unaccountably lost," Eayrs agreed to pay $250 for each casualty to the company "in compensation for the surviving family and relatives."

Every fur acquired would be accurately recorded in an account book kept by the Russian crew chiefs, and Captain Eayrs would certify the accuracy of this account when the furs were loaded aboard his ship. Eayrs would share with the Russian crew chiefs a concern for the furs' preservation. When the *Mercury* returned—either to Kodiak Island or to New Archangel, whichever Captain Eayrs found most convenient—the sea otter pelts, "obtained with God's help," would be divided into two equal halves between the RAC and the captain. If the vessel and cargo had any accident, Eayrs agreed not to claim damages from the RAC or Baranov, "but only to divide the salvaged furs . . . [as earlier specified]," and each side was to "incur losses according to the will of Providence."

This contract also covered personal relations aboard ship. No one from the vessel's crew, Eayrs agreed, would interfere with the Alutiiq hunters. Only the company's agents would be in charge, "none of whom is to be offended or disturbed in the slightest." If any of the hunters committed an offense, the company agents would punish the offender. Moreover, "the women should have complete freedom and security from impertinence and bold invitations to debauchery from the ship's crew." The Russian agents were to have "the complete right to protect these women in every instance." In case any disagreements should arise between the captain and his crew, the RAC agents were not to be involved in any way. They were not to interfere with the ship's orders, and Baranov pledged them to support the captain, "whose authority they must always defend."

Contract clauses also dealt with the possibilities for trade during the voyage. All areas from Sitka Sound south to San Francisco should be considered open to joint trade by Captain Eayrs and the RAC agents. But the RAC, Baranov said, did not want to interfere with trade in Spanish California, from San Francisco southward, "since it is prohibited." This area would be left to Eayrs and his partners. With peace existing at the time between the Spanish government and the U.S. government, Eayrs might find it possible to trade with permission from the Spanish authorities. If so, Baranov hoped he would obtain a cargo of various foodstuffs to supply the RAC's Alaskan settlements. Baranov agreed to purchase these products at prices set forth on an accompanying list, to be paid from the RAC's share of furs obtained by this expedition. If there were any problems because of orders from the Spanish government, Captain Eayrs was to deal with them on his own, not involving the RAC, "and without exposing Chief Manager Baranov to any losses, disputes, or accountability."

These provisions demonstrate Aleksandr Andreevich's business experience and his careful attention to detail. They also indicate his continued concern for the well-being of his employees, both the Russian crew chiefs and the Alutiiq partovshchiks. He, like Rezanov, was well aware of the dangers to which the RAC's Native hunting crews had been exposed during their expeditions to the Alaskan mainland and especially during their incursions into Tlingit territory. Certainly, he understood the hardships imposed on their families and home villages when fatal calamities struck hunting party members. On these California excursions, Baranov hoped to assure their safety as much as possible. It is interesting to see that his concern included an effort to safeguard the morality of the Alutiiq working wives, who were likely to be the only women aboard ship. And though, unknown to Captain Eayrs, Baranov meanwhile was forming other plans that might result in direct RAC trade with the Hispanic Californians, Baranov's eagerness for such exchanges led him to encourage Eayrs in this possibly dangerous venture.[25]

* * *

While these joint trading ventures were proceeding, Baranov urged the RAC board of directors to secure Aleksandr I's permission to establish a Russian settlement in northern California. RAC board chairman Mikhail Buldakov sent this request to Count Nikolai Rumiantsev, minister of commerce and foreign affairs, with his endorsement. Count Rumiantsev in turn recommended the proposal to the emperor, who approved it in November 1809.[26] News of this approval likely did not reach New Archangel until late 1810. At that point the chief manager further intensified RAC hunting and reconnaissance efforts in northern California.

Soon after Timofei Tarakanov's rescue and safe return to New Archangel, Baranov again sent him southward. In the winter of 1810–11 he led a hunting crew with forty-eight baidarkas aboard the *Isabella*, commanded by Captain William Heath Davis. When Davis departed for Hawaii, Tarakanov and his partovshchiks made camp on the north side of San Francisco Bay. They were soon joined by another hunting party of sixty baidarkas carried aboard the *Albatross* by Captain Nathan Winship. In February or March 1811 a third hunting crew of twenty-two baidarkas came from Bodega Bay, where Ivan Kuskov had arrived aboard the American-built RAC schooner *Chirikov*, but found the hunting very poor. Working together, these three groups must have wiped out the remaining sea otter population of San Francisco Bay. Kuskov returned to Sitka after three months with more than twelve hundred pelts. In September Captain Davis and the *Isabella* also reached Sitka with Tarakanov and his hunting crew, probably accompanied by the hunters from the *Albatross*, bringing to Baranov another substantial haul of California sea otter skins.[27]

After the return of these parties, the chief manager launched his major project for establishing an RAC post north of San Francisco Bay. Once again he placed Ivan Kuskov in charge. Sailing in the *Chirikov* commanded by Captain K. M. Benzeman, the expedition included sixty Alutiiqs in forty baidarkas along with twenty-five Russian promyshlenniks, mostly craftsmen. Because of Baranov's earlier desire that Tarakanov take a major role in the failed 1808 expedition and his recent success as a crew chief, he too must have been included. In fact, he seems to have served as Kuskov's principal deputy in managing the Alutiiq partovshchiks and dealing with the Native people of Bodega Bay and the Fort Ross region.

No official reports concerning this founding voyage and the early months of the RAC settlement at Bodega Bay and Fort Ross have yet come to light.

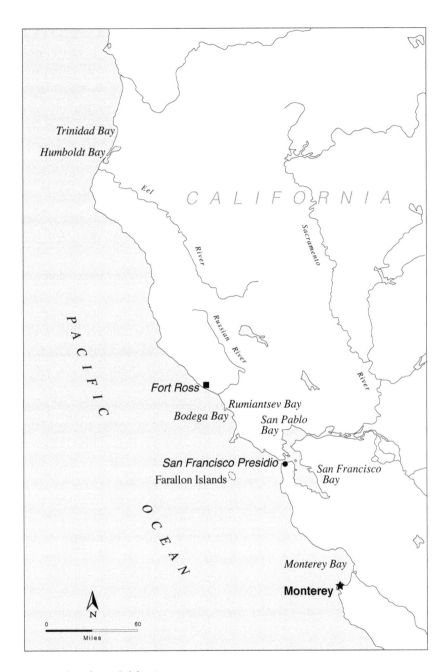

MAP 4. Northern California

According to historian Khlebnikov, the expedition departed from Sitka in November 1811 aboard the *Chirikov*, although an account by an anonymous Russian author says that the departure date was not until February 1812, arriving in mid-March.[28] Once ashore at Rumiantsev Bay, an area without trees, Kuskov sent out his men to find a better settlement site. One party headed by Sysoi Slobodchikov examined on foot the country between Bodega Bay and the Russian (Slavianka) River but saw no good location. A second group, traveling by baidarka, went farther north. They reached the coastal timber belt about ten miles north of the Russian River and found there a small sandy cove situated below an easily defensible knoll, watered by a stream and with nearby natural pasturage as well as abundant timber. In June Kuskov moved the *Chirikov* to this location, had the schooner pulled onto the beach, and started construction for Fort Ross.

Sometime during these same months, Tarakanov met with headmen of the Native communities at Bodega Bay and the Fort Ross area. According to a Native account recorded by a Franciscan missionary, Tarakanov presented gifts to a Kashaya Pomo leader near Fort Ross: three blankets, three pairs of trousers, beads, two hatchets, and three hoes. He also gifted a Bodega Miwok headman with "an Italian-style cape, a coat, trousers, shirts, arms, three hatchets, five hoes, sugar, three files, and beads."[29]

Most writers have viewed these transactions as commercial real estate deals, saying that the Russians purchased a right of settlement from the Miwok at Bodega Bay and, at the Fort Ross site, purchased the land itself from the Kashaya community.[30] It is more accurate to say that Tarakanov acted on Kuskov's behalf to help assure friendship and cooperation between these Natives and the RAC colonists. Tarakanov and Kuskov were beginning to build a mutually beneficial, reciprocal relationship with these California peoples, one that would endure for the entire three decades of Russian colonization at Bodega Bay, Fort Ross, and surrounding areas. Gifts were critical in creating good relations, not primarily for their economic value but for their noneconomic worth as a symbol of friendly regard and respect.

Except in international diplomatic disputes, land title or settlement rights were not an issue. The Russians had already determined to occupy the locations most suitable for their northern California settlement project. As Baranov had instructed Kuskov in 1808, he believed that RAC agents had a valid right to hunt or establish settlements in any part of New Albion not already held by "other enlightened powers."[31] As for Native land claims, in northern California, just as in Tlingit territory, no Russian official during

Baranov's era conceived that America's indigenous peoples had any sort of a valid title or possessory right that needed be taken into account.

The more essential goal, however, was for the small RAC contingent to establish with neighboring Native communities a relationship of mutual support and assistance. There is every indication that the Bodega Miwok and the Kashaya Pomo from the start were pleased to have the RAC newcomers settle nearby. As allies, the Russians provided security against the persistent threat of Spanish raids on Native settlements. As trading partners, they brought highly desirable articles to the California peoples, including new types of clothing, metal tools and weapons, decorative jewelry items, and luxury foods such as sugar, molasses, and candy, as well as tea and distilled liquors. Soon they became employers, paying Native people in trade goods for their labor as hunters and fishers, builders, farmers, herders, and domestic servants. Just as soon, Russian and Alutiiq men formed intimate bonds with California Native women, establishing family ties that added to the well-being of the newcomers and fostered a stable, comfortable familiarity among the members of these newly fashioned multiethnic, polycultural communities.

After two and a half centuries' experience in meeting and mixing with indigenous societies in Siberia and the maritime North Pacific, the Russians had become adept at this process of social amalgamation. Both Kuskov and Tarakanov were, like Baranov, married to Alaskan Native women in what turned out to be enduring and harmonious pairings.[32] They understood the social and cultural dynamics—and the mutual benefits—of forming cordial, intimate relationships with people of different cultural identity. A practiced generosity was essential. Alike for individuals, their families, and communities, gifting was an unmistakable sign of amity, cutting across barriers of language and ethnicity.

When Vasilii Golovnin, a Russian navy captain, visited Port Rumiantsev and Fort Ross in 1818, he found himself involved in a gift exchange with the headman of the local Miwok community. After Captain Golovnin anchored his ship, this dignitary came on board to visit him. "He brought gifts consisting of various parts of their regalia, arrows, and household items," Golovnin recorded, "and asked to be taken under Russian protection." With an Alutiiq who had lived among the Miwok for more than a year serving as interpreter, the chieftain said that he definitely wanted more Russians to settle among his people "in order to protect them from Spanish oppression." He also asked earnestly for a Russian flag, which "he wanted to raise . . . as a sign of friendship and peace whenever Russian ships should appear near the shore."[33]

Saying nothing about any putative purchase of settlement rights, Captain Golovnin declared that from all this evidence of Native friendship "it would be contrary to justice and reason to assert that the Russians occupied land belonging to someone else and settled on the shores of New Albion without having any right to do so." In another account of this visit, Lieutenant Fyodor Matiushkin described Golovnin's reciprocal presents: axes, knives, and a Russian military flag, with the promise of more gifts whenever the Miwoks displayed the flag to welcome other visiting Russian vessels.[34]

* * *

At first living in tents, Kuskov and his men made rapid progress in constructing the wooden ramparts of Fort Ross and completing the structures they needed for protection and comfort: a manager's house, barracks, storehouses, and outbuildings for cattle and farming operations. Lieutenant Gabriel Moraga visited the new post in 1812 and again in 1814, making friendly contact with the Russian commander while surveying the site for the benefit of Governor Arrillaga. He described the log-walled square palisade with its two cannon towers on the southwestern and northeastern corners. Within, he reported, was "an attractive roof construction with partitions—the lower part is used as a barracks; the upper as a storehouse." He also mentioned a separate building used as a workspace for "artisans," presumably a blacksmith, carpenters, and perhaps also rope makers and riggers. He made particular note of the manager's large house, which he shared with a ship pilot. It was "in very good condition—filled with windows—on a lower floor is the wine storehouse; other things can be kept upstairs." He also mentioned a roofed structure in the draw leading to the small beach, which he termed "a sort of supply area or equipment storage since in it they had the rigging and other things for ships."[35] By the time of his 1814 visit, the RAC men had also constructed another walled compound between the fort and the beach, which they were using as a corral for both cattle and horses.

In reporting his observations, Lieutenant Moraga warned that "if the need should arise to attack them," the approach must be carefully planned since it would be no easy matter for soldiers even to reach the fort. "Further," he cautioned, "these are very astute people as shown by the factories [trading structures] they have built in such a short time and the differences that are found from one day to the next."[36] With Alta California's Spanish soldiery few in number, unpaid and poorly supplied during a period of continuing political upheaval in the mother country and Mexico, and with both Fran-

FORT ROSS in 1817. This view of Fort Ross shows the palisaded compound with its two gun towers and various buildings. At the water level on the right is the small sandy beach suitable for baidarkas. The edge of the region's woodlands and the coastal mountain range frame the view. Fruit orchards and extensive cattle herds were later additions. It is evident why Hispanic Californians thought this a strong defensive position for the RAC outpost.

ciscan missionaries and government officials pleased to have opportunities for clandestine trade with the nearby Russians, Governor Arrillaga had no intention of attacking the RAC's new outpost.

Still, appearances had to be maintained. The governor sent Kuskov a letter stating his objections to the Russians' invasion of what he claimed was Spanish territory and demanding RAC withdrawal forthwith. In reply, Kuskov adopted a tactic of deliberate delay and obfuscation. Writing with formal politeness, he explained that he could not really understand Arrillaga's message because he could neither read nor write Spanish. And while the message bearer, Lieutenant Moraga, had tried to explain the governor's demand, "his explanations were hardly sufficiently clear," Kuskov stated, "as we had no interpreter to justify me in taking official action on the premises."

Then Kuskov changed the subject, asking Arrillaga about the return of certain "Kodiak men" held by the Spanish at the San Francisco presidio. It appeared, he said, that these men had done no wrong, but had simply been trying to save themselves from the surf in San Francisco Bay when they were captured by Spanish troops. Two other Alutiiq men and two women—apparently members of an earlier hunting party—had also been unjustly detained in 1813, Kuskov pointed out. Though Governor Arrillaga had supposedly ordered the return of these people to the RAC, Kuskov concluded that "whether this is true or not, [only] time will tell."[37]

For the time being, this stalemate seemed to satisfy everyone, Russian and Spanish. Two years later a new governor, Don Pablo Vicente de Solá, felt the need to restate his government's formal objection to the Russian intrusion into Alta California, a territory that extended, according to Madrid authorities, all the way north at least to the Columbia River or even to Nootka Sound on Vancouver Island. His opportunity came when the brig *Rurik* commanded by Captain Otto von Kotzebue, a Russian navy lieutenant, entered San Francisco Bay in early October 1816.

More than a year into a voyage of Pacific exploration that would last two more years, Captain Kotzebue had no instructions or specific orders to deal with matters concerning Russia's imperial boundaries and borders on the Pacific coast of North America. Nonetheless, after Governor Solá came from Monterey to meet him, Kotzebue and his officers listened with apparent sympathy to the governor's complaints about Kuskov's Russian establishment at Bodega Bay and Fort Ross. This territory, Solá said, was indisputably the property of the Spanish empire. Kotzebue replied that he could only regret that he lacked instructions to remedy the wrong imposed upon Spain by the RAC officials, Baranov and Kuskov. But he did send a message by baidarka to Fort Ross, requesting Kuskov to come meet with him and Governor Solá for a conference on this difficult matter.

Within a few days Kuskov arrived with a company in seven baidarkas. As arranged by Captain Kotzebue, the diplomatic conference took place the following day, October 26, at the San Francisco presidio. After the governor stated his case and demanded that Kuskov abandon the RAC's illegal occupation, Kuskov made a careful reply. The sense of his words was recorded by Adelbert von Chamisso, the *Rurik*'s naturalist who was serving as the conference secretary. "Without going into the question of law, which was not his concern," Chamisso wrote, Mr. Kuskov "manifested the greatest willingness to depart from Port Bodega as soon as he was empowered to do so by his superior, Mr. Baranov, who had ordered him here." In apparent exasperation, Governor Solá then called on Captain Kotzebue as the emperor's representative to intervene and secure the evacuation of Bodega. The captain declared that, unfortunately, he lacked jurisdiction to act, "though the justice of the case seemed so clear that it merely had to be stated to be recognized." So, Chamisso commented, "we were as far as we had been before."[38]

The proceedings were not yet concluded. The participants agreed to draft a joint statement about the day's negotiations and send it in proper form to the Spanish king and the Russian emperor. Chamisso, put in charge of editing this document, rejected a first draft and explained his reasoning to Governor Solá. By informing both sovereigns and expecting the Russian emperor to act by punishing those responsible, he said, "you are divesting yourself of the right you indisputably have of taking action into your own hands against the invader, and then must not anticipate the high decision of the monarchs." In other words, for Solá to actually do anything about Kuskov's establishment might prove to be a usurpation of the power of either the Spanish or the Russian ruler. It was an ingenious quibble, a brilliant justification for letting the situation remain as it was.

Solá agreed and even praised Chamisso for his insight. When the document was finally prepared and signed at the presidio two days later, the governor "gave his solemn word of honor not to undertake any act of force on his own initiative against the aforesaid Kuskov and the Russian settlement in Port Bodega and to leave affairs *in statu quo* until the decision of the high courts was made."

After a "festive farewell dinner" in the tents of the *Rurik*'s officers, Kuskov and his fleet of baidarkas departed for Bodega and Fort Ross early on the morning of October 29. (Two baidarkas of his men had meanwhile gone sea otter hunting at the distant eastern end of the bay, well out of sight from the presidio.) Later that day Governor Solá rode away on horseback, heading back to his Monterey capital.

For two more days the *Rurik*'s people occupied themselves in bringing aboard animals along with a great supply of fresh water, fresh vegetables, and fruit. They also loaded a cask of Monterey wine, a gift from the governor. Sea-ready, on the morning of November 1, All Saints' Day, while their Spanish friends were walking to church, the *Rurik*'s crew weighed anchor and set sail, heading westward toward the Hawaiian Islands and points beyond.

Even without the Spanish governor having sworn his oath not to attack the RAC in northern California, Chamisso said in retrospect, "he would hardly have opened hostilities and undertaken a campaign against the Russian fort at Port Bodega." His record of the San Francisco conference proceedings did in time reach St. Petersburg "and, without ever being acted upon, was consigned to the files in the appropriate ministry."[39]

Neither Baranov nor any of his successors ever believed that RAC occupancy gave Russia a title to lands at Bodega Bay and Fort Ross. These posts remained secure above all because of Spanish and later Mexican military weakness, combined with a mutual reluctance to cause political problems between two friendly nations. The situation remained much as Captain Hagemeister described it in 1817. "All the Spaniards, even including the Viceroy," he said, "are indifferent about the new settlement of the Russian American Company, Ross. In fact, they even commend its organization. . . . By extending a helping hand to each other in the New World," the Spanish and the Russians "may strengthen the friendship which was firm in the Old World, and with cooperative efforts we will be in a position to expel unwelcome guests." The hatred that Spanish officials felt for Americans and English because of the aid they had given the revolutionary insurgents, he added, "leads them to feel that our proximity is a lesser evil."[40] After the Mexican rebels gained independence two years later, they too were willing to accept their RAC neighbors as a lesser evil, compared to the incipient danger from aggressive Yankee frontiersmen.

* * *

While no Spanish authority could officially countenance the RAC establishment at Rumiantsev Bay and Fort Ross, unofficially the frontier between Russian California and Spanish California was quite permeable. Kuskov's men early began building their cattle and horse herds with breeding stock from the Franciscan missions. Sheep and hogs presumably came from the same sources. Sapling fruit trees, grape vines, and seed for garden vegetables and grain crops likewise must have been secured in barter with the obliging friars. Because of local weather conditions along this coast, with dense fog throughout the summer, farming at Fort Ross was never a great success. Small-scale kitchen gardens and the natural reproduction of beef cattle and other domestic animals helped feed the RAC residents, yet Russian hopes were never fully realized for a large locally grown agricultural surplus to supply posts in Alaska and Kamchatka.

By the time of Fort Ross's founding, predatory hunting had drastically reduced California's sea otter population. For a few years the Winship brothers and other Yankee shipmasters continued their hunting partnerships with

Baranov, but with fewer pelts each season to show for their efforts. The New Englanders then turned elsewhere, many to trade sandalwood with King Kamehameha in the Hawaiian Islands. Kuskov sent Alutiiq and Russian hunters northward along the coast as far as Humboldt Bay, both to explore and to raid the remnant sea otter population, but with scant results.

While Kuskov remained at Fort Ross, Tarakanov returned to New Archangel at least once. In January 1814 he headed a crew of fifty-nine Alutiiq hunters sent to California aboard the brig *Il'mena* (formerly Captain Brown's *Lydia*, purchased by the RAC a few months earlier), under Captain William Wadsworth, who had joined the service of the RAC.[41] Apparently, he remained at Bodega Bay or Fort Ross until April 1816. He then he boarded the *Il'mena* with his hunting crew for a return trip to New Archangel, leaving California for the last time.[42] Once at sea, however, Captain Wadsworth discovered his ship leaking dangerously. Needing repairs, Wadsworth made the shorter, safer voyage to the Hawaiian Islands, arriving at Honolulu in May, with consequences described in the following chapter.

The Fort Ross commander also dispatched a small hunting crew to live for a while on the Farallon Islands while they killed fur seals and sea lions, the one for their skins, the other to help feed the Fort Ross garrison. But these efforts were insignificant in producing profits for the RAC.

With neither farming nor marine hunting as an economic mainstay, Fort Ross became most useful as a base for the RAC's covert trade with northern California's Franciscan missions. Situated inland from the coastal weather regime, these missions with their large unfree Native labor forces resembled in some ways the huge serf-run estates of Russia's black-earth region. They produced abundant crops of wheat and other grains for which there was only a limited local market, feeding Alta California's undermanned military posts and its four small civilian settlements. Bartering with the RAC brought the Franciscans a welcome supply of scarce manufactured goods and luxury items that they could not get from New Spain.

Because it could not be approved in Mexico City, Alta California's officials kept this Russian trade out of the documentary record. A rare account is preserved in the journal of a Russian naval officer visiting San Francisco on a round-the-world voyage in January 1821. This officer, Lieutenant Nikolay Shishmaryov aboard the sloop *Blagonamerenni* (*Good Intent*), recorded the arrival of the RAC brig *Golovnin* in January. Coming from the Bodega Bay, the ship exchanged salutes with the fort as it sailed into the bay and reached an anchorage. "The reason for its coming here," the lieutenant wrote, "was trade with the Spaniards; it had various goods from Sitka, such as coarse cloth, linen, taffeta, a variety of shawls, mirrors, and various other things that had to be exchanged for wheat." Business could not begin, however, until the San Francisco presidio commandant gained permission from the governor at Monterey. "Although trade is forbidden here," Shishmaryov explained, "circumstances have forced them to permit it." Chief among these circumstances was a raid by Mexican insurgents who had recently destroyed a large part of Monterey. "Although a very high price was set on the goods," he tells us, "these circumstances forced them to give [in exchange] 5,000 puds [about 90 tons] of grain."[43]

Soon after this event, the struggle for Mexican independence enabled the Hispanic Californians to establish their own virtual independence. For a while these changed circumstances worked for the advantage of the RAC. Largely as Rezanov and Baranov had envisioned, California's mission-grown wheat and other grain crops made possible an improvement in diet far more agreeable to Alaska's Russian population than were the fish, shellfish, and marine mammals that had sustained everyone during the early years of Aleksandr Andreevich's administration.[44] The RAC's Russian and Alutiiq personnel, as well as the company's stockholders in the home country, were thus beneficiaries of Aleksandr Baranov's move southward beyond Alaska.

XI

AVERTING DISASTERS

✦━━━━━━━━━━━━━━━━━✳━━━━━━━━━━━━━━━━━✦

Despite Baranov's often repeated wish to be replaced, circumstances and misfortune kept him at his North American post through the period of the Napoleonic Wars in Europe and the U.S. war against Great Britain that began in 1812. The longer he remained, the more difficult he found it to keep RAC operations running smoothly and profitably. The threat of a bloody mutiny at New Archangel, an awkward short-term partnership with John Jacob Astor's Pacific Fur Company, and a violent confrontation with one of Astor's agents, the erratic Wilson Price Hunt, all added to his burdens. Perhaps most disappointing was a totally mismanaged effort to reach a closer understanding with King Kamehameha I, the ruling monarch of the Hawaiian Islands, whose friendship with the Russians was heavily damaged by the arrogant behavior of a German naturalist who Baranov had unwisely appointed to represent the RAC in the island kingdom.

✦━━━━━━━━━━━━━━━━━✳━━━━━━━━━━━━━━━━━✦

AS SEA OTTER RETURNS FROM CALIFORNIA BEGAN TO DECLINE, Aleksandr Baranov faced new, often challenging problems. In part, these problems were personal. More than ever, he felt his strength failing and his vitality lagging, and he suffered under the burden of work his position imposed on him. Moreover, he worried about the future well-being of his two children as well as their mother. From year to year he hoped for the appearance of a new administrator to take over the leadership of Russian America. Yet his experience with possible replacements must have been discouraging.

The first man sent out in that role was his friend Emel'ian Larionov, the Irkutsk merchant who in 1797 had become a partner in the United American Company. Accompanied by his wife and daughter, Larionov traveled to Unalaska to manage that new district in 1798. Although Baranov recommended him as a successor the following year, RAC company directors ignored this proposal. Larionov remained in that same post until his illness and death in 1806.[1]

Ivan Banner was the next person who seemed a plausible candidate for the chief manager's post. A Dane with experience in the Russian mining service, he befriended Kirill Laksman and Baranov at Irkutsk during the 1780s. Banner became a trader with the Chukchi alongside the Baranov brothers and also served as a rural police chief in northeastern Siberia. In 1797, with Baranov's urging, he joined Shelikhov's Northeastern Company, expecting to establish a trading post on the American shore of the Bering Sea, opposite the Chukchi Peninsula. When he reached Unalaska in 1802, however, Larionov sent him instead to Pavlovskaia to become Baranov's understudy. In that role he took command of the Kodiak district when Aleksandr Andreevich left to begin the campaign against the Sitka Tlingits in 1804.

At Pavlovskaia, Banner and his Russian wife gained a reputation for their hospitality. He was interested in America's natural history and also promoted the advance of learning at the company settlement. Some of his peers, however, thought him too genial and lax in discipline with his RAC subordinates. After his wife's death in 1806, he married a young Alutiiq woman. He died of an unrecorded illness ten years later, apparently without ever having been given further consideration as the RAC's chief manager.[2]

When Rezanov arrived in Russian America in 1805, he found that Baranov then hoped to make Ivan Kuskov his successor. He described Kuskov as "very deserving and of good morals." As a reward for his services, Rezanov presented Kuskov with a gold medal, but Baranov's assistant was reluctant to stay in Alaska. Both Baranov and Kuskov had good reasons for wanting to leave, and to the RAC directors Rezanov explained, "You must excuse them." Given the state of affairs in the company's American territory, Rezanov thought that it would be hard to find someone to take charge, and by the time a new man learned the job, the company might suffer irreparable losses. "Such is the ugly organization of our trading business," he declared.[3]

With Kuskov ruled out, the RAC directors made two more attempts to provide someone to take over Baranov's post. The first, appointed in 1810, was Ivan Kokh, a German-born physician and government official in Irkutsk and Okhotsk. After working as the director of a state textile factory, he took an assignment with the RAC to sail to America and take over the chief manager's duties. On the way in January 1811, he died in Kamchatka of unknown causes.[4]

The following year the board of directors found another likely candidate. Tertii Bornovolokov was a native of northern Russia and the owner of a small estate. He had a lengthy record of military service and employment with both the State Treasury and the Ministry of Justice in St. Petersburg. A minor official, remarks historian Richard A. Pierce, he was honest and therefore poor. Seeking a more lucrative position, Bornovolokov impressed two RAC directors with his ideas for improving the company's organization. Early in 1812 the board unanimously agreed to make him Baranov's assistant, paying him well and designating him to eventually succeed the veteran chief manager.

Bornovolokov prepared for the new assignment by reading everything about Russian America he could find in St. Petersburg. He then set out across Siberia during the spring of 1812. In mid-August he reached Okhotsk and boarded the aging RAC ship *Neva*, now commanded by Lieutenant Iakov Podushkin, another young naval officer in company service. It departed from the Okhotsk roadstead far too late in the season for safe sailing across the North Pacific. With constant storms and an outbreak of scurvy on board, this prolonged voyage was doomed from the start. In January 1813 the *Neva* ran aground and broke up on a rocky island at the foot of Mount Edgecumbe, nearly in sight of Sitka. Bornovolokov died in the wreck. Lieutenant Podushkin, thrown senseless on the shore, was one of twenty-five survivors.[5]

* * *

With these repeated disappointments, Baranov comforted himself with the thought that it must be God's will for him yet to remain as the emperor's viceroy in Russian America. But the job had dangers beyond the perils of Alaskan sea travel and the risks of battle with hostile Natives. In 1809, as historian Khlebnikov described it, "several stormy and deluded spirits" among the promyshlenniks plotted a mutiny that would start with the murder of the chief manager. The two leaders, Vasilii Naplavkov, who had come from Siberian criminal exile, and a former peasant named Ivan Popov, recruited ten others in a scheme to kill Baranov and everyone in his home. They would then seize all the guns at New Archangel and try to incite other promyshlenniks to join them. Those who refused would be imprisoned or killed. Once in control of the garrison, the plotters planned to steal the richest furs and put them aboard a new ship then anchored in Sitka Sound, whence they would sail away toward Hawaii and the South Seas. To complete this proletarian fantasy, they intended to take along one young girl for each mutineer and at least an additional fifteen women.

Three of the men first contacted by the head plotters secretly reported the scheme to Aleksandr Andreevich, who devised a plot of his own to catch the evildoers red-handed. He waited until the would-be mutineers had gathered one evening and written down their plan in the form of a contract, which they all signed. At that point one of Baranov's loyal informers began singing a certain song. At this signal the chief manager and a squad of armed men burst into the room, seized the ringleaders and others, and clamped them all in irons.

Baranov presided at a hearing that exposed the details of the plot. It had been inspired, according to one of the guilty men, by the example of an earlier mutiny at Kamchatka. When questioned about their motive, the prisoners complained about a shortage of food and what they considered unjust punishments. The two chief conspirators and four accomplices remained under guard until they could be sent to the military commandant at Kamchatka, accompanied by a full report from Aleksandr Andreevich about their bloody-minded intrigue.[6] Unfortunately, no reports are available to show what happened to them, but it cannot have been a pleasant outcome for the inept ringleaders.

* * *

The competition from Yankee shipmasters trading with the Tlingits for sea otter peltry remained vexing. After Baranov sent Kuskov and Tarakanov to New Albion and northern California on their abortive 1808 expedition, RAC fur hunting virtually ended in southeastern Alaska. The Tlingits, sometimes backed by American mariners, were successful in forestalling Baranov's partovshchik expeditions into their home waters. Even when accompanied by company ships for protection, these hunting parties found it a dangerous effort with little reward. After returning from his first trip to California, in May 1810 Kuskov led a hunting expedition with two ships and more than a hundred baidarkas southward toward the Queen Charlotte Islands. Although he returned in early August with fourteen hundred pelts, his men had met heavy, well-armed opposition from the Haida wherever they went.

Subsequently, no more RAC parties ventured into these waters until 1815. Lieutenant Podushkin, having survived the 1813 wreck of the *Neva*, then sailed the *Otkrytie* (*Discovery*) into the home waters of the southern Tlingits on a trading excursion, but the returns were disappointing: only 340 large sea otters and another 146 yearlings and pups, while his Alutiiq hunters delivered but 349 pelts of all sizes. The following year hunting parties brought back a mere 63 sea otter pelts. In the Sitka area, the local Tlingits sold to the RAC a total of 163 pelts between 1815 and 1818.[7] These figures mark the end of Baranov's effort to exploit the dwindling fur resources of southeastern Alaska, henceforth controlled entirely by the Tlingits, the Haida, and their Yankee trading partners.

During the first decade of sea otter hunting along the California coast, the returns, even shared with the Winships and other New England captains, nicely offset the diminishing hunting results from the Northwest Coast. From 1809 through 1813, the RAC gained more than 7,000 pelts from this source. California expeditions led by Kuskov and Tarakanov in company ships during these same years yielded an additional 3,500 sea otter skins. After the founding of Fort Ross, hunters searching the northern coastal waters brought back 857 pelts of all sizes from 1812 through 1814, 250 in 1815 and 1816, and only 55 in 1817, mute evidence of the demographic collapse of the population. To explain this decline, however, historian Khlebnikov mentioned the growing opposition of the Spanish authorities to Russian and Yankee incursions, but he also ungraciously said that it was the fault as well of the Alutiiq partovshchiks, "who caused the sea otters to disperse."[8]

To offset the rapid drop in sea otter returns both in southeastern Alaska and in California, Chief Manager Baranov increasingly relied on fur seal skins from the Pribylov Islands. A bounty system for Russian hunters had resulted in the slaughter of immense numbers of fur seals early in Baranov's administration. Thousands of skins had accumulated, simply stacked on beaches in the open. At least eight thousand had spoiled, and another large number were all but worthless by the time they reached Irkutsk. As the result of a killing moratorium imposed by the RAC directors for nearly a decade, a renewed demand for these skins by Russian and Chinese buyers made them once more an important item of commerce by 1814. Although an individual fur seal skin was not nearly as valuable as a sea otter pelt, averaging only a dollar or so per hide in Canton, Baranov was able to trade them with American skippers in very large numbers at favorable prices.

Lured by the RAC's sea otter pelts and fur seal hides, according to an important recent study of the Russian-American trade in the North Pacific, seventeen American ships visited New Archangel between 1801 and 1809, delivering an estimated five hundred thousand rubles worth of goods in exchange for Baranov's furs.[9] It was this trade that enabled the chief manager to keep his operations prosperous and fairly well supplied despite the hardships caused by a continuing lack of support from Russia.

During and after the period of the Napoleonic Wars, sandalwood from the Hawaiian Islands became another greatly valued commodity in the Pacific trade. Highly aromatic, it was prized for burning as incense in joss houses throughout eastern Asia. Growing in abundance at lower elevations, it could be cut and sold only under the authority of the local monarchs. King Kamehameha's growing authority was based in no small part on his royal sandalwood monopoly, with immense cargoes carried to market by New England and British captains who catered to the monarch's tastes. An immediate, virtually cost-free source of wealth, it tempted Kamehameha into heedless cutting and exorbitant spending until the sandalwood groves were all but eradicated. Learning of the money to be made in this trade from visiting shipmasters, Aleksandr Andreevich considered how to gain a share of it for the RAC.

* * *

Beginning in late 1807 the Jefferson and Madison administrations, prompted by war conditions in Europe, enacted the first in a series of measures to restrict U.S. trade with Britain and France. Lacking a navy, the two presidents and Congress hoped to force the belligerent sea powers to respect the neutral rights of American shipping by economic coercion. After the United States declared war against Great Britain in 1812, the Enemy Trade Act and, in 1813, the new Embargo Act set national policy. Both economically and politically, these various measures restricting trade proved disastrous to the young American republic. They failed to influence seriously the warring European nations, but badly crippled the northeastern merchant shipping interests and fueled antiadministration sentiment among the Federalists of New England.

These measures had a mixed effect on Russian America. While the Napoleonic Wars continued, fewer Boston-based ships reached Alaska. Meanwhile, a small group of New England and New York sea captains shifted their trading patterns to remain in the Pacific, away from their home ports, where they were relatively safe from British or French interference. With Honolulu as a major port of call, their voyages linked New Archangel into a commercial network that included Valparaiso, San Diego, Monterey, San Francisco, Bodega Bay, and Fort Ross, as well as Macao and Canton. Manila in the Philippine Islands, Batavia in the Dutch East Indies, Petropavlovsk in Kamchatka, and even Okhotsk might also figure in their evolving, improvised series of commercial exchanges. Many of these seagoing traders, beginning with the Winship brothers and their family connections, became familiar, trusted friends for Baranov at New Archangel. But others continued the arms trade with the Tlingits, exasperating everyone in Russian America.

Cut off from European Russia, the chief manager broadened his dependence on cooperative Yankee merchant captains, using Pribylov Island seal skins as his customary capital in securing provisions and supplies for Russian America. Among those supplies was an ample stock of alcohol. Visiting traders often commented on Baranov's delight in social drunkenness. Captain John Ebbets of the *Enterprise*, an agent for the wealthy American fur merchant John Jacob Astor, in 1811 told Astor that liquor must be a significant part of every cargo meant for Aleksandr Andreevich. "Without any," he reported, "we should have been unwelcome guests." At New Archangel, Ebbets said, "it is the *Idol* of the Common people as they all drink an astonishing quantity G[overnor] B[aranov] himself not excepted, and I assure you it is no small tax on a person's health that does business with him."[10]

A year later Peter Corney, first mate on the North West Company schooner *Columbia*, described his experience. While his captain went ashore to enjoy the convivial society of Aleksandr Andreevich and other guests, Corney had to remain aboard ship. "It is the custom of Governor Baranoff," he wrote, "to make his visitors drunk, when they dine with him. On these occasions he will commence firing guns, which must be answered by the ships, and I have been obliged to fire upwards of fifty guns in a day."[11] Clearly, the RAC headquarters under Baranov's management was as much a drunken republic during these years as Chamberlain Rezanov had earlier discovered, to his dismay.

* * *

Responding to Baranov's complaints about the Yankee sea captains' clandestine dealing with Northwest Coast Native peoples on the borders of Russian America, RAC officials repeatedly protested against such activities to the U.S. consul general in St. Petersburg. By 1808, when the leaders of both nations were hoping to enlarge a trade in American sugar and cotton in exchange for Russian manufactures, these protests had become diplomatically significant.[12] RAC directors once again urged that the American captains' commerce with the Tlingits be officially prohibited. Consequently, a new Russian consul general, Andrei Dashkov, arrived in the United States with instructions to give all possible support to the company's commercial interests. He was to be, in effect, the RAC's diplomatic agent.

After spending a few months in the United States, Dashkov told Chief Manager Baranov what he had learned. The key difficulty, he wrote, was that the American republican government lacked authority to regulate the business practices of its citizens in the overseas trade. Even if the national authorities had such power, he added, they would be totally unable to enforce any restraints on the Yankee shipmasters. As the RAC main administration quoted him, "The government of the United States does not have either the desire or the power to put an end to this illegal trade."[13]

But Dashkov believed a solution was at hand. He had discussed the problem at length with John Jacob Astor, the wealthy New Yorker whose American Fur Company dominated the U.S. fur business in the northern Great Lakes and upper Missouri country. Astor was now forming a new organization, the Pacific Fur Company, and planning to establish a permanent trading post near the mouth of the Columbia River. Though neither he nor any members of the federal administration envisioned an immediate move to colonize settlers along the Pacific coast, the establishment of a prosperous trading station would be a first move in the complicated diplomatic chess game that might ultimately decide sovereign claims to the Oregon Country and the Northwest Coast.

According to Dashkov, Astor favored a commercial alliance with Baranov and the RAC. He would send two or three ships a year to New Archangel with the supplies needed by Baranov's colony, exchange them for furs, and take the Russian furs along with his own to market at Canton. He would trade exclusively with Baranov, not with the Tlingits or other Native people, adhering to a mutually agreeable list of prices and exchange rates. In this way, with a pledge not to intrude on each other's trading region, Astor claimed that his new company and the RAC could monopolize the Northwest Coast trade, undercutting the Boston men and blocking further advance into the Oregon Country by the Montreal-based North West Company, Astor's Pacific Coast rivals.[14]

With Consul Dashkov's encouragement, and even before completing any formal agreement, Astor sent to New Archangel one of the ships outfitted for the Pacific trade and supplying his new post, Astoria, on the lower Columbia River. This ship was the *Enterprise*, with John Ebbets as captain.[15] Ebbets was well acquainted with Baranov; he had been one of the captains who rescued survivors from the 1802 Tlingit attack on the Sitka fort. His arrival at New Archangel with a cargo of goods for the RAC came as a pleasant surprise for the chief manager.

The first Baranov learned of Dashkov's discussions with Astor was in a letter from Dashkov delivered by Captain Ebbets. Although Astor had loaded the *Enterprise* with trade goods recommended by Dashkov, Baranov was not well pleased with the cargo. While he was interested in some items—among them certainly the rum and brandy—he thought Ebbets's prices were too high. The captain, however, thought that Baranov was asking too much for his furs, a view later seconded by Astor. Even so, Baranov and Ebbets negotiated a deal for part of the New Yorker's goods and an arrangement for Ebbets to carry RAC furs valued at sixty-five thousand dollars to Canton, where he would trade them for specified Chinese merchandise.

Since China's imperial authorities still refused to allow Russian traders access to the Canton market, Aleksandr Andreevich found this plan an alluring advantage to an Astor connection. So too was the virtual guarantee of a regular supply of needed manufactures and food items that the New York merchant seemed to be offering. The trade with Baranov, Astor anticipated, would prove a profitable addition to his project for monopolizing the fur trade of the Columbia River drainage and the Oregon Country. Working together, he believed the RAC and his Pacific Fur Company could monopolize the fur trade opportunities north of California along the entire northwest coast. Baranov seemed to agree. But both the chief manager in New Archangel and Consul Dashkov at Philadelphia referred any international negotiation to the imperial authorities in Russia.

Demonstrating apparent goodwill on both sides, the relationship between Astor and the RAC was formalized in May 1812 by an agreement made in St. Petersburg by Astor's son-in-law, the Danish consul Adrian Bentzon, and the RAC's executive committee led by board chairman Mikhail Buldakov. Buldakov and his colleagues suspected that Astor and Bentzon had an ulterior motive. What interested them most was not trade with Russian America, they thought, but the possibility of bringing other furs from North America into Russia duty-free. The RAC directors exercised their monopoly rights to block such a concession. Even so, with Emperor Aleksandr's approval, the directors reached an agreement with Bentzon, to be good for four years.

The agreement's main features included a division of the Pacific Coast fur territories between the RAC and the American Fur Company and a ban on arms trading with Native peoples by both parties. The American Fur Company agreed to send on its own ships "all the supplies and other articles, staples, and apparatus and materials" ordered by the RAC chief manager, and the RAC agreed not to buy these items from anyone else, with certain exceptions: if, after an agreement on a specific cargo, the supplies did not arrive because of a shipwreck or other misfortune or "in the unlikely event that the American Fur Company demands clearly exorbitant prices."

The two companies promised to cooperate to remove any outsiders from their territory and to cooperate "in any cases in which they may find themselves subject to disadvantages or dangers." Finally, the American Fur Company ships would carry RAC furs to Canton for reasonable freight charges "and sell these on Russian account . . . and bring back Chinese goods to the Russian colonies for an agreed-upon charge." All RAC payments to the American Fur Company for supplies and services would be payable at St. Petersburg or in the colonies with furs at prices fixed by the chief manager.[16]

Astor's optimistic expectations for cooperation with Baranov and the RAC were not fully realized. Captain Ebbets aboard the *Enterprise* admirably carried out his orders, making two trading voyages between New Archangel and Canton in 1811 and 1812 before returning safely to New York. But the next ship Astor sent to the Pacific, the *Tonquin* under Captain Jonathan Thorn, was destroyed with most of its cargo while trading with Nootkans at Clayoquot Sound, near Nootka Sound on Vancouver Island.[17] A greater calamity was the coming of war between the United States and England in 1812, a turn of events that came as a complete surprise to Astor. Before he could take any defensive measures, his partners at Astoria sold out the fort and its inventory very cheaply to the North West Company, whose agents raised the British flag and renamed it Fort George.[18] Although Astor tried unsuccessfully to regain the post after the peace in 1815, eventually he withdrew from any further Oregon Country trade ambitions, while his captains became more active in trade with China and the Hawaiian Islands.

In 1813 Astor's ship *Lark* drifted ashore and wrecked on Maui, losing five men and its full cargo, most of it meant for New Archangel.[19] Although this loss was another major setback for Astor, when the RAC directors learned of the *Lark*'s destruction—undoubtedly through Baranov—they considered themselves lucky. "We are extremely sorry for Astor's loss," the directors wrote, "but at the same time we must admit that the cargo would have been disastrous for the Company." Included was a very large amount of rum and other items that were useless to the RAC they said. "Baranov did not want them, and had not ordered them, but they were sent, in great quantities, and at prices we could not agree to." If the chief manager had taken this cargo, they said, "Astor would have been the only person to profit." There had been an informal agreement of sorts regarding the types of goods and prices, but Astor "had apparently tried to reap the profits he craved, from us," they wrote, "for useless items which it would have been shameful for Baranov to accept." Not even the rum in the cargo was needed. If Baranov had taken it, his supply would have been enormously increased "because the rum previously delivered [by Captain Ebbets] is still in the warehouse and is evaporating."[20]

Another of Astor's ships, the *Beaver* commanded by Captain Cornelius Sowle, arrived at New Archangel in mid-August 1812. On board was Wilson Price Hunt, one of Astor's partners coming from Astoria. Hunt, by all accounts, was a difficult man, an eastern merchant with no previous wilderness or seagoing experience. He had been the nominal leader of Astor's disastrous 1811 overland expedition, sent from St. Louis with men and supplies for the founding of Astoria, an expedition that became lost, splintered into four parties, and after great suffering arrived at Astoria up to half a year late.[21]

At New Archangel, Hunt and Sowle together bargained with Baranov for the *Beaver*'s cargo, at length selling him goods for $56,400 that were part of a cargo invoiced in New York at $22,342.[22] Payment was to be made in seal skins. Since none were on hand at New Archangel, Captain Sowle took the *Beaver* to St. Paul Island, one of the Pribylov Islands in the Bering Sea, which was the RAC's main sealing station. There, despite being blown off the coast by a gale, the ship loaded over 74,500 skins.

Though Astor had ordered the *Beaver* to return directly to his Columbia River post before heading for Canton, Hunt instead told Captain Sowle to sail to the Hawaiian Islands. They made port at Oahu, took on provisions, secured needed repairs, and on New Year's Day 1813 Sowle departed for Canton. Hunt stayed behind, taking advantage of the pleasant Hawaiian winter season.[23] At Canton, Captain Sowle belatedly learned of the U.S. declaration of war against Great Britain, which had come in mid-June 1812. To avoid capture by British vessels, he remained blockaded at the Chinese neutral port until war's end; yet in a fluctuating market the captain failed to make a sale of his seal hides.

Astor's other ships continued to call at New Archangel from time to time during the war years, nominally fulfilling the terms of the 1812 St. Petersburg agreement. The bulk of this trade was seal skins from the Pribylov Islands in exchange for provisions and goods from China and India, California, the Hawaiian Islands, and some South American ports as well. A frequent visitor in this trade was Captain William Pigot, master of the *Forester*, a brig purchased for Astor in London that sailed under British colors to evade capture.

Hunt returned to New Archangel in 1814 as master of the *Pedlar*. This ship was a Boston brig purchased in Hawaii by Hunt after he learned about the loss of the *Lark*. He reached Sitka Sound after spending a month or more at Astoria, now Fort George, concluding there the affairs of the Pacific Fur Company on Astor's behalf. Following his earlier visit to New Archangel in company with Captain Sowle, Hunt apparently thought that he knew how to get the best of Baranov in his commercial dealings. But from an RAC perspective, according to the board of directors his negotiating style was characterized by "trickery and low arguments and objections."[24]

Hunt's 1814 appearance coincided with the arrival of the *Forester*. From Captain Pigot, Hunt secured a supply of trade goods and two thousand dollars in cash. Pigot then sailed for Hawaii, having agreed with Baranov to pick up a cargo of provisions for delivery to the new Russian establishment in northern California.[25] Hunt, however, remained in Sitka Harbor, declaring that he needed to repair his ship. (He was also remaining safe from the danger of British cruisers.) He claimed that Astor was sending him another ship with goods for Russian America; yet sixteen months later, after the return of peace in Europe, he was still there. Meanwhile, the RAC ship *Suvorov*, commanded by Lieutenant Mikhail Lazarev of the regular navy, arrived from Kronstadt, resuming the series of round-the-world voyages that marked a growing interest in Russian America on the part of the navy's high command. Hunt became a frequent visitor to the *Suvorov*'s officers' quarters, socializing with Lazarev and his uniformed colleagues while undoubtedly sharing many a convivial toast. As Baranov had learned during his earlier visit, Hunt was a heavy drinker, well able to match the navy men glass for glass.

There followed a series of events that linked together Hunt and the Russian naval officers in a cabal of sorts opposing Aleksandr Baranov. The chief manager began putting aboard the *Suvorov* a cargo of furs to be carried to Russia, the first in at least three years. Then, rather late in the loading process, he ordered Lieutenant Lazarev to take the ship to the Pribylov Islands for a cargo of seal skins, which had become by now Russian America's most abundant export. Lazarev seems to have resented this assignment, not the least because it was ordered by the merchant Baranov.

After the ship's return to Sitka Sound, Hunt suddenly stepped forward and claimed these seal skins on behalf of Captain Pigot. Baranov, so Hunt claimed, had contracted these items to Pigot. Hunt said that he was acting in Pigot's place, to secure the seal hides before the contract expired. Meanwhile, Hunt and the *Suvorov* officers also devised various plans for having one of these men take command of Hunt's ship, raise a Russian flag, and sail to the Hawaiian Islands. There they might acquire from King Kamehameha a cargo of sandalwood for sale at Macao. This voyage, they expected, would bring huge profits. The profits, we might suppose, seemed greater and ever more certain as the evening grew later around the rum keg.

Baranov refused to endorse any of these plans. Captain Pigot soon reappeared in the *Forester*, took the contested seal skins aboard, and in mid-July 1815 put to sea. Officers from the *Suvorov* accompanied him some distance outside the harbor. As they made ready to return in their small boats, Pigot brought out a keg of gunpowder and put it into one of these craft, entrusting it to an English navigator employed by the RAC. Pigot told him to deliver it to Hunt's ship without informing Baranov. But an RAC clerk aboard the same boat witnessed the whole business and immediately let Baranov know.

By this time Hunt and some of his men had been living onshore in tents for weeks, outside New Archangel's stockade. Baranov suspected they were trading with the Tlingits for peltry, but he had no proof. When he heard about the secret gunpowder delivery, he was outraged. In the hands of the Tlingits, this explosive was an immediate threat to the Russian establishment. He could envision an attack on his fort, just as had occurred in 1802 with the destruction of Fort Mikhailovskii. Aleksandr Andreevich had always tried to be friendly with the Yankees, but this incident was a breaking point. Something more needed to be done.

The chief manager sent two trusted men, one of them the assistant supercargo on the *Suvorov*, to the *Pedlar* to ask Hunt for an explanation about why he had accepted the gunpowder in Sitka Sound while attempting to hide the transaction. He told his men to confiscate the powder keg in question, so it might be compared with some gunpowder recently seized from a group of armed Tlingits. Aboard the *Pedlar*, Hunt resisted Baranov's demands and harassed his men. They appealed for help from the officers of the *Otkrytie*, another visiting RAC ship with the *Suvorov* naval officers aboard at the time. "But," said the RAC report on this incident, "not only did the officers refuse help, they remained silent as if they had heard nothing."[26]

Hearing a "terrible shout" from Hunt's ship, four Russian promyshlenniks rowed out from shore to help their comrades. In response, some twenty sailors and officers from other foreign ships anchored nearby came swarming aboard to aid Hunt and his men. A general fight broke out, the two groups pounding each other with their fists. As the battle continued, Baranov decided to intervene, armed with his sturdy cane and taking along two assistants. When he came aboard and asked why the fighting, Hunt refused an answer, returned to his cabin, and shouted that he would surrender his ship to Baranov as a prize. He then gathered together most of his men and abandoned the ship, taking refuge on another American vessel. Left in possession, Baranov ordered the *Pedlar*'s cannons spiked, threw overboard some of the firearms he found on the ship, and confiscated four kegs of gunpowder, including the one from Captain Pigot, which he sent ashore and placed under guard in a company warehouse.

Leaving the *Pedlar* with his men guarding the cabin and the ship's hold, Baranov now took his assistants and rowed to the ship where Hunt had taken refuge. At first Hunt refused to appear; then, "in a very resentful mood," holding a pistol half hidden beneath his shirt, he entered the cabin where Baranov was standing. As he neared Baranov, Aleksandr Andreevich struck Hunt with his cane, disarming the angry Yankee. A few of his countrymen then grabbed Hunt and dragged him away. The day's violence had come to an end.

Was Hunt drunk during this melee? Probably. It would be hard to credit a sober man with such antic behavior. Was he guilty of the charges leveled against him by Baranov? Certainly. On inspection, all four powder kegs proved to be from the same source, as did the gunpowder recovered from the hostile Tlingits. Hunt, as Baranov suspected, had been secretly trading with the Sitka Tlingits, securing sea otter pelts in exchange for various trade items supplied by Captain Pigot, including gunpowder. Given the circumstances, as the RAC directors later said, Baranov's precautions were altogether necessary.[27]

During the next few days the conflict between Hunt and Baranov deescalated into a war of words, with an exchange of letters in which Hunt claimed that the chief manager had made him a prisoner and seized his ship. As a precaution, Baranov appointed a commission to inventory the *Pedlar* and its cargo. This group included Lieutenant Podushkin, commander of the *Otkrytie*, and Lieutenant S. I. Unkovskii of the *Suvorov*, as well as a few junior officers from American merchant ships. Baranov also heard reports that some Americans were so angry about his treatment of Hunt that they wanted to come ashore at night, raid the RAC warehouse, and blow up the gunpowder. He doubled his guards and sent orders to Lieutenant Lazarev to bring the *Suvorov* closer to the fort to defend it, if necessary, against any hostilities.

The outcome was an incident that neither Chief Manager Baranov nor Lieutenant Lazarev ever reported to their superiors, apparently not wanting to admit their mutual foolishness. Lazarev refused to comply with Baranov's order. In reply, an angry Baranov threatened to strip Lazarev of his command. Defying the chief manager, Lazarev had his sailors weigh anchor and the *Suvorov* began to slip out of Sitka Harbor. Reacting hastily, Aleksandr Andreevich ordered his cannoneers to fire a few shots across the ship's bow, thinking that he might force Lazarev to return. Despite the threat, the ship kept sailing. On a fair wind, the *Suvorov* left Sitka Sound and took a course toward northern California. This departure under fire, with the chief manager having his men lob cannonballs toward a company vessel under naval command, was an event unique in RAC history. In retrospect, it did no credit either to Lieutenant Lazarev or to Aleksandr Baranov.

Three months later, much calmer, Captain Hunt agreed to resume command of the *Pedlar* with its cargo intact and departed at last from New Archangel toward Hawaii. Meanwhile both Baranov and his superiors in St. Petersburg had concluded that Astor, despite his claims, never had any intention of blocking New England sea captains from trading with the Tlingits and other Northwest Coast native peoples. When the St. Petersburg agreement negotiated by Adrian Bentzon expired, Astor made no effort to renew it. The general peace in Europe and North America by 1816 made a Russian-American commercial pact superfluous for the New York merchant.

* * *

Among the company employees who had arrived aboard the *Suvorov* in November 1814 was Dr. Georg Schäffer, an adventure-seeking physician from Bavaria who had contracted with the RAC to serve as the ship's surgeon. When Lieutenant Lazarev hastily left Sitka Harbor, Schäffer gladly remained behind. A man of some learning, proficient in Russian, and with an engaging manner, he became a frequent guest at Baranov's table. With Kuskov and Tarakanov on duty in northern California and Banner needed as the head administrator at the Kodiak settlement, Aleksandr Andreevich turned to the German for assistance with a new problem, this one in the Hawaiian Islands.

In January 1815 the company ship *Bering* wrecked on Kauai. The island's monarch, Kaumualii, appropriated the cargo, principally furs. Anxious to reclaim this RAC property, Baranov believed that his friend King Kamehameha, who claimed authority over all the islands, would come to his assistance. Schäffer agreed to serve as Baranov's emissary to retrieve the furs and other company property. Failing that, according to Baranov's instructions, he should secure a cargo of sandalwood as compensation. In October 1815

Schäffer left for Hawaii aboard the American ship *Isabella*, confident of success. His only companions were two young Alaskan creoles, one of them Antipatr Baranov, Aleksandr Andreevich's son, then eighteen years old.

At Honolulu Schäffer soon antagonized King Kamehameha and aroused the suspicion of the American shipmasters—including John Ebbets and Wilson Price Hunt—who advised the monarch on matters of trade and foreign relations.[28] In early May 1816 Schäffer received reinforcement with the arrival from New Archangel of the company ship *Otkrytie* under Captain Podushkin. Eight days later further support came, unexpectedly, when the company-owned ship *Il'mena*, under Captain Wadsworth, arrived from Bodega Bay, leaking badly and needing repairs. Crowded aboard were twenty-four Alutiiq hunters supervised by Timofei Tarakanov. They had left California to return to Sitka, but once at sea, Captain Wadsworth realized that his ship had been so severely damaged when leaving the bay that he opted to make the shorter, safer voyage to Honolulu.

Shortly after the *Il'mena*'s appearance, Schäffer and the newcomers all moved to Kauai's south shore and anchored at Waimea Bay. There Kaumualii, now supposedly an ally and supporter of King Kamehameha, welcomed the German and his men. A few days later Kaumualii offered Baranov's emissary a dazzling proposition. Not only would he give the Russians all the remaining cargo salvaged from the *Bering*, but he would pledge allegiance to Emperor Aleksandr I, allow the RAC exclusive trading privileges on Kauai, and permit Russian trading posts to be located anywhere on his island. In exchange, Schäffer promised him Russia's imperial protection, backed by an armed ship when a first cargo of Kauai sandalwood was ready. He also presented the king a silver medal and an officer's commission in the Russian navy.

Schäffer had no authority to agree to any of these arrangements. His negotiation with Kaumualii was an amazing act of diplomatic hubris. We can only conclude that the ambitious German, always on the lookout for the main chance, had been enthralled by the Hawaiian ruler's friendly reception and the prospect of personal reward. The king in turn was eager to cultivate Russian favor as a counterbalance to the more powerful Kamehameha I. The fact that he had sworn allegiance to Kamehameha six years earlier was simply ignored by Kaumualii, who hoped with Russian aid to regain his independence and the restoration of what he regarded as his lawful patrimony as Kauai's hereditary monarch, which included the right to log off the island's sandalwood for his own exclusive profit.

For some months Schäffer could think himself the master of events. Kaumualii granted him land and villagers for his personal plantations and made smaller grants to other Russians, including a village with eleven families alongside the Hanapepe River for Tarakanov. On the first of July, Schäffer and Kaumualii completed a secret treaty that would have deposed Kamehameha altogether. Kaumualii agreed to raise an army of five hundred to be placed under Schäffer's command for the conquest of all the islands, with a fort to be constructed on each island. Schäffer would supply ammunition and ships from the RAC for this army of conquest. The RAC would receive half of Oahu, Kamehameha's principal base, additional land on other islands, and all of Oahu's sandalwood. The two men also agreed to ban trade with American citizens. As an extravagant added gesture, the Hawaiian monarch ostensibly elevated Baranov to become "first chief of the Sandwich [Hawaiian] islands" in appreciation for the promises of protection by Emperor Aleksandr I. The king also granted to Baranov and his family, "free from taxes for all time," a royal village in a specified district at the port of Honolulu—perhaps the very last place in the islands where one could expect Kaumualii's authority to replace Kamehameha's strong rule.[29] For any responsible observer, it would all seem a rather absurd mockery of international diplomacy.

Even though the *Otkrytie* had already sailed back to Sitka with reports for Baranov, additional manpower arrived in August 1816 aboard the company ship *Kad'iak*. Tarakanov became Schäffer's trusted deputy on Kauai, taking charge of a Russian and Alutiiq workforce at Waimea and constructing a rock-walled bastion called Fort Elizabeth, while Schäffer busied himself with expanding his claims and authority elsewhere.

As soon as Baranov and Kamehameha learned something about the schemes of Schäffer and Kaumualii, they both took steps to counter this challenge to the Hawaiian status quo. Early in 1817, apparently by way of the ship *Cossack* coming from Sitka Sound, Aleksandr Baranov sent word repudiating Schäffer's various business transactions. He demanded the return of the two Russian ships already in Hawaii as well as the money he had entrusted to Schäffer. The chief manager also ordered Tarakanov to return to New Archangel with his Alutiiq hunters. Schäffer ignored Baranov's commands and refused to let Tarakanov and his crew leave. "I will hold you," Tarakanov remembered him saying, "until Alexander Andreevich sends an intelligent, sober, and experienced man in your place."[30]

Compelled to disobey Baranov's order, Tarakanov was highly distressed. His conduct up to that point, he believed, had been exemplary, but now he was placed in a situation "from which, with my simple soul, I could not find any way out." How, he asked rhetorically, "was I to escape this pigheadedness?" Indeed, he declared, "Life was very hard."

He went to his residence, asked for a glass of vodka, then another, and took to bed. The next day he did the same, and so it went for more than a week. Whenever Schäffer asked for him, he was told that Tarakanov was drunk. At first the other Russians made excuses for him. He was not a young man, they said, and should not be ashamed of "a little relaxation" after having served the company for such a long time. But then, as Tarakanov later candidly reported, everyone started to wonder at his prolonged drinking bout, "knowing that I had always considered drunkenness as one of the worst vices." His excuse was his feeling that, he later explained, "everything I undertook [for the RAC] was done in vain."

Simultaneously, Kamehameha, with coaching from his American advisors, began to put pressure on Kaumualii to end his Russian alliance. Because of this coercion, in May 1817 the Kauai monarch forced Tarakanov and his crew to leave Waimea and Fort Elizabeth. At Hanalei, on the north side of the island, Schäffer announced that he would remain there to await the two warships and other reinforcements that, he said, would be arriving soon from Sitka. In June he drafted a most extraordinary document, a manifesto of sorts meant to bolster the spirits of his beleaguered Russian and Alutiiq command, declaring his resolve to stay at Hanalei. He was determined, he wrote, to "show these Indian bandits what Russian honor is and that it cannot be treated lightly."[31] Particularly, the German boasted, "I will show these barbarians that a Russian staff officer can put down rebellion." First among those who joined in signing this bombastic pronouncement was Tarakanov, now restored to duty.

In the face of Kaumualii's continued opposition, however, Schäffer left Kauai a month later and took Tarakanov and his men to Honolulu. There Kamehameha and his Yankee advisors were determined to end the Russian bid for trade and influence in the islands. By this time the RAC employees, responding to Baranov's earlier orders, also had decided that Schäffer's meddling in Hawaii's royal politics had made him a liability. In July 1817 Tarakanov headed a council that persuaded Schäffer—likely against his wishes—to board a Yankee ship heading for Canton, with the understanding that he would proceed to St. Petersburg and report on the Hawaiian situation to the RAC directors and the Russian government.

With Schäffer gone, Tarakanov took charge of efforts to salvage a difficult situation for the RAC. He was on good terms with most of the American captains who had opposed the German. Determined to retrieve the remaining company assets on Kauai and return to New Archangel, he prepared an inventory of RAC property, including the plantations on Kauai presented or promised to the Russians by Kaumualii. With the help of his old friend Captain William Heath Davis, Tarakanov in October arranged with Captain Myrick of the *Cossack* to take back to Sitka two Russians and the Alutiiq hunters who had come with him from California. To pay their way, they would first return to California with Myrick for a sea otter hunt under the customary share arrangement.[32] A short time later Tarakanov, probably sailing with Davis aboard his new ship the *Eagle*, also departed for New Archangel, reaching the RAC headquarters a few days before Christmas, 1817.[33]

Russia's Hawaiian misadventure was not yet concluded. On his return to New Archangel, Tarakanov learned that Captain-Lieutenant Leontii Hagemeister, a naval officer dispatched by the RAC directors, had come to Alaska to review Aleksandr Baranov's administration. A month later, as described in the following chapter, Hagemeister formally took command, allowing Baranov to retire, as the aging chief manager had so long desired.[34] Among other concerns, Hagemeister was eager to clear up the tangled situation left in Hawaii by Schäffer. And he was not at all pleased with Tarakanov's initiative in sending his hunting crew to California with Captain Myrick. He believed that Tarakanov, the former serf, did not have the necessary authority to make this agreement, which, the new chief manager said, "was contrary to instructions from superiors."[35]

Hagemeister, schooled in navy discipline, believed in strict rules and a meticulously businesslike management of the RAC colonies. Concerning affairs in Hawaii, he directed Lieutenant Podushkin, captain of the *Otkrytie*, to sail back to the islands accompanied by Tarakanov. They had orders to reestablish cordial relations with King Kamehameha and bargain with him for all the company property that could possibly be retrieved. Reacting to stories about Tarakanov's drinking, Hagemeister also cautioned Podushkin to monitor the veteran employee's behavior, which according to rumors reaching him "were not so advantageous for the company because of carelessness regarding property, and prejudicial to his character because of licentiousness."[36] But Hagemeister also told Podushkin to help Tarakanov in collecting the company's property so that later no one could claim that any obstacle had been put in his way.

Seven months later Hagemeister reported the disappointing results of this expedition. Captain Podushkin had succeeded in returning the RAC people left in Hawaii except for two fugitives who remained in the islands. But "none of the property squandered by the Doctor was recovered. The plantations are desolate, and not being returned; the vessel *Kad'iak* has been abandoned because it is unfit. The tackle and several sails and whatever could be dismantled from the vessel [have] been brought back."[37] In other words, despite the best efforts of Tarakanov and Podushkin, the RAC's risky intrusion in Hawaiian politics ended as a debacle. Kiril Khlebnikov, Hagemeister's assistant in auditing Baranov's accounts, estimated the monetary loss at more than two hundred thousand rubles.[38]

* * *

Despite Baranov's growing sense of weariness, his declining health, and his frustrations during the last years of his administration, he had avoided disasters that might have truly imperiled the RAC's future in North America. He had thwarted a mutiny, adapted RAC finances to declining returns of sea otter peltry, and kept Russian Alaska and the Fort Ross colony amply supplied even amid turbulent wartime conditions. At New Archangel he had also dealt with the erratic behavior of John Jacob Astor's agent, Wilson Price Hunt, despite Hunt's insolence and the defiance of a small cadre of Russian naval officers in company service. Perhaps least successfully, he had extricated the RAC from the Hawaiian political mess created by his irresponsible agent, Dr. Georg Schäffer. Guiding his administration through these difficult times was in itself something of a triumph. But increasingly, as he would discover, Baranov's style of personal management and his determination to keep the RAC profitable were at odds with the official mentality and the aims of his superiors in St. Petersburg.

XII

CLOSING THE BARANOV ERA

✳

After the Napoleonic Wars, the Russian navy's high command began to view Russian America as a potential resource for training its officers in the art of colonial administration. This interest spread to decision makers in Aleksandr I's government, who realized that great fortunes could no longer be made in the North Pacific fur business. With resumption of the navy's round-the-world voyages in 1817, Captain-Lieutenant Leontii Hagemeister arrived in New Archangel to inspect Baranov's management of Russia's overseas empire. Aleksandr Andreevich convinced Hagemeister to allow him at last to retire. After a detailed audit of his accounts, the aged administrator departed for Russia with Hagemeister. Unfortunately, following a prolonged delay in fever-ridden Batavia, Baranov sickened and died at sea on April 16, 1819, seventy-one years old. His death closed an adventurous, highly profitable era in the history of Russia's overseas empire. Results of his achievements and elements of his legacy, social and cultural, remain evident today throughout maritime Alaska and as far away as Fort Ross State Historic Park on California's north coast.

✳

B Y THE TIME THE RAC MAIN OFFICE LEARNED OF THE DEATH of Tertii Bornovolokov, the last person the directors had appointed to replace Baranov as chief manager, Napoleonic France was no longer a danger. The allied powers had placed Napoleon in exile; peace had arrived in Russia and throughout western Europe. The board of directors now hesitated to remove their aging North American administrator. Because of his continued success in producing profits, Baranov might still be thought indispensable. But the end of Europe's wars encouraged a reappraisal of the very character of the RAC and the company's role within the imperial regime. Aleksandr I had become Europe's leading champion of autocracy, devoting his rule to a continuing struggle against liberalism in all its forms. His government acted to fortify the influence of Russia's landed elite and enhance their role within imperial society, thus accumulating more power in the hands of the powerful.

In this setting, the emphasis in imperial policy for the North Pacific continued to shift farther from the concerns of the Siberian merchant oligarchy. Irkutsk had given way to St. Petersburg as the center of authority in managing the RAC's colonial empire. In Aleksandr I's government, it was no longer true that St. Petersburg was interested only in the money. Imperial officials were looking toward the sort of professional management that Rezanov had advocated a decade earlier. In particular, the regular officers of the Russian imperial navy, well-trained and disciplined—and as contemptuous as always of the merchant class—were becoming covetous of the RAC's Pacific maritime monopoly.[1]

* * *

The navy's encroachment on RAC authority was gradual. It began with the company's need for aid in sailing the North Pacific. At the request of Natalia Shelikhova, in 1801 Emperor Paul I authorized the Admiralty to assign junior officers to command RAC ships sailing from Okhotsk. Even though such a posting would double their salary, it could not have been popular duty. Some of these navy skippers, like Navigator Bulygin, were less than skilled shipmasters. Others, notably Lieutenant Talin and Fleet-Lieutenant Lazarev, were openly scornful of Aleksandr Baranov and the merchant culture that sustained the RAC. Even so, the services of these navy officers—including even the notorious drunkards—eased somewhat the chronic shortage of qualified shipmasters that hampered the company's operations all through Baranov's administration. These navy men shared responsibility for the alarmingly high rate of shipwrecks that plagued RAC operations during these years. But at this historical distance, given the extreme hazards of North Pacific navigation, it is all but impossible to distinguish between the incompetent and the able but unfortunate among them.

The start of the navy's round-the-world voyages in 1803 had great significance in bringing the RAC's commercial empire to the attention of European Russia. Since the time of Peter the Great, a tour of duty with the British navy had been requisite for ambitious young Russian officers. The round-the-world voyages evoked the renowned expeditions of Captain James Cook, Great Britain's famed Pacific explorer. Emulating Cook's voyages, the Russian Admiralty authorized these expeditions to be sea journeys of intellectual

discovery, voyages of enlightenment, often complete with shipboard comple-
ments of naturalists, physical scientists, and artists who would contribute to
Europe's knowledge of the more remote non-European areas of the globe.
For striving young officers, a posting to one of these expeditions was a prized
assignment.

Sailing from Kronstadt, the Russian navy's headquarters on the Baltic Sea
near St. Petersburg, these voyages came to the aid of Russian America by
carrying cargoes of foodstuffs and supplies to Alaska and returning with cargoes of furs. On the first of these voyages, Captain Lisiansky's timely arrival
at Sitka Sound aboard the *Neva* in 1804 had further importance. By rescu-
ing Baranov's timorous RAC attackers from potential disaster during the
assault on the Tlingit fort, Lisiansky and his men fostered RAC dependence
on the navy's military power. And when Captain Lisiansky, still emulating
Cook, published a detailed account of his experiences, he set an example
for all Russian expedition commanders who would follow. The volumes that
issued from the early round-the-world voyages were an elementary course
in empire for European Russia's educated elite, introducing them to the glory
of their nation's North Pacific possessions.

The great prestige of the Russian navy's officer corps made its interest in
Russian America a fashionable concern in St. Petersburg. After the return
of peace in 1814, the resumption of round-the-world voyages on a regular
basis had another important effect. The Russian navy's high command came
to value these lengthy cruises as an integral part of naval training. They
regarded Russian America as an asset not because of the profits it made for
its stockholders. (These profits, to be sure, were declining despite Baranov's
best efforts.) Nor were most of these men especially interested in the society
and culture of Russia's overseas colonies. Rather, for ranking navy officers,
the RAC outposts had importance as administrative units, places to practice
command skills for a generation of well-born men training to be commanders.

From a St. Petersburg perspective, Aleksandr Baranov was not the sort
of properly educated expert who should manage Russia's overseas empire.
Despite his decorations and honors, he remained the son of a provincial
merchant, a person with a habit of moral laxity and a regrettable lack of
social polish, married to an Alaskan Native woman of no status. Rezanov
had written in 1805 that "Baranov is a quite unique and happy creation of
nature," giving the chief manager great praise for his bravery and accomplishments.[2] Yet he also said that when Russian America was reorganized

along professional lines, someone younger and better prepared for the job must take over. Despite Rezanov's 1807 death in Siberia, the RAC's higher management after 1815 seemed to be following a script written by their late, much admired colleague.

* * *

Leontii Andreevich Hagemeister was a native of Livonia province in modern Latvia, born of a Baltic German family with a landed estate. His father had received an army major's commission and served as a state official. His mother too came from a distinguished family. At age fifteen, in 1795 young Hagemeister volunteered for Russia's Baltic fleet, receiving an appointment as a midshipman. Seven years later, after voyages in the North Sea and the Baltic, he gained a place as a junior officer in the British navy, sailing in the Mediterranean, along Africa's west coast, and in the West Indies. He distinguished himself in battle against a Spanish convoy, earning a commendation from Admiral Horatio Nelson before returning to the Russian fleet in 1805.

The following year the navy's high command placed him in charge of the *Neva* on its second round-the-world voyage. Avoiding French cruisers, he sailed from Kronstadt to Brazil, turned eastward to reach the Cape of Good Hope, continued on to Port Jackson, Australia, touched briefly at the Galapagos Islands, and reached Sitka Sound in mid-September 1807. After wintering at Pavlovskaia, he spent the next year and a half shuttling supplies back and forth to the Hawaiian Islands, Kamchatka, Kodiak, and New Archangel. At Petropavlovsk in May 1810 he left the *Neva*, turning command over to a younger officer, took a transport ship to Okhotsk, and began the long overland journey to St. Petersburg. There he was promoted to captain-lieutenant, and his exploits aboard the *Neva* made him one of the most prominent and celebrated officers in the imperial navy.

During the next few years Hagemeister, mainly for personal reasons, returned to Irkutsk to supervise ship construction on Lake Baikal and manage provisions and cargo being put aboard the RAC's ships sailing from Okhotsk. By 1814 he was ready to return to sea. Encouraged by his friend Captain Vasilii Golovnin, the RAC's main office appointed him to command another round-the-world voyage to Russian America. After a lengthy search he found at Le Havre an appropriate vessel, a 525-ton American ship that he purchased, renamed the *Kutuzov*, and readied for an expedition to New Archangel. To accompany his vessel, he also supervised the outfitting of the *Suvorov*, commanded by Lieutenant Zakhar Panafidin. Leaving Kronstadt in September 1816, the two ships made a leisurely voyage by way of Brazil, Cape

Horn, and Peru. Sailing from Callao, the *Suvorov* reached Sitka in late July 1817. After stopping at Bodega Bay and Fort Ross, Hagemeister arrived with the *Kutuzov* in November.[3]

The RAC's main administration the previous spring had drafted a series of dispatches for Chief Manager Baranov about affairs in Russian America. These messages concerned official authorization for trade with Spanish California ("be patient"); Georg Schäffer ("no longer to be entrusted"); Fort Ross ("build up agriculture, livestock breeding, poultry raising, the planting of fruits and vegetables, and establish plantations"); personnel matters at Sitka ("organize this however God may guide you"); his troubles with Lieutenant Lazarev (his court martial "is already in session at Kronstadt"); a set of new regulations for visiting skippers ("you may use this regulation to take action"); and education for creoles ("send two or three bright young lads here to study," but only after they have been vaccinated against smallpox).[4] Other dispatches about maintaining order, the main administration said, had been sent recently via Okhotsk and forwarded to him aboard the *Konstantin*. Baranov should refer to these dispatches and, the administrators advised, "pray God to strengthen you in health and force so these instructions can be carried out."[5]

Almost as if an afterthought, this simple statement was included by the main administration: "When Leontii Hagemeister reaches you . . . he will take over part of your responsibilities."[6] Here was the first intimation Baranov received that he might actually be allowed to surrender his official duties. But this cryptic sentence told Aleksandr Andreevich less than the full truth. Chief Director Buldakov and his colleagues had told Captain Hagemeister to evaluate the situation in New Archangel and ordered him, if he thought conditions warranted, to relieve Baranov of his duties and become Russian America's chief manager on an interim basis.

We cannot be certain just when Aleksandr Andreevich learned the full extent of Hagemeister's mandate. Kiril Khlebnikov had reached New Archangel in July as the supercargo aboard the *Kutuzov*. In his biography of Baranov he said that while the chief manager was happy to have the foodstuffs and other necessities brought from California by Hagemeister, "he was angered and openly protested that the Company had ignored his persistent requests, and refused to replace him, forcing him to continue under his heavy burden." It was Baranov's "despairing complaints," according to Khlebnikov, that "eventually persuaded Captain Hagemeister to himself assume the duties of Chief Manager of the colonies."[7] Hagemeister had already unloaded his cargo toward the end of December and was taking on board a consignment of furs when he informed Baranov of this decision.

Hagemeister's delay, according to Khlebnikov, was based on experience. Having seen Baranov in action during his first visit to Alaska in 1808, he was "reluctant to accept these new and arduous duties, strewn with so many cares, worries and discords." But, Khlebnikov informs us, "one particular circumstance seemingly decided him to act: The respected and tireless Simeon Ianovskii, first lieutenant on the *Suvorov*, was courting Baranov's daughter and had agreed to remain in Sitka for two years."[8]

At that time Lieutenant Ianovskii was twenty-nine years old; Irina Baranova was thirteen or fourteen. It is left to our imaginations to fill in the details of their brief courtship, but who can doubt that the worldly Russian navy officer in his handsome uniform, trimmed with gold braid and shiny brass buttons, set aflutter the heart of this sheltered young woman. And as Baranov's daughter, assured of inherited wealth and a position in Russian society, she might well have seemed a perfect marriage partner for the lieutenant when he came courting.

On January 7, 1818, just at the end of the Christmas holidays, Irina and Lieutenant Ianovskii were joined in holy matrimony at St. Michael's Church in New Archangel. Performing the service must have been Father Aleksei Sokolov, who had arrived in 1816 to become Sitka's first Russian Orthodox priest. Four days later, Captain Hagemeister officially took over the colony's administration, "replacing Baranov's easy-going regime with one more disciplined and businesslike," according to historian Richard A. Pierce.[9]

Hagemeister immediately appointed Khlebnikov as the colony's office manager. A capable and experienced administrator and a self-taught scholar with literary ambitions—and also a survivor of many dangerous Siberian wilderness adventures on the company's behalf—Khlebnikov had sailed aboard the *Kutuzov* expecting to be named chief clerk of the RAC's American administration upon Baranov's retirement. His first job was to audit Baranov's books and make a complete report on all his accounts regarding the company's property, then to take charge of that property. Working with him closely for months, Khlebnikov developed a great admiration for Aleksandr Andreevich. He was inspired to start asking the veteran administrator about his experiences, gathering information into a set of notes that eventually became the basis for Khlebnikov's biographical account of the chief manager's career.[10]

Although Captain Hagemeister objected to the number of pigs running loose at New Archangel, he maintained a cordial relationship with Baranov. Within weeks he was urging Aleksandr Andreevich to return to Russia with him aboard the *Kutuzov* "for the good of the colonies."[11] Joining the *Suvorov*'s skipper in his appeal was another eminent navy officer, Baranov's old acquaintance Vasilii Golovnin. Now a captain-lieutenant and Hagemeister's senior in rank, Golovnin was the official head of this 1817–18 round-the-world expedition. He reached New Archangel in July 1818 aboard the sloop *Kamchatka*, a heavily armed fighting ship of nine hundred tons. Prussian in background, Golovnin personified a man born to command. One youngster who served under him described him as stiff, unbending, and unapproachable, always dressed in uniform. It was said that he never displayed either pleasantness or kindness. "Everyone feared him," according to this source, "but at the same time all valued his impartiality and honesty."[12] After his arrival, while Hagemeister was also at New Archangel with the *Kutuzov*, Captain Golovnin must have added considerable weight to Hagemeister's efforts at persuading Baranov to go to St. Petersburg.

Aleksandr Andreevich found the decision difficult, Khlebnikov later wrote. The future well-being of Anna and their son, Antipatr, were important concerns. He must also have been reluctant to leave longtime friends and colleagues, including some men who had been with him since the early days and who had stood with him through countless crises. Habit, Khlebnikov said, inclined Baranov to remain in Alaska and settle in Pavlovskaia. But the settlement's isolation, the likelihood of boredom, and the damp climate all argued for a different location. One alternative would have been to move back to Siberia and make a place for himself in Chukchi country with his only remaining sibling, Petr. He also thought sometimes about moving to the Hawaiian Islands and ending his days on the plantation given to him by his friend King Kamehameha, still considered his property despite the Schäffer debacle.

But finally he responded once again to the appeal to his sense of duty by his superiors. He agreed to return to Russia with Hagemeister and report in person to the RAC directors. Captain Golovnin assured him that the directors would recognize their debt to him and "would undoubtedly undertake to provide him with all the perquisites of a peaceful and pleasant life." And in St. Petersburg "he could still benefit the company through knowledge of colonial affairs and his advice."[13] Such subtle flattery and the appeal to his ego must also have helped sway Aleksandr Andreevich's decision to end his days back in his homeland.

To expedite his departure, Baranov made personal arrangements at Pavlovskaia. Anna agreed to go live under the protection of Father German, now installed on Elovoi Island in a virtual hermitage that he called New Valaam. This plan, supported financially by Aleksandr Andreevich, must have satisfied both Father German and Anna, who became a devout assistant to her husband's onetime adversary. The future for Antipatr, now twenty-one, was assured when he received the promise of an appointment to the Russian naval cadet corps in Kronstadt. Captain Golovnin presumably had a hand in arranging it. In late August 1818 the young man left Sitka aboard the *Kamchatka* under Golovnin's command, saying farewell to his family and friends three months before his father's departure.

Circumstances delayed Aleksandr Andreevich's leave-taking until the end of November. Most important was his need to work with Khlebnikov in auditing the RAC's financial records and accounting for all company property in his safekeeping. The transfer of funds, the handover of property, and the preparation of reports lasted until September. When finished, Khlebnikov's summary showed that during Baranov's administration the company's capital increased in value from 1.3 million rubles to almost 4.8 million rubles. Physical assets in the colonies by this reckoning were worth an additional 2.5 million rubles, which included the value of goods, munitions, raw materials, ships, buildings, and all other RAC property relinquished by Baranov. The company's returns to Russia in furs and other goods could only be approximated. According to figures Khlebnikov obtained from the main office, between 1808 and 1818 the net proceeds totaled some 15 million rubles, while the directors had sent only 2.8 million rubles worth of supplies, ships, and provisions to Russian America.

This huge profit, Khlebnikov explained, "was because Baranov, without demanding imports [from Russia], bartered goods for goods and traded with the foreigners." In this fashion, "he put into the storehouses in Kad'iak and Sitka up to 5,000 sea otters, 4,000 beaver tails, 10,000 river beavers, and up to 4,000 fur seals, worth in all about 1,200,000 rubles."[14] In addition, said Khlebnikov, he had acquired five ships by barter: the *Juno, Kad'iak, Il'mena, Bering,* and *Amethyst.* (The *Cossack* and the *Sv. Nikolai* should also have been on this list.) But when he turned over everything to Khlebnikov, including nine hundred thousand rubles in cash and remaining furs valued at approximately two hundred thousand rubles, only three company vessels were still fit for use, all built elsewhere by Yankee craftsmen.[15]

Various detractors, Khlebnikov indicated, had doubted Aleksandr Andreevich's fiscal honesty. Yet he found in the record many examples that showed "Baranov's painstaking, unselfish, and fruitful care for the Company's interests."[16] His investigation, basically a thorough internal audit, proved that the suspicions of Baranov's critics were completely groundless.

While the accounting slowly proceeded, Captain Hagemeister sailed to California with the *Kutuzov* for provisions. As one of his first reforms as interim chief manager, he persuaded the company promyshlenniks to accept a change in their method of payment. Under the old system their wages were based on shares in kind for all the furs gathered by the workforce. Rezanov and Baranov had both urged that this practice be abandoned and the men paid a set amount based on their term of service. The main office had eventually agreed to this change, with the company also contracting to supply the workforce with provisions on a monthly basis. And of course these Russians wanted bread, fresh vegetables, and meat, not dried fish. So did the large contingent of hungry sailors and ships' officers at Sitka and Kodiak.

Hagemeister's expedition to California was primarily for trade with the Franciscan missions. Leaving in June, he returned in early October carrying 15,000 puds (270 tons) of grain and a great quantity of other fresh supplies.[17] Once again the Spanish authorities, while still officially prohibited from such dealings, had welcomed the chance to exchange their province's foodstuffs for the handicrafts and manufactures brought by the Russians, including some acquired by trade with China and with New England shipmasters.

After Hagemeister returned, he outfitted the *Kutuzov* for the voyage back to Russia. As Baranov's departure drew near, he hosted many farewell visits. Khlebnikov witnessed some of these scenes and summarized them with the utmost empathy:

> Not without tears did he part from his former employees and colleagues, who had so often willingly shared his labors and hardships, and followed him boldly into danger, Many of his colleagues were grey haired and aged like himself. They who had shared his adventures and campaigns now sobbed like children as they parted forever from their beloved leader. Many of those who now surrounded him had grown up under his administration. He was godfather to many, and had taught most of the younger

ones. He had been above all a benefactor, and now, bidding farewell, he left
them all forever.[18]

Among those who came to wish him well was K'alyáan, the man who had
led the Sitka Kiks.ádis' destruction of Fort Mikhailovskii. Since his people's
retreat from the Russian danger in 1804, he had returned to the New Archangel area with some followers, who were trading with Baranov's workers
on a limited basis. The two men had made peace, and Baranov now introduced him to Lieutenant Ianovskii, urging his successor to respect the Tlingit
leader's intelligence and ability.

Other Tlingit headmen from the Sitka district also gathered to bid good-
bye to their Russian former enemy. One of these, Naawushkeitl of the Kiks.
ádis, had become particularly friendly with Baranov. Aleksandr Andreevich,
as a sign of his own respect, presented to Naawushkeitl his Russian-made
chain mail vest, the light armor worn under this shirt that had protected him
from danger over the years.[19] It was a gesture of peace and friendship that
must have been greatly appreciated by some, if not all, Sitka Tlingits.

Before leaving New Archangel, Baranov arranged another remarkable gift
to the Kiks.ádis. He commissioned the construction of an elaborate brass hat
based on the design of a ceremonial Northwest Coast cedar-bark and spruce-
root dancing hat, ornamented with sea lion whiskers and Russian beads.
A decade later this metal hat, known ever since as the Baranov Peace Hat,
arrived in New Archangel, perhaps in the care of Governor Ferdinand von
Wrangel. Finely polished and stamped with the name of the Russian foundry
responsible for crafting it, the Peace Hat was presented to "Chief Michael,"
representing the Point House Kiks.ádis whose descendants became the cus-
todians of this valuable ceremonial object. It was the last visible memento of
Baranov's long, eventful administration to reach Russian America.[20]

* * *

The *Kutuzov* sailed away from New Archangel on November 27, 1818. Traveling with Baranov were his chief clerk and three servants. His nephew from
Kargopol', Afanasii Kuglinov, who had worked under his uncle's direction
for a number of years, also accompanied the party. They would have been
a companionable group when gathered aboard ship for drinks and dinner,
maybe at the captain's table.

Captain Hagemeister took an unusual course toward home. In late
December he skirted past the Hawaiian Islands, ignoring the chance to stock
up on fresh provisions. From there he steered westward toward the Philippine Islands, but unseasonably stormy weather with strong winds kept him

from making port at Manila. Needing supplies, he returned east to Guam and late in January anchored at Umatac, a small village with a harbor on the southwest coast of the island. Perhaps not yet having all the provisions he needed, Hagemeister departed three days later, taking a general southeastern course toward the Cape of Good Hope.

For more than a month he threaded his way through the islands of Micronesia, past the southern Philippines, and tacked his way across the Celebes Sea and the Java Sea. On March 7, 1819, he reached Batavia, a teeming port that was the capital of the Dutch East Indies—the modern Jakarta, capital of Indonesia. There Hagemeister dropped anchor and stayed for thirty-six days, preparing for the last leg on his long voyage home. Along with needing supplies, his ship may have required repairs for damage sustained in heavy weather.

At Batavia, Baranov had to endure a protracted stay in an unfamiliar place, under conditions that must have been especially hard for someone who had not lived outside Alaska for decades. Jakarta's average daily temperatures in March and April range between lows in the midseventies to highs around ninety degrees Fahrenheit, with extreme humidity. Rather than stay aboard ship, Aleksandr Andreevich lodged ashore at an inn, where the food was probably better and his room more comfortable than a warship's cabin. We may hope that he found the ancient Javanese city interesting during his lengthy visit. But he was not feeling well, suffering "bouts of illness" while ashore.[21]

On April 12 the *Kutuzov* again put out to sea. Four days later, April 16, 1819, while Captain Hagemeister was navigating through the straits of Sunda, the ailing old man breathed his last. What was the specific cause of Baranov's death? Khlebnikov explained simply that "the mortal poison of the [Batavian] climate infected him."[22] That mortal poison, beyond doubt, was yellow fever. Carried by the *Aedes aegypti* mosquito, which only survives at temperatures well above freezing, the yellow fever virus is endemic throughout Southeast Asia. It is especially dangerous to the aged and frail. Since the virus takes four or five days to incubate, Aleksandr Andreevich must have contracted it while ashore in Batavia. Like Captain Hagemeister and all the seamen on the *Kutuzov*, the shipboard members of his party evidently spared themselves the intense disease exposure that Baranov suffered because of his wish for comfortable quarters.

The following day, while sailing near Prince Island in the Indian Ocean, Captain Hagemeister led a funeral service. At its conclusion, the *Kutuzov*'s sailors lowered Baranov's mortal remains over the side. Everyone must have watched the body sink beneath the waters. It was a sadly ironic ending for a man of the north who had never before traveled anywhere farther south than Moscow or Sitka.

* * *

Except among the relatively small circle of his family, colleagues, and closest friends, news of Baranov's death had no great consequences. He had outlived nearly all contemporaries and his siblings except for Petr, still a trader living with his wife in northeastern Siberia, where he died in 1844.[23] Aleksandr Andreevich's surviving Alaskan comrades and associates had already made their emotional adjustment to his departure. Their added sadness when they learned of his passing, while sincere, cannot have been overwhelming. Since he was not a familiar figure in St. Petersburg, it is difficult to imagine that he was deeply mourned when Captain Hagemeister arrived with a report of his demise.

Baranov had survived long enough to become a figure from an earlier generation, known for his bold rule over a declining industry, controlling a distant enterprise in a rough-edged manner no longer in style. He was a commercial empire builder, but his empire had now passed into very different hands. Surely, the directors of the RAC felt regret for the loss of Aleksandr Andreevich and his experienced advice. He was, after all, the man who had made all of them rich. These wealthy gentlemen had only to look around their finely appointed company offices near the imperial palace to be reminded of their debt to him. At the company's shareholders meeting in 1822, Chief Director Buldakov succinctly recognized this debt. "Baranov alone," he said, "is responsible for building up new capital for the Company."[24] It was not much of a eulogy.

Kiril Khlebnikov was one of the people who knew Baranov best at the end of his days. After working closely with him and encouraging the retiring chief manager to describe his career for posterity, Khlebnikov gained an appreciation for Aleksandr Andreevich's accomplishments that has informed all later appraisals of the man and his works. In his biography of Baranov, published in Russia shortly before Khlebnikov's death in 1838, the author praised his late friend as an architect of empire. From Shelikhov's one original settlement at Three Saints Harbor, he wrote, Baranov managed to take control over a vast area extending from the lower Alaska Peninsula, the area around Kenai Bay, the whole of Chugach Bay, southward to Yakutat and Sitka Sound, and much farther south to include Fort Ross and Bodega Bay. In 1818, Khlebnikov pointed out, Baranov left a main factory at Sitka, permanent branches at

Kodiak, Unalaska, and Ross, and separate hunting posts at Kenai Bay and Chugach Bay and on the Pribylov Islands.

Not all of Aleksandr Andreevich's projects were successful. The New Russia colony—Shelikhov's grandiose scheme for creating a showcase agricultural settlement—was a miserable failure. Chamberlain Rezanov's hope for a long-term trading agreement with the Spanish Californians was stymied by international politics and the unyielding opposition to foreign trade by Madrid's royal authorities. The RAC's tenuous partnership with Astor's American Fur Company, forced on the chief manager by his St. Petersburg superiors, led to the strange conflict involving Wilson Price Hunt and Lieutenant Mikhail Lazarev. And Baranov's hope for securing a steady source of Hawaiian-grown provisions and profit from sandalwood shipments was destroyed by the outrageous behavior of his agent, Dr. Georg Schäffer, whose appointment in a position of trust Baranov came to regard as the worst mistake of his career.

His improvised California policy, however, turned out well. The sea otter hunting partnerships with Yankee captains proved quite profitable, especially since they gained access to the Canton market for RAC fur cargoes. Unlike the miscarried designs of Shelikhov, Rezanov, and Schäffer, the chief manager's plans for establishing RAC settlements at Rumiantsev Bay and Fort Ross also paid off. For more than two decades Fort Ross flourished as a depot for sub-rosa exchanges with the Franciscan missions. Meanwhile, a workforce mostly of Alutiiqs and Pomo people began growing garden crops and raising livestock to sustain themselves and improve Russian America's food supply.

* * *

While praising Baranov, Khlebnikov had little of substance to say about the chief manager's relationships with Alaska's Native peoples. He emphasized the role of disease in accounting for Native population decline, but he completely ignored the great loss of life among the long-distance hunting parties from Kodiak Island that had touched off the 1801 Alutiiq rebellion. And he remained vague in discussing Baranov's relations with the Tlingit clans at Yakutat and Sitka. Yet he stated a conviction that, if the Russians were patient, a time would come "of itself, when through trade and imitation" of their habits, "through social mixing and a result of education and intermarriage, and through the almighty action of God's Mercy, attitudes will soften."[25]

Maybe, or maybe not. In May 2004, two hundred years after the fighting at Shis'gi Noow, the Kiks.ádis hosted a two-day conclave at Sitka to commemorate the 1805 peace with the Russians. They called the central first-day

ceremony "the removal of grief." It was a grand affair all around. The program included stirring addresses both in Tlingit and in English, display of
significant historical objects including Kʻalyáan's blacksmith hammer and his
battle-scarred raven hat and also the Baranov Peace Hat, much ceremonial
dancing and singing, and a gracious talk in Russian by a young woman visiting from Moscow who is Antipatr Baranov's descendant. It ended with an
epic potlatch staged at the Sitka's Centennial Hall on the waterfront. It was
an event long to be remembered, marking a significant stage in the multigenerational renaissance of traditional Tlingit culture.[26] But, it has been said,
there are some hard-liners among the older Tlingits who believe that it is still
way too early for forgiveness.

There is also a cultural renaissance among the Alutiiq people. The vital
center is the Alutiiq Museum and Archaeological Repository located in
downtown Kodiak. Among other activities, the museum staff provides online
weekly lessons in the Alutiiq language. Although many Russian names are
found on the roll of its founding directors, the interpretive program largely
ignores Baranov and his era. In general, the museum's public outreach tends
to credit the Russian Orthodox Church as the principal defender and advocate of Alaskan Native interests, to the detriment of Aleksandr Andreevich's
reputation. Chief Manager Baranov, in the words of one commentator, "was
the Stalin of Alutiiq history."[27]

This view reflects attitudes of a later time. Following the U.S. purchase
of Alaska in 1867, the Russian Orthodox faith gained many adherents and
greater popularity among Alutiiqs and other Native Alaskans. The Church's
ministry, many of them Native men and others married to Native women,
became a bulwark against the anti-Indian bias brought north by the territory's new Anglo-American rulers. With some sixty congregations active
today in Alaskan towns and villages, the Church's overly reverent attitude
toward the monks in the 1794 spiritual mission has greatly affected historical perceptions.

The result has been a misreading of history, ignoring much of the documentary record and portraying events as they never were. Despite the early
controversies, the misunderstandings, and a few angry encounters, Aleksandr Baranov was no enemy of the Church or the churchmen. He should
properly be understood as a friend, generous supporter, and liberal patron of
the spiritual mission's educational and humanitarian activities, even while
serving as an unwitting agent of the mercantile imperialism that disrupted
Native cultures and cut short Native lives in Russian America, as everywhere

else in Europe's borderland colonies from the fifteenth century forward.

We all need to recognize that neither Baranov nor any of the churchmen had it in their power to safeguard North America's Native peoples from the cumulative onslaught of Western civilization in the forms that reached the Pacific world during the eighteenth and nineteenth centuries. The fatal impact of newly introduced diseases, the undermining and impoverishment of traditional economies, the alteration of customary marriage practices, family relationships, and social forms, along with the relocation of entire communities and a pervasive sense of cultural malfunction—all these consequences were inescapable. Baranov was their unconscious instrument; but in a no less significant way, so too were the self-assured emissaries of Orthodox Christian religion, despite their sincere, totally admirable efforts to soften the blows of outrageous fortune on Native Alaskan societies. The suffering victims might be consoled, perhaps, but not protected.

* * *

Even though Khlebnikov extolled Baranov as an empire builder, a view adopted in a recent popular publication by two Alaskan authors, the chief manager never advocated expansion of the Russian empire for its own sake.[28] He remained always a merchant, in charge of a for-profit commercial operation. His goal was to boost the flow of soft gold from North America toward Irkutsk and the flow of money to St. Petersburg. Grigorii Shelikhov had vaguely outlined a grand plan for expansion southward along the Alaskan coast. Baranov implemented parts of this plan wholly as a means to reach new sea otter hunting grounds and, in northern California, advantageous trade connections. From time to time, as seen in his correspondence, he articulated a sense of duty toward the emperor and the fatherland. But these abstract sentiments, though quite sincere, never trumped his commercial calculations. Serving usually as his own bookkeeper, he kept close track of the bottom line for every aspect of his administration.

Throughout his North American career, the chief manager received a shocking lack of support from company directors and shareholders. He had to contend with problems made far worse by isolation and the uncertainty of communications with superiors in Irkutsk and St. Petersburg. Perhaps most damaging was the company's frequent loss of ships with their crews and cargoes. The North Pacific in Baranov's time was a deadly marine graveyard. Each loss came as a blow to the company treasury and a setback to his administration that Aleksandr Andreevich had to try somehow to offset.

His solution was to turn elsewhere for trading partners and for captains, crews, and ships. This policy became more practical after Baranov built New Archangel with its convenient, easily accessible harbor facilities. When Rezanov agreed with him to buy John D'Wolf's *Juno* with all its cargo in 1805, the way was opened for a regular commerce with the Boston-based shipmasters that continued vigorously to the end of Baranov's career. The purchase of British-built and American-built ships became commonplace by 1812. Compared to the galiots turned out by the Okhotsk shipyards, these were better constructed and better designed vessels: larger, faster, and more agile to sail in all sorts of weather. The employment of their captains and crews by the RAC during the last few years of Baranov's tenure also eased his personnel problems. The American captains proved much easier to manage, and better company, than many of the cantankerous Russian navy officers who resented and resisted the chief manager's authority.

Aided by the increased trade with foreign merchant captains and also by friendly exchanges with Hispanic Californians, the economy of Russian America became steadily more diversified during the closing years of Baranov's administration. Aleksandr Andreevich encouraged a variety of handicraft industries to make goods for barter, and he was pleased with gains in farming and livestock raising that supplemented the provisions from other, non-Russian localities. By the time Captain Hagemeister relieved him from the heavy responsibilities of office, Russian America was well on its way to becoming economically independent. In maritime Alaska and at Fort Ross, Baranov's management had fostered a village-based society and economy not so very different from the Russian north.

Throughout his American career, many visitors from Russia and elsewhere respected Aleksandr Andreevich as a person to be admired not just for his accomplishments but even more for what he was forced to endure. Lieutenant Gavrill Davydov met Baranov in 1803, just when the *Feniks* was lost. "All this work, these obstacles, sorrows, deprivation and failure," he wrote, "had not blighted the spirit of this rare man, although it had naturally had an influence on him and thereby made him rather somber in manner."[29] We should not wonder that Baranov liked to take his ease with a few glasses of brandy or rum or that he came to enjoy a frolic at a drunken dinner party as he grew older. These occasions became more frequent and apparently more bibulous with the passing years. In North America, as in Russia, alcohol was an all-purpose remedy for whatever might be ailing the veteran chief manager.

* * *

Baranov's retirement marked the end of an era in Russian America. It brought a change in administration that replaced his intensely personal management style and the crude ways of the fur hunting and trading era with a highly formal, punctilious, and class-conscious supervision by naval officers, trained in imperial Russia's most aristocratic service. This new style of empire was a state-funded enterprise, run by navy officers for the benefit of the navy and its highborn patrons. From 1820 onward these men served fixed five-year terms as governors. Keeping the common people at a social distance, they did not form strong ties with the communities they were governing. By the time the navy took command of Russian America, the fur profits had virtually disappeared from the empire made by Aleksandr Baranov. It was a tipping point in the history of Russia's overseas colonies. Subsequently, Alaska's naval caretakers had no interest in any assets that might be marketed for a profit.

By the 1850s Russia's top policy makers had become concerned that Alaska's untapped natural wealth—in coal deposits, fish, timber, and ice—and its excellent seaports were becoming dangerous liabilities. They were too attractive to American entrepreneurs, some feared, too liable to invite an influx of aggressive Yankee frontier capitalists who would easily take possession of Russia's North American colonies, and, as one official predicted, "we shall never be in a position to regain them."[30] This fear even impelled Baron Ferdinand von Wrangel, a former RAC governor, to recommend in 1857 the cession of Alaska to the United States government as a matter of *"anticipatory prudence."*[31]

* * *

In our time, Sitka, once New Archangel, though still a small town, has become one of Alaska's most popular tourist locations. Despite the ever-present possibility of rain, the town's gorgeous setting and its historic sites make it a favorite port of call for folks traveling along Alaska's marine highway. As many as four or even five cruise ships a day may anchor there during the peak summer season, each bringing hundreds of visitors to the harbor front. They arrive from their huge ships aboard small lighters and land at pier side with a few hours to inspect the town. In most cases they will watch a brief Russian-themed presentation put on by costumed townsfolk in Centennial Hall. Almost certainly they will peer into St. Michael's Russian Orthodox cathedral and maybe trek up Castle Hill, once the site of an official governor's mansion remembered as Baranov's Castle (though built after Aleksandr Andreevich's departure), now designated a National Historic Site. Many will take a guided tour through the Bishop's House, built as a residence for Father Veniaminov, the "Apostle of Alaska," and later used as a school, hospital, and orphanage. This imposing structure has now been carefully restored by the U.S. National Park Service. The more energetic may hike to the south end of town, past the campus of the former Sheldon Jackson College, and walk along the Totem Trail that leads through the impressive scenery of Sitka National Historic Park and near the place where the Tlingits' Shis'gi Noow fort once stood.

Perhaps before returning to their ship, some tourists will stop to gaze at a bronze statue of Aleksandr Andreevich Baranov, larger than life, located close to the waterfront. Its rests atop a high granite pedestal facing the harbor. The monument portrays a man somewhat younger and certainly a good bit slimmer than the portly veteran it represents. He sits looking seaward in a position of thoughtful determination, wrists on his thighs with elbows confidently spread, holding a rolled manuscript in his right hand. An inscription quotes these words from one of his messages: "That we may dwell in amity and peace forever in this region." It is an apt quotation, highlighting Baranov's hope for a good life for himself and many others, newcomers and Natives, in a wide expanse of maritime Alaska, creating an ethnically and culturally diverse borderland society we may still recognize as Russian America.

* * *

Away from Alaska, far to the south at Fort Ross on the northern California coast, is located a virtual monument to Baranov. Today the physically restored Fort Ross includes a log palisade with two gun towers, a Russian Orthodox chapel and bell tower, a barracks and storeroom building, and a functional wooden windmill. Its one remaining original structure, Manager Aleksandr Rotchev's house, is listed on the National Register of Historic Places. During recent years the site has received substantive assistance from the voluntary Fort Ross Interpretive Association and a newer group, the Fort Ross Conservancy. The Russian ambassador to the United States and, in 2010, the then Russian president Dmitri Medvedev have shown strong interest in supporting this showcase property of the California State Historic Park and Recreation system, which has been threatened with closure because of cuts in the state parks budget.

Aleksandr Andreevich never reached Fort Ross, but he was solely responsible for founding this most distant outpost of Russia's nineteenth-century Pacific empire. The place today is well known in Russia. Irkutsk has a dedicated group of Fort Ross history buffs. In the Russian north there is a car dealership in Vologda, not far from Baranov's birthplace, that announces its name FORT ROSS in red neon characters shining through the night. A modest Baranov monument erected in Kargopol', close to the Baranov family property, is perhaps more likely to catch the attention of the few history-minded tourists who make the trip.

When state park employees at Fort Ross host a special observance such as an ethnic heritage weekend or a harvest festival, crowds gather for colorful events: dancing, singing, booming cannon salutes, and maybe a Russian Orthodox priest leading a procession down the path to the cove below for a blessing of the boats. Many visitors are costumed to take a part in the spectacle. And a great many, arriving by car or van and in busloads from the San Francisco Bay Area, are Russian, chatting in their native language and buying piroshki for an afternoon snack. There are no statues of Baranov at Fort Ross. But as a strong-voiced male choir sings an anthem or light-footed young women swirl and twirl together in their bright skirts, it takes no great imagination to sense that Aleksandr Andreevich too is visiting here in spirit.

ABBREVIATIONS:
RUSSIAN ARCHIVAL REPOSITORIES

ARGO.   Arkhiv Russkogo geograficheskogo obshchestva (Archive of the Russian Geographical Society), St. Petersburg.

AVPRI.   Arkhiv vneshnei politiki Rossiiskoi imperii (Archive of the Foreign Policy of the Russian Empire), Moscow.

GAAO.   Gosudarstvennyi arkhiv Arkhangelskoi oblasti (State Archive of the Archangel Region), Archangel.

GAIO.   Gosudarstvennyi arkhiv Irkutskoi oblasti (State Archive of the Irkutsk Region), Irkutsk.

GAPO.   Gosudarstvennyi arkhiv Permskoi oblasti (State Archive of the Perm' Region), Perm'.

GARF   Gosudarstvennyi arkhiv Rossiiskoi Federatsii (State Archive of the Russian Federation), Moscow.

GAVO.   Gosudarstvennyi arkhiv Vologodskoi oblasti (State Archive of the Vologda Region), Vologda.

OR RNB.   Otdel rukopisei Rossiiskoi natsional'noi biblioteki (Manuscript Division of the Russian National Library), St. Petersburg.

RGA DA.   Rossiiskii gosudarstvennyi arkhiv drevnikh aktov (Russian State Archive of Ancient Acts), Moscow.

RGA VMF.   Rossiiskii gosudarstvennyi arkhiv voenno-morskogo flota (Russian State Archive of the Navy), St. Petersburg.

RGB OR.   Rossiiskaia gosudarstvennaia biblioteka, Otdel rukopisei (Russian State Library, Manuscript Division), Moscow.

RGIA.   Rossiiskii gosudarstvennyi istoricheskii arkhiv (Russian State Historical Archive), St. Petersburg.

RG VIA.   Rossiiskii gosudarstvennyi voenno-istoricheskii arkhiv (Russian State Archive of Military History), Moscow.

NOTES

PREFACE AND ACKNOWLEDGMENTS

1   The first of these other volumes is Hubert Howe Bancroft's *History of Alaska* (1886), a standard account that nevertheless in many places is opinionated and factually unreliable. This volume was written for Bancroft mainly by a shady character, an immigrant Russian newspaper writer and researcher known to Bancroft as Ivan Petrov. He held strongly anticlerical views, and he freely blended invented documentary fictions into his factual narrative. In 1942 another journalist, named Hector Chevigny, published *Lord of Alaska: Baranov and the Russian Adventure*. Chevigny's sensationalist style and often imaginary claims promoted a distorted view of the Baranov era that has now deservedly fallen into obscurity.

1. A MAN OF THE NORTH

1   The early development of the Pomory territory is summarized in Terence Armstrong, *Russian Settlement in the North* (Cambridge: Cambridge University Press, 1965), 41–46. See also T. A. Bernshtam, "Promyslovye zveroboinye arteli pomorov zimnego berega Belogo moria vo vtoroi polovine XIX–pervoi treti XX vv." ("The Organization of Hunting Villages on the Winter Shore of the White Sea, from the Second Half of the Nineteenth Century to the Early Twentieth Century") (Ph.D. diss., Kunstkamera, St. Petersburg, 1968), 7–8.

2   Petr A. Kolesnikov, ed., *Istoriia severnogo krest'ianstva* (*History of Northern Peasantry*) (Vologda: Severo-Zapadnoe knizhnoe izdatel'stvo, 1984), 1:225–45.

3   On the history of enserfment, see the introductory chapter of Peter Kolchin, *Unfree Labor: American Slavery and Russian Serfdom* (Cambridge, Mass.: Harvard University Press, 1987). Kolchin's discussion of the regional distribution of serfdom rests on the careful statistical analysis in Ia. E. Vodarskii, *Naselenie Rossii v kontse XVII–nachale XVIII veka (Chislennost', soslovno-klassovyi sostav, razmeshchenie)* (*The Population of Russia at the End of the Seventeenth to the Beginning of the Eighteenth Century [Numbers, Estate-Class Composition, Distribution]*) (Moscow: Nauka, 1977). See also Jerome Blum, *Lord and Peasant in Russia, from the Ninth to the Nineteenth Century* (Princeton, N.J.: Princeton University Press, 1961), 480, 504–23.

4   F. A. Brokgauz and I. A. Efron, *Encyclopedia* (St. Petersburg: I. A. Efron, 1895), 14:480.

5   Kolesnikov, *Istoriia severnogo krest'ianstva*, 1:290.

6   Patriarch Nikon, metropolitan of Novgorod, in the mid-seventeenth century banned further use of the tent tower form in Orthodox churches. While the patriarch was not consistent in applying this design dictum to his own building projects, he was effective in seeing it applied to church architecture throughout Russia. William C. Brumfield, *A History of Russian Architecture* (Cambridge: Cambridge University Press, 1993), 164–67.

7   For examples, including views of log houses and wooden churches in the Kargopol' area and discussion of wooden windmills, see Alexander Opolovnikov and Yelena Opolovnikova, *The Wooden Architecture of Russia: Houses, Fortifications, and Churches*, ed. David Bruxton (New York: Harry N. Abrams, 1989), 60–74, 217–25. Other examples from the William C. Brumfield Collection of Russian architectural photography may be seen on the Meeting of Frontiers website created by the Library of Congress: international.loc.gov/intldl/mtfhtml/mfdigcol/mfdcphot.html. Additional pictures and a valuable historical survey appear in appendix 1, "Russian Wooden Architecture," in Brumfield, *A History of Russian Architecture.*

8   John T. Alexander, *Catherine the Great: Life and Legend* (New York: Oxford University Press, 1989), 191–92.

9   Concerning Kargopol''s origins, see G. P. Gunn, *Kargopol'e-Onega* (Moscow: Iskusstvo, 1989), 15–16. According to one authority, the most likely explanation for the name refers to the arable land for grain crops in this area, unusual in the Russian north. Others link the name to a Finno-Ugric word derivation that identifies this site as the place of the bears.

10   For Peter's administrative reorganization efforts, see Robert K. Massie, *Peter the Great: His Life and World* (New York: Alfred A. Knopf, 1980), 748–56. The system's reorganization by Catherine II is described in Alexander, *Catherine the Great*, 185–89.

11   With no census statistics from the period for guidance, this population estimate is an informed guess, based on the town's physical size, number of churches, and social structure. For general discussion of population trends in Russia, see Blum, *Lord and Peasant*, 277–81. Kargopol''s population had declined to an estimated three thousand people by 1900, with twenty-two churches and two monasteries. The town today numbers approximately twelve thousand residents. It is now well outside the main lines of travel, having been bypassed by railroad construction, with river traffic no longer important and no nearby major population centers or the improved road connections necessary for attracting tourists.

12   This summary of Kargopol' town history and particularly its architectural heritage relies heavily on the excellent work of architectural historian William C. Brumfield of Tulane University. See in particular his article "Architectural Monuments of the Sol'vychedosk and Kargopol' Regions of Arkhangel'sk Province," in *La mort et ses representations: Monde slave et Europe du Nord, Cahiers slaves*, no. 3 (Paris: Université de Paris-Sorbonne, 2001), available online at www.recherches-slaves. paris-sorbonne.fr/Cahier3/Brumfield.htm.

13   F. 647, op. 1, d. 254, l. 1–10b., Russian State Historical Archive, St. Petersburg (RGIA). Much of the following information is drawn from the Baranov family genealogical

sketch by M. N. Kriuchkova, *Pravitel' Russkoi Ameriki i ego potomki* (*The Governor of Russian America and His Heirs*) (Moscow: Gramota, 1997).

14 Extract from the book of [Kargopol'] town residents, F. 994, op. 3, d. 5, l. 173, State Archive of the Archangel Region, Archangel (GAAO).

15 Extracts from the book of [Kargopol'] town residents, F. 994, op. 3, d. 5, l. 173; F. 29, op. 30, d. 2, l. 45, GAAO.

16 The most comprehensive and balanced treatment of birth-order traits is Frank J. Sulloway, *Born to Rebel: Birth Order, Family Dynamics, and Creative Lives* (New York: Pantheon, 1996). Although Sulloway does not specifically cross-match birth order and gender as independent variables, see his discussions on testing birth-order claims and genetic sources of sibling diversity (71–79, 86–118). His data indicate that middle children in upper- and middle-class families are far more inclined than first children to be receptive to innovation and to travel abroad, personality traits much stronger in Aleksandr Baranov than in his siblings.

17 The Baranov sons had already reached manhood when Empress Catherine introduced the Russian nation to smallpox inoculation by the technique of variolation, brought to St. Petersburg at her request by an English physician in 1768. An informative account of the empress's farsighted action, emphasizing her personal bravery in insisting that she become the royal exemplar for this procedure, may be found in Alexander, *Catherine the Great*, 143–48.

18 The region's fisheries are surveyed in L. P. Sabaneev, *Sobranie sochinenii* (*Collected Works*) (Moscow: A. A. Kartseva, 1892), 2:201. The nelma is widely distributed in the Arctic Ocean basin from the White Sea to the Bering Sea and inflowing rivers including the Onega and the Northern Dvina, as well as in the Mackenzie and Yukon River systems in North America. It is highly prized as food fish. L. S. Berg, *Fishes of Fresh Waters of USSR and Adjacent Countries* (Moscow: U.S.S.R. Academy of Sciences, 1948), 1:321–26.

19 Baranov to the Emperor, [New Archangel,] August 24, 1805, in *A History of the Russian-American Company*, by P. A. Tikhmenev, vol. 2, *Documents*, trans. Dmitri Krenov, ed. Richard A. Pierce and Alton S. Donnelly (Kingston, Ontario: Limestone Press, 1979), no. 37: 144.

20 Brumfield, "Architectural Monuments" (unpaged).

21 F. 647, op. 1, d. 24, l. 1–10b., RGIA.

22 Contract, Aleksandr Andreevich Baranov and Ivan Grigor'ev Pozdeev, June 26, 1777, F. 647, op. 1, d. 24, l. 2–20b., RGIA, trans. Alexander Yu. Petrov. Unless otherwise credited, all translations of Russian documents are Petrov's work.

23 Kiril Khlebnikov, *Baranov, Chief Manager of the Russian Colonies in America*, trans. Colin Bearne, ed. Richard A. Pierce (Kingston, Ontario: Limestone Press, 1973), 1.

24 Kriuchkova, *Pravitel' Russkoi Ameriki*, 14.

25 Extract from the book of [Kargopol'] town residents, F. 994, op. 3, d. 5, l. 173, GAAO.

26 Kiril Khlebnikov, *Notes on Russian America*, pt. 1, *Novo-Arkhangel'sk*, comp. Svetlana G. Fedorova, trans. Serge LeCompte and Richard A. Pierce, ed. Richard A. Pierce (Kingston, Ontario: Limestone Press, 1994), 7; Richard A. Pierce, *Russia's Hawaiian Adventure, 1815–1817* (Berkeley: University of California Press, 1965), 210; Pierce,

Russian America: A Biographical Dictionary (Kingston, Ontario: Limestone Press, 1990), 274.

27   Extract from the book of [Kargopol'] town residents, F. 994, op. 3, d. 5, l. 173, GAAO.

28   Kriuchkova, *Pravitel' Russkoi Ameriki*, 14.

29   F. 647, op. 1, d. 254, l. 2–20b., RGIA.

30   F. 647, op. 1, d. 254, l. 1–10b., RGIA.

2. SIBERIAN MERCHANT CAPITALIST

1   W. Bruce Lincoln, *The Conquest of a Continent: Siberia and the Russians* (New York: Random House, 1994), 142.

2   For a highly descriptive overview of travel on the Great Siberian Post Road, see Harmon Tupper, *To the Great Ocean: Siberia and the Trans-Siberian Railroad* (Boston: Little, Brown and Company, 1965), 7–20; *Istoriia Sibiri (The History of Siberia)* (Leningrad: Nauka, 1968), 2:25–109, 163–81; and V. I. Shunkov, *Ocherki po istorii zemledeliia Sibiri (XVII v.) (Essays on the History of Agriculture in Siberia [Seventeenth Century])* (Moscow: Nauka, 1956), 34–35, 314, 417. Siberian travel conditions improved at a slow rate. In 1857 a resilient pair of American tourists, speeding in a three-horse sleigh and stopping only briefly in a few towns to rest, arrived at Irkutsk fifty-seven days after leaving Moscow, having used more than seven hundred horses while changing teams and drivers 210 times: Perry McDonough Collins, *Overland Explorations in Siberia, Northern Asia, and the Great Amoor River Country; Incidental Notices of Manchooria, Mongolia, Kamschatka, and Japan* (New York: D. Appleton and Company, 1864), 46. Three decades later, just before construction of the Trans-Siberian Railroad, the American observer George Kennan claimed that imperial couriers could travel between Irkutsk and St. Petersburg by sleigh in sixteen days, with 212 changes of horses and drivers. This feat could only be achieved by a nonstop trip, Kennan pointed out, during which drivers would eat, drink, and sleep in their sleighs, to make an average speed of ten miles an hour for nearly four hundred consecutive hours. Tupper, *To the Great Ocean*, 13n.

3   An authoritative summary of the Vitus Bering and Aleksei Chirikov expedition appears in Basil Dmytryshyn, E. A. P. Crownhart-Vaughan, and Thomas Vaughan, trans. and eds., *Russian Penetration of the North Pacific Ocean, 1700–1797: A Documentary Record*, vol. 2 of *To Siberia and Russian America: Three Centuries of Russian Eastward Expansion* (Portland: Oregon Historical Society, 1988), xxxvi–xxxix.

4   The history of this route is the focus of James R. Gibson, *Feeding the Russian Fur Trade: Provisionment of the Okhotsk Seaboard and the Kamchatka Peninsula, 1639–1856* (Madison: University of Wisconsin Press, 1969). For a detailed narrative regarding the development of the Yakutsk-Okhotsk track, see 78–102.

5   Although this route had more traffic by 1801, travel conditions had scarcely improved. The Russian-American Company clerk N. I. Korobitsyn spent all of the month of May escorting a cargo of merchandise from Irkutsk to Yakutsk. After a week's forced delay, he started for Okhotsk with two companions on June 12 and reached his destination on July 29, having been so delayed by rainy weather and high water that the three

men exhausted their food supply and finished the trip eating nothing but the meat of a small bull they purchased on the way from some Yakuts herders. "Journal of N. I. Korobitsyn, Clerk of the Russian-American Company, for the Period of 1795–1807," in *Russian Discoveries in the Pacific and in North America in the Eighteenth and Nineteenth Centuries: A Collection of Materials*, ed. A. I. Andreev, trans. Carl Ginsburg (Ann Arbor, Mich.: J. W. Edwards for the American Council of Learned Societies, 1952).

6   A good many of the sons of these unions, particularly in eastern Siberia, followed their father's profession, becoming promyshlenniks in the Aleutian and Alaskan fur business. The difficulty in estimating the ethnic composition of the workforce in Russian America is made clear in Svetlana G. Fedorova, *The Russian Population in Alaska and California, Late Eighteenth Century–1867*, trans. Richard A. Pierce and Alton S. Donnelly (Kingston, Ontario: Limestone Press, 1973).

7   This discussion of the Siberian fur business and its regulation depends heavily on Benson Bobrick, *East of the Sun: The Epic Conquest and Tragic History of Siberia* (New York: Poseidon Press, 1992), 67–78.

8   Ibid., 68–70.

9   Basil Dmytryshyn, E. A. P. Crownhart-Vaughan, and Thomas Vaughan, trans. and eds., *Russia's Conquest of Siberia, 1558–1700: A Documentary Record*, vol. 1 of *To Siberia and Russian America: Three Centuries of Russian Eastward Expansion* (Portland: Oregon Historical Society Press, 1985), lxi. For the impact of the Kiakhta trade on Russia, including the adoption of tea as Russia's national nonalcoholic drink, see James R. Gibson, "Russian Expansion in Siberia and America: Critical Contacts," in *Russia's American Colony*, ed. S. Frederick Starr (Durham, N.C.: Duke University Press, 1987), 32–40.

10 A scholarly overview of these voyages is found in Raisa V. Makarova, *Russians on the Pacific, 1743–1799*, trans. and ed. Richard A. Pierce and Alton S. Donnelly (Kingston, Ontario: Limestone Press, 1975).

11 An excellent narrative account of Kiakhta's creation and its trade appears in Lincoln, *Conquest of a Continent*, 143–47. A detailed physical description of Mai-mai-cheng and Kiakhta may be found in Bobrick, *East of the Sun*, 329–30.

12 Four hundred miles long and 20–50 miles wide, with an average depth of 2,400 feet and a maximum depth of 5,300 feet, Lake Baikal gathers its immense waters from hundreds of springs, streams, and rivers that drain central Siberia and northern Mongolia. So huge that it creates its own atmospheric conditions, the lake has a unique biology. Its denizens include the small *golomyanka*, or oil fish; the famously tasty *omul'*; the Baikal sturgeon; and the *nerpa*, or Baikal seal, the world's only freshwater seal species. The Angara River is its single outlet. Flowing northeast, the Angara eventually joins the Yenisey River and continues more than 1,500 miles north to the Kara Sea and the Arctic Ocean. Situated at 1,460 feet in elevation, Lake Baikal never freezes at the Angara's source even in the coldest weather, since a warm upflow from the lake's depths creates an ice-free zone that extends far downstream. A detailed account of the lake's geology and its flora and fauna is Mikhail Kozhov, *Lake Baikal and Its Life* (The Hague: Dr. W. Junk Publishers, 1963).

13 V. P. Shakherov, "Osobennosti formirovaniia krupnogo kapitala v Iugo-vostochnoi Sibiri v kontse XVIII–pervoi treti XIX veka" ("Peculiarities in Large Capital Formation in Southeast Siberia at the End of the Eighteenth to the Early Nineteenth Century"), in *Sibir' v proshlom, nastoiashem, buduiushchem (Siberia's Past, Present, and Future)* (Novosibirsk, 1981), 48.

14 Bobrick, *East of the Sun*, 304.

15 Siberia's governmental history is summarized in John A. Harrison, *The Founding of the Russian Empire in Asia and America* (Coral Gables, Fla.: University of Miami Press, 1971), 96–100.

16 Collins, *Overland Explorations in Siberia*, 48; Bobrick, *East of the Sun*, 330–31; Lincoln, *Conquest of a Continent*, 147–48.

17 F. 447, op. 1, d. 2, l. 103, State Archive of the Irkutsk Region, Irkutsk (GAIO).

18 Baranov to Natalia Shelikhova, June 10, 1798, F. RAK, op. 888, d. 121, Archive of the Foreign Policy of the Russian Empire, Moscow (AVPRI).

19 K. G. Laksman entry in *Great Soviet Encyclopedia*, ed. A. M. Prokhorov, 3rd. ed., English translation (New York: Macmillan, 1976), 14:179.

20 The exact Russian measures were 9 desiatinas (1 desiatina equals 2.7 acres), 10 square *sazhens* (1 sazhen equals approximately 7 feet), and 300 desiatinas for the settlement of twenty exile workers, providing 15 desiatinas (40.5 acres) for each.

21 F. 447, op. 1, d. 2, l. 107, GAIO.

22 Ibid.

23 F. 447, op. 1, d. 2, l. 108, GAIO.

24 Baranov to G. I. Shelikhov, Irkutsk, June 5, 1789, F. RAK, op. 888, d. 747, l. 5–6, AVPRI.

25 Baranov to G. I. Shelikhov, Irkutsk, June 15, 1789, F. RAK, op. 888, d. 747, l. 7–7ob., AVPRI.

26 Baranov to Emel'ian Larionov, [Pavlovskaia Harbor,] March 3, 1798, in Tikhmenev, *Documents*, no. 24: 97.

27 Katharina (Ekaterina) Laksman to M. Buldakov, July 2, 1799, F. 10, op. 1, d. 34, l. 1, Vologda State Art and History Museum.

28 F. 447, op.1, d. 2, l. 187, GAIO.

29 F. 447, op.1, d. 2, l. 143, GAIO; F. 447, op.1, d. 1, l. 82–82ob., GAIO.

30 Note of third guild merchant Maxim Alekseevich Sibiriakov, December 15, 1789, for 189 rubles; note of Moscow merchant Nikolai Ivanovich Rybinskii, January 2, 1790, for 1,136 rubles, both in F. 447, op. 1, d. 3, l. 91–92ob., GAIO.

31 F. 447, op. 1, d. 2, l. 2ob., GAIO. The identity of Mr. Gomukov and the nature of his relationship with Baranov remain unknown.

32 F. 70, op. 1, d. 11, l. 23, GAIO.

33 F. 446, op. 1, d. 3, l. 34–34ob., GAIO. It is possible that Baranov originally borrowed this money to secure the funds needed for paying off Krasnogorov, but then the renegotiation of the Krasnogorov loan enabled him to return the three thousand rubles to Lebedev-Lastochkin. A biographical sketch of Lebedev-Lastochkin, who had originally come to Irkutsk from Yakutsk, appears in Pierce, *Russian America*, 301–3.

34 For a biographical sketch of Golikov, see Pierce, *Russian America*, 172–73. A fuller

account of his life and career appears in A. V. Zorin, ed., *Kurskie kuptsy Golikovy* (*The Golikovs, Merchants from Kursk*) (St. Petersburg: VIRD, n.d.), 16–40.

35 The scattered biographical information concerning Shelikhov is concisely presented by Richard A. Pierce in his extensive introduction to the English edition of Grigorii Shelikhov, *A Voyage to America, 1783–1786*, trans. Marina Ramsay, ed. Richard A. Pierce (Kingston, Ontario: Limestone Press, 1981). For a summary see Pierce, *Russian America*, 454–59.

36 New evidence concerning Natalia Alekseevna's parentage and her marriage is presented in Katerina G. Solovjova and Aleksandra A. Vovnyanko, *The Fur Trade: Essays and Documents on the History of Alaska at the End of the Eighteenth Century*, trans. Richard L. Bland and Katya S. Wessels (Anchorage, Alaska: Phenix Press, 2002), 98–103. Formerly, it was generally supposed that she was a widow with a considerable fortune of her own at the time of her marriage to Grigorii Shelikhov. Some scholars, skeptical of the argument made by Solovjova and Vovnyanko, still endorse this hypothesis even though it is entirely at odds with her age at the time of the marriage.

37 F. 50, op. 7, d. 5, l. 2290b., GAIO.

38 For additional detail on this very interesting woman, whom scholar Alexander Yu. Petrov has termed "Russia's first businesswoman," see Pierce, *Russian America*, 459–60; Alexander Yu. Petrov, *Obrazovanie Rossiisko-Amerikanskoi Companii (Formation of the Russian-American Company)* (Moscow: Nauka, 2000), 80–123; and *Natalia Shelikhova: Russian Oligarch of Alaska Commerce*, trans. and ed. Dawn Lea Black and Alexander Yu. Petrov (Fairbanks: University of Alaska Press, 2010).

39 Solovjova and Vovnyanko, *The Fur Rush*, 102–3.

40 F. 447, op. 1, d. 104, l. 89, GAIO. To the confusion of historians, this partnership was often identified simply as the Shelikhov Company or the Golikov-Shelikhov Company, especially after the death of Mikhail Golikov in 1788. The Northeastern Company is easily confused with other companies within the one encompassing the Golikov-Shelikhov partnership. The Northeastern Company was reorganized with a new charter on August 14, 1790, the Predtechenskaia on the same date, the Unalashkinskaia in August 1791, the Northern Company on July 31, 1794, and the Kurile Company on September 3, 1795. For details on capitalization of all these companies, the formation of the Golikov-Shelikhov partnership, and the contract of 1781, see Petrov, *Obrazovanie Rossiisko-Amerikanskoi Companii*, 45–49, 134. For biographical information on the Golikovs, see Pierce, *Russian America*, 172–73; and Zorin, *Kurskie kuptsy Golikovy*, 41–43. Although Mikhail Golikov has often been identified as a nephew of Ivan Golikov, Zorin fixes his identity as a cousin of the older man. Both Golikovs, like Baranov, were licensed to sell alcoholic spirits in Siberia.

41 Shelikhov's report, including the requests to Catherine's government, is conveniently available in English in Shelikhov, *A Voyage to America*. An excellent alternative translation of his account of his voyage and the conquest of the Kodiak Alutiiq people is published in Dmytryshyn, Crownhart-Vaughan, and Vaughan, *Russian Penetration*, no. 49: 296–320. This same volume also includes a special report from Grigorii Shelikhov, "Requesting Special *Privileges* for His Company in North America," apparently intended for the ministers of Catherine II and dated May–November 1787, and

a separate "Petition to Empress Catherine II from Grigorii Shelikhov and Ivan L. Golikov, Requesting Support for Their Company in North America," February 1788; see *Russian Penetration*, no. 57: 344–47 and no. 59: 361–64.

42 Governor General I. V. Iakobii to Empress Catherine II, "Concerning Activities of the Golikov-Shelikhov Company on Islands in the North Pacific," November 30, 1787, in Dmytryshyn, Crownhart-Vaughan, and Vaughan, *Russian Penetration*, no. 58: 348–60.

43 "Citation, Given Shelikhov by the Governing Senate," October 11, 1778, in Tikhmenev, *Documents*, 18–19; "A Decree from the Governing Senate Granting Golikov and Shelikhov Medals and Prohibiting Promyshlenniks from Provoking Arguments with the Chinese," September 12, 1788, in Dmytryshyn, Crownhart-Vaughan, and Vaughan, *Russian Penetration*, no. 60: 365–67.

44 Shelikhov's detailed account of this meeting can be found in Shelikhov, *A Voyage to America*, 50–51. A brief mention appears in his report to Irkutsk governor-general I. V. Iakobii, April 19, 1787, in Dmytryshyn, Crownhart-Vaughan, and Vaughan, *Russian Penetration*, no. 52: 331. The agreement between Shelikhov and Peters is published in A. I. Andreev, comp., *Russkie otkrytiia v Tikhom okeane i Severnoi Amerike v XVIII–XIX Vekakh: Sbornik documentov* (*Russian Discoveries in the Pacific Ocean and North America in the Eighteenth and Nineteenth Centuries: A Collection of Materials*) (Moscow: Nauka, 1948), 199–200. A less complete 1944 version of this volume, published under wartime conditions, has been translated by Carl Ginsburg: Andreev, *Russian Discoveries in the Pacific and in North America*. This volume contains Shelikhov's separate "Memorandum on Trade with the English on Kamchatka" (72–76), also written in April 1767, but it does not include the Shelikhov-Peters agreement.

45 A copy of this contract is preserved in F. 447, op. 1, d. 104, l. 1700b.–171, GAIO.

46 Pierce, *Russian America*, 397. It is highly likely that Baranov then invested these funds in his project for trade with the Chukchi, summarized below.

47 Baranov to Shelikhov, Irkutsk, December 12, 1787, F. RAK, op. 888, d. 443, l. 1–20b., AVPRI.

48 Baranov to Shelikhov, Irkutsk, December 29, 1788, F. RAK, op. 888, d. 440, l. 1–20b., AVPRI.

49 The official authorization and detailed orders appear in "Instructions from Catherine II and the Admiralty College to Captain Lieutenant Joseph Billings for His Expedition [1785–1794] to Northern Russia and the North Pacific Ocean," 1785, in Dmytryshyn, Crownhart-Vaughan, and Vaughan, *Russian Penetration*, no. 47: 268–89.

50 Baranov to Shelikhov, Irkutsk, December 12, 1787, F. RAK, op. 888, d. 443, l. 1–20b., AVPRI; Baranov to Shelikhov, Irkutsk, December 29, 1788, F. RAK, op. 888, d. 440, l. 1–20b., AVPRI; Baranov to Shelikhov, Irkutsk, July 20, 1789, F. RAK, op. 888, d. 747, l. 8–90b., AVPRI.

51 The empress had made clear her deep concern about mistreatment of Native peoples in the North Pacific in 1787: "A Personal Ukaz from Empress Catherine II to Ivan V. Iakobii, Governor General of Siberia, Approving the Investigation into Cruelties Perpetrated by Russian Promyshlenniks Against Natives on Islands in the North Pacific Ocean," August 13, 1787, in Dmytryshyn, Crownhart-Vaughan,

and Vaughan, *Russian Penetration*, no. 54: 336. The substance of Britiukov's charges appears in "A Confidential Report to the Governing Senate from Ivan Alferevich Pil, Acting Governor General of Irkutsk and Kolivan, Transmitting Information on Conditions in Russian Possessions in Alaska and the Aleutian Islands," September 19, 1789, in Dmytryshyn, Crownhart-Vaughan, and Vaughan, *Russian Penetration*, no. 63: 379–82. Britiukov had sailed to Kodiak with Shelikhov as an assistant surgeon aboard the *Tri Sviatitelia* in 1783, only to be dismissed by the merchant just prior to his return; Pierce, *Russian America*, 70–71. Additional information on Britiukov's charges and their resolution is available in Mary E. Wheeler, "Origins and Formation of the Russian-American Company" (Ph.D. diss., University of North Carolina at Chapel Hill, 1965), 96–98. For later charges—and denials—of mistreatment of Natives by Shelikhov company workers, recorded by Captain Sarychev based on the testimony of three Aleuts from Unalaska, see "Complaints Made by Natives of the Unalaska District to Russian Government Inspectors about Treatment by Russian Promyshlenniks and Seamen; Responses to These Charges from Those Named by the Natives," June 7, 1789–July 5, 1790, in Dmytryshyn, Crownhart-Vaughan, and Vaughan, *Russian Penetration*, no. 61: 368–72. Fathers Herman and Gideon later affirmed the substance of these charges, as described in Chapter 6.

52   Baranov to Shelikhov, Irkutsk, July 20, 1789, F. RAK, op. 888, d. 747, l. 8–90b., AVPRI.

53   F. 994, op. 2, d. 828, RGIA. Baranov's continuing concern for his goddaughter Aleksandra is exemplified in his letter to Natalia Shelikhova, June 10, 1798, F. RAK, d. 19, l. 7, AVPRI. In time Aleksandra married Gavril Politkovskii, a senior Russian official. Their son Vladimir subsequently became chief director of the RAC, and all his immediate family members became company shareholders.

54   Baranov to Shelikhov, Irkutsk, December 29, 1788, F. RAK, op. 888, d. 440, l. 1–20b., AVPRI.

55   Natalia Shelikhova to Shelikhov, Irkutsk, July 20, 1789, F. RAK, d. 801, l. 12–13, AVPRI.

56   Evidence regarding other contracts between Baranov and Shelikhov appears in F. 447, op. 1, d. 3, l. 103; and F. 447, op. 1, d. 104, l. 1980b., GAIO.

57   F. 70, op. 1, d. 1126, l. 36, GAIO.

58   A report on their explorations along the Aniui and Anadyr Rivers by servitors Semen Dezhnev and Nikita Semenov, dated April 1655, appears in Dmytryshyn, Crownhart-Vaughan, and Vaughan, *Russia's Conquest*, no. 87: 317–33.

59   Waldemar Bogaras, *The Chukchee*, in *Memoirs of the American Museum of Natural History*, vol. 11, ed. Franz Boas (Leiden: E. J. Brill, Ltd., 1909), 53–54.

60   Ibid., 56–58.

61   F. 447, op. 1, d. 2, l. 1050b.; F. 70, op. 1, d. 1087, l. 49, GAIO.

62   F. 70, op. 1, d. 1087, l. 42, 108, GAIO.

63   F. 70, op. 1, d. 35, l. 28, GAIO.

64   F. 70, op. 21, d. 1087, l. 32; d. 1126, l. 3, GAIO. The minimum requirement for classification as a meshchane according to the reform of 1775 was 550 rubles.

65   F. 70, op. 1, d. 1087, l. 48, GAIO.

66   F. 70, op. 1, d. 1126, l. 36, GAIO. Baranov's associates in this proposal were two mer-

chants from Velikiy Ustyug, seven from Tot'ma, and two from Solvychegodsk, all commercial centers in northern Russia.

67   Ibid.

68   F. 50, op. 7, d. 5, l. 262ob., GAIO.

69   F. 50, op. 7, d. 5, l. 269ob., GAIO.

70   Kriuchkova, *Pravitel' Russkoi Ameriki*, 14–15. The author mentions just two children, Appolonii and Afanasiia.

71   F. 590, op. 3, d. 37, GAIO.

72   F. 50, op. 7, d. 33, l. 540ob., GAIO.

73   F. 50, op. 7, d. 7, l. 267ob., 282ob., 302, GAIO.

3. MOVING TO AMERICA

1   Contractual agreement between Baranov and Kuskov, May 20, 1790, F. 204, kart. 32, d. 1, l. 1–10b., Russian State Library, Manuscript Division, Moscow (RGB OR).

2   Baranov to the Kargopol' City Council, Kodiak, June 10, 1798, F. 647, op. 1, d. 25, l. 2, RGIA.

3   In 1812 Ekaterina Laksman sold the factory to the Irkutsk merchant Iakov Soldatov. After his death the factory came into the hands of other Irkutsk merchants. During the Soviet era, it was designated as a state enterprise called Pokrovskii and remained in operation until the mid-1950s. At this point dam construction for the Irkutsk hydroelectric power station flooded the factory site. The equipment was handed over to the Tulunskii glass plant, located also in the Irkutsk region. Presently, the area where Baranov and Laksman once built their factory has been made into an open-air museum devoted to the native wooden architecture, with a main office in Irkutsk.

4   Baranov to Shelikhov, Yakutsk, June 19, 1790, F. RAK, op. 888, d. 447, l. 11–12, AVPRI. Baranov sent two separate letters from Yakutsk, dated June 18 and June 19, which Shelikhov received at Okhotsk on July 17.

5   F. RAK, d. 74, l. 1–7, AVPRI. This document has been published almost in its entirety in *Russkie ekspeditsii po izucheniiu severnoi chasti Tikhogo okeana vo vtoroi polovine XVIII veka* (*Russian Expeditions of Exploration in the North Pacific Ocean in the Second Half of the Eighteenth Century*) (Moscow: Nauka, 1989), 277–80. The main agenda items for Baranov in this document are summarized in P. A. Tikhmenev, *A History of the Russian-American Company*, trans. and ed. Richard A. Pierce and Alton S. Donnelly (Seattle: University of Washington Press, 1996), 28–29. The provision for Baranov's ten full-ownership shares as his reward for assuming the chief manager's position is recorded in Khlebnikov, *Baranov*, 2.

6   The agreement was submitted to the Second Department of the Okhotsk council, with a confirmation that it had been written and signed by the eminent citizen of the city of Ryl'sk and partner in the North America company Grigorii Ivanovich Shelikhov and by Irkutsk guest Aleksandr Andreevich Baranov. According to customs regulations, after the signing took place the document was confirmed and recorded on December 1, 1790, by Collegiate Assessor Ivan Kokh, the governor of Okhotsk guberniia, along with secretary Prokopii Syromiatnikov and clerk Andrei Pribylov.

7   Instructions, Collegiate Assessor I. G. Kokh, acting commandant of Okhotsk, to Baranov, no. 18, August 14, 1780, in Tikhmenev, *Documents*, no. 6: 22.

8   Instructions, Kokh to Baranov, no. 19, August 14, 1780, in Tikhmenev, *Documents*, no. 7: 23–24.

9   Cox's career and this privateering episode are recounted in detail in Pierce, *Russian America*, 101–3.

10   Vasilii N. Berkh, *A Chronological History of the Discovery of the Aleutian Islands; or, The Exploits of Russian Merchants, with a Supplement of Historical Data on the Fur Trade*, trans. Dmitri Krenov, ed. Richard A. Pierce (Kingston, Ontario: Limestone Press, 1974), 63. Berkh traveled to Russian America aboard the *Neva* in 1804. He published this work in 1823.

11   In 1794 Shelikhov sent Governor-General Pil a detailed critique of Okhotsk's deficiencies as a port and ship construction site, urging that an effort be made to find a better location on the coast of the Sea of Okhotsk, with a more convenient overland route to that place. Unfortunately, as experience would demonstrate, a better location simply did not exist. "A Report from Grigorii I. Shelikhov to Ivan A. Pil, Governor General of Irkutsk, concerning the Establishment of Settlements on the Northwest Coast of North America," November 18, 1794, in Dmytryshyn, Crownhart-Vaughan, and Vaughan, *Russian Penetration*, no. 75: 460–62.

12   Gavrill Davydov, *Two Voyages to Russian America, 1802–1807*, trans. Colin Bearne, ed. Richard A. Pierce (Kingston, Ontario: Limestone Press, 1977), 68. A graduate of the Russian Naval Academy who had served briefly with the British fleet, young Davydov brought a professional navy officer's disdain to his assessment of the ships and shipmasters he encountered in the North Pacific fur business. His career is described in Pierce, *Russian America*, 112–14.

13   Regarding Bocharov, see Pierce, *Russian America*, 64–65. The more correct translation of *Tri Sviatitelia* is *Three Hierarchs*, but here we follow the common practice among historians. The ship's full name identified each of the hierarchs: *Tri Sviatitelia: Vasilii Velikii, Grigorii Bogoslov i Ioann Zlatoust* (Vasilii the Great, Gregory the Divine, and John Chrysostom).

14   Quoted in Berkh, *Chronological History*, 69–70.

15   The original report on this voyage is preserved in the Archive of the Foreign Policy of the Russian Empire (AVPRI) in Moscow. It was first published in Grigorii Shelikhov's 1791 volume *A Voyage to America, 1783–1786*, subsequently translated by Marina Ramsay and edited by Richard A. Pierce, 83–106. A recent translation with an interpretive note appears in Solovjova and Vovnyanko, *The Fur Rush*, app. 1, 268–83. It includes a discussion of the expedition and its maps (185–87).

16   Baranov to Shelikhov, Koshiginskaia Bay, Unalaska Island, September 1, 1790, F. RAK, op. 888, d. 447, l. 15–16ob., AVPRI. The problem demonstrates either incompetent or dishonest management at the Irkutsk shipyards.

17   Located at the eastern end of the Aleutians, the largest of the Fox Island group, Unalaska had become familiar to Russia's Siberian merchants following its discovery by Vitus Bering in 1741. A first trading expedition under Stepan Glotov was active there from 1759 to 1762. A second expedition under Ivan Solov'ev arrived in 1763, only

to encounter the united hostility of the Fox Island Aleuts, who attacked and killed 175 of the Russians. In reprisal, Solov'ev's men carried out a bloody campaign that crushed Aleut resistance. By the time Baranov and his men arrived, the surviving Aleut people had become accustomed to trade and friendly interchange with Russian hunters, who came in search of both sea otters and fox peltry.

18   The term *baidara* was used in eastern Siberia for hide-covered riverboats and sailing skiffs. Naval historian Berkh describes them as "a boat whose frame is made of young trees. It has a pointed stern and instead of planking it has the hides of sea animals sewn together and stretched on these frames. These vessels are very handy and can carry up to sixty men, but it is easy to imagine how dangerous it is to make a long journey in these leather boats." Berkh, *Chronological History*, 54. In 1783 Shelikhov had a few Siberian baidaras aboard the *Tri Sviatitelia*. Apparently, three of these serviceable craft were carried on deck to serve as ship's boats during this 1790 voyage.

19   For the career of Potap Zaikov, see Pierce, *Russian America*, 550–51. He died on Unalaska in the spring of 1791, presumably not long after Baranov's departure. Regarding the identity of this ship and its owner, see Makarova, *Russians on the Pacific*, 215. This voyage, Makarova points out, had begun ten years earlier. On the *Aleksandr Nevskii*'s arrival at Okhotsk, the value of the cargo was registered as 238,700 rubles, which was the last substantial fur return from the Unalaska district. Skipper Ivan Orekhov, with his profits, immediately retired from the North Pacific fur business. Berkh's admittedly incomplete listing of Russian ships in the North Pacific trade does not include the *Aleksandr Nevskii* during this period, although he records this ship's extremely successful voyage from 1781 to 1786. Berkh, *Chronological History*, 60, 62, 104–5.

20   During their visit, Billings and his men gathered detailed stories from the Fox Island Aleuts concerning their recent mistreatment by Russian traders and hunters, including promyshlenniks in the Orekhov Company as well as a party of Shelikhov's people led by Evstratii Delarov. According to this testimony, the Russians had seized sea otter and sea lion pelts without paying the Aleut hunters, forced them to hunt, and stolen their women and sometimes cruelly abused them for their own pleasure. Not all Russian companies, however, were included in this indictment. Specifically exempted were the companies of Kamchatka merchant Leontii Nagaev and Tot'ma trader Stepan Cherepanov. Typescript copy, Billings expedition, F. 1605, op. 1, d. 367, l. 1–7, Russian State Archive of Ancient Acts, Moscow (RGADA); Pierce, *Russian America*, 84–85, 374–75.

21   Baranov to Shelikhov, Koshiginskaia Bay, Unalaska Island, September 1, 1790, F. RAK, op. 888, d. 447, l. 15–160b., AVPRI.

22   Thirty years later the Russian Orthodox missionary Ioann Veniaminov recorded the existence of an Aleut village at Koshigin Bay, but there is no direct evidence that such a village existed at the time of Baranov's visit. Ioann Veniaminov, *Notes on the Islands of the Unalashka District*, trans. Lydia T. Black and R. H. Geoghegan, ed. Richard A. Pierce (Kingston, Ontario: Limestone Press, 1991), 130.

23   Baranov to Shelikhov, Koshiginskaia Bay, Unalaska, April [24?], 1791, F. RAK, op. 888, d. 78, l. 1–80b., AVPRI.

24 Khlebnikov, *Baranov*, 2.

25 Ibid., 2–3.

26 Baranov to Shelikhov, Koshiginskaia Bay, Unalaska, April [24?], 1791, F. RAK, op. 888, d. 78, l. 1–80b., AVPRI.

27 *Barabara* (or *barabor*) is a term derived from a Kamchadal word for a Native hut erected for summer camping. In Alaska it came to designate a permanent dwelling with a dugout construction topped by a wooden or bone frame and covered in hides or thatched with brush and grass.

28 Khlebnikov, *Baranov*, 3. When Molev volunteered for this hazardous journey, Baranov promised to pay him one hundred rubles. Baranov to Shelikhov, Koshigin-skaia Bay, Unalaska, April [24?], 1791, F. RAK, op. 888, d. 78, l. 1–80b., AVPRI.

29 Khlebnikov, *Baranov*, 3. Koshigin Bay was notable in early times for its abundance of salmon. The earliest species to arrive each year are the king (chinook) salmon, which appear in February and continue through mid-April. Sockeye (red) salmon, the species preferred for the Natives' drying process, do not make their spawning run until late summer. See Douglas W. Veltre and Mary J. Veltre, *Resource Utilization in Unalaska, Aleutian Islands, Alaska*, Technical Paper no. 58 ([Bethel]: Alaska Department of Fish and Game, Division of Subsistence, 1982), 78, 80–82.

30 Baranov to Shelikhov, Koshiginskaia Bay, Unalaska, April [24?], 1791, F. RAK, op. 888, d. 78, l. 1–80b., AVPRI. For Medvednikov's eventful Alaskan career, see Pierce, *Russian Alaska*, 349–50.

31 Khlebnikov, *Baranov*, 3. Because their diet included fresh meat and shellfish along with roots and plants rich in vitamin C, no one came down with scurvy—although the reasons for their good health were not understood by Aleksandr Andreevich or any of his men. Captain James Cook had devised successful antiscorbutic dietary measures to prevent scurvy aboard ship during his second and third Pacific voyages in the 1770s, yet none of Baranov's contemporaries in Russian America came to understand the relationship between the disease and diet. Consequently, this affliction would continue to endanger Russian workers and officials when fresh foods were lacking The year after Baranov and his men wintered at Koshigin Bay, for example, the two ships of the Billings expedition remained anchored in Captain's Bay from late August until the following May, with the loss of at least fourteen men from scurvy. Every person in the command except one was more or less affected, and at one point three-quarters of the men were down sick in their hammocks. "The chief cause of this malady," declared Captain Gavriil Sarychev, expressing a common misunderstanding, "was the damp and unfavourable weather, which continued almost uninterruptedly during the whole of our stay at this place." The survivors began recovering their health in March and April when they added fresh salmon and a new growth of wild mustard greens to their diet. The singular healthy exception through the entire winter was the expedition physician, Dr. Martin Sauer, an Englishman who was apparently familiar with Captain Cook's success. Sauer described in detail his efforts to avoid scurvy with a supply of antiscorbutics that included salads made of fresh cress, rock fish that he caught for himself, and spruce beer laced with corn brandy and flavored with berries, sugar, and pepper. For the fatalities and Captain Sarychev's

remarks, see Gavriil Sarychev, *Account of a Voyage of Discovery to the North-East of Siberia, the Frozen Ocean, and the North-East Sea, by Gawrila Sarytschew, Translated from the Russian* (London: J. G. Barnard, 1806; reprint, 2 vols. in 1, New York: Da Capo Press, 1969), 2:68–69. Sauer's description is in Martin Sauer, *An Account of a Geographical and Astronomical Expedition to the Northern Parts of Russia . . . [and] the Islands in the Eastern Ocean, Stretching to the American Coast. Performed . . . by Commodore Joseph Billings, in the Years 1785, &c. to 1794* (London: A. Strahan for T. Cadell, Jun. and W. Davies, 1802), 262–63. 269–70. Biographical sketches of Captain Sarychev and Sauer may be found in Pierce, *Russian America*, 442–45.

32 The description in Khlebnikov's biography, a primary source for this account, relies both on Baranov's 1818 recollections and on his letter of late April 1791 to Shelikhov. Khlebnikov, *Baranov*, 4.

33 These last quotations come from the first page in the English-language manuscript version of Khlebnikov's biography, translated presumably by Khlebnikov himself as described in the preface to this volume. The corresponding paragraph in the published Colin Bearne translation contains an expanded, embroidered version of Baranov's remarks. According to historians Katerina G. Solovjova and Aleksandra A. Vovnyanko, the Northeastern Company's acting chief manager, Evstratii Delarov, had spent the winter of 1789–90 on Unalaska Island, presumably on the northeastern end of the island, where he created a temporary hunting outpost that must have taken a heavy toll on the remaining sea otter population in those waters. Solovjova and Vovnyanko, *The Fur Rush*, 79. Baranov made no mention of this expedition in his accounts of his Unalaska sojourn during the following winter.

34 Baranov to Shelikhov, Koshiginskaia Bay, April [24?], 1791, F. RAK, op. 888, d. 78, l. 1–8ob., AVPRI. Bocharov's baidara, Baranov mentions, was thirty-seven feet in length, apparently about the same size as Baranov's own, so a journey to Okhotsk may not have been entirely impractical. In earlier times, fur hunters had frequently sailed baidaras from Okhotsk or Kamchatka to the most western Aleutian Islands, the so-called Near Islands. Included in Bocharov's party, probably in charge of the smaller third baidara, was the hunter Vasilii Medvednikov.

35 Baranov to Shelikhov, Kapistanskaia Harbor, Unalaska Island, April 28, 1791, F. RAK, op. 888, d. 83, l. 1–2ob., AVPRI. Khlebnikov's biography gives the departure date as April 21, 1791, a small error.

36 For the identity of this ship and its captain, see Makarova, *Russians on the Pacific*, 215. This voyage, Makarova points out, had begun ten years earlier. On the *Aleksandr Nevskii*'s arrival at Okhotsk, the value of the cargo was registered as 238,700 rubles, which was the last substantial fur return from the Unalaska district. Apparently, Orekhov retired from the North Pacific trade following this fur bonanza.

37 Baranov to Shelikhov, Kapistanskaia Harbor, Unalaska Island, April 28, 1791, F. RAK, op. 888, d. 83, l. 1–2ob., AVPRI; Baranov to Shelikhov, Cook Harbor, Unalaska Island, April 29, 1791, F. RAK, d. 80, l. 2, AVPRI; Baranov to Shelikhov, Cook Harbor, Unalaska Island, May 14, 1791, F. RAK, op. 888, d. 447, l. 17–18ob., AVPRI. All of Baranov's letters to Shelikhov from Unalaska Island reached him in Okhotsk on July 8, 1791.

38 For the identification of Issanakh Strait with False Pass, see Donald J. Orth, *Dictionary of Alaska Place Names* (Washington, D.C.: Government Printing Office, 1967), 461.

39 The Russian outpost at Karluk dated to the period of Shelikhov's original colonization of Kodiak Island. Shelikhov had wintered there in 1785–86. The Karluk River was notable for its abundant runs of king salmon in July and silver (coho) and sockeye salmon in September. The Karluk settlement became an important resource to the Russians both for its salmon and for a supply of willing Native workers, not the less because Baranov's Alutiiq consort—later wife—came from Karluk.

40 The date Baranov reached the settlement at Three Saints Harbor has sometimes been given as July 27, 1791. But since he wrote to Shelikhov from this site in a letter dated July 2, 1791, we must conclude that he actually arrived there on June 27. This conclusion is verified by Khlebnikov's biography. Thus the trip from Cook's Harbor took six weeks. The confusion in dates can be explained by the difficulty in distinguishing the names of the two months in the handwritten Cyrillic script of the time.

41 Bocharov's mapping accomplishments are discussed in "The Lost and Forgotten Maps of Alaska of the Northeastern Company Navigators," in Solovjova and Vovnyanko, *The Fur Rush*, 173–201. His map of the Alaska Peninsula, located in F. 419, d. 240, Russian State Archive of Military History, Moscow (RG VIA), is reproduced by Solovjova and Vovnyanko as figure 105 on page 193.

42 Quoted in Khlebnikov, *Baranov*, 4.

43 Baranov manuscript, in ibid., [1–2].

44 Quoted in Khlebnikov, *Baranov*, 5.

4. TAKING COMMAND

1 Pierce, *Russian America*, 115–17.

2 Sauer, *An Account*, 174; Pierce, *Russian America*, 116–17.

3 The total number of general shares for each voyage was fixed by the number of contract workers, plus a few shares—usually from five to ten—assigned to the ship's captain, the ship's clerks, and perhaps other company officers. One or two additional shares were set aside to provide a charitable donation to some worthy cause in Siberia. It was also common practice for each company to agree that a small number of bonus shares might be awarded to company members either for bravery or for acts of singular benefit to the company such as the discovery of a new hunting territory. A detailed explanation of this system is contained in Natalia Shelikhova's "Note on the Essential Meaning of Maritime Shares [Pai] in Animal-Hunting Companies and on the State of the Company of the Late Shelikhov," November 1, 1799, in Black and Petrov, *Natalia Shelikhova*, 143–47.

4 Baranov to Shelikhov, Kodiak Island, June 2, 1791, F. RAK, op. 888, d. 90, l. 1–20b., AVPRI.

5 Baranov to Shelikhov, Kodiak Island, July 2, 1791, F. RAK, op. 888, d. 90, l. 1–20b., AVPRI. Sauer recorded some of the same complaints voiced by the company hunters to the visiting officers of the Billings expedition in 1790. While Shelikhov's men made

extraordinarily high pay, six hundred to one thousand rubles a year, Sauer understood, his company also charged exorbitant prices for everything the men needed
to purchase, "so that their expenses (they not being allowed to trade) exceed their
salaries. Some men bitterly complained of this." Sauer, *An Account*, 174. According
to testimony recorded in the expedition's official report, Shelikhov and other traders
customarily charged for their goods a four hundred percent markup over Okhotsk
prices: Billings report, F. 1605, op. 1, d. 367, l. 1–7, RGA DA.

6   Baranov to Ivan Kuskov, [Pavlovskaia Harbor,] June 9, 1797, F. 204, kart. 32, d. 2, l.
    18–25, RGB OR.

7   In a letter to Baranov following Shelikhov's death, the interim office manager at
    Okhotsk reemphasized the need to avoid the slightest appearance of compulsory
    iasak collection from the Alutiiq. According to the decree from the imperial ruling
    senate, such a levy should not be taken even as a gift. "If you have already collected
    iasak you should return it to those from whom you collected it. You have to prohibit
    [even] mentioning it orally." Ivan Shelikhov to Baranov, Okhotsk, August 20, 1795, F.
    RAK, op. 888, d. 118, l. 16–19, AVPRI.

8   *The Round the World Voyage of Hieromonk Gideon, 1803–1809*, trans. Lydia T. Black,
    ed. Richard A. Pierce (Kingston, Ontario: Limestone Press, 1989), 63. Father Gideon's
    report was first published in Russian in 1894 as part of the Valaam Monastery cen-
    tennial volume, much translated and published as *The Russian Orthodox Religious
    Mission in America, 1794–1837*, trans. Colin Bearne, ed. Richard A. Pierce (Kings-
    ton, Ontario: Limestone Press, 1978). The 1989 edition contains additional materials,
    including marriage and birth registers, translated by Professor Black from docu-
    ments in the Shur Collection at the U.S. Library of Congress.

9   The term *kaiur* was another Russian introduction from Kamchatka, where it referred
    to hired laborers, specifically dog-team drivers. Davydov, *Two Voyages*, 191.

10 Baranov to Kuskov, [Pavlovskaia Harbor,] June 9, 1797, F. 204, kart. 32, d. 2, l. 18–25,
    RGB OR.

11 Gideon, *Round the World Voyage*, 61–62.

12 Davydov, *Two Voyages*, 178.

13 Ibid., 191, 193.

14 Archimandrite Ioasaf to Shelikhov, Kadiak Island, May 15, 1795, in Tikhmenev, *Docu-
    ments*, no. 33: 80. It is likely that on such occasions Baranov, who loved to sing, joined
    in with a rendition of his song of the Russian hunters.

15 Baranov to Emel'ian Larionov, [Pavlovskaia Harbor,] March 22, 1801, in Tikhmenev,
    Documents, no. 31: 127.

16 Information for this treatment of the sea otter is drawn from the following principal
    sources: Karl W. Kenyon, *The Sea Otter in the Eastern Pacific* (Washington D.C.:
    Bureau of Sport Fisheries and Wildlife, 1969); John A. Love, *Sea Otter* (Golden, Colo.:
    Fulcrum Publishing, 1992); Roy Nickerson, *Sea Otters, a Natural History and Guide*
    (San Francisco: Chronicle Books, 1989); and Alvin Silverstein, Virginia Silverstein,
    and Robert Silverstein, *The Sea Otter* (Brookfield, Conn.: Millbrook Press, 1995).

17 Russian hunters never really became adept at hunting from baidarkas; they relied
    on their muskets, though this was less efficient because they were able to retrieve a

much smaller percentage of the dead animals than the Native hunters.

18 Shelikhov to Baranov, Okhotsk, August 10, 1792, F. RAK, op. 888, d. 96, l. 1–20b., AVPRI.

19 This dilemma is the central theme of Arthur F. McEvoy, *The Fisherman's Problem: Ecology and Law in California Fisheries, 1850–1980* (New York: Cambridge University Press, 1988).

20 Merkul'ev to Shelikhov, Three Saints Bay, May 2, 1789, quoted in James F. Lander, *Tsunamis Affecting Alaska, 1737–1996* (Boulder, Colo.: National Geophysical Data Center, National Environmental Satellite, Data and Information Service, U.S. Department of Commerce, 1996), 33–34.

21 Ibid.; Davydov, *Two Voyages*, 206.

22 Journal of Joseph Billings, June 27, 1790, F. 913, op. 1, d. 170, l. 120–25, Russian State Archive of the Navy, St. Petersburg (RGA VMF). From his shipboard vantage, Captain Sarychev succinctly described the company's establishment as containing only "several pithouses, one barn, and two huts." Quoted in Solovjova and Vovnyanko, *The Fur Rush*, 84. Dr. Carl Heinrich Merck, the expedition's German naturalist, added to this description: "On the banks of the harbor, close to the mountains," he wrote, "there are some Russian dwellings, storage places, a bath house, and a large cabin for a large number of the islanders' boys and girls who are kept there as hostages." At the time, in late July, Dr. Merck observed, only some "merchant's helpers" and twenty promyshlenniks lived in the settlement. *Siberia and Northwestern America, 1788–1792: The Journals of Carl Heinrich Merck, Naturalist with the Russian Scientific Expedition Led by Captains Joseph Billings and Gavriil Sarychev*, trans. F. Jaensch, ed. Richard A. Pierce (Kingston, Ontario: Limestone Press, 1980), 96–97.

23 Sauer, *An Account*, 173. Luka Voronin, an artist with the Billings expedition, made a detailed drawing that nicely supplements these descriptions. Voronin pictured about twenty low-built structures situated quite close to the shoreline, where they must have been exceedingly vulnerable to further damage from high water. There is no trace of the high palisade that Shelikhov originally had constructed around the site. Voronin's drawing also depicts two tents erected onshore by the expedition, one used as an astronomical observatory and the other serving as the expedition's "traveling church," according to Sauer. Though temporary, this canvas sanctuary was the first designated place of Christian worship in Russian North America.

24 Baranov to Shelikhov, Chugach Sound, July 24, 1793, in Tikhmenev, *Documents*, no. 9: 36.

25 Ibid.

26 Shelikhov and Aleksei Polevoi to Baranov, Okhotsk, August 9, 1794, in Tikhmenev, *Documents*, no. 17: 54–55.

27 Now a small fishing port with a predominately Alutiiq population, Old Harbor has survived later seismic upheavals, rebuilding even after the 1964 Great Alaskan Earthquake destroyed nearly all the town's structures except the Russian Orthodox church. In 1990 the population was 284. See the online text for *Looking Both Ways*, www.mnh.si.edu/lookingbothways/text/villages/oldHarbor.html.

28 Davydov, *Two Voyages*, 103.

29   Ibid., 105. The only British ship known to be trading on the Northwest Coast dur-
      ing the 1802 season was the *Cheerful*, commanded by Henry Barber. It arrived on
      the coast from Macao in 1801, wintered over, and continued its trade in 1802. F. W.
      Howay, *List of Trading Vessels in the Maritime Fur Trade, 1785–1825*, ed. Richard A.
      Pierce (Kingston, Ontario: Limestone Press, 1973), 44, 49. The supposition that Cap-
      tain Barber met Baranov and traded with him in 1802 is reinforced by later events. In
      1804 as captain of the *Unicorn*, he rescued twenty-three Russian and Native survivors
      of the Sitka Massacre and ransomed them to Baranov. In 1807 he again arrived at
      Pavlovskaia Harbor commanding still another British trading ship, the *Myrtle*, which
      he sold to Baranov with all its cargo. Renamed the *Kad´iak*, this vessel took a promi-
      nent part in Baranov's program of expansion to California, as described below.

30   Davydov, *Two Voyages*, 107.

31   Baranov's office, combined with the company warehouse, was apparently the most
      imposing of the new structures. According to local tradition, part of this pioneer
      edifice, built of square logs, was incorporated in the building subsequently known as
      the Erskine House, now the home of the Kodiak Historical Society, at the corner of
      Marine Way and Center Street. But a National Park Service architectural survey has
      dated this building to 1825 and later, well after Baranov's departure. It is identified as
      KOD-00123 in the Alaska Heritage Resources Survey (AHRS) inventory maintained
      by the State of Alaska, Department of Natural Resources.

32   Journal of N. I. Korobitsyn, July 1, 1804, in Andreev, *Russian Discoveries in the Pacific*,
      168–69.

33   Shelikhov, *A Voyage to America*, 15.

34   The native village of Nanwalek (English Bay) is located now at the Aleksandrovsk
      site.

35   Baranov to Shelikhov, Chugach Sound, July 24, 1793, in Tikhmenev, *Documents*, no.
      9: 27–36.

36   Kolomin's account of Konovalov's disreputable behavior appears in letters to Baranov
      published in Tikhmenev, *Documents*: Kolomin to Lebedev-Lastochkin and other
      partners [1791], no. 11: 39–40; Kolomin to Baranov, November 22, 1791, no. 12: 40–41;
      Kolomin to Baranov, March 11, 1792, no. 13: 42–43. An excellent general history
      of the Lebedev-Lastochkin Company appears as the first chapter in Solovjova and
      Vovnyanko, *The Fur Rush*, 7–42. This work quotes also recently discovered letters
      from Vasilii Malakhov, a Northeastern Company crew chief, to Baranov, found in F.
      RAK, op. 888, d. 861, l. 40b., 50b., AVPRI.

37   Malakhov to Baranov, March 1792, quoted in Solovjova and Vovnyanko, *The Fur Rush*,
      13; Archimandrite Ioasaf to Shelikhov, Kodiak Island, May 18, 1795, in Tikhmenev,
      Documents, no. 19: 84.

38   Baranov to Shelikhov and Polevoi, Pavlovskaia Harbor, May 20, 1795, in Tikhmenev,
      Documents, no. 18: 65–66.

39   Baranov to Shelikhov, Chugach Sound, July 24, 1793, in Tikhmenev, *Documents*, no.
      9: 32–33.

40   Baranov to Shelikhov, Pavlovskaia Harbor, May 20, 1795, in Tikhmenev, *Documents*,
      no. 18: 61.

41   Regarding the common identify of the Kodiak and Chugach Alutiiq people, see Aron
      L. Crowell, Amy F. Steffian, and Gordon L. Pullar, eds., *Looking Both Ways: Heritage
      and Identity of the Alutiiq People* (Fairbanks: University of Alaska Press, 2001).

42   Baranov to Shelikhov, Chugach Sound, July 24, 1793, in Tikhmenev, *Documents*, no.
      9: 28.

43   Captain Moore had made at least two trading voyages to the Northwest Coast with
      the *Phoenix* between 1792 and 1794. Judge Howay calls the *Phoenix* "one of the mys-
      tery ships of the trade." Howay, *List of Trading Vessels*, 17, 23, 28–29, 168.

44   Baranov to Shelikhov, Chugach Sound, July 24, 1793, in Tikhmenev, *Documents*, no.
      9: 28. Richard spoke good English, Baranov relates, and he quickly learned Russian.
      Subsequently, in gratitude for his "splendid service and trustworthiness," Aleksandr
      Andreevich allowed him to sail for his homeland aboard an American trading vessel.
      Baranov to Emel'ian Larionov, Kadiak, July 24, 1800, in Tikhmenev, *Documents*, no.
      29: 114.

45   Baranov to Shelikhov, Chugach Sound, July 24, 1793, in Tikhmenev, *Documents*, no.
      9: 28.

46   Ibid., no. 9: 30. Baranov concluded this section of his report with generous praise for
      the bravery of the Russians who were with him, adding that more than half of them
      were new to the country.

47   Ibid. This account differs slightly from the version from Baranov's 1818 recollections
      recorded in Khlebnikov, *Baranov*, 8–9.

48   According to ethnohistorian Andrei V. Grinev, it is not possible to determine the
      precise number of Tlingits at the end of the eighteenth century. Navy lieutenant
      Yuri Lisiansky provided an estimate of ten thousand in 1804, but he failed to indicate
      whether women and children were included in this figure. Grinev provides a table of
      the various Tlingit population estimates from the nineteenth century to the 1930s.
      Andrei V. Grinev, *The Tlingit Indians in Russian America, 1741–1867*, trans. Richard
      L. Bland and Katerina G. Solovjova (Lincoln: University of Nebraska Press, 2005),
      28–29. A detailed map of the Tlingit homeland appears in *Anóoshi Lingít Aaní Ká,
      Russians in Tlingit America: The Battles of Sitka, 1802 and 1804*, ed. Nora Marks
      Dauenhauer, Richard Dauenhauer, and Lydia T. Black, vol. 4 of *Classics of Tlingit
      Oral Literature* (Seattle: University of Washington Press; Juneau, Alaska: Sealaska
      Heritage Institute, 2008), xi–xii.

49   Cf. Grinev, "The Tlingit Indians before Contact with Europeans," chap. 1 in *Tlingit
      Indians in Russian America*, 15–89; and Frederica de Laguna, "Tlingit," in *Northwest
      Coast*, ed. Wayne P. Suttles, vol. 7 of *Handbook of North American Indians*, ed. Wil-
      liam G. Sturtevant (Washington, D.C.: Smithsonian Institution, 1990), 203–28.

50   Warren Cook, *Flood Tide of Empire: Spain and the Pacific Northwest, 1543–1819* (New
      Haven, Conn.: Yale University Press, 1975), 41–84; Solovjova and Vovnyanko, *The Fur
      Rush*, app. 2, "Russo-Hispanic Contacts, by Enriqueta Vila Vilar," trans. Richard L.
      Bland, 284–301.

51   A brief biography of Shields appears in Pierce, *Russian America*, 461–63. A fuller
      treatment appears in Solovjova and Vovnyanko, *The Fur Rush*, 244–66.

52   Shelikhov to Baranov, [September 1791], quoted in Tikhmenev, *History*, 33.

53 Baranov to Shelikhov, Chugach Sound, July 24, 1793, in Tikhmenev, *Documents*, no. 9: 30–31; Solovjova and Vovnyanko, *The Fur Rush*, 248, 256–57, 259.

54 Baranov to Shelikhov, Chugach Sound, May 20, 1795, in Tikhmenev, *Documents*, no. 18: 66.

55 Baranov to Shelikhov, Chugach Sound, July 24, 1793, in Tikhmenev, *Documents*, no. 9: 31.

56 Ibid., no. 9: 37.

57 George Vancouver, *The Voyage of George Vancouver, 1791–1795*, ed. W. Kaye Lamb, 4 vols. (London: Hakluyt Society, 1984), 4: 1243–44. The fullest biography of Vancouver, with a detailed summary of this expedition, is Bern Anderson's *Surveyor of the Sea: The Life and Voyages of Captain George Vancouver* (Seattle: University of Washington Press, 1960).

58 Baranov to Shelikhov and Polevoi, Pavlovskaia Harbor, May 20, 1795, in Tikhmenev, *Documents*, no. 18: 64.

59 Ibid., no. 18: 60.

60 Skipper Fedor Rodionov, he was quick to report, "had remained inflexible," joined by other men loyal to Baranov and the company management. Ibid., no. 18: 63.

61 Baranov to the Hunters and Employees of the Company, May 1794, in Tikhmenev, *Documents*, no. 10: 37–39.

62 Baranov to Shelikhov and Polevoi, Pavlovskaia Harbor, May 20, 1795, in Tikhmenev, *Documents*, no. 18: 60.

63 Ibid., no. 18: 62–63, 67. An alternative translation appears in Solovjova and Vovnyanko, *The Fur Rush*, 250.

64 Personal communication, May 6, 2009. The drawing, found in the Russian State Archive of the Navy (RGA MVF), is reproduced in Solovjova and Vovnyanko, *The Fur Rush*, 249, fig. 134.

65 Natalia Shelikhova to Count Platon Zubov, [Irkutsk,] November 22, 1795, in Tikhmenev, *Documents*, no. 20: 87.

66 Baranov to Shelikhov, Pavlovskaia Harbor, May 20, 1795, in Tikhmenev, *Documents*, no. 18: 62–63, 67. An alternative translation appears in Solovjova and Vovnyanko, *The Fur Rush*, 250. The vedro was a standard unit of measure in imperial Russia. It equaled 3.2 U.S. gallons (12.3 liters). With so many workmen sharing the libations, one suspects that more than one vedro of this alcoholic concoction was responsible for the results described by Baranov.

67 No further information about these two craft can be found in the surviving documents. Not even their names reappear in any correspondence or reports known to scholars.

68 Baranov to Purtov, June 6, 1793, F. 1605, op. 1, d. 352, l. 1–3, RGA DA.

69 Egor Purtov and Demid Kulikalov to Baranov, Pavlovskaia Harbor, August 9, 1794, in Tikhmenev, *Documents*, no. 16: 47. Kulikalov apparently served as Purtov's scribe in preparing the report.

70 Ibid., no. 16: 50.

71 Ibid., no. 16: 49.

72 Ibid., no. 16: 49–51.

73 Ibid., no. 16: 51. Judge Howay identifies the *Jackal*, along with the *Prince Lee Boo*, as companion vessels to the *Butterworth*, all under the joint command of William Brown, trading on the Northwest Coast in 1792 and 1793. Howay, *List of Trading Vessels*, 13, 19.

74 Purtov and Kulikalov to Baranov, Pavlovskaia Harbor, August 9, 1794, in Tikhmenev, *Documents*, no. 16: 50.

75 Baranov to Shelikhov and Polevoi, Pavlovskaia Harbor, May 20, 1795, in Tikhmenev, *Documents*, no. 18: 60.

76 Solovjova and Vovnyanko, *The Fur Rush*, 251.

5. CALAMITIES AND CATASTROPHES

1 Tikhmenev, *History*, 36. The ship's full name was the *Three Hierarchs: Vasilii the Great, Gregory the Divine, and John Chrysostom*. For the career of Izmailov, a native of Yakutsk who had been educated in the Irkutsk navigation school founded by Catherine the Great, see Pierce *Russian America*, 205–7. He also receives prominent attention in Solovjova and Vovnyanko *The Fur Rush*, emphasizing his skills as a navigator and mapmaker: see 109–11, 280–83.

2 "Personal Instructions from Empress Catherine II to Ivan A. Pil, Governor General of Irkutsk, Authorizing Him to Assign Siberian Exiles to the Shelikhov-Golikov Company as Artisans and Farm Settlers," December 31, 1793; "A Report from Ivan A. Pil, Governor General of Irkutsk, to Empress Catherine II, concerning Sending Exiles to Settle in Areas Claimed by Russia in America and on the Kuril Islands," March 1, 1794, both in Dmytryshyn, Crownhart-Vaughan, and Vaughan, *Russian Penetration*, no. 70: 415; no. 71: 416. Governor-General Pil provided very detailed instructions to Shelikhov concerning the prospective settlement and the treatment of the exile settlers prior to their departure from Okhotsk. "Instructions from Ivan A. Pil, Governor General of Irkutsk, to Grigorii I. Shelikhov, concerning Establishment of Settlements in North America," in ibid., no. 73: 420–32.

3 Pribylov's adventurous career is summarized in Pierce, *Russian America*, 412–13.

4 Baranov to Shelikhov and Polevoi, Pavlovskaia Harbor, May 20, 1795, in Tikhmenev, *Documents*, no. 18: 64. Polevoi was office manager for Shelikhov in Okhotsk. Pierce, *Russian America*, 403. Baranov dismissed Polevoi as nothing but a clerk and grumbled to Shelikhov about having to take instructions from such a person.

5 Baranov to Shelikhov and Polevoi, Pavlovskaia Harbor, May 20, 1795, F. RAK, op. 888, d. 447, l. 24–250b., AVPRI.

6 Shelikhov and Polevoi to Baranov, Okhotsk, August 9, 1794, in Tikhmenev, *Documents*, no. 17: 53.

7 Ibid., no. 17: 54. Although the details are not clear, Shelikhov had obtained from other investors in Lebedev-Lastochkin's operations a power of attorney, which he sent to Baranov apparently without the knowledge of Lebedev-Lastochkin, thus demonstrating his own well-known skills as a "deep politician."

8 A Tomsk merchant, Polomoshnoi may have sailed with Shelikhov to Kodiak Island in 1783. He subsequently succeeded Vasilii Merkul'ev as company clerk at Three Saints

Harbor. Apparently, in 1794, he accompanied the colonists aboard the *Tri Ierarkha* from Okhotsk. Pierce, *Russian America*, 405.

9 Shelikhov and Polevoi to Baranov, Okhotsk, August 9, 1794, in Tikhmenev, *Documents*, no. 17: 55.

10 Ibid., no. 17: 56–57.

11 Ibid., no. 17: 57–58.

12 Baranov to Shelikhov and Polevoi, Pavlovskaia Harbor, May 20, 1795, in Tikhmenev, *Documents*, no. 18: 59.

13 Ibid., no. 18: 62.

14 Ibid., no. 18: 67, 72.

15 Ibid., no. 18: 72.

16 Ibid., no. 18: 67.

17 Ibid. Until the advent of penicillin therapy in the 1940s, mercury remained the most efficacious treatment for syphilis.

18 Baranov to Shelikhov and Polevoi, Pavlovskaia Harbor, May 20, 1795, in, F. RAK, op. 888, d. 447, l. 24–250b., AVPRI. This passage does not appear in Tikhmenev's published version of the letter.

19 Baranov to Shelikhov and Polevoi, Pavlovskaia Harbor, May 20, 1795, in Tikhmenev, *Documents*, no. 18: 68.

20 Regarding Anna Grigor'evna's background see Pierce, *Russian America*, 416. Her identity with Karluk remains a strong tradition among Karluk people and other Alutiiqs, a fact confirmed by ethnologist Lydia T. Black. Oral communication, Kodiak, September 15, 2004. Father Ioasaf passed on to Shelikhov the scandalous story that one of the Alutiiq former students at the missionaries' Pavlovskaia school had been made to run the gauntlet as punishment for his affair with Anna Grigor'evna. He had been further humiliated by having his hair and eyebrows shaved off and the front of his parka cut off. He had then been exiled to another settlement, where he worked and got "nothing for it but whipping." Archimandrite Ioasaf to Shelikhov, Kodiak Island, May 18, 1795, in Tikhmenev, *Documents*, no. 19: 79.

21 Fedorova, *The Russian Population in Alaska and California*, 147–53.

22 Baranov to Shelikhov and Polevoi, Pavlovskaia Harbor, May 20, 1795, in Tikhmenev, *Documents*, no. 18: 70.

23 Khlebnikov, *History*, 13–14.

24 Baranov to Shelikhov and Polevoi, Pavlovskaia Harbor, May 20, 1795, in Tikhmenev, *Documents*, no. 18: 71.

25 Baranov to Shelikhov and Polevoi, Pavlovskaia Harbor, May 20, 1795, F. RAK, op. 888, d. 447, l. 24–250b., AVPRI.

26 Baranov to Shelikhov and Polevoi, Pavlovskaia Harbor, May 20, 1795, in Tikhmenev, *Documents*, no. 18: 76. As Baranov had earlier indicated, he was convinced that Captain Bocharov, a notorious drunkard, had filled Shelikhov's ears with complaints about his conduct.

27 I. P. Shelikhov and S. Zakharov to V. P. Merkurev and I. F. Popov, August 18, 1796, F. RAK, op. 888, d. 118, l. 75–800b., AVPRI.

28 Pierce, *Russian America*, 458; Black and Petrov, introduction to *Natalia Shelikhova*, xliv.

29   Baranov to Shelikhov and Polevoi, Pavlovskaia Harbor, May 20, 1795, in Tikhmenev, *Documents*, no. 18: 73. Shelikhov assured Baranov that the company directors had provided sufficient food and other supplies for the colonists, but Polomoshnoi apparently understood the need for rationing until they could begin raising their own. This policy did nothing to increase the popularity of either Polomoshnoi or Baranov with the unhappy newcomers.

30   Natalia Shelikhova to Count Platon Zubov, [Irkutsk,] November 22, 1795, in Tikhmenev, *Documents*, no. 20: 86.

31   Baranov's 1796 census counted 3,221 men and 2,985 women, for a total population of 6,206. Presumably these figures included infants and children. He reported that the Kodiak Alutiiqs had as many as seven hundred baidarkas engaged in sea otter hunting under company direction. Khlebnikov, *Baranov*, 18.

32   This narrative was included in Baranov's letter to Shelikhov and Polevoi, Pavlovskaia Harbor, May 20, 1795, in Tikhmenev, *Documents*, no. 18: 73. Apparently with Father Ioasaf's agreement, Baranov had moved two of the offending exiles and their families to the Nikolaevsk outpost at English Bay, ostensibly to experiment there with farming. A third was sent to Chugach Sound or near Cape St. Elias, which Shelikhov had suggested as a potential settlement site.

33   Baranov's survey is described by Dmitrii Tarkhanov in his journal of 1796, translated by Lydia T. Black and published in Dauenhauer, Dauenhauer, and Black, *Anóoshi Lingít*, 69–71.

34   Tikhmenev, *History*, 43–44. A somewhat different account appears in Dmitrii Tarkhanov's journal, cited above. Tarkhanov, a mining engineer, was one of the hostages left among the Yakutat Tlingits in 1795.

35   Baranov to Larionov, Kadiak, July 24, 1800, in Tikhmenev, *Documents*, no. 29: 109.

36   Baranov to Polomoshnoi, Kadiak, April 28, 1798, in Tikhmenev, *Documents*, no. 23: 92–93.

37   Ibid., no. 23: 93.

38   Baranov to Larionov, Kadiak, July 24, 1800, in Tikhmenev, *Documents*, no. 29: 109.

39   Khlebnikov, *Baranov*, 26. A similar epidemic, Baranov wrote, was also raging in Kenai Bay, a piece of information that increases the probability that it was a highly virulent strain of influenza.

40   Partners of the United Company to Baranov, July 19, 1797, in Tikhmenev, *Documents*, no. 21: 90–91.

41   Baranov to Kuskov, Pavlovskaia Harbor, October 24–28, 1797, F. 204, kart. 32, d. 2, l. 7–80b., RGB OR; Baranov to Larionov, [Pavlovskaia Harbor,] March 3, 1798, in Tikhmenev, *Documents*, no. 24: 94–97; Baranov to Polomoshnoi, Kadiak, April 28, 1798, in Tikhmenev, *Documents*, no. 23: 92–93; Black and Petrov, *Natalia Shelikhova*, 165–66.

42   Black and Petrov, introduction to *Natalia Shelikhova*, xv–xliv.

43   Baranov to Larionov, [Pavlovskaia Harbor,] March 3, 1798, in Tikhmenev, *Documents*, no. 24: 96–97.

44   Ibid., no. 24: 97.

45   Ibid.,

46   Tikhmenev, *History*, 45. Unfortunately, Tikhmenev confused the name of the *Tri*

Ierarkha, built in Okhotsk in 1794, with the galiot *Tri Sviatitelia*, wrecked in 1790 on Baranov's voyage to America.

47 Khlebnikov, *Baranov*, 23; Baranov to Larionov, Kadiak, July 24, 1800, in Tikhmenev, *Documents*, no. 29: 107. The dispute between Baranov and Talin is documented from Baranov's perspective in his May 1799 letter to Talin printed in Tikhmenev, *Documents*, no. 25: 98–101.

48 Tikhmenev, *History*, 45; Baranov to Larionov, [Pavlovskaia Harbor,] March 3, 1798, in Tikhmenev, *Documents*, no. 24: 95–96. Talin and his crew in time reached Pavlovskaia by baidarkas after rescue by Alutiiq hunters and Russian promyshlenniks. Aboard the smaller *Olga* Baranov was caught in the same storm that struck the *Orel*, but his seamanship enabled him and his crew to reach safety.

49 Baranov to Vasilii Malakhov, [Pavlovskaia Harbor,] June 11, 1800, in Tikhmenev, *Documents*, no. 28: 105. Malakhov was then acting as foreman of the company crew at Kenai Bay. In another account, the chief manager states that the wreck probably occurred in the fall of 1799, though "still we are not sure." Baranov to Larionov, [Pavlovskaia Harbor,] March 22, 1801, in Tikhmenev, *Documents*, no. 31: 122–23.

50 In an 1804 report to the Russian Orthodox Governing Synod, the remaining four missionaries claimed that they still knew nothing about Bishop Ioasaf's death at sea because the Russian-American Company withheld from them any news of ship departures. "A Report to the Holy Governing Synod of the Russian Orthodox Church from Missionaries in Russian America Detailing Complaints against Aleksandr A. Baranov," [Pavlovskaia,] August 1, 1804, in Dmytryshyn, Crownhart-Vaughan, and Vaughan, *Russian American Colonies*, no. 10: 62. The most complete report is contained in Baranov's letter of May 28, 1807, addressed to Father Gideon, which appeared in Father Gideon's manuscript report published in [Valaam Monastery,] *The Russian Orthodox Religious Mission*, 174–75. Along with details about the wreckage recovered at various localities, Baranov stated that he had received a report from the American captain Joseph O'Cain about Natives in the Otter Bay region who possessed whole suits of European clothes and ragged fox furs assumed to be Russian, such as they could not have obtained either through trading or hunting.

51 Tikhmenev, *History*, 59.

52 Khlebnikov, *Baranov*, 23, 26–27. It was Father Gideon in his manuscript account of the Alutiiqs and the spiritual mission who stated that 140 men died as a result of eating shellfish on this 1799 journey and that 40 more died from other causes. [Valaam Monastery,] *Russian Orthodox Religious Mission*, 143.

53 With Egor Purtov, Mikhail Kondakov had been a coleader of the 1794 hunting and exploration expedition to Yakutat Bay. He was also one of the leaders of the 1796 expedition to Sitka Sound. For a summary of his career, see Pierce, *Russian America*, 251.

54 A report of this 1800 disaster appears in the manuscript of Father Gideon, in [Valaam Monastery,] *Russian Orthodox Religious Mission*, 143. For the site of Tugidak (Tukidok), see Sonja Luehrmann, *Alutiiq Villages under Russian and U.S. Rule* (Fairbanks: University of Alaska Press, 2008), 24, 29. Tugidak was abandoned by 1849, with the consolidation of the remaining Alutiiq village populations into six settlements.

6. THE MISSIONARY MONKS AND THE CHIEF MANAGER

1 "A Report from Grigorii I. Shelikhov, Requesting Special Privileges for His Company in North America," May–November 1787, in Dmytryshyn, Crownhart-Vaughan, and Vaughan, *Russian Penetration*, no. 57: 345.

2 "A Decree from the Governing Senate Approving the Request of Ivan L. Golikov and Grigorii I. Shelikhov to Build Churches in Order to Propagate the Orthodox Christian Faith among Natives of North America," June 20, 1793, in Dmytryshyn, Crownhart-Vaughan, and Vaughan, *Russian Penetration*, no. 69: 413–14.

3 Four years later, after Shelikhov's death, Metropolitan Gavriil stated that he had sent five missionaries to America. There is no apparent reason for this discrepancy. "A Report from Metropolitan Gavriil of Novgorod to Field Marshal Count Platon Aleksandrovich Zubov concerning the Activity of Ivan L. Golikov in Alaska and the Work of the Russian Orthodox Missionaries," February 18, 1793, in Dmytryshyn, Crownhart-Vaughan, and Vaughan, *Russian Penetration*, no. 81: 494–95.

4 "A Report by the Monk Herman to Father Nazarii concerning the Work of the Russian Orthodox Missionaries on Kodiak and Other Islands in the North Pacific Ocean," [Pavlovskaia,] May 19, 1795, in Dmytryshyn, Crownhart-Vaughan, and Vaughan, *Russian Penetration*, no. 78: 482; Archimandrite Ioasaf to Elder Igumen Nazarii, Pavlovskaia Harbor, May 1795, in *Alaskan Missionary Spirituality*, ed. Michael Oleksa (New York: Paulist Press, 1987), 38. With some interpolations, this letter may also be found in [Valaam Monastery,] *Russian Orthodox Religious Mission*, 41–43.

5 In the Russian Orthodox Church, the title hieromonk denotes a monk who has been consecrated as a priest. A hierodeacon is a junior figure, in effect an apprentice monk, likewise with authority to administer the holy sacraments. An archimandrite is a supervisory official who, like a monk, has taken vows of celibacy. All monks in Orthodox Church parlance are considered to be in the black clergy, unlike the regular priests, called white clergy, who serve congregations and are expected to marry.

6 Pierce, *Russian America*, 201.

7 Baranov to Shelikhov and Polevoi, Pavlovskaia Harbor, May 20, 1795, in Tikhmenev, *Documents*, no. 18: 68.

8 Archimandrite Ioasaf to Shelikhov, Kodiak Island, May 18, 1795, in Tikhmenev, *Documents*, no. 19: 80. An alternative translation of this letter, based on a copy in the Yudin Collection of the Library of Congress Manuscript Division, is available in Dmytryshyn, Crownhart-Vaughan, and Vaughan, *Russian Penetration*, no. 76: 465–75. Another partial translation by Lydia T. Black is published in Oleksa, *Alaskan Missionary Spirituality*, 58–63. Varying in some details from the other two translations, Professor Black's version overall presents Father Ioasaf's statements in a much milder tone, and it omits various passages, including the final ten paragraphs that appear elsewhere. These omitted sections include many of Father Ioasaf's most outlandish charges against the chief manager.

9 Archimandrite Ioasaf to Shelikhov, Kodiak Island, May 18, 1795, in Tikhmenev, *Documents*, no. 19: 81.

10 Baranov to Natalia Alekseevna Shelikhova, [Pavlovskaia Harbor,] June 10, 1798, F. RAK, op. 888, d. 121, AVPRI.

11 Archimandrite Ioasaf to Shelikhov, Kodiak Island, May 18, 1795, in Tikhmenev, *Documents*, no. 19: 80.

12 Ibid.

13 Baranov to Shelikhov and Polevoi, Pavlovskaia Harbor, May 20, 1795, Tikhmenev, *Documents*, no. 18: 71.

14 Archimandrite Ioasaf to Shelikhov, Kodiak Island, May 18, 1795, in Tikhmenev, *Documents*, no. 19: 81–82.

15 Ibid., no. 19: 81.

16 Ibid. At the same time he wrote to Shelikhov, Father Ioasaf also sent a report to the archbishop of Irkutsk, describing the mission's situation in North America and seeking to enlist the archbishop's aid in his campaign to have Baranov recalled. "A Report from Arkhimandrit Ioasaf to His Archbishop concerning Conditions in the Russian Settlement on Kodiak Island," Pavlovskaia, May 19, 1795, in Dmytryshyn, Crownhart-Vaughan, and Vaughan, *Russian Penetration*, no. 77: 476–81. In this report he describes the difficulties faced by the missionaries in their effort to end plural marriages among the Alutiiqs and also the high prevalence of venereal disease among the Native population. This report went to the bishop of Irkutsk, who summarized it and forwarded it to the archbishop with a comment on Father Ioasaf's effort to have Baranov removed. "Whether or not the company will decide to recall him I do not know," he said, "for he is a capable person and indispensable for local business matters." "A Report from Veniamin, Bishop of Irkutsk and Nerchinsk, to the Archbishop of Irkutsk, concerning Baptism of Natives on Kodiak Island by Russian Orthodox Missionaries," November 22, 1795, in Dmytryshyn, Crownhart-Vaughan, and Vaughan, *Russian Penetration*, no. 80: 492–93.

17 [Valaam Monastery,] *Russian Orthodox Religious Mission*, 50. An alternative translation appears as "A Report from Arkhimandrit Ioasaf to His Archbishop concerning Conditions in the Russian Settlement on Kodiak Island," [Pavlovskaia,] May 19, 1795, in Dmytryshyn, Crownhart-Vaughan, and Vaughan, *Russian Penetration*, no. 77: 476–81.

18 Baranov manuscript, in Khlebnikov, *Baranov*, [29].

19 Baranov to Natalia Shelikhova, [Pavlovskaia Harbor,] June 10, 1798, F. RAK, op. 888, d. 121, AVPRI. As Father Michael Oleksa remarks, the Russian Orthodox Church has canonized as saints two of the clerics—Father German and Father Juvenalii—who Baranov called "willful and rude people." Personal communication, February 15, 2014.

20 A detailed listing of the missionaries' local food sources was provided in 1819 by Father German, writing to the abbot of Valaam. The holy father emphasized the extraordinary quantities of different fish species. "But whales," he declared, "are considered the best." [Valaam Monastery,] *Russian Orthodox Religious Mission*, 114.

21 Ibid., 60. Father Gideon was obviously the author.

22 Baranov to Kuskov, [Pavlovskaia Harbor,] June 10, 1796, F. 204, kart. 32, d. 2, l. 1–2, RGB OR.

23 Baranov to Kuskov, Aleksandrovskaia Outpost, July 20, 1797, F. 204. kart. 32, d. 2, l. 5–50b., RGB OR.

24 Archimandrite Ioasaf to Father German, [Pavlovskaia Harbor,] June 8, 1798, in [Valaam Monastery,] *Russian Orthodox Religious Mission*, no. 18: 112.

25 Father Afanasii, the oldest, was forty-three in 1798, while Father German was two years younger. Father Nektarii was twenty-eight years old, and Father Ioasaf was twenty-nine. These figures are calculated from Father Gideon's report to the metropolitan of Moscow, June 2, 1806, published in [Valaam Monastery,] *Russian Orthodox Religious Mission*, 150.

26 Archimandrite Ioasaf to Father German, June 8, 1798, in [Valaam Monastery,] *Russian Orthodox Religious Mission*, no. 18: 111.

27 Baranov to Larionov, Kadiak, July 24, 1800, in Tikhmenev, *Documents*, no. 29: 116.

28 Archimandrite Ioasaf to Valaam Monastery, [Valaam Monastery,] *Russian Orthodox Religious Mission*, 50. An alternative translation appears as "A Report from Arkhimandrit Ioasaf to His Archbishop concerning Conditions in the Russian Settlement on Kodiak Island," [Pavlovskaia,] May 19, 1795, in Dmytryshyn, Crownhart-Vaughan, and Vaughan, *Russian Penetration*, no. 77: 476–81. Baranov's own census at that time counted just over sixty-two hundred Kodiak Alutiiq people, men and women.

29 Father German to Valaam Monastery, [Pavlovskaia, May 19, 1795,] in [Valaam Monastery,] *Russian Orthodox Religious Mission*, 44. For an alternative translation see "A Report by the Monk Herman to Father Nazarii concerning the Work of the Russian Orthodox Missionaries on Kodiak and Other Islands in the North Pacific Ocean," [Pavlovskaia,] May 19, 1795, in Dmytryshyn, Crownhart-Vaughan, and Vaughan, *Russian Penetration*, no. 78: 482–84.

30 Father German to Valaam Monastery, [Pavlovskaia, May 19, 1795,] in [Valaam Monastery,] *Russian Orthodox Religious Mission*, 44.

31 Baranov specifically reported to Natalia Shelikhova that "Father Juvenalii started for some unexplored lands of Alaska without asking his chief [Father Ioasaf] for permission." Baranov to Natalia Shelikhova, [Pavlovskaia Harbor,] June 10, 1798, F. RAK, op. 888, d. 121, AVPRI.

32 [Valaam Monastery,] *Russian Orthodox Religious Mission*, 47.

33 In December 1797 Father Makarii sent the Church's ruling synod a vividly written account of the brutalities committed against the Unalaska Aleuts by local agents of the Golikov-Shelikhov Company, writing: "The Shelikhov-Golikov Company treats the native islanders in the most barbaric manner. They have no humane instincts. They take the wives and young daughters [of Native men] as their sexual partners. They kill any who refused to hunt sea otters, and early in the spring they send out the healthy and the sick alike, against their will." The principal target of Father Makarii's charges was a crew chief of the Golikov-Shelikhov Company. "A Report from Ieromonk Makarii, Head of the Russian Orthodox Mission in Alaska [*sic*], to the Holy Governing Synod, Detailing the Treatment of Natives by Russians," [Yakutsk,] October 5, 1797, in Dmytryshyn, Crownhart-Vaughan, and Vaughan, *Russian Penetration*, no. 83: 497–502. Another translation appears in Oleksa, *Alaskan Missionary Spirituality*, 287–90.

34 Father Michael Oleksa in the introduction to his documents collection emphasizes this obligation as central to the monastic calling. Oleksa, *Alaskan Missionary Spirituality*, 6.

35   When Baranov learned of Father Makarii's activities, he interpreted them as part
of the struggle for control over the late Shelikhov's trading empire. Father Makarii,
he judged, was being used by the Kiselev brothers and their men as a pawn in an
effort to discredit Shelikhov's management. Besides, Baranov assured Ivan Kuskov,
the complaints were directed principally at V. P. Merkul'ev, a company foreman who
had taken eighty Aleut families to the Pribylov Islands, where nearly half of them
perished. Baranov to Kuskov, Pavlovskaia Harbor, October 28, 1797, F. 204, kart. 32,
d. 2, l. 7–80b., RGB OR; Pierce, *Russian America*, 355. Baranov's interpretation is
reinforced by details of the Kiselevs' plotting in Tikhmenev, *History*, 50.

36   Father Makarii's efforts in Irkutsk and Siberia are recounted in [Baranov,] Kadiak
Office of the Russian-American Company to Navigator V. P. Petrov, October 12,
1802, in Tikhmenev, *Documents*, no. 33: 132–33. This document quotes at length the
emperor's directive that censured Father Makarii "with instructions not to leave the
islands in the future without consent of his superior." His transgression this time,
added the emperor, was forgiven "as per request of the Aleuts."

37   A detailed account of Father Makarii's miscarried crusade for justice on behalf of the
Aleuts appears in Pierce, *Russian America*, 324–25.

38   Writing to the abbot of Valaam in 1819, Father German stated that there was still
no reliable information about the location and circumstances of Father Juvenalii's
death. Father German to Abbot Ionafan, December 13, 1819, in [Valaam Monastery,]
Russian Orthodox Religious Mission, no. 26: 115. Tikhmenev (*History*, 47) states only
that in 1795 "he was killed by natives at Lake Iliamna." Captain Yuri Lisiansky in an
1814 account of his visit to Russian America in 1804 repeated another hearsay version
from a Native source. Though of a quiet disposition, he wrote, the people of the Kenai
Bay district so disliked our priests that they threatened to kill the first who dared
to come among them. This dislike began in 1796 [1795], he said, "in consequence of
the imprudent zeal of one of our missionary monks, who, having prevailed on many
of them to embrace Christianity, had too rigidly insisted on their throwing aside,
all at once, their native prejudices and customs, and, by authority of his holy office,
compelled some of them to marry in conformity to the Greek church. Provoked at
last by the daring encroachments of this fanatic stranger, they put him to death, and
vowed at the same time perpetual hatred to the whole Russian priesthood." Yuri
Lisiansky, *Voyage Round the World in the Years 1803, 1804, 1805, and 1806* (London:
John Booth, 1814; repr., Edgewood, N.J.: Gregg Press, 1968), 187.

39   As part of Bancroft's historical staff, Ivan Petrov served as a principal writer as well
as researcher for the volume. His dodgy career, which included a substantial number of legitimate, well-done translations alongside a handful of patent forgeries, has
received thorough critical study. See "Ivan Petrov's Fraudulent Tarakanov Document," in *The Wreck of the Sv. Nikolai: Two Narratives of the First Russian Expedition
in the Oregon Country, 1808–1810*, ed. Kenneth N. Owens, trans. Alton S. Donnelly
(Portland: Western Imprints, the Press of the Oregon Historical Society, 1985), 77–87;
and the various articles by Morgan B. Sherwood, Richard A. Pierce, and Theodore
C. Hinkley and Caryl Hinkley cited therein, note 4. The most amazing feature in this
tale of documentary mendacity is the willingness of so many authors over the years

to accept without question the authenticity of Petrov's supposed Juvenalii journal, a crude forgery that flunks every standard test of textual criticism.

40 Michael Oleksa, "The Death of Hieromonk Juvenaly," in *Russia in North America: Proceedings of the Second International Conference on Russian America*, ed. Richard A. Pierce (Kingston, Ontario: Limestone Press, 1990), 322–57.

7. GOVERNMENT MEN, MONKS, AND THE ALUTIIQ REBELLION

1 Baranov to Navigator Talin, [Pavlovskaia Harbor,] May 1799, in Tikhmenev, *Documents*, no. 25: 98–99.

2 Baranov to Larionov, Kadiak, July 24, 1800, in Tikhmenev, *Documents*, no. 29: 110.

3 Baranov to Larionov, [Pavlovskaia Harbor,] March 22, 1801, in Tikhmenev, *Documents*, no. 31: 124.

4 Ibid., no. 31: 124–25.

5 Ibid., no. 31: 125.

6 Ibid., no. 31: 125–26.

7 Father Gideon to Metropolitan [Amvrosii], June 2, 1806, [Valaam Monastery,] *Russian Orthodox Religious Mission*, 147.

8 Ibid.

9 Baranov to Larionov, [Pavlovskaia Harbor,] March 22, 1801, in Tikhmenev, *Documents*, no. 31: 127.

10 Ibid., no. 31: 126. The clergymen's two accounts make no mention of these incidents.

11 Ibid., no. 31: 127. Baranov's threat to wall off the clerics' house and the adjoining church strongly suggests the policy originally advised by Grigorii Shelikhov in his fantasy plan for the colony's agricultural settlement.

12 Father Gideon is the author of this missionary narrative of the confrontation, which he wrote at the beginning of his inspection of the American religious mission. Father Gideon to Metropolitan [Amvrosii], Kadiak, June 2, 1805, marked "secret," in [Valaam Monastery,] *Russian Orthodox Religious Mission*, 147–48.

13 Baranov to Larionov, [Pavlovskaia Harbor,] March 22, 1801, in Tikhmenev, *Documents*, no. 31: 127.

14 Ibid., no. 31: 126.

15 Father Gideon to Metropolitan [Amvrosii], Kadiak, June 2, 1805, in [Valaam Monastery,] *Russian Orthodox Religious Mission*, 148. The published missionary account names this village as Togodatsk. It is identified as Tugadok in Luehrmann, *Alutiiq Villages*, 25, 29.

16 Father Gideon manuscript, in [Valaam Monastery,] *Russian Orthodox Religious Mission*, 148.

17 Ibid.

18 Ibid., 149.

19 Pierce, *Russian America*, 412, 497; Father Gideon to Father German, June 1, 1807, in [Valaam Monastery,] *Russian Orthodox Religious Mission*, 171. Kristofor Prianishnikov, interpreter Prianishnikov's creole son, earned a reward of eighty rubles for his school achievements, the money coming from Aleksandr Baranov's contribution

of three hundred rubles. Apparently, Kristofor, with his own father absent from the settlement, had become a ward of Father German. He later served as a subdeacon of the Pavlovskaia church.

20   Baranov to Kadiak Spiritual Mission, September 25, 1802, published in Gideon, *Round the World Voyage*, 82–83. Some writers have unfortunately confused this occasion and Baranov's authorization of the prescribed oath with the earlier controversy initiated by Father Afanasii.

21   These conciliatory moves are recorded in Father Gideon to Metropolitan Amvrosii, June 2, 1805, published in Gideon, *Round the World Voyage*, 79; and in [Valaam Monastery,] *Russian Orthodox Religious Mission*, 149–50.

22   Father Gideon's background is summarized by Lydia T. Black in Gideon, *Round the World Voyage*, ix. He was the father-confessor to Emperor Aleksandr I. His reports from Pavlovskaia would go directly to the emperor. His account of his outward journey aboard the Russian navy ship *Nadezhda* (*Hope*) forms the first chapter in this small volume. His narrative of his sojourn at the Pavlovskaia settlement and his ethnological observations are virtually identical to those published in the Valaam Monastery history of the religious mission in America.

23   Ivan Banner to the Kadiak Religious Mission, [Pavlovskaia,] January 23, 1805, and Hieromonk Gideon to the RAC Kadiak Company Office, [Pavlovskaia,] March 11, 1805, both published in [Valaam Monastery,] *Russian Orthodox Religious Mission*, 154–55.

24   Hieromonk Gideon to Metropolitan Amvrosii, [Pavlovskaia,] June 2, 1805, in Gideon, *Round the World Voyage*, 75–81.

25   Gideon to Nikolai Rezanov, Pavlovskaia Harbor, April 14, 1806, in Gideon, *Round the World Voyage*, 96.

26   His wife, Anna Grigor'evna, in July 1801 had given birth to a son, named Petr. On October 2, 1802, she was delivered of a daughter, christened Olga, but died twelve days later, presumably of childbed fever. Pierce, *Russian America*, 419.

27   As Father Michael Oleksa points out, the villages in which the monks carried out their campaign of baptism remain solidly faithful to their Orthodox Christian beliefs to this day. Personal communication, February 15, 2014.

28   Rezanov to the RAC Board of Directors, New Archangel, November 6, 1805, in Tikhmenev, *Documents*, no. 42: 168–69.

29   Ibid., no. 42: 167.

30   Ibid., no. 42: 168.

31   According to Father Oleksa, Father Gideon initiated a program in the school to establish literacy in Sugpiaq, the language of the Kodiak Alutiiqs, producing a Sugpiaq grammar and translating biblical and liturgical texts. Oleksa, *Alaskan Missionary Spirituality*, 11–12, 120.

32   Father Gideon to Metropolitan Amvrosii, Kadiak, June 2, 1805, in [Valaam Monastery,] *Russian Orthodox Religious Mission*, 150; Rezanov to the RAC Board of Directors, New Archangel, November 6, 1805, in Tikhmenev, *Documents*, no. 42: 168.

33   Rezanov to the RAC Board of Directors, New Archangel, November 6, 1805, in Tikhmenev, *Documents*, no. 42: 168.

34   Ibid., no. 42: 169.

35   Ibid., no. 42: 170.

36   Father Gideon to Baranov, [Pavlovskaia,] May 17, 1807, in [Valaam Monastery,] *Russian Orthodox Religious Mission*, 165. The gist of this letter's critical comments about Father Afanasii is quoted also in Pierce, *Russian America*, 2.

37   Father Gideon to Baranov, [Pavlovskaia,] May 17, 1807, in [Valaam Monastery,] *Russian Orthodox Religious Mission*, 165–66.

38   According to Father German, six months after their arrival at Pavlovskaia the missionaries still intended to make the mainland settlement their final destination. "A Report by the Monk Herman to Father Nazarii concerning the Work of the Russian Orthodox Missionaries on Kodiak and Other Islands in the North Pacific Ocean," [Pavlovskaia,], May 19, 1795, in Dmytryshyn, Crownhart-Vaughan, and Vaughan, *Russian Penetration*, no. 78: 482.

39   Rezanov to the [RAC] Board of Directors, [New Archangel,] February 15, 1806, in Tikhmenev, *Documents*, no. 43: 175.

40   Quoted in Oleksa, *Alaskan Missionary Spirituality*, 309–10. Father Oleksa interprets Father German's appeal as a call for total reform of the colony and its treatment of Kodiak Alutiiqs. Personal communication, February 14, 2014. For the close ties that developed between Father German and Lieutenant Ianovskii, see Simeon Ianovskii to Igumen Damascene of Valaam, November 22, 1865, in Oleksa, *Alaskan Missionary Spirituality*, 46–55.

41   Lieutenant Ianovskii later wrote a lengthy account of his conversion experience and his relationship with Father German, whom he called "my true benefactor." Simeon Ianovskii to Damascene, Abbot of Valaam, November 22, 1865, in [Valaam Monastery,] *Russian Orthodox Religious Mission*, 80–89.

8. THE RUSSIAN-AMERICAN COMPANY

1   Natalia Shelikhova to His Eminence [Platon Zubov], [Irkutsk,] November 22, 1795, F. Gl, Archive II-3, op. 34, years 1784–96, d. 1, l. 15–230b., RGA DA. For an alternative translation, see Tikhmenev, *Documents*, no. 20: 85–89.

2   Details in this narrative are excerpted from the entries on Rezanov and Natalia Shelikhova in Pierce, *Russian America*, 418–19, 459–60.

3   An alternative possibility is that Natalia Shelikhova and her family came to Velikiy Ustyug, where Avdot'ia met Buldakov and where the couple married. Personal communication from Alexander Yu. Petrov, September 10, 2013.

4   Mary E. Wheeler, "The Russian American Company and the Imperial Government: Early Phase," in Starr, *Russia's American Colony*, 57.

5   Missing from these provisions, however, was a limited liability feature, which guarantees that in case of business failure, stockholders will suffer no greater loss than the amount of their original investment. This feature had become standard in the charters of French and English joint stock trading companies by the late eighteenth century. It was placed into the RAC charter in 1821, when the imperial administration of Aleksandr I granted the firm a twenty-year extension.

6   Dated December 27, 1799, the imperial decree from Emperor Paul I granting special privileges to the Russian-American Company for a period of twenty years is in Dmytryshyn, Crownhart-Vaughan, and Vaughan, *Russian American Colonies*, no. 3: 18–23.

7   "Ukaz, Granting Nobility to Madam Shelikhova and Her Descendants," February 15, 1798, in Tikhmenev, *Documents*, no. 22: 91.

8   Buldakov would retain this position until his death a quarter century later. For a sketch of his life, see Pierce, *Russian America*, 73–74.

9   Ibid., 19–20.

10 Khlebnikov, *Baranov*, 47.

11 According to the imperial table of ranks, designation as collegiate counselor equaled the rank of an army colonel. That position made Baranov unquestionably superior in authority and precedence to the Russian navy lieutenants and captains who arrived in Russian America.

12 Rezanov to the RAC Board of Directors, New Archangel, November 6, 1807, in Tikhmenev, *Documents*, no. 42: 170.

13 Baranov to the Emperor, [New Archangel,] August 24, 1805, in Tikhmenev, *Documents*, no. 37: 144.

14 Pierce, *Russian America*, 253.

15 Rezanov to the RAC Board of Directors, New Archangel, November 6, 1805, in Tikhmenev, *Documents*, no. 42: 169.

16 Baranov to D. I. Kulikalov, April 29, 1805, in Tikhmenev, *Documents*, no. 36: 142–43.

17 Davydov, *Two Voyages*, 102.

18 Ibid., 105. A substantial biographical sketch of Lieutenant Davydov appears in Pierce, *Russian America*, 112–15.

19 Ibid., 121–22.

20 Ibid., 164–65.

21 Ibid., 171.

22 Davydov identified this disease only as "some kind of contagious fever" that had broken out in Okhotsk and was carried aboard the *Aleksandr Nevskii* by infected crewmen. The Russian seamen transmitted the disease to Atkha Island, where it ran its course only after decimating the Native inhabitants. Davydov, *Two Voyages*, 105.

23 This sentiment, as Father Michael Oleksa has observed, gave strong evidence of the company's continued oppression and exploitation of the Alutiiq villagers, which remained a grievance long after the Alutiiq rebellion. Personal communication, February 14, 2014.

24 Davydov, *Two Voyages*, 105–6.

25 This figure, 1.2 million rubles, appears in Khlebnikov, *Baranov*, 41. A larger figure is given in Davydov's account, *Two Voyages*, 105–6.

26 The two men began traveling together two years earlier aboard the Russian navy ship *Nadezhda*, one of two English-built vessels purchased by the imperial government and outfitted at Copenhagen for Russia's first round-the-world expedition. After various complications, including a lengthy, fruitless attempt by Rezanov to establish diplomatic relations with the Japanese imperial government, they had reached Pet-

ropavlovsk and found the *Maria* at anchor, ready to sail to Kodiak Island. Impatient to reach North America, Rezanov ordered the RAC skipper to take him and his companion along. At Pavlovskaia, Ivan Banner was acting as Baranov's deputy.

27 Georg H. von Langsdorff, *Voyages and Travels in Various Parts of the World during the Years 1803, 1804, 1805, 1806, and 1807* (London: Henry Colburn, 1814), 2:67–68.

28 Ibid., 2:69–70.

29 As part of the deal, D'Wolf also secured the loan of another small RAC vessel to take him and his remaining crew to Okhotsk, where he would start overland across Siberia to reach St. Petersburg and redeem his notes on the RAC. See John D'Wolf, *A Voyage to the North Pacific and a Journey through Siberia More than Half a Century Ago* (Cambridge, Mass.: Welch, Bigelow, and Company, 1861; repr., Fairfield, Wash.: Ye Galleon Press, 1968). An extensive summary of Wolf's volume appears in Pierce, *Russian America*, 129–32.

30 D'Wolf, *A Voyage to the North Pacific*, 22.

31 Rezanov to the RAC Board of Directors, New Archangel, November 6, 1805, in Tikhmenev, *Documents*, no. 42: 170

32 Ibid., no. 42: 171.

33 Quoted in Khlebnikov, *Baranov*, 43.

9. THE SITKA SOUND WAR

1 Report, Egor Purtov and Demid Kulikalov to Baranov, Pavlovskaia Harbor, August 9, 1794, in Tikhmenev, *Documents*, no. 16: 51–52. Purtov reported that the English commander had insisted on reinforcing Purtov's men, sending along a whaleboat with six sailors armed with small cannons to help rescue two interpreters and some Alutiiq hostages.

2 Baranov to Larionov, [Pavlovskaia Harbor,] March 3, 1798, in Tikhmenev, *Documents*, no. 24: 95.

3 A description of Shields's 1796 excursion by Filipp Kashevarov, his second in command, appears in "Answers to K. T. Khlebnikov's Questionnaire about the Years 1794–1800," trans. Lydia T. Black, in Dauenhauer, Dauenhauer, and Black, *Anóoshi Lingít*, 91–98.

4 Baranov to Larionov, [Kadiak Island,] July 24, 1800, in Tikhmenev, *Documents*, no. 30: 121. As a result, Baranov was left without a woolen coat or cape; he asked his friend to send him some woolen cloth to help restore his wardrobe.

5 Baranov to Larionov, Kadiak, July 24, 1800, in Tikhmenev, *Documents*, no. 29: 111–12.

6 Ibid., no. 29: 112–13. Baranov wrote that the exchange rate was one dollar to one ruble, twenty kopeks. The dollar was originally a Spanish silver coin, also known as a piece of eight, that was popular in international circulation during the eighteenth and nineteenth centuries and that became the basic unit of U.S. currency in the Coinage Act of 1794.

7 Ibid., no. 29: 113. No doubt this exchange and other socializing were expedited by the services of Baranov's talented young interpreter, the East Indian Richard, whom he had received from Captain Moore in 1792.

8   Ibid., no. 29: 113–14.

9   Baranov to Medvednikov, [New Archangel,] April 19, 1800, in Richard A. Pierce, ed., *Documents on the History of the Russian-American Company*, trans. Marina Ramsay (Kingston, Ontario: Limestone Press, 1976), no. 8: 115.

10 Ibid., no. 8: 116.

11 Deposition of Ekaterina Pinnuin of Chiniak Village, wife of the Russian Zakhar Lebedev, 1802, in Tikhmenev, *Documents*, no. 34: 138.

12 Deposition of Abrosim [Abram] Plotnikov, 1802, in Tikhmenev, *Documents*, no. 34: 135.

13 Andrew P. Johnson, "The Tlingit and the Russians' Battles," told in English and recorded between 1974 and 1977, transcribed by Richard Dauenhauer, in Dauenhauer, Dauenhauer, and Black, *Anóoshi Lingít*, 162.

14 The details of their pursuit, capture, and gruesome execution remained fixed in Tlingit oral tradition until the 1970s. Ibid., 162–63.

15 W. W. Schumacher, "Aftermath of the Sitka Massacre of 1802: Contemporary Documents with an Introduction and Afterword," *Alaska Journal* 9 (1979): 60.

16 Khlebnikov, *Baranov*, 39–40.

17 Tikhmenev, *History*, 65–66; Grinev, *Tlingit Indians in Russian America*, 120–21. According to Tikhmenev's account, Captain Barber learned that Russia and England were at war only after leaving Pavlovskaia and reaching the Hawaiian Islands. Reportedly, he became furious at missing an opportunity for plunder and decided to return immediately to Kodiak "with hostile purposes." Then the news arrived of peace between the two powers, "and his wish to destroy the Russian colony came to nothing."

18 Ethnohistorian Andrei V. Grinev provides a comparative view of the differing accounts in *Tlingit Indians in Russian America*, 127–33.

19 Professor Richard Dauenhauer, the foremost academic authority on Tlingit history and culture, says that the documentary and oral history evidence that these other communities took part in the 1802 battle remains unclear. In Sitka, Professor Dauenhauer adds, "there is no documentation that warriors other than Kiks.ádi were involved, although civilians and other clan members experienced 'collateral damage.'" Personal communication, January 14, 2014.

20 Kiril Khlebnikov, *Notes on Russian America*, pts. 2–5, *Kadiak, Unalaska, Atkha, the Pribylovs*, comp. Roza G. Liapunova and Svetlana G. Fedorova, trans. Marina Ramsey, ed. Richard A. Pierce (Kingston, Ontario: Limestone Press, 1994), 8. Tikhmenev says in his authorized company history that 20 Russians and 130 Aleuts (Alutiiqs) perished in the fighting at Fort Mikhailovskii. Tikhmenev, *History*, 65.

21 Kuskov to Baranov, Yakutat, July 1, 1802, in Pierce, *Documents*, 128–29.

22 Dauenhauer, Dauenhauer, and Black, *Anóoshi Lingít*, 157–69.

23 Johnson, "The Tlingit and the Russians' Battles," in Dauenhauer, Dauenhauer, and Black, *Anóoshi Lingít*, 165.

24 Khlebnikov, *Baranov*, 39.

25 See the seminal treatment of the turbulent frontier phenomenon in imperial history by John S. Galbraith, "The 'Turbulent Frontier' as a Factor in British Expansion,"

Comparative Studies in Society and History 2, no. 2 (January 1960): 150–68. In brief, *turbulent frontier* refers to situations in which an imperial power wields a greater ability to assert military power over a borderland district than it has administrative capacity to establish and maintain a stable government for the district. In most cases, Galbraith points out, the invaders are tempted to a further effort at conquest in order to control the frontier district. They thus fall into the practice, as other historians have called it, of imperial overreach.

26 Khlebnikov, *Baranov*, 44–45.

27 Tikhmenev's *History of the Russian-American Company* (69–73) succinctly describes the origin of this first round-the-world voyage. Lisiansky recorded his experiences in *Voyage Round the World*.

28 Lisiansky, *Voyage Round the World*, 155.

29 Andrew P. Johnson, "Part Two: The Battle of 1804" (undated), in Dauenhauer, Dauenhauer, and Black, *Anóoshi Lingít*, 259–60.

30 Ibid., 258–59; Lisiansky, *Voyage Round the World*, 155, 163.

31 Lisiansky published a drawing of this structure, the only known representation, in *Voyage Round the World*, 162–63; his description of this unique fort is on 163.

32 Ibid., 164; Khlebnikov, *Baranov*, 48–49.

33 Lisiansky, *Voyage Round the World*, 159.

34 Ibid., 162.

35 Thomas P. Thornton, "Postscript," in Dauenhauer, Dauenhauer, and Black, *Anóoshi Lingít*, 280.

36 Lisiansky, *Voyage Round the World*, 220–21.

37 Ibid., 221–24. The Tlingit love of dancing on every occasion drew Lisiansky's particular notice. "These people are so fond of dancing," he wrote, "that I never saw three of them together without their feet being in motion" (223–24).

38 Ibid., 224.

39 Ibid., 225.

40 Johnson, "Part Two: The Battle of 1804," in Dauenhauer, Dauenhauer, and Black, *Anóoshi Lingít*, 263.

41 Ibid., 263–64. See also the translated bilingual accounts by Alex Andrews (Kooxíchx'), "The Battle at Indian River," and by Sally Hopkins (Shxaastí), "The Battle of Sitka," both in Dauenhauer, Dauenhauer, and Black, *Anóoshi Lingít*, 343–44 and 365–67. These two traditional oral recollections confirm many of the details in Johnson's narrative of the 1805 peacemaking.

42 Personal communication from Alexander Yu. Petrov, October 10, 2013.

43 Herb Hope, "The Kiks.ádi Survival March of 1804," in Dauenhauer, Dauenhauer, and Black, *Anóoshi Lingít*, 273.

44 Rezanov to Minister of Commerce, New Archangel, June 17, 1806, in Tikhmenev, *Documents*, no. 46: 222–23.

45 Rezanov to [RAC] Board of Directors, [New Archangel,] February 15, 1806, marked "secret," in Tikhmenev, *Documents*, no. 43: 174.

46 Ibid., no. 43: 187.

10. BEYOND ALASKA

1 Mary Malloy, *"Boston Men" on the Northwest Coast: The American Maritime Fur Trade, 1788–1844* (Kingston, Ontario: Limestone Press, 1998), 137–38; Elton Engstrand, *Joseph O'Cain: Adventurer on the Northwest Coast* (Juneau: Alaska Litho Printers, 2003).

2 Khlebnikov, *Baranov*, 41–42; Adele Ogden, *The California Sea-Otter Trade, 1784–1848* (Berkeley: University of California Press, 1941), 46–47. Captain O'Cain also took from California an additional seven hundred skins he had secured in trade with the Spanish on his own account.

3 D'Wolf, *A Voyage to the North Pacific*, 25–34.

4 Rezanov to Minister of Commerce Nikolai Rumiantsev, New Archangel, June 17, 1806, published with a modern translation in Dmytryshyn, Crownhart-Vaughan, and Vaughan, *Russian American Colonies*, no. 19: 112–48.

5 Ibid., no. 19: 119.

6 Langsdorff, *Voyages and Travels*, 2:183.

7 Ibid., 2:220.

8 Ibid., 2:181.

9 Pierce, *Russian America*, 420.

10 Khlebnikov, *Baranov*, 67–68.

11 Ogden, *California Sea-Otter Trade*, 50, 196n16, citing Luis Antonio Argüello to Governor Arrillaga, San Francisco, March 31 and May 15, 1807, in manuscript series Californias, vol. 51, no. 12, Bancroft Library, University of California, Berkeley.

12 Malloy, *"Boston Men,"* 93; Ogden, *California Sea-Otter Trade*, 50; Khlebnikov, *Notes on Russian America*, pt. 1: 9.

13 Baranov's roster for the voyage is contained in his instructions to Navigator Bulygin, September 2, 1808, F. 204, kart. 32, d. hr. 8, l. 1–4, RGB OR. It may be compared with Tarakanov's list of the survivors in Owens, *Wreck of the* Sv. Nikolai, 65.

14 Baranov to Tarakanov, September 18, 1808, New Archangel, F. 204, kart. 32, ed. hr. 7, l. 1–2., RGB OR; instructions from Baranov to Kuskov, New Archangel, October 14, 1808, in Dmytryshyn, Crownhart-Vaughan, and Vaughan, *Russian American Colonies*, no. 25: 168.

15 Kuskov to Baranov, [New Archangel,] October 5, 1809, in *So Far from Home: Russians in Early California*, by Glenn J. Farris (Berkeley, Calif.: Heyday Books; Santa Clara, Calif.: Santa Clara University, 2012), 58–60.

16 Report from Luis Argüello to Governor Arrillaga, San Francisco, February 16, 1809, in Farris, *So Far from Home*, 61.

17 Baranov to Kuskov, October 14, 1808, in Dmytryshyn, Crownhart-Vaughan, and Vaughan, *Russian American Colonies*, no. 25: 172.

18 Owens, *Wreck of the* Sv. Nikolai.

19 Kuskov to Baranov, [New Archangel,] October 5, 1809, in Farris, *So Far from Home*, 58–60.

20 Archibald Campbell, *A Voyage Round the World, from 1806 to 1812*, facsimile reprint (Honolulu: University of Hawaii Press for the Friends of the Library of Hawaii, 1967), 88.

21   Lieutenant-Captain Hagemeister to the Directors of the Russian-American Company, 1809, paraphrased, in Pierce, *Russia's Hawaiian Adventure*, 38.

22   Hagemeister to the RAC Main Office, April 6, 1818, in Pierce, *Russia's Hawaiian Adventure*, 155.

23   Khlebnikov, *Notes on Russian America*, pt. 1: 10, 11; Khlebnikov, *Baranov*, 71. Presumably because of a copyist's error, the two tables Khlebnikov presents do not quite agree.

24   Contract between Aleksandr A. Baranov and Captain George Washington Eayrs, St. Paul's Harbor, Kodiak Island, May 19/30 [*sic*], 1808, reproduced in an English translation, in *The United States and Russia: The Beginnings of Relations, 1765–1815*, ed. Nina N. Bashkina et al. (Washington, D.C.: U.S. Department of State, [1998]), 311–16. The original is Baranov's certified copy in Russian, archived in F. 204, 32.11, l. 1–6, RGB OR.

25   For a detailed account of Eayrs's adventurous trading career in California, see Robert Ryal Miller, *A Yankee Smuggler on the Spanish California Coast: George Washington Eayrs and the Ship* Mercury (Santa Barbara, Calif.: Santa Barbara Trust for Historical Preservation, 2001). In June 1813 a Spanish privateer captured the *Mercury* near Santa Barbara. The ensuing legal case occupied Captain Eayrs the remainder of his life, to no avail.

26   The text of Rumiantsev's report, with the emperor's approval, is in Bashkina et al., *The United States and Russia*, 618–21. A different translation appears in Dmytryshyn, Crownhart-Vaughan, and Vaughan, *Russian American Colonies*, no. 27: 184–89. See also Buldakov's request to Rumiantsev dated December 20, 1809, in Dmytryshyn, Crownhart-Vaughan, and Vaughan, *Russian American Colonies*, no. 28: 190.

27   Malloy, "Boston Men," 67, 113.

28   Khlebnikov, *Baranov*, 83; Farris, *So Far from Home*, 76–77.

29   Farris, *So Far from Home*, 65–66. It is Farris, an expert on Fort Ross history and ethnology, who has identified Tarakanov as the Russian agent called Talicani in the Miwok account. Miwok speakers, he points out, consistently substitute *l* for *r* when transliterating from other languages. Regarding the time of these meetings, they must have occurred in 1812 after the arrival of the *Chirikov*; Tarakanov's gifts included hoes, farming tools that would not have been carried to California on earlier RAC hunting expeditions.

30   Ibid., 63–74. During Captain Golovnin's 1818 visit, Kuskov did give him a document that Golovnin characterized as "a copy of the deed which confirms that this land was ceded to the Russians by the Indians." Vasilii M. Golovnin, *Around the World on the* Kamchatka, *1817–1819*, trans. Ella Lury Wiswell (Honolulu: Hawaiian Historical Society and the University Press of Hawaii, 1979), 161. Important as it was to the Russians in view of the Spanish challenge to their right of occupancy, it is difficult to conceive what such a piece of paper in the Russian language might have meant to the Kashaya people.

31   Dmytryshyn, Crownhart-Vaughan, and Vaughan, *Russian American Colonies*, no. 25: 171.

32   Kuskov's "Kolosh" wife, Ekaterina Prokhorovna, was with him at Fort Ross, though they were not married in a church until they returned to New Archangel in 1823. An

unknown artist painted matched portraits of the two at Fort Ross apparently in 1813. After his retirement, she accompanied him to Tot'ma, his birthplace. They had no children, but the descendants of other Kuskov family members still live in Tot'ma. After Kuskov's death in 1823, Ekaterina married a local official. Tarakanov's wife, Aleksandra Ignatova, was an Alutiiq woman fifteen years his junior, reputedly from Karluk. They had one son named Aleksei, born in 1819. After Tarakanov's forced retirement in 1820 or 1821, he took his wife and son with him to Kursk, his hometown. There, in 1834, Tarakanov, who was born into serfdom, and his wife and son were added to the class of townspeople. Pierce, *Russian America*, 281–85, 499; Kenneth N. Owens, "Frontiersman for the Tsar: Timofei Tarakanov and the Expansion of Russian America," *Montana: The Magazine of Western History* 56, no. 3 (Autumn 2006): 20.

33 Golovnin, *Around the World*, 165.

34 Farris, *So Far from Home*, 71.

35 Report of Gabriel Moraga and Gervasio Argüelello's visit to Fort Ross, San Francisco, July 30, 1814, in Farris, *So Far from Home*, 80.

36 Ibid., 81.

37 Kuskov to Governor Arrillaga, [Fort Ross,] June 9, 1814, in Farris, *So Far from Home*, 82–83.

38 Adelbert von Chamisso, *A Voyage Around the World with the Romanzov Exploring Expedition in the Years 1815–1818 in the Brig* Rurik, *Captain Otto von Kotzebue*, trans. and ed. Henry Katz (Honolulu: University of Hawaii Press, 1986), 108.

39 Ibid., 108–9. Since he never saw either Bodega Bay or Fort Ross, it is understandable that Chamisso conflated the identity of these two posts.

40 Report from Captain Hagemeister, Commander of the Kutuzov, to the Main Administration of the Company, [Callao,] April 18, 1817, in Dmytryshyn, Crownhart-Vaughan, and Vaughan, *Russian American Colonies*, no. 44: 231.

41 Regarding Captain Wadsworth's career, see Pierce, *Russian America*, 537.

42 Historian Adele Ogden reports the supposed capture of Tarakanov and eleven Aleuts by the Spanish when they went ashore near San Pedro. This totally erroneous report comes from a patently forged document, a pencil-written manuscript in English found in the Bancroft Library with the title "Statement of My Captivity among the Californians by a Russian Fur-Hunter," supposedly written by one Vasilii Petrovich Tarakanov, a fictitious figure loosely modeled on Tarakanov. Like the fake Juvenalii diary, this document is another of the forgeries passed off on Hubert Howe Bancroft in the 1870s by the translator, researcher, and writer who called himself Ivan Petrov. See "Ivan Petrov's Fraudulent Tarakanov Document," in Owens, *Wreck of the Sv. Nikolai*, and works by other scholars cited therein. Pertinent also is another manuscript forgery in the Bancroft Library, an account of a sea otter hunting expedition north to Eureka Bay supposedly written by an author named Zakhar Chichinev. This man and this expedition are also figments of Petrov's fertile imagination.

43 Lieutenant Nikolay Shishmaryov, excerpts from a journal of a visit to [Alta California], November 1820–February 1821, in *California through Russian Eyes, 1806–1848*, comp., trans., and ed. James R. Gibson (Norman: Arthur H. Clark Company, an imprint of the University of Oklahoma Press, 2013).

44   It should be noted, however, that this system of covert trade did not long endure. A decade after Mexican independence, anticlerical political leaders began to secularize the Alta California missions, freeing most of their Native workers from Franciscan control. Because of the rapid decline in the missions' agricultural output, RAC administrators during the late 1830s began to look for an alternative source to raise the farm products they needed to feed their American colonists. That role was soon taken by the Puget Sound Agricultural Company, a Pacific Northwest subsidiary of the British Hudson's Bay Company. Fort Ross then became a surplus property, no longer useful for the RAC's operations. The 1841 sale of all the fort's buildings, movable property, livestock, and other tangible assets to Captain John Sutter on credit for thirty thousand dollars was a fortuitous stroke of business management, even though Sutter was never able to pay off his debt. Albert L. Hurtado, *John Sutter: A Life on the North American Frontier* (Norman: University of Oklahoma Press, 2006), 95–100. For the complex negotiations that led to a commercial treaty between Russia and Great Britain in 1839, a treaty that made Fort Ross a redundant Russian holding, see John S. Galbraith, *The Hudson's Bay Company as an Imperial Factor, 1821–1869* (Berkeley: University of California Press, 1957), 135–53.

11. AVERTING DISASTERS

1   Pierce, *Russian America*, 294–95.

2   Ibid., 19–20.

3   Rezanov to the RAC Board of Directors, New Archangel, November 6, 1805, in Tikhmenev, *Documents*, no. 42: 155.

4   Pierce, *Russian America*, 247–48.

5   Ibid., 66–67, 402.

6   Khlebnikov, *Baranov*, 72–74; RAC Main Administration to Aleksandr I, September 22, 1810, in Dmytryshyn, Crownhart-Vaughan, and Vaughan, *Russian American Colonies*, no. 29: 191–92.

7   Khlebnikov, *Notes on Russian America*, pt. 1: 7–8.

8   Ibid., pt. 1: 11–12.

9   Alexander Yu. Petrov, "Vzaimodeistvie Rossii i Soedinennykh Shtatov na severo-zapade Ameriki v nachale XIX veka" ("Interactions between Russia and the United States on the Northwest Coast of America at the Beginning of the Nineteenth Century"), *Novaia i noveishaia istoriia* (*New and Contemporary History*) 5 (2013): 170–82.

10   John Ebbets to Astor, Macao, January 11, 1811, in *John Jacob Astor, Business Man*, by Kenneth Wiggins Porter, 2 vols. (New York: Russell and Russell, 1966), vol. 1, doc. 48: 451.

11   Peter Corney, *Early Voyages in the North Pacific, 1813–1818* (Fairfield, Wash.: Ye Galleon Press, 1965), 116.

12   Nikolai P. Rumiantsev to Levett Harris, St. Petersburg, May 17, 1898; Levett Harris to James Madison, June 1, 1808; Rumiantsev to Aleksandr I, St. Petersburg, November 12, 1809, all in Bashkina et al., *The United States and Russia*, no. 260: 510–11; no. 262:

516–17; no. 312: 618–21. Statement from the Directors of the RAC, April 21, 1808, in Dmytryshyn, Crownhart-Vaughan, and Vaughan, *Russian American Colonies*, no. 23: 159–62.

13   Andrei Ia. Dashkov to Baranov, October 7, 1809; Report from the Main Administration of the RAC, December 23, 1816, both in Dmytryshyn, Crownhart-Vaughan, and Vaughan, *Russian American Colonies*, no. 26: 175–79; no. 37: 226. Adrian Bentzon to Astor, Washington, July 9, 1810; Fedor P. Pahlen to Rumiantsev, Philadelphia, July 9, 1810, both in Bashkina et al., *The United States and Russia*, no. 344: 674–75; no. 346: 677–79.

14   Statement of RAC Directors M. M. Buldakov and Benedikt Kramer, April 21, 1808; Andrei Ia. Dashkov to Baranov, October 7, 1809, both in Dmytryshyn, Crownhart-Vaughan, and Vaughan, *Russian American Colonies*, no. 23: 159–62; no. 26: 175–83. Porter, *John Jacob Astor*, 1:129–213.

15   Astor to Captain John Ebbets, New York, November 4, 1809, in Bashkina et al., *The United States and Russia*, no. 306: 601–3.

16   Convention between the American Fur Company and the Russian-American Company, St. Petersburg, April 20/May 2, 1812, in Bashkina et al., *The United States and Russia*, no. 421: 841–43.

17   The destruction of the *Tonquin* is one of the classic tales in the annals of the Northwest Coast fur trade. After unloading part of the ship's cargo at the new Astoria post in July 1811, Captain Thorn hurried to the Nootka Sound area to trade for sea otter skins. By his arrogance and deliberately insulting behavior at Clayoquot Sound he angered the local Nootka chieftain. In a surprise attack, the Nootkans seized the *Tonquin*, killing Thorn and most of his men. The next day, while the Nootkans were roaming the ship, a survivor below deck set alight the powder magazine, blowing everything and everyone to kingdom come. A detailed contemporary account of the voyage and the disaster is in Gabriel Franchére, *Narrative of a Voyage to the Northwest Coast of America, in the Years 1811, 1812, 1813, and 1814; or, The First American Settlement on the Pacific* (New York: Redfield, 1854).

18   In 1812, while still unaware that Astoria had been lost, Astor planned to send all the post's goods and supplies to New Archangel, thinking that it would be safe from British depredation in Baranov's hands as a caretaker. He simply assumed that Aleksandr Andreevich would cooperate with this emergency measure. This plan came too late.

19   Porter, *John Jacob Astor*, 1:232.

20   RAC Directors to Andrei Dashkov, October 16, 1814, in Dmytryshyn, Crownhart-Vaughan, and Vaughan, *Russian American Colonies*, no. 36: 218–19. Apparently, rum evaporated as readily as vodka in Russian America.

21   Porter, *John Jacob Astor*, 1:183–85, 202–3.

22   A full accounting of the *Beaver*'s cargo sold to Baranov appears in ibid., vol. 1, doc. 58: 513–22. Topping the list were 362 barrels of flour, 40 barrels of cornmeal, 15 hogsheads of sugar, 20 hogsheads of molasses, 70 casks of pilot bread, and 7 hogsheads of tobacco. Included also were 10 casks of brandy, 10 casks of rum, 5 casks of gin, and 16 quarter casks of Tenerife wine. Among the many other items were soap, writing paper, canvas, bar lead, Swedish steel, shoe leather, plates and dishes, iron kettles, men's wool hats, men's strong shoes, cotton bandannas, and 52 gross of metal and

gilt buttons for coats and vests, as well as a large supply of sewing needles. Barrels and barrels of paint, turpentine, rosin, and tar added to the cargo. In essence, this account demonstrates, the *Beaver* served as a wholesale supply house for the diverse needs of the RAC colony and its residents, with many of these items being placed presumably in the company stores at New Archangel and Pavlovskaia.

23   Ibid., 1: 406–7.

24   "A Report from the Main Administration of the Russian American Company concerning Current Trade with the North Americans," [St. Petersburg,] December 23, 1816, in Dmytryshyn, Crownhart-Vaughan, and Vaughan, *Russian American Colonies*, no. 37: 229.

25   Subsequently, a Spanish corvette captured the *Pedlar* at San Luis Obispo, where the Spanish captain charged Captain Pigot with engaging in smuggling. The charge could not be proved in court, so the California authorities released the ship and its crew after a two-month detention. Porter, *John Jacob Astor*, 2:643–44.

26   "A Report from the Main Administration of the RAC concerning Current Trade with the North Americans," [St. Petersburg,] December 23, 1816, in Dmytryshyn, Crownhart-Vaughan, and Vaughan, *Russian American Colonies*, no. 37: 232. This document, obviously based on Baranov's report, is the only substantial source describing this 1815 imbroglio at New Archangel.

27   Ibid., no. 37: 233–34. In compiling this report, the RAC main office mistakenly inferred that Captain Pigot was an Englishman who had traded with the American Hunt. In fact, as earlier noted, Pigot was an American sailing, like Hunt, with Astor's backing, but with his ship under a British flag as a wartime expedient to avoid capture.

28   Pierce, *Russia's Hawaiian Adventure*.

29   "Award of Chief's Rank to Baranov by King Kaumualii, July 1, 1816," in Pierce, *Russia's Hawaiian Adventure*, 73–74.

30   Report of Tarakanov to Captain-Lieutenant Hagemeister, received at Sitka, February 12, 1818, in Pierce, *Russia's Hawaiian Adventure*, 97, 99.

31   "Declaration, Schäffer et al., June 1, 1817, of a Decision to Make a Stand at Hanalei," in Pierce, *Russia's Hawaiian Adventure*, 93.

32   In *The Russian-American Company: Correspondence of the Governors, Communications Sent, 1818*, trans. and ed. Richard A. Pierce (Kingston, Ontario: Limestone Press, 1984): Captain-Lieutenant Hagemeister, "Instructions to Mr. Skipper Benseman," January 17, 1818, no. 16: 3; Hagemeister, "Proposal to the NA Office," January 17, 1818, no. 15: 3; "Translation of a Letter to the Governor of New California, Don Pablo Vicente De Sala," January 18, 1818, no. 19: 6.

33   George Young et al. to Schäffer, December 29, 1816, in Pierce, *Russia's Hawaiian Adventure*, 83–84. The letter has the notation "Delivered by Tarakanov, December 20, 1817, at Novo-Arkhangel'sk." On William Heath Davis and the *Eagle*, see Malloy, *"Boston Men,"* 97.

34   Hagemeister, report, NA Office [of the RAC] to the Main Office, January 11, 1818, in Pierce, *Correspondence of the Governors*, no. 1: 1. On Hagemeister's American career, see Pierce, *Russian America*, 185–87.

35   Hagemeister, "Instructions to Mr. Skipper Benseman"; Hagemeister, "Proposal to the

NA Office"; "Translation of a Letter to the Governor of New California, Don Pablo Vicente De Sala," in Pierce, *Correspondence of the Governors*, nos. 16, 15, 19: 3–6.

36   Hagemeister, "Instructions to the Commander of the RAC Vessel *Otkrytie*, Fleet-Lieutenant and Cavalier Iakov Anikeevich Podushkin," February 9, 1818, in Pierce, *Correspondence of the Governors*, no. 51: 27–28.

37   Hagemeister, undated letter to the RAC main office [July 13/18], 1818; Hagemeister to the main office, August 18, 1818, both in Pierce, *Correspondence of the Governors*, nos. 207–8: 121–22.

38   Khlebnikov, *Baranov*, 94.

12. CLOSING THE BARANOV ERA

1   This theme is developed with great insight in Ilya Vinkovetsky, *Russian America: An Overseas Colony of a Continental Empire, 1804–1867* (Oxford: Oxford University Press, 2011).

2   Rezanov to the RAC Board of Directors, New Archangel, November 6, 1805, in Tikhmenev, *Documents*, no. 42: 153–73; Dmytryshyn, Crownhart-Vaughan, and Vaughan, *Russian American Colonies*, no. 53: 105–8.

3   The details of Hagemeister's background and career are provided in Pierce, *Russian America* (185–87), where he is identified as Ludwig von Hagemeister. His description of the voyage as far as Callao, with his observations on the struggle between the Spanish imperial regime and insurgents throughout Latin America, is contained in "A Report to the Main Administration of the Company," Callao, April 1817, in Dmytryshyn, Crownhart-Vaughan, and Vaughan, *Russian American Colonies*, no. 44: 249–54.

4   RAC Main Administration to Baranov, St. Petersburg, March 22, 1817, in Dmytryshyn, Crownhart-Vaughan, and Vaughan, *Russian American Colonies*, no. 39: 239; no. 40: 239–40; no. 41: 241–45; no. 42: 244–45.

5   Ibid., no. 41: 242.

6   Ibid.

7   Khlebnikov, *Baranov*, 96.

8   Ibid., 97.

9   Pierce, *Russian America*, 186.

10   Ibid., 229–30; and Khlebnikov, *Notes on Russian America*, pt. 1: xv–xxii.

11   Pierce, *Russian America*, 186.

12   F. P. Litke, at one time a midshipman on the *Kamchatka*, quoted in ibid., 176.

13   Khlebnikov, *Baranov*, 98.

14   Ibid., 106–7. This accounting leaves fox pelts out of consideration, and it may underestimate the total return on sea otter pelts. In a later calculation, historian S. B. Okun reported that the Northeastern Company and the RAC between 1797 and 1818 secured a total of 80,271 sea otter pelts and 1,493,626 fur seal skins. S. B. Okun, *The Russian-American Company*, ed. B. D. Grekov, trans. Carl Ginsburg (Cambridge, Mass.: Harvard University Press, 1951), 58.

15   These were the ships *Otkrytie*, the brig *Il'mena*, and the schooner *Chirikov*.

16   Ibid., 109.

17   Ibid., 97.

18   Ibid., 98.

19   "The Baranov Chain Mail," app. 5, and "Naawushkeitl," app. 6, both in Dauenhauer, Dauenhauer, and Black, *Anóoshi Lingít*, 399–400, 401–2; Grinev, *Tlingit Indians in Russian America*, 151–52. Carefully restored, this chain mail vest is now in the collections of the National Museum of American History in Washington, D.C. It is pictured in Dauenhauer, Dauenhauer, and Black, *Anóoshi Lingít*, 399, fig. 36.

20   Dauenhauer, Dauenhauer, and Black, *Anóoshi Lingít*, xlvi and fig. 3; n. 23, xlix, and also color plates 18–22.

21   Khlebnikov, *Baranov*, 99.

22   Ibid.

23   Pierce, *Russian America*, 25.

24   Khlebnikov, *Baranov*, 108.

25   Ibid., 103. This statement sounds very much like a direct quotation from one of Baranov's messages concerning his policy toward the Native Alaskans.

26   Dauenhauer, Dauenhauer, and Black, *Anóoshi Lingít*, xliii–xlvii.

27   Personal communication, Father Michael Oleksa, February 14, 2014.

28   Elton Engstrand and Allan Engstrand, *Alexander Baranov and a Pacific Empire* (Juneau, Alaska: Elton Engstrand and Allan Engstrand, 2004). This volume offers a sketchy, highly episodic account of Russian America during Baranov's time, relying principally on Khlebnikov's original Baranov biography for its factual matter about the chief manager.

29   Davydov, *Two Voyages*, 104.

30   Grand Duke Constantine to Prince Gorchakov, December 7, 1857, Manuscript Division, U.S. Library of Congress, quoted in Howard I. Kushner, *Conflict on the Northwest Coast: American-Russian Rivalry in the Pacific Northwest, 1790–1867* (Westport, Conn.: Greenwood Press, 1975), 135–36.

31   Baron Ferdinand von Wrangel, "Concerning the Cession of the American Colonies to the Government of the United States," April 9, 1857, quoted in Kushner, *Conflict on the Northwest Coast*, 136.

BIBLIOGRAPHY

RUSSIAN ARCHIVAL SOURCES

Archangel

GAAO. Gosudarstvennyi arkhiv Arkhangelskoi oblasti (State Archive of Archangel Region).

Irkutsk

GAIO. Gosudarstvennyi arkhiv Irkutskoi oblasti (State Archive of the Irkutsk Region).

Ten collections, among them: Fond 50, Irkutsk Diocese; Fond 70, Irkutsk State Duma, and Fond 336, Irkutsk State Magistrate.

Muzei G. I. Shelikhova (Grigorii I. Shelikhov Museum).

Exhibition of material culture related to Aleksandr A. Baranov; Records on Shelikhov-Baranov Relations.

Muzei Taltsy (Taltsy Museum).

Exhibition of material culture related to Aleksandr A. Baranov.

Kargopol'

Kargopol'skii gosudarstvennyi istoriko-khudozhestvennyi muzei-zapovednik (Kargopol' State Art and Historical Museum).

Miscellaneous collections, with records of birth, possessions, and trade, devoted to Aleksandr A. Baranov.

State Archive of Krasnodar Region.

Records of birth, possessions, and trade, devoted to Russian Greeks and Cossacks.

Moscow

AVPRI. Arkhiv vneshnei politiki Rossiiskoi imperii (Archive of the Foreign Policy of the Russian Empire).

Fond RAK, 341, Russian-American Company, op. 888. Miscellaneous papers concerning the history of Russian America, collections of documents regarding Russian-British relations, Russian-American relations.

GARF. Gosudarstvennyi arkhiv Rossiiskoi Federatsii (State Archive of the Russian Federation).

Collection 5325, papers regarding archival collections on Russian America.

RGA DA. Rossiiskii gosudarstvennyi arkhiv drevnikh aktov (Russian State Archive of Ancient Acts).

Preobrazhenskii prikaz; correspondence of various individuals.

Yudin Collection; Vorontsov Collection; Senate Collection; Miller files; Siberian prikaz.

RGB OR. Rossiiskaia gosudarstvennaia biblioteka, Otdel rukopisei (Russian State Library, Manuscript Division).

Fond 204, Collection Obshchestvo istorii i drevnostei rossiskikh.

RG VIA. Rossiiskii gosudarstvennyi voenno-istoricheskii arkhiv (Russian State Archive of Military History).

VUA (Voenno-ucheny arkhiv). Odessa, Ukraine

Library of Odessa State University. Vorontsov Collection; Schilder Collection; Stroganov Collection.

Odessa State Library, named after Maxim Gorky. Division of Regional Studies; Division of Rare Books and Manuscripts.

Perm'

GAPO. Gosudarstvennyi arkhiv Permskoi oblasti (State Archive of the Perm' Region).

Fond 445, Kiril T. Khlebnikov Collection.

St. Petersburg

ARGO. Arkhiv Russkogo geograficheskogo obshchestva (Archive of the Russian Geographical Society).

Fond 99, Veselago Collection.

OR RNB. Otdel rukopisei Rossiiskoi natsional'noi biblioteki (Manuscript Division of the Russian National Library).

Voenskii and Olenin Collections.

RGA VMF. Rossiiskii gosudarstvennyi arkhiv voenno-morskogo flota (Russian State Archive of the Navy).

Kushelev Collection; miscellaneous papers related to the history of Russian America.

RGIA. Rossiiskii gosudarstvennyi istoricheskii arkhiv (Russian State Historical Archive).

Materials from twenty-seven collections, among them documents from Fond 1263, Committee of Ministers; Fond 583, Special Chancellery, about the Credit Matters; Fond 13, Commerce College; Fond 560, Special Chancellery of the Minister of Finance; Fond 18, Department of Manufactures and Internal Trade; and Fond 15, Main Office of the Russian-American Company.

Vologda

GAVO. Gosudarstvennyi arkhiv Vologodskoi oblasti (State Archive of the Vologda Region).

Fond 671, miscellaneous papers regarding the activity of the Russian-American Company.

Vologda State Art and History Museum.

Fond 10, Buldakov-Shelikhov Collection.

PUBLISHED PRIMARY SOURCES

Andreev, A. I., ed. *Russian Discoveries in the Pacific and in North America in the Eighteenth and Nineteenth Centuries: A Collection of Materials.* Translated by Carl Ginsburg. Ann Arbor, Mich.: J. W. Edwards for the American Council of Learned Societies, 1952.

Bashkina, Nina N., et al., eds. *The United States and Russia: The Beginnings of Relations, 1765–1815.* Washington, D.C.: U.S. Department of State, [1998].

Black, Dawn Lea, and Alexander Yu. Petrov. Introduction to *Natalia Shelikhova: Russian*

Oligarch of Alaska Commerce. Edited and translated by Dawn Lea Black and Alexander Yu. Petrov. Fairbanks: University of Alaska Press, 2010.

Busch, Briton C., and Barry M. Gough, eds. *Fur Traders from New England: The Boston Men in the North Pacific, 1787–1800; The Narratives of William Dane Phelps, William Sturgis, and James Gilchrist Swan.* Spokane, Wash.: Arthur H. Clark Company, 1997.

Campbell, Archibald. *A Voyage Round the World, from 1806 to 1812.* Facsimile reprint. Honolulu: University of Hawaii Press for the Friends of the Library of Hawaii, 1967.

Chamisso, Adelbert von. *The Alaskan Diary of Adelbert von Chamisso, Naturalist on the Kotzebue Voyage, 1815–18.* Translated and edited by Robert Fortuine. Anchorage, Alaska: Cook Inlet Historical Society, 1986.

———. *A Voyage Around the World with the Romanzov Exploring Expedition in the Years 1815–1818 in the Brig* Rurik, *Captain Otto von Kotzebue.* Translated and edited by Henry Katz. Honolulu: University of Hawaii Press, 1986.

Collins, Perry McDonough. *Overland Explorations in Siberia, Northern Asia, and the Great Amoor River Country; Incidental Notices of Manchooria, Mongolia, Kamschatka, and Japan.* New York: D. Appleton and Company, 1864.

Corney, Peter. *Early Voyages in the North Pacific, 1813–1818.* Fairfield, Wash.: Ye Galleon Press, 1965.

Dauenhauer, Nora Marks, Richard Dauenhauer, and Lydia T. Black, eds. *Anóoshi Lingít Aaní Ká, Russians in Tlingit America: The Battles of Sitka, 1802 and 1804.* Vol. 4 of *Classics of Tlingit Oral Literature.* Seattle: University of Washington Press; Juneau, Alaska: Sealaska Heritage Institute, 2008.

Davydov, Gavrill. *Two Voyages to Russian America, 1802–1807.* Translated by Colin Bearne. Edited by Richard A. Pierce. Kingston, Ontario: Limestone Press, 1977.

Dmytryshyn, Basil, E. A. P. Crownhart-Vaughan, and Thomas Vaughan, trans. and eds. *Russia's Conquest of Siberia, 1558–1700: A Documentary Record.* Vol. 1 of *To Siberia and Russian America: Three Centuries of Russian Eastward Expansion.* Portland: Oregon Historical Society Press, 1985.

———. *Russian Penetration of the North Pacific Ocean, 1700–1797: A Documentary Record.* Vol. 2 of *To Siberia and Russian America: Three Centuries of Russian Eastward Expansion.* Portland: Oregon Historical Society, 1988.

———. *The Russian American Colonies, 1798–1867: A Documentary Record.* Vol. 3 of *To Siberia and Russian America: Three Centuries of Russian Eastward Expansion.* Portland: Oregon Historical Society, 1989.

D'Wolf, John. *A Voyage to the North Pacific and a Journey through Siberia More than Half a Century Ago.* Cambridge, Mass.: Welch, Bigelow, and Company, 1861; repr., Fairfield, Wash.: Ye Galleon Press, 1968.

Franchére, Gabriel. *Journal of a Voyage on the North West Coast of North America during the Years 1811, 1812, 1813, and 1814.* Translated by Wessie Tipping Lamb. Edited by W. Kaye Lamb. Toronto: Champlain Society, 1969.

———. *Narrative of a Voyage to the Northwest Coast of America, in the Years 1811, 1812, 1813, and 1814; or, The First American Settlement on the Pacific.* New York: Redfield, 1854.

Gibson, James R., comp., trans., and ed. *California through Russian Eyes, 1806–1848.*

Norman: Arthur H. Clark Company, an imprint of the University of Oklahoma Press, 2013.

Gideon. *The Round the World Voyage of Hieromonk Gideon, 1803–1809*. Translated by Lydia T. Black. Edited by Richard A. Pierce. Kingston, Ontario: Limestone Press, 1989.

Golovnin, Vasilii M. *Around the World on the* Kamchatka, *1817–1819*. Translated by Ella Lury Wiswell. Honolulu: Hawaiian Historical Society and the University Press of Hawaii, 1979.

———. "Memorandum of Captain Second Rank Golovnin on Condition of the Aleuts in the Settlements of the Russian-American Company and on Its Promyshlenniki." Translated by Katherine Arndt. *Alaska History* 1, no. 2 (1985–86): 59–71.

Holmberg, Heinrich Johan. *Holmberg's Ethnographic Sketches*. Edited by Marvin W. Falk. Translated by Fritz Jaensch. Fairbanks: University of Alaska Press, 1985.

Khlebnikov, Kiril. *Colonial Russian America: Kyrill T. Khlebnikov's Reports, 1817–1832*. Translated by Basil Dmytryshyn and E. A. P. Crownhart-Vaughan. Portland: Oregon Historical Society, 1976.

———. *The Khlebnikov Archive: Unpublished Journal (1800–1837) and Travel Notes (1820, 1822, and 1824)*. Edited by Leonid Shur. Translated by John Bisk. Fairbanks: University of Alaska Press, 1990.

———. *Notes on Russian America. Pt. 1, Novo-Arkhangel'sk*. Compiled by Svetlana G. Fedorova. Translated by Serge LeCompte and Richard A. Pierce. Edited by Richard A. Pierce. Kingston, Ontario: Limestone Press, 1994.

———. *Notes on Russian America. Pts. 2–5, Kadiak, Unalaska, Atkha, the Pribylovs*. Compiled by Roza G. Liapunova and Svetlana G. Fedorova. Translated by Marina Ramsey. Edited by Richard A. Pierce. Kingston, Ontario: Limestone Press, 1994.

Korobitsyn, N. I. "Journal of N. I. Korobitsyn, Clerk of the Russian-American Company, for the Period of 1795–1807." In *Russian Discoveries in the Pacific and in North America in the Eighteenth and Nineteenth Centuries: A Collection of Materials*, edited by A. I. Andreev, translated by Carl Ginsburg. Ann Arbor, Mich.: J. W. Edwards for the American Council of Learned Societies, 1951.

Kotzebue, Otto von. *A New Voyage Round the World*. 2 vols. London: Colburn and Bentley, 1830.

———. *A Voyage of Discovery into the South Sea and Beering's Straits, Undertaken in the Years 1815 to 1818*. 3 vols. London: Longman, 1821.

Krusenstern, A. J. von. *A Voyage Round the World, in the Years 1803, 4, 5 and 6, by Order of His Imperial Majesty Alexander I, on Board the Ships* Nadeshda *and* Neva. Translated by R. B. Hoppner. 2 vols. London: John Murray, 1813.

Langsdorff, Georg H. von. *Langsdorff's Narrative of the Rezanov Voyage to Nueva California*. Reprint of 1927 ed. Fairfield, Wash.: Ye Galleon Press, 1988.

———. *Voyages and Travels in Various Parts of the World during the Years 1803, 1804, 1805, 1806, and 1807*. 2 vols. London: Henry Colburn, 1814.

La Pérouse, Jean-François de Galaup, comte de. *A Voyage Round the World, Performed in Years 1785, 1786, 1787, and 1788 by the* Boussole *and* Astrolabe. 2 vols. Amsterdam, N. Israel; New York: Da Capo Press, 1968.

Ledyard, John. *A Journal of Captain Cook's Last Voyage to the Pacific Ocean, and in Quest of North-West Passage between Asia and America (1776–1779)*. Hartford, Conn.: N. Patten, 1783.

Lisiansky, Yuri. *Voyage Round the World in the Years 1803, 1804, 1805, and 1806*. London: John Booth, 1814; repr., Edgewood, N.J.: Gregg Press, 1968.

Mahr, August. C. *The Visit of the "Rurik" to San Francisco in 1816*. Stanford University, Calif.: Stanford University Press, 1932.

Merck, Carl Heinrich. *Siberia and Northwestern America, 1788–1792: The Journals of Carl Heinrich Merck, Naturalist with the Russian Scientific Expedition Led by Captains Joseph Billings and Gavriil Sarychev*. Translated by F. Jaensch. Edited by Richard A. Pierce. Kingston, Ontario: Limestone Press, 1980.

Pierce, Richard A., ed. *Documents on the History of the Russian-American Company*. Translated by Marina Ramsay. Kingston, Ontario: Limestone Press, 1976.

———, trans. and ed. *The Russian-American Company: Correspondence of the Governors, Communications Sent, 1818*. Kingston, Ontario: Limestone Press, 1984.

Sarychev, Gavriil. *Account of a Voyage of Discovery to the North-East of Siberia, the Frozen Ocean, and the North-East Sea, by Gawrila Sarytschew, Translated from the Russian*. London: J. G. Barnard, 1806; repr., 2 vols. in 1, New York: Da Capo Press, 1969.

Sauer, Martin. *An Account of a Geographical and Astronomical Expedition to the Northern Parts of Russia . . . [and] the Islands in the Eastern Ocean, Stretching to the American Coast. Performed . . . by Commodore Joseph Billings, in the Years 1785, &c. to 1794*. London: A. Strahan for T. Cadell, Jun. and W. Davies, 1802.

Shelikhov, Grigorii. *A Voyage to America, 1783–1786*. Translated by Marina Ramsay. Edited by Richard A. Pierce. Kingston, Ontario: Limestone Press, 1981.

Shelikhova, Natalia. *Natalia Shelikhova: Russian Oligarch of Alaska Commerce*. Translated and edited by Dawn Lea Black and Alexander Yu. Petrov. Fairbanks: University of Alaska Press, 2010.

Tupper, Harmon. *To the Great Ocean: Siberia and the Trans-Siberian Railroad*. Boston: Little, Brown and Company, 1965.

[Valaam Monastery.] *The Russian Orthodox Religious Mission in America, 1794–1837*. Translated by Colin Bearne. Edited by Richard A. Pierce. Kingston, Ontario: Limestone Press, 1978.

Vancouver, George. *The Voyage of George Vancouver, 1791–1795*. Edited by W. Kaye Lamb. 4 vols. London: Hakluyt Society, 1984.

Veniaminov, Ioann. *Notes on the Islands of the Unalashka District*. Translated by Lydia T. Black and R. H. Geoghegan. Edited by Richard A. Pierce. Kingston, Ontario: Limestone Press, 1991.

SECONDARY SOURCES

Afonsky, Georgii (The Right Reverend Gregory, Bishop of Sitka and Alaska). *A History of the Orthodox Church in Alaska (1794–1917)*. Kodiak, Alaska: St. Herman's Theological Seminary, 1977.

Alexander, John T. *Catherine the Great: Life and Legend*. New York: Oxford University Press, 1989.

Anderson, Bern. *Surveyor of the Sea: The Life and Voyages of Captain George Vancouver.* Seattle: University of Washington Press, 1960.

Armstrong, Terence. *Russian Settlement in the North.* Cambridge: Cambridge University Press, 1965.

Baker, Emily Reynolds. *Caleb Reynolds, American Seafarer: Based on the Papers of Caleb Reynolds, 1771–1858.* Kingston, Ontario: Limestone Press, 2000.

Bancroft, Hubert Howe. *History of Alaska, 1730–1855.* San Francisco: A. L. Bancroft, 1886.

———. *History of California.* 7 vols. San Francisco: A. L. Bancroft, 1884–90; repr., Santa Barbara, Calif.: W. Hebberd, 1966.

———. *History of the Northwest Coast, 1543–1867.* 2 vols. San Francisco: A. L. Bancroft, 1884.

Barratt, Glynn. *Russia in Pacific Waters, 1715–1825: A Survey of the Origins of Russia's Naval Presence in the North and South Pacific.* Vancouver: University of British Columbia Press, 1981.

———. *Russian Shadows on the British Northwest Coast of North America, 1810–1890.* Vancouver: University of British Columbia Press, 1984.

Beaglehole, J. C. *The Exploration of the Pacific.* London: Oxford University Press, 1947.

Berg, L. S. *Fishes of Fresh Waters of USSR and Adjacent Countries.* 2 vols. Moscow: USSR Academy of Sciences, 1948.

Berkh, Vasilii N. *A Chronological History of the Discovery of the Aleutian Islands; or, The Exploits of Russian Merchants, with a Supplement of Historical Data on the Fur Trade.* Translated by Dmitri Krenov. Edited by Richard A. Pierce. Kingston, Ontario: Limestone Press, 1974.

Bernshtam, T. A. "Promyslovye zveroboinye arteli pomorov zimnego berega Belogo moria vo vtoroi polovine XIX–pervoi treti XX vv." ("The Organization of Hunting Villages on the Winter Shore of the White Sea, from the Second Half of the Nineteenth Century to the Early Twentieth Century"). Ph.D. diss., Kunstkamera, St. Petersburg, 1968.

Black, Lydia T. "The Russian Conquest of Kodiak." *Anthropological Papers of the University of Alaska* 24, nos. 1–2 (1992): 165–82.

———. *Russians in Alaska.* Fairbanks: University of Alaska Press, 2004.

Blum, Jerome. *Lord and Peasant in Russia, from the Ninth to the Nineteenth Century.* Princeton, N.J.: Princeton University Press, 1961.

Bobrick, Benson. *East of the Sun: The Epic Conquest and Tragic History of Siberia.* New York: Poseidon Press, 1992.

Bogaras, Waldemar. *The Chukchee.* In *Memoirs of the American Museum of Natural History*, vol. 11, edited by Franz Boas. Leiden: E. J. Brill, Ltd., 1909.

Bolkhovitinov, Nikolai N. *Rusia y América (ca. 1523–1867) (Russia and America [ca. 1523–1867]).* Madrid: Editorial MAPFRE, 1992.

Bradley, H. W. "The Hawaiian Islands and the Pacific Fur Trade, 1785–1813." *Pacific Historical Review* 30 (1939): 275–99.

Brokgauz, F. A., and I. A. Efron. *Encyclopedia.* Vol. 14. St. Petersburg: I. A. Efron, 1895.

Brumfield, William C. *A History of Russian Architecture.* Cambridge: Cambridge University Press, 1993.

Cook, Warren. *Flood Tide of Empire: Spain and the Pacific Northwest, 1543–1819.* New Haven, Conn.: Yale University Press, 1975.

Crowell, Aron L., Amy F. Steffian, and Gordon L. Pullar, eds. *Looking Both Ways: Heritage and Identity of the Alutiiq People*. Fairbanks: University of Alaska Press, 2001.

de Laguna, Frederica. "Tlingit." In *Northwest Coast*, edited by Wayne Suttles. Vol. 7 of *Handbook of North American Indians*, edited by William G. Sturtevant. Washington, D.C.: Smithsonian Institution, 1990.

———. *Under Mount St. Elias: The History and Culture of the Yakutat Tlingit*. Washington, D.C.: Smithsonian Institution Press, 1972.

Dmytryshyn, Basil. "The Administrative Apparatus of the Russian-American Company, 1798–1867." *Canadian-American Slavic Studies* 28, no. 1 (1994): 1–52.

———. "The Visit of the Russian Ship *Juno*, March 28–May 10, 1806." Unpublished paper, undated. Courtesy of the author.

Drucker, Philip. *Indians of the Northwest Coast*. Garden City, N.Y.: Natural History Press, 1963.

Emmons, George Thornton. *The Tlingit Indians*. Edited by Frederica de Laguna. Seattle: University of Washington Press, 1991.

Engstrand, Elton. *Joseph O'Cain: Adventurer on the Northwest Coast*. Juneau: Alaska Litho Printers, 2003.

Engstrand, Elton, and Allan Engstrand. *Alexander Baranov and a Pacific Empire*. Juneau, Alaska: Elton Engstrand and Allan Engstrand, 2004.

Essig, E. O., Adele Ogden, and Clarence John Dufour. *Fort Ross: California Outpost of Russian Alaska, 1812–1841*. Edited by Richard A. Pierce. Kingston, Ontario: Limestone Press, 1991.

Farris, Glenn J. *So Far from Home: Russians in Early California*. Berkeley, Calif.: Heyday Books; Santa Clara, Calif.: Santa Clara University, 2012.

———. "Talacani, the Man Who Purchased Fort Ross." *Fort Ross Interpretive Association Newsletter*, September–October 1993.

Fedorova, Svetlana G. "Ethnic Processes in Russian America." Translated by Antoinette Shalkop. Occasional Paper no. 1. Anchorage, Alaska: Anchorage Historical and Fine Arts Museum, 1975.

———. *The Russian Population in Alaska and California, Late Eighteenth Century–1867*. Translated by Richard A. Pierce and Alton S. Donnelly. Kingston, Ontario: Limestone Press, 1973.

Fisher, R. H. *The Russian Fur Trade, 1550–1700*. Berkeley: University of California Press, 1943.

Galbraith, John S. *The Hudson's Bay Company as an Imperial Factor, 1821–1869*. Berkeley: University of California Press, 1957.

———. "The 'Turbulent Frontier' as a Factor in British Expansion." *Comparative Studies in Society and History* 2, no. 2 (January 1960): 150–68.

Gibson, James R. "European Dependence upon American Natives: The Case of Russian America." *Ethnohistory* 25, no. 4 (1978): 359–85.

———. *Feeding the Russian Fur Trade: Provisionment of the Okhotsk Seaboard and the Kamchatka Peninsula, 1639–1856*. Madison: University of Wisconsin Press, 1969.

———. *Imperial Russia in Frontier America: The Changing Geography of Supply of Russian*

America, 1784–1867. New York: Oxford University Press, 1976.

———. *Otter Skins, Boston Ships, and China Goods: The Maritime Fur Trade of the Northwest Coast, 1785–1841*. Seattle: University of Washington Press, 1992.

———. "Russian Expansion in Siberia and America: Critical Contacts." In *Russia's American Colony*, edited by S. Frederick Starr. Durham, N.C.: Duke University Press, 1987.

Golder, Frank Alfred. *Russian Expansion on the Pacific, 1641–1850: An Account of the Earliest and Later Expeditions Made by the Russians along the Pacific Coast of Asia and North America; Including Some Related Expeditions to the Arctic Regions*. Gloucester, Mass.: P. Smith, 1960 [ca. 1914].

Gough, Barry. *Fortune's River: The Collision of Empires in Northwest America*. Madeira Park, B.C.: Harbour Publishing, 2007.

Gregory (Bishop). *Sitka and St. Michael's Cathedral*. [Platina, Calif.]: St. Herman's Press, the Diocese of Alaska of the Orthodox Church in America, 1974.

Grinev, Andrei V. *The Tlingit Indians in Russian America, 1741–1867*. Translated by Richard L. Bland and Katerina G. Solovjova. Lincoln: University of Nebraska Press, 2005.

Gunn, G. P. *Kargopol'e-Onega*. Moscow: Iskusstvo, 1989.

Harrison, John A. *The Founding of the Russian Empire in Asia and America*. Coral Gables, Fla.: University of Miami Press, 1971.

Hinckley, Ted C. *The Canoe Rocks: Alaska's Tlingit and the Euramerican Frontier, 1800–1912*. New York: University Press of America, 1996.

Howay, F. W. *List of Trading Vessels in the Maritime Fur Trade, 1785–1825*. Edited by Richard A. Pierce. Kingston, Ontario: Limestone Press, 1973.

Hurtado, Albert L. *John Sutter: A Life on the North American Frontier*. Norman: University of Oklahoma Press, 2006.

Istomin, Alexei. *The Indians at the Ross Settlement: According to the Censuses by Kuskov, 1820–1821*. Institute of Ethnology and Anthropology, Moscow. Fort Ross, Calif.: Fort Ross Interpretive Association, 1992.

Ivashintsov, N. A. *Russian Round-the-World Voyages, 1803–1849; With Summaries of Later Voyages to 1867*. Translated by Glynn Barratt. Edited by Richard A. Pierce. Kingston, Ontario: Limestone Press, 1980.

Iversen, Eve. *The Romance of Nikolai Rezanov and Concepción Argüello: A Literary Legend and Its Effect on California History*. Edited and with historical notes by Richard A. Pierce. Kingston, Ontario: Limestone Press. 1998.

Khlebnikov, Kiril. *Baranov, Chief Manager of the Russian Colonies in America*. Translated by Colin Bearne. Edited by Richard A. Pierce. Kingston, Ontario: Limestone Press, 1973.

Kliment (Kapalin), Metropolitan. *Russkaia Pravoslavnaia tserkov' na Aliaske do 1917 goda*. (*The Russian Orthodox Church in Alaska before 1917*). Moscow: Olma Media Group, 2009.

Kolchin, Peter. *Unfree Labor: American Slavery and Russian Serfdom*. Cambridge, Mass.: Harvard University Press, 1987.

Kolesnikov, Petr A., ed. *Istoriia severnogo krest'ianstva* (*History of Northern Peasantry*). 2 vols. Vologda: Severo-Zapadnoe knizhnoe izdatel'stvo, 1984.

Kozhov, Mikhail. *Lake Baikal and Its Life*. The Hague: Dr. W. Junk Publishers, 1963.

Kriuchkova, M. N. *Pravitel' Russkoi Ameriki i ego potomki (The Governor of Russian America and His Heirs)*. Moscow: Gramota, 1997.

Kushner, Howard I. *Conflict on the Northwest Coast: American-Russian Rivalry in the Pacific Northwest, 1790–1867*. Westport, Conn.: Greenwood Press, 1975.

Kuykendall, Ralph S. *The Hawaiian Kingdom, 1778–1854: Foundation and Transformation*. Honolulu: University of Hawaii Press, 1947.

Lander, James F. *Tsunamis Affecting Alaska, 1737–1996*. Boulder, Colo.: National Geophysical Data Center, National Environmental Satellite, Data and Information Service, U.S. Department of Commerce, 1996.

Lightfoot, Kent G., Thomas A. Wake, and Ann M. Schiff, eds. *The Archaeology and Ethnohistory of Fort Ross, California*. Berkeley: Archaeological Research Facility, University of California at Berkeley, 1991.

Lincoln, W. Bruce. *The Conquest of a Continent: Siberia and the Russians*. New York: Random House, 1994.

Luehrmann, Sonja. *Alutiiq Villages under Russian and U.S. Rule*. Fairbanks: University of Alaska Press, 2008.

Mackay, David. *In the Wake of Cook: Exploration, Science, and Empire, 1780–1801*. London: Croom Helm, 1985.

Makarova, Raisa V. *Russians on the Pacific, 1743–1799*. Translated and edited by Richard A. Pierce and Alton S. Donnelly. Kingston, Ontario: Limestone Press, 1975.

Malloy, Mary. *"Boston Men" on the Northwest Coast: The American Maritime Fur Trade, 1788–1844*. Kingston, Ontario: Limestone Press, 1998.

Massie, Robert K. *Peter the Great: His Life and World*. New York: Alfred A. Knopf, 1980.

McCoy, Patrick. *Archaeological Research at Fort Elizabeth, Waimea, Kauai, Hawaiian Islands*. Honolulu: Hawaiian State Parks Department, 1972.

McEvoy, Arthur F. *The Fisherman's Problem: Ecology and Law in California Fisheries, 1850–1980*. New York: Cambridge University Press, 1988.

Mehnert, Klaus. *The Russians in Hawaii, 1804–1817*. Honolulu, 1939.

Miller, Robert Ryal. *A Yankee Smuggler on the Spanish California Coast: George Washington Eayrs and the Ship* Mercury. Santa Barbara, Calif.: Santa Barbara Trust for Historical Preservation, 2001.

O'Brien, Bickford, Diane Spencer-Hancock, and Michael S. Tucker. *Fort Ross: Indians, Russians, Americans*. Sacramento: Fort Ross Interpretive Association, 1980.

Ogden, Adele. *The California Sea-Otter Trade, 1784–1848*. Berkeley: University of California Press, 1941.

Okun, S. B. *The Russian-American Company*. Edited by B. D. Grekov. Translated by Carl Ginsburg. Cambridge, Mass.: Harvard University Press, 1951.

Oleksa, Michael, ed. *Alaskan Missionary Spirituality*. New York: Paulist Press, 1987.

———. "The Death of Hieromonk Juvenaly." In *Russia in North America: Proceedings of the Second International Conference on Russian America, Sitka, Alaska, August 19–22, 1987*, edited by Richard A. Pierce, 322–57. Kingston, Ontario: Limestone Press, 1990.

Opolovnikov, Alexander, and Yelena Opolovnikova. *The Wooden Architecture of Russia: Houses, Fortifications, and Churches*. Edited by David Bruxton. New York: Harry N. Abrams, 1989.

Orth, Donald J. *Dictionary of Alaska Place Names*. Washington, D.C.: Government Printing Office, 1967.

Owens, Kenneth N. "Frontiersman for the Tsar: Timofei Tarakanov and the Expansion of Russian America." *Montana: The Magazine of Western History* 56, no. 3 (Autumn 2006): 3–21.

———, ed. *The Wreck of the Sv. Nikolai: Two Narratives of the First Russian Expedition in the Oregon Country, 1808–1810*. Translated by Alton S. Donnelly. Portland: Western Imprints, the Press of the Oregon Historical Society, 1985.

Pethick, Derek. *First Approaches to the Northwest Coast*. Vancouver: J. J. Douglas, 1976.

Petrov, Alexander Yu. *Obrazovanie Rossiisko-Amerikanskoi Companii (Formation of the Russian-American Company)*. Moscow: Nauka, 2000.

———. "Vzaimodeistvie Rossii i Soedinennykh Shtatov na severo-zapade Ameriki v nachale XIX veka" ("Interactions between Russia and the United States on the Northwest Coast of America at the Beginning of the Nineteenth Century"). *Novaia i noveishaia istoriia (New and Contemporary History)* 5 (2013): 170–82.

Pierce, Richard A. *Builders of Alaska: The Russian Governors, 1818–1867*. Kingston, Ontario: Limestone Press, 1986.

———, ed. *Russia in North America: Proceedings of the Second International Conference on Russian America, Sitka, Alaska, August 19–22, 1987*. Kingston, Ontario: Limestone Press, 1990.

———. *Russian America: A Biographical Dictionary*. Kingston, Ontario: Limestone Press, 1990.

———. *Russia's Hawaiian Adventure, 1815–1817*. Berkeley: University of California Press, 1965.

Porter, Kenneth Wiggins. *John Jacob Astor, Business Man*. 2 vols. New York: Russell and Russell, 1966.

Prokhorov, A. M., ed. *Great Soviet Encyclopedia*. 3rd. ed., English translation. 32 vols. New York: Macmillan, 1973–83.

Rich, Edwin E. *The History of the Hudson's Bay Company, 1670–1870*. 3 vols. London: Blackwell, 1958–59.

Richard, Rhys. *Captain Simon Metcalfe: Pioneer Fur Trader in the Pacific Northwest, Hawaii, and China, 1787–1794*. Edited by Richard A. Pierce. Kingston, Ontario: Limestone Press, 1991.

Ronda, James P. *Astoria and Empire*. Lincoln: University of Nebraska Press, 1990.

Russkie ekspeditsii po izucheniiu severnoi chasti Tikhogo okeana vo vtoroi polovine XVIII veka (Russian Expeditions of Exploration in the North Pacific Ocean in the Second Half of the Eighteenth Century). Moscow: Nauka, 1989.

Sabaneev, L. P. *Sobranie sochinenii (Collected Works)*. 2 vols. Moscow: A. A. Kartseva, 1892.

Saul, N. E. *Distant Friends: The United States and Russia, 1763–1867*. Lawrence: University of Kansas Press, 1991.

Schumacher, W. W. "Aftermath of the Sitka Massacre of 1802: Contemporary Documents with an Introduction and Afterword." *Alaska Journal* 9 (1979): 58–61.

Shakherov, V. P. "Osobennosti formirovaniia krupnogo kapitala v Iugo-vostochnoi Sibiri v kontse XVIII–pervoi treti XIX veka" ("Peculiarities in Large Capital Formation in

Southeast Siberia at the End of the Eighteenth to the Early Nineteenth Century"). In *Sibir' v proshlom, nastoiashem, buduiushchem* (*Siberia's Past, Present, and Future*). Novosibirsk, 1981

Shunkov, V. I. *Ocherki po istorii zemledeliia Sibiri (XVII v.)* (*Essays on the History of Agriculture in Siberia [Seventeenth Century]*). Moscow: Nauka, 1956.

Shur, L. A. *Russian Sources on American History.* Fairbanks, Alaska: Elmer E. Rasmuson Library, 1990.

Smith, Barbara S. *Russian Orthodoxy in Alaska: A History, Inventory, and Analysis of the Church Archives in Alaska with an Annotated Bibliography.* [Anchorage]: Published for the Alaska Historical Commission, 1980.

Smith, J. L. *Russians in the Pribilof Islands, 1786–1867.* Anchorage, Alaska: White Stone Press, 2001.

Solovjova, Katerina G., and Aleksandra A. Vovnyanko. *The Fur Rush: Essays and Documents on the History of Alaska at the End of the Eighteenth Century.* Translated by Richard L. Bland and Katya S. Wessels. Anchorage, Alaska: Phenix Press, 2002.

Starr, S. Frederick. *Russia's American Colony.* Durham, N.C.: Duke University Press, 1987.

Sulloway, Frank J. *Born to Rebel: Birth Order, Family Dynamics, and Creative Lives.* New York: Pantheon, 1996.

Suttles, Wayne P., ed. *Northwest Coast.* Vol. 7 of *Handbook of North American Indians*, edited by William G. Sturtevant. Washington D.C.: Smithsonian Institution, 1990.

Tikhmenev, P. A. *A History of the Russian-American Company.* Translated and edited by Richard A. Pierce and Alton S. Donnelly. Seattle: University of Washington Press, 1996.

——. *A History of the Russian-American Company.* Vol. 2, *Documents*, translated by Dmitri Krenov, edited by Richard A. Pierce and Alton S. Donnelly. Kingston, Ontario: Limestone Press, 1979.

Vaughan, Thomas, and Bill Holm. *Soft Gold: The Fur Trade and Cultural Exchange on the Northwest Coast of America.* 2nd ed. Portland: Oregon Historical Society Press, 1990.

Veltre, Douglas W., and Mary J. Veltre. *Resource Utilization in Unalaska, Aleutian Islands, Alaska.* Technical Paper no. 58. [Bethel]: Alaska Department of Fish and Game, Division of Subsistence, 1982.

Vinkovetsky, Ilya. *Russian America: An Overseas Colony of a Continental Empire, 1804–1867.* Oxford: Oxford University Press, 2011.

Vodarskii, Ia. E. *Naselenie Rossii v kontse XVII–nachale XVIII veka (Chislennost', soslovno-klassovhyi sostav, razmeshchenie)* (*The Population of Russia at the End of the Seventeenth to the Beginning of the Eighteenth Century [Numbers, Estate-Class Composition, Distribution]*). Moscow: Nauka, 1977.

Wheeler, Mary E. "Empires in Conflict and Cooperation: The 'Bostonians' and the Russian-American Company." *Pacific Historical Review* 40 (1971): 419–41.

——. "Origins and Formation of the Russian-American Company." Ph.D. diss., University of North Carolina at Chapel Hill, 1965.

——. "The Russian American Company and the Imperial Government: Early Phase." In *Russia's American Colony*, edited by S. Frederick Starr. Durham, N.C.: Duke University Press, 1987.

Zorin, A. V., ed. *Kurskie kuptsy Golikovy* (*The Golikovs, Merchants from Kursk*). St. Petersburg: VIRD, n.d.

INDEX

Note: page numbers in *italics* refer to illustrations